D0984763

Man

European Perspectives
A Series of the Columbia University Press

Man

His Nature and Place in the World

by Arnold Gehlen

Translated by
Clare McMillan and
Karl Pillemer

with an Introduction by
Karl-Siegbert Rehberg

Columbia University Press
NEW YORK   1988

Acknowledgement is gratefully extended by the Press to Inter Nationes for a special grant supporting this publication.

Library of Congress Cataloging-in-Publishing Data
Gehlen, Arnold, 1904-
  Man, his nature and place in the world.
  Translation of: Mensch, seine Natur und seine Stellung in der Welt.
  Includes index.
  1. Man. 2. Language and languages   Origin.
3. Psychology. I. Title.
GN24.G3813 1988 128   87-23859
ISBN 0-231-05218-9

Columbia University Press
New York   Guildford, Surrey

Title of the original German edition: *Der Mensch* copyright © 1974 by Anthenaion, Frankfurt, with authorization of Akademische Verlagsgesellschaft, Athenaion, Wiesbaden, FR-Germany. First edition copyright 1950.

Clothbound Columbia University Press editions are Smyth-sewn and printed on permanent and durable acid-free paper

Book design by Ken Venezio

Contents

Part III. The Laws Governing Human Impulses; Character; the Problem of the Mind

Translators' Preface

The translation of Arnold Gehlen's major work, *Man: His Nature and Place in the World,* has been an undertaking of major proportions, for Gehlen's discussion ranges widely: from ethology to the origins of language; from Gestalt psychology to symbolic interactionism; from the fossil remains of primitive man to modern institutions. Gehlen draws on myriad sources, many of which have not been translated into English and remain virtually unknown today. The breadth of his frame of reference proved a continual challenge to the translators.

Gehlen's style may also seem somewhat foreign to English readers. It is at times ponderous and didactic. Further, the reader may be struck by a certain degree of repetitiousness; key ideas are reiterated almost word-for-word over a series of chapters. While the translators have always aimed to make the work readable, we have remained true to Gehlen's own presentation as much as possible, even where it becomes stylistically difficult.

One dilemma that confronted us as translators was the question of sexist language. The reader will note that we have generally translated the term *Mensch* as "man," and employed the pronoun "he" for that term. The alternative was to translate *Mensch* invariably as "human being" and to use a construction such as "he or she," "s/he." However, it seems clear that Gehlen himself would have employed the term "man" and the masculine pronoun. To revise the book's language to avoid sexist terminology would add a contemporary cast to the text that, in our opinion, would not be appropriate.

The translation of a few specific terms deserves mention here. Gehlen begins his argument with the assertion that the human being is the "not yet determined animal" *(das noch nicht festgestellte Tier),* a phrase employed by Nietzsche. Gehlen uses this phrase to emphasize his point that man's existence is not "determined" by a strict set of instincts, as an animal's is;

the human being enjoys a high degree of plasticity *(Plastizität)*, in that he is not adapted to a specific environment, in the sense that an animal is. This is the positive side of Gehlen's characterization of the human being as a "deficient being" *(Mängelwesen)*, whose lack of specialized features constitutes an overwhelming burden.

Gehlen highlights two aspects of this basic human condition. On the one hand, in contrast to animals, human beings are *weltoffen,* a term Gehlen borrowed from Max Scheler. We have rendered it literally as "world-open" to convey Gehlen's idea that man is open to experiencing the world in a way that animals are not. At the same time, however, this world-openness means that the human being is highly vulnerable to stimulation and impressions from the outside world; it places a great burden on him, from which he must seek "relief" *(Entlastung)*. We have translated this key concept simply and directly as "relief," but the reader should bear in mind that the German term carries the even stronger connotation of the removal of a burden.

A word on the special difficulties that are posed by part 1 of *Man* is also in order. Although Gehlen provides a footnote in which he defines such terms as anthropoid, pongid, etc., his own use of these terms is not consistent. When, for example, it is apparent that Gehlen does not mean "anthropoid" but rather "early hominid," we have substituted the correct term. Second, many of Gehlen's sources in this part of the book date from the 1920s and 1930s and are consequently outdated. At places in the text where recent archaeological findings have proven Gehlen's presentation to be in error, we have taken care to indicate so.

Finally, in any undertaking such as this one, it is inevitable that assistance is required from experts in a number of fields. In particular, we would like to express our gratitude to Professors Tamara Dembo, Walter Wright, and Walter Schatzberg of Clark University, and Professor Jonathan Imber of Wellesley College. We owe a great debt to Professor Peter Bogucki of the University of Massachusetts in Boston for his careful reading of part 1 of the book. And, finally, Professor Kurt H. Wolff of Brandeis University deserves special thanks: to his original encouragement we owe our involvement in this translation.

Clare A. McMillan
Karl A. Pillemer

Arnold Gehlen's Elementary Anthropology—An Introduction

by Karl-Siegbert Rehberg

I

More than forty years after its original publication in Germany, *Man: His Nature and Place in the World*—the major anthropological work of the German philosopher, anthropologist, and sociologist Arnold Gehlen—is available for the first time in English. The publication of the English edition marks the translation of an important document of twentieth-century German social philosophy. At the same time, however, the question inevitably arises as to the relevance of such a book. This question is ambiguous, however, for it could be asked equally of the scientific findings of Gehlen's "elementary anthropology," of its reception, of the critical objections raised against it, of the resurrection of old approaches to problems, or of the political implications of Gehlen's basic premises.

In the 1930s and 1940s, anthropological issues were the "philosophical theme of the day." At that time, following in the footsteps of Max Scheler, philosophers professed an interpretation of the human being which took strict issue with an exclusively zoological anthropology, while at the same time taking into consideration the findings of modern biological science. This anthropological question became topical again decades later, in a completely different context—in the debates over the possibilities for a "new human being" which took place during the student protest movements of the sixties and early seventies. Such debates usually culminated in a rejection of all those anthropological viewpoints that held that certain invariable elements in human nature were of utmost importance to human life. All this is evidence of how a way of thinking can remain relevant in different ways. I believe that, as far as the impact of Arnold Gehlen's book in Germany is concerned, it is by no means insignificant that his views became the target of a leftist critique of anthropology. This critique stressed the ideological implications of the underlying assumptions and consequences of Gehlen's "image of the human being." At the same time, however, it also served to bring to light many of his insights as well as his view of reality, which is both imaginative and grounded in experience.

There are other ways in which Gehlen's book remains relevant today: for example, in the widespread rise of neoconservatism at the beginning of the eighties. Apart from all such changing trends, however, Gehlen's thought has shown itself to be a reflection on fundamental social philosophical issues, which on the one hand has remained a firm component of philosophical knowledge (it forms, for example, part of the teaching canon of philosophical institutes and is included in lexica and handbooks) and on the other hand, has remained unique, in that there has been no direct continuation to date of this particular line of anthropological inquiry. Thus, as is true as well of his impact on postwar German sociology, Gehlen's reception has been contradictory, for he is simultaneously a "classical thinker" and an outsider. The reasons for this are first and foremost biographical and will be documented later; other factors have to do with the many-faceted nature of such a book, which makes it difficult to categorize in terms of individual disciplines.

Gehlen's views sparked a variety of attempts at a new formulation of anthropological issues and research objectives, including such attempts as were not so much concerned with identifying invariable elements as with using anthropological methods to document variations in human lifestyles. The debate brought about by this "philosophical anthropology" led to the development of "historical" and "sociological" anthropology and, in many respects, the advances made in defining psychohistorical concepts and in the theory of action have benefited from Gehlen's work. Thus, I believe one could argue that it is not so much the ways in which this science of anthropological foundations has been applied (in pedagogery, for example), as in fact the critical responses to Gehlen's work that have shed new light on his thought and opened up the possibility of developing it further.

II

Gehlen put forth his anthropological approach in lectures and essays dating from 1935 on; in 1940, he consolidated it for the first time and presented it to the public, and ten years later, he reworked it extensively once more. He described his approach as "elementary," based on his argument that the fundamental features that distinguish the human species are "extraordinarily far-reaching," and that only by studying these can we hope to get a clear picture of the "special place" occupied by the human being. Gehlen did not want to propose a "naturalistic" or "biological" theory of man, but preferred instead to refer to his approach as an "anthropobiological" one, which allows the human being to be viewed as a "complete project of Nature." To accomplish this, it was not enough to focus simply on the physical features of the human being; instead, it was necessary to identify the basic requirements for man's existence. This meant in turn that the nature of human morphology, that is, the peculiar features of the species, had to be documented first. Thus, the book was intended to lay the groundwork for a fundamental science of the human being. Gehlen's approach made it necessary to cull findings from many different scientific disciplines concerned with man, which could not then simply be all lumped together, but instead had to be synthesized in order to come up with an all-encompassing perspective on the conditions necessary for human existence. The fruit of this philosophical thought, supported by a variety of other sciences, would in turn indicate new areas of research for all the individual disciplines concerned with the study of the human being. Thus, above all, certain areas of inquiry were to be sketched out and then given back to the individual sciences. Gehlen therefore intended to present a program for research as well as for thought, to which he gave the often criticized title of an "empirical philosophy."

"Philosophical anthropology" had already been formulated in the twenties and thirties by Max Scheler, Helmuth Plessner, and others as a new beginning for philosophy. Gehlen, however, did not wish simply to derive this new anthropology from the excess of reflection in academic philosophy, but argued instead that this sort of contemplation of the nature of the human being was in fact part of human nature. He accordingly spoke of the human being as a "being who must form attitudes," a being who could not survive without some sort of self-interpretation or "self-view." Gehlen saw herein a problem fundamental to human existence which he expressed, in a phrase borrowed from Nietzsche, by describing man as the "not yet determined animal" *(noch nicht festgestelltes Tier)*. Gehlen's anthropology is concerned with "determining" the human being in a dual sense: on the one hand, based on the human need for self-interpretation, philosophical and scientific assertions are intended to make our statements or "determinations" about the human being more certain and substantial; on the other, this "deficient being" who has been denied a secure existence guided by instincts and who lacks all innate forms of adaptation to the environment as well as organic specialization, is to be "determined" by means of lifestyles that provide a secure orientation. This threatened and vulnerable being, who of necessity must lead a hazardous life, first manages to establish a long-term basis for survival by creating interlocking systems of order—primarily "institutions."

This anthropological interpretation thus focuses right from the start on a program of social stabilization. Gehlen wanted his approach to be understood as "objective" in the strictest sense of the word—that is, above all, as free from all political influences. However, the initial, introductory presentation of his elementary anthropology already clearly reveals that this understanding of the human being also has a political side to it. The author bases his theories of the need for firmly rooted systems of order on assumptions which are developed only in the course of the anthropological discussion in the book. Nonetheless, even in this first topic of the "undetermined nature" of the human being, we can recognize this connection, which is then explored in greater depth in part 3 of the book.

The "anthropological scheme" that Gehlen proposes is based on the concept of action; it describes the human being as a "creature of discipline" (*Zuchtwesen*) whose undetermined nature compels him to undergo a process of formation. This vulnerable and labile being, who suffers an ever-present threat of perishing, owes the possibility of his survival to one crucial fact: to a decisive reversal in his circumstances. He is "anticipatory." Thus, the human being is a Prometheus—living for the future, for the distant, and not exclusively in the here and now.

On the biological level, Gehlen focuses on human "deficiencies"—i.e., that humans are not adapted to a specific environment, that they are unspecialized, and that they posses certain primitive traits; on the nature of human organs; and above all on the "life-threatening lack of true instincts." This idea of the imperiled nature of the human being is based primarily on the "incomparably long period of neediness during infancy and childhood."

After a discussion of this theory of the "deficient being," which draws on the anthropology of Johann Gottfried Herder as well as on the findings of contemporary biology, Gehlen brings up Max Scheler's understanding of the human being as "world-open" (*weltoffen*), that is, as free of "the animal's adaptation to a specific environment." This concept of world-openness highlights the productive side of the human being's "unfinished" nature, i.e., human freedom, plasticity, and capacity for development. To be sure, Gehlen does not go on from here to formulate a philosophy of the "upright gait," that is, a philosophy of human dignity founded upon human freedom, such as Ernst Bloch, for example, has developed from similar considerations of human morphology, with a view toward the capacity for contradiction, the possibility of revolting against and improving social conditions. Gehlen, in contrast, prefers to focus his gaze on the new dangers that are brought about by the human being's erect posture, on the human being's now precarious existence. One of his major themes in this respect is the "flood of stimulation" experienced by the human being, who lives in a "field of surprises, full of unpredictable structures" from which he must find "relief." Thus, in their orientation toward the future, humans must master the world and themselves, for only by transforming nature can they create a human world, "culture," which constitutes a "second Nature" for the human being.

This line of reasoning suggests a human compulsion to act; in other words, human beings are compelled to transform Nature, within themselves and outside themselves; they must create the conditions necessary for survival. According to Gehlen, the sources for this transformation lie in the individual's own activity which in turn provides the foundation for Gehlen's central category—action. In light of this, one can understand why Gehlen's dynamic model of existence, which accords to the human being firmly established "social regulatory forces" and institutional bonds, is closely related to Nietzsche's concept of "more out of life" *(Mehr an Leben)*.

The human being is therefore understood as a being whose basic impulses pose dangers at the same time as they provide the means for him to gain control over existence and achieve some sort of stability. This point comes across clearly in Gehlen's discussion of the relationship between impulses and action, in which he brings up the concept of an "excess of impulses," making reference both to Max Scheler and to Freud.

The category of action refers to the human need to transform the world, without which the human being would be unable to survive. This same idea has been take up by idealist philosophy (as formulated by Fichte and Hegel), with its interest in the objectifications and manifestations of human activity, and by the American Pragmatists, who were influenced in turn by the German philosophical tradition. The term "pragmatic" in this sense can also be applied to Karl Marx's concepts of "work" and "praxis." Thus, as far as the emphasis on the instrumentality of actions is concerned, there are many similarities between Gehlen and Marx; however, the philosophical, political, and ideological chasm between the two remains unbridgeable.

Indeed, Gehlen was able to employ some concepts such as Georges Sorel's "syndicalism" which played intermediary roles in a certain sense.

Early on, Gehlen allied himself with those cognitive theoretical positions that treated the intellectual understanding of the world and the active mastery of it as interrelated; he cites Nietzsche, "We can only understand what we can do, if there is any understanding at all." Gehlen finds support for his views in many thinkers, from Thomas Hobbes to Kant, Friedrich Heinrich Jacobi, Schelling, Novalis, and even Goethe, as evidenced in the following maxim: "In the sciences as well, one cannot really know anything; it must always be done." Gehlen was probably familiar with the development of this thought in the philosophy of pragmatism (particularly in the works of Charles S. Peirce, William James, and John Dewey) through Max Scheler's critique of it in his *Erkenntnis und Arbeit* (Knowledge and Work). Scheler accepted the pragmatic axioms that knowledge is bound up with action and truth with utility as being valid for our "knowledge of achievement or mastery of Nature," but he did not believe these were the foundations for our knowledge of "truth" or the "idea of knowledge in itself"— and certainly not for a "knowledge of salvation." For Scheler, the "spirit that permeated pragmatism [was] the same spirit that spoke from the eleven-story buildings of Chicago, from the verses of Walt Whitman—a spirit that must have remained left over from the unrestrained puritan work ethic, which created America in the first place and which, as Max Weber said, brought forth the 'age of heroes of early capitalism' in Geneva and Holland, after its original, christian-calvinist superstructure was destroyed."

With less distance than Max Scheler, Gehlen embraced this activist, technologically oriented perspective which bypassed all the strictures of "old Europe," just as he had seized upon the "pragmatic" themes in Nietzsche's work. On the political level, this category of "action," chosen so skillfully from an analytical perspective as a unit of execution, can be incorporated into the myths of "struggle" and "act" in Germany during this period. Gehlen often lamented the fact that the levelheadedness of the fundamental ideas of Pragmatism found so little acceptance in Germany; in fact, the reduction of all intellectual achievements, all ideas, and "truths" to the substratum of actions and interests (that is, the unrelenting question of "cui bono?") is probably one thing Gehlen's empiricism did achieve. However, we must not forget that in the Germany of the 1930s, the political right, with its affirmation of deeds, favored the reception of Pragmatism. Gehlen was certainly inspired as well by Eduard Baumgarten (his successor to the chair of philosophy at Königsberg) who in 1938 wrote insightfully and bc sympathetically about *The Intellectual Foundations of American Community,* that is, the "pragmatism" of R. W. Emerson, James, and Dewey. Although Baumgarten's interpretation had a political focus (his reference to the "power instinct," for example), he did examine all the fundamental and methodological aspects of American pragmatism, which Gehlen then explored in detail. In the first edition of *The Human Being* in 1940, Gehlen examined the tradition of "pragmatic" cognitive theory, which he felt began with Hobbes and which he had discussed in earlier essays, and followed it up to John Dewey. In revising the book in 1950, he added a discussion of George Herbert Mead, introducing him to German audiences. Particularly in his analysis of "play" and "game," and of the key concept of "taking the role of the other" (from *Mind, Self and Society*), Mead became forGehlen the authority on the social components of the human being's active understanding of the world. Through the execution of actions and the adoption of the "alter ego," the forms and rules of interaction are inculcated into the individual. In this fashion, Gehlen was able to expand his original ideas, although he did not fully exhaust Mead's notion of "intersubjectivity." Gehlen's theory of action has its greatest strength in its description of the dynamic and self-reflexive development of man's contact with things. He broadened this model to include other participants which in a certain sense function as objects of and obstacles to action. Of course, from his reading of Mead, Gehlen does not conclude that it is necessary to revise fundamentally his ideas; he does not draw the conclusion that "interaction" should be understood as the most fundamental category of human understanding of the world and ourselves, because man's possibilities for action are themselves always founded on intersubjectivity and communication.

From an anthropological perspective, Gehlen sees action as the decisive point of departure from which the traditional dualism of body and soul can be overcome. Scheler had also envisioned this possibility, which he expressed in his model of the graduated psychical structure of all life. Gehlen believed, in contrast, that the relationship between the "inside" and "outside," between cognitive, mental, and physiological abilities, could best be expressed in the concept of "action."

In addition to the category of action, there is the category of "relief," which Gehlen also derives from the constitutional deficiencies of the human being. The concept of relief refers to Gehlen's view that the human being is able to increase the possibilities and the means for survival by shifting behavior toward those functions that require no effort and are purely suggestive. In other words, whatever we "grasp" or appropriate through our senses, in the course of experiences involving our hands, that is, the sense of touch, we transform mentally in such a way that we can then recognize certain aspects of a thing's nature (such as its weight) through sight alone, which we previously could experience only through direct physical contact. It can be assumed that some animals possess the rudiments of this ability to transcend and rework situations and things; however, as a fundamental method of representing the contents of the world, it exists only in the human being. According to Gehlen, the central medium that provides this relief is language (see the discussion of part 2 of Gehlen's book in section 6 of this introduction).

Gehlen insightfully describes the "increasingly indirect nature of human behavior," which is closely tied in with his notion of relief. By indirectness, Gehlen means that "intermediate elements" are interpolated between an action and its goal (that is, the gratification of the needs and orientations that direct the action). Gehlen thus identifies habit and tradition (that is, all means of habitualizing behavior) as very important instruments for achieving relief. At this point, out of the initial concept designed to avoid any dualism, a new and equally fundamental opposing thought is developed—the incompatibility of the execution of action and reflection. This theme runs throughout Gehlen's book, affecting every phase of the development of his thought. Reflecting consciousness is understood as a process of turning inward, which inhibits action. This idea can be detected in Gehlen's early philosophical writings, in his existentialist attempt to overcome the self-centeredness of the individual through the "we"-relationship, in the national socialist notion of stabilization through community, and even in the conservative Gehlen's late polemical tirades against intellectuals. Consciousness is of course understood as "a means in the quest for perfection of the organic process," to the extent that it remains focused beyond itself. However, as self-reflection, that is, as the attempt to see through this very process, it will—as Gehlen has argued in his analysis of Schopenhauer's philosophy—stifle action completely, inhibit it entirely, in the sense of the English phrase "self-consciousness."

III

Before I undertake to discuss in greater detail the line of argument Gehlen pursues in this book, I would like to comment first on his methods, taking note of certain similarities between Arnold Gehlen's anthropology with its orientation toward action theory and the views of Vilfredo Pareto, as put forth in the latter's *Trattato di sociologia generale (The Mind and Society*, ed. by Arthur Livingston, New York: Harcourt, Brace, 1935), also based on a sociological theory of action.

As Gehlen expressly emphasized in the revised fourth edition of the present work (1950), he is concerned with finding "categories," that is, with un-covering in his analysis those "fundamental characteristics of the human being that cannot be further reduced." This aim presupposes a dissecting analysis of objects, a "phenomenological" analysis, for if all meta-physical derivations are to be avoided (as Gehlen in strict contrast even to Max Scheler advocates), then penetrating analyses must be carried so far until they hit upon "residues that cannot be further reduced." There is an important connection here with the work of Vilfredo Pareto, whose theory of action was also concerned with an analysis of residues. Gehlen was greatly impressed by Pareto's work; in 1941, he published a comprehensive article on his theory of action—at the time he even planned to bring out a German-language edition of Pareto's work. He also showed a similarity with Pareto for a while in presenting categorical findings in the form of classifications. His analysis of actions, his search for the foundations of human drives and residual motivating forces, along with his unmasking of the logical super-structure, without which action is inconceivable, all point up many simi-larities between Pareto and Gehlen. Furthermore, a difference cannot be found in the fact that Gehlen wishes to present a theory of the fundamental nature of the human being, for he is thereby advocating the formulation of categories in the sense that has been discussed here, and not as some form of metaphysics. Thus, Gehlen is in complete agreement with Pareto's strong rejection of a philosophy of essences *(Wesensphilosophie)*. Pareto made a strict distinction between the "value as logical, experimental truths" held by interpretations and "theories" about given actions, and their "value as convictions, suggestions, or propaganda." In discussing Pareto's views, Geh-len goes back to a common source of influence upon them both—Nietzsche's philosophy. Nietzsche similarly differentiated between the truth of a state-ment and its "value for action or vital value." Gehlen, however, is quick to add that "in comparison to Nietzsche, Pareto's theory is far more sensible, certain, productive in terms of concrete results, more sober, and political, and on the whole is without prophetic or sacerdotal, even without anti-sacerdotal, gestures, characterized by an ancient classical serenity and freedom."

As far as the formulation of the categories of action and the insights gained through the execution of actions are concerned, Gehlen's premise is in my opinion considerably more differentiated than is Pareto's theory of action. Ultimately, it will prove to be more of an advantage that Gehlen did not develop his theory of action along the lines of a system of classification. He did remain fascinated, however, by Pareto's "historical" vision—that is, by the wealth of concrete examples and illustrations of Pareto's theory of action in his *Trattato*. Here, "history" means something similar to both thinkers: it did not refer to changes in a historical process—not even when understood as the history of evolution—but instead history became a reservoir of the realizations of fundamental types, as defined in terms of the theory of action, of directions of impulses, and "rationalizations." Thus—as was true for Machiavelli, for other historians of the nineteenth century, and for Nietzsche as well—history is understood by Pareto and Gehlen as a tableau upon which the educated and historically informed individual can record continually new variations in the basic pattern of human action, whereby the wealth of human possibilities is illustrated before one's eyes as, to borrow one of Nietzsche's phrases, an "eternal return," that is, "a circulation of absolutely identical sequences." This also leads to patterns of historical change: the model of the "circulation of elites" could serve as an example here, or perhaps even Gehlen's notion of the stagnation of life in modern industrial society. The principal components of this society no longer change; all that is conceivable is the technical perfection of what is essentially an unalterable process. This state of affairs, described by Gehlen as "cultural crystallization," refers again—and not only because of the origin of the borrowed phrase—to Pareto. The similar political orientations of both thinkers is also striking and is the reason why Gehlen uses Pareto's work as a source for his own illustrations, as for example when he attacks the demands for equality made by those who do not stand on top, arguing that these represent the concealed wishes of the individuals to ascend in the ranks themselves.

IV

Part 1 (i.e., chapters 10–12) of *Man* should be understood, as Gehlen's own introduction indicates, as an extensive digression intended to provide substantiation for his theory of the evolution of "deficient being." To anyone interested in the philosophical findings of Gehlen's anthropology, this discussion, although important for its analysis of theories of the natural sciences on the development of the human being, will appear to be less relevant. In part 1, Gehlen argues that the human being's organic deficiencies, or the "peculiarities of organs" and their "primitive traits," should be understood as evidence of his failure to specialize. One critical aspect of his argument is his opposition to the evolutionary theories proposed in the wake of Darwin, that is, to the "classical" viewpoints on evolution, according to which the human being is directly descended from already specialized great ape species. Gehlen also takes issue with the theory of "domestication" (as advanced in particular by Konrad Lorenz), which holds that human versatility, openness to different impressions, and failure to specialize are to be interpreted not so much as fundamental morphological characteristics of the species than as signs of a process of deterioration taking place over the course of evolutionary history. The human being's unspecialized nature becomes for Gehlen "the acid test of every theory of evolution." Gehlen's views on this are founded in great measure upon the theories of Louis Bolk, particularly his theory of endogenous "retardation." His stance is further supported by the views of the Swiss zoologist Adolf Portmann, who interpreted the human being's lack of specialized features along with the great plasticity and ability to learn as embryonic characteristics, and expressed this idea in his catch-phrase of the "extra-uterine period of prematurity."

V

Part 2 of Gehlen's book is devoted primarily to the dynamic and versatile nature of human achievements, with a central focus on a "theory of the roots of language" (chs. 19–24). The fundamental model Gehlen proposes here for language, as well as for all actions, is that of the "circular process,"

wherein functions direct their course by referring back to themselves. It is in language that this increase in the intensity of human capabilities, based on their reciprocity and self-motivated reinforcement, is demonstrated most clearly. Language thereby becomes the fundamental model for human interaction in the world and for man's experience of himself, as well as a model for action, which in this sense is always "analogous to language" (sprachmässig). Gehlen often stressed that he developed this notion of the circle of action independently of other thinkers; most likely, it was an idea whose time had come and which later really came into its own in cybernetics.

The advantage that such a dynamic theory of action possesses is illustrated clearly in the following passage from Talcott Parson's correspondence with Alfred Schütz, 1940–1941 (Richard Grathoff, ed., *The Theory of Social Action: The Correspondence of Alfred Schütz and Talcott Parsons* Bloomington and London: Indiana University Press, 1978, p. 120): "At the time that Alfred Schütz and I were discussing these problems, what is now frequently called the cybernetic point of view was scarcely on the horizon. This seems to me, however, to have served immensely to clarify this kind of consideration, essentially by introducing a component of what one might call limited reversibility."

On this point, and particularly in the basic premises of his philosophy of life, Gehlen had already gone a significant step further than other more systematic conceptual schemes. In particular, his approach treated the execution of actions differently; it was intended to overcome the gap between internal and external, thus to achieve a "neutralization of the dualism of body and soul," which Gehlen expressed in the phrase "psychophysically neutral." Proceeding from this basis, then, Gehlen was also able to understand action in terms of its general course and could therefore show that it is in the actual execution of an action that its direction and efficiency first become clear. Thus, unlike many other theories of action, Gehlen's theory does not reduce action to the simple execution of plans and the setting of goals.

VI

The theory of language that Gehlen presents—a theory that could serve to define many hitherto untreated (even in linguistic circles) areas of inquiry—begins with a discussion of the different roots of language. On this point, Gehlen stands squarely in the tradition of those theories of the origin of language that have been put forth since the eighteenth century (for example, by Rousseau and Condorcet in France, Hamann and Herder in Germany) and elaborated in Wilhelm von Humboldt's writings on language. Gehlen concentrates on Herder's *Essay on the Origin of Language* (1966); there are countless instances in which he adopts and paraphrases Herder's arguments. Gehlen does avoid any attempt to present a theory of the historical origins of language, however, which points out how misleading the label of "theory of origin" that is often applied to such theories can be. Gehlen does not make claims about the sources from which language evolved. Thus, for example, he rejects Herder's idea of the historical origin of language, according to which the words of language represent attempts to repeat sounds found in nature, although he does adhere to Herder's theory of the structure of language in almost every other respect. The roots of language that Gehlen identifies are "anthropological" in the sense that they are all related to the constitution of the human being. Gehlen discusses five such fundamental conditions for the acquisition of language ("roots of language"); in doing so, in accordance with his all-encompassing interpretation, he proceeds from the human being's own productive activity.

He begins with the "life of the sound," which both Humboldt and Herder also recognized as fundamental. Gehlen stresses the aspect of "self-communication" in language, the way in which sound is both produced and perceived by man; it echoes back to man via the ear. Gehlen wants to call attention to a form of sensory response that is at the same time a constant theme in human development. It exists as well in the structure of tactile movemets, which similarly perceive a sensory stimulus and at the same time process the "experience" and "impressions" gained through touch in such a way that the sensitivity of the sense of touch is also further enhanced. The same holds true for the production of sounds. As a small child performs its babbling monologues, it simultaneously hears and gives structure to these; ultimately, the child discovers that he himself is the "cause" of his sounds. This discovery then makes possible repetition, intensification, and changes in sound which to a certain extent form the basic repertoire of possible ways to produce sounds.

This theory of automatic reinforcement is carried further in the discussion of the second root of language, which Gehlen describes as "sound-motor communication with visual impressions." To a great extent, a child responds in sound to those stimuli in its environment that it perceives through sight in sound, and it thereby functionalizes (although Gehlen does not explain exactly how this occurs) its heretofore purely self-communicative production of sounds.

The third root of language, closely related to the second, is recognition, that is, a firmer connection between a sound movement and the external datum it represents. In this context, Gehlen discusses the "birth of the name," the retention of what has been recognized in the form of a sound. According to Gehlen, this constitutes the fundamental function of language as far as the conduct of human life and the nature of human actions (characterized as "analogous to language") are concerned. Recognition enables human beings to appropriate the world in a relieved form, to suspend it and "keep it to themselves." This is the most important example of the process of relief: things are represented in the human mind not only as individual isolated objects, but also in their interrelationships with each other. Language permits systems of interconnection and categorization; it allows relationships in time and reality to be suspended. Gehlen interprets this power of language as "excessive in its results," because the perception

xxii GEHLEN'S ELEMENTARY ANTHROPOLOGY

of oneself and the perception of the world blend together with a wide range of different individual achievements. Access to the things in the world in this relieved form has in addition the important characteristic "that even in the simple act of naming, something is 'taken care of' or accomplished." With the "estranged self-awareness" brought about by the retroactively perceived production of sounds and with this "communicative process of self-enjoyment" as the basis, and continuing with the objectification achieved through communication with others, our linguistic representation of the world is developed. At this point, Gehlen again cites Herder, who states, that in this manner, "all states of the soul become analogous to language."

The "call" constitutes the fourth root of language and signifies the externalization of desires or inner impulses. Through the call, our inner life finds articulation; our needs and impulses are expressed. In a manner that is not sufficiently systematic, Gehlen links these considerations to the communicative aspects of play (see ch. 21). The call, as the expression of internal state of being, can be imagined without partners, as a self-reflexive act; this idea stresses the "playful element" in the sense that, in complete accordance with Gehlen's theory of the production of sounds and the self-communication indulged in by a small child, exercises in movement are "rewarded" with retroactively experienced sensations and new experiences. However, play has a social side as well, and Gehlen accordingly connects in this respect the "excess of results" produced by such playfulness to the social components in the sequences of actions related to play and the invention of rules. In revising the book in 1950, Gehlen brought in at this point the model of taking the role of the other, as developed by George Herbert Mead.

The fifth root of language is "sound gestures," the "expressive motor accompaniment" to actions and movements. Once again, Gehlen does not follow the traditional argument of the origin of language; unlike Noiré (*Der Ursprung der Sprache*, 1778) and Herder, he realizes that this is not the sole root of human language, although he does demonstrate how such "sound gestures" can serve to hold fast actions and communications as practical experiences involving interaction with things and other beings.

Gehlen envisioned these roots of language as the "preintellectual" foundations for the development of language (see ch. 27). His anthropological theory of language, however, must describe the functions and the gains in achievement and ability that become possible with this basis. This he does primarily in chapters 28–37, in which he traces the development of ideas and de-actualized as well as intentional memories and images and describes language as the medium in which mental processes and external data come together. To clarify his conceptual scheme, Gehlen borrows an expression from Novalis, the "inner outer-world."

Taken together, these chapters provide us with the key to Gehlen's anthropological model, for actions are seen as being "analogous to language," in the sense that, like language, they develop from playful movement, initially without purpose, and at the same time, actions facilitate the development of additional functions, up to and including conscious and planned actions and the direction of actions. Gehlen's model of action includes the element of the symbolic, which also figures into his theory of language; in other words, a thing or an event can be represented by an expression, a metaphor, a sound, so that the semiotic character of human actions, which always have a communicative and symbolic aspect, becomes apparent.

VII

With these categorical definitions of human impulses and the characterization of the nature of actions as analogous to language as the basis, Gehlen goes on to argue that man is subject to a compulsion to form and to order: the "not yet determined" animal is to be firmly established in reality. Gehlen begins this avenue of his examination with a discussion of one particular aspect of the nature of human impulses which he believes is fundamental to the structure of human needs. Since human needs cannot be satisfied by pursuing the shortcut available to animals through their instincts, the idea suggests itself that the human being must be able to defer needs in order to be able to find enduring gratification for them. This means that a void is created which must be actively bridged time and time again, a "hiatus" between needs and the conditions necessary for their gratification. Gehlen sees this break with the direct gratification of drives as responsible not only for the indirect nature of the human being's choice of goals and means, but also in general for that artificial means of existing, of changing and transforming nature, that is called "culture." Gehlen thus rejects all theories of established drives, such as those that catalogue "fundamental drives." He prefers instead to stress the "world-open" nature of human impulses and the necessity for controlling and imposing "discipline" *(Zucht)* on these, since even with their openness, their capacity for development, their adaptability, and the capacity for sublimation made possible (and even necessary) in them, these impulses still cannot completely compensate for the absent "certainty of instincts." One important aspect of relief is that it is fragile to a certain degree; drives evince a readiness "to degenerate and deteriorate . . . to run rampant." The answer to the problem of how human beings can survive despite the excessive nature of their impulses and their lack of true instincts can therefore be found by carrying further the insights gained in the theory of action and language and arguing that human beings are compelled to make their own creations valid components of the external world and to orient themselves by these. Indeed, human beings are even forced to subject themselves to the very order they have created. This suggests the idea that human impulses are channeled in certain directions and given form by certain obligations; thus, Gehlen's "elementary anthropology" is linked to an examination of culture, which is derived from it, and of the forms of social life as well—an examination that, because it takes these very assumptions into account, is termed "philosophical." This social theory was proposed in the first edition of the present book (1940) as the doctrine of the "highest directing systems" *(oberste Führungssysteme)* and, at least as far as terminology is concerned, was grouped with the expression of the "image of discipline," as used by Alfred Rosenberg, the manufacturer

of the national socialist world-view. These "directing systems" were viewed on the one hand as "ultimate contexts for interpreting the world" (for example, religions, or world-views) and, on the other, as "forming actions." The basis for these are the "interests of powerlessness," from which antidotes are developed against failure, suffering, death, and the vagaries of chance. These "directing systems" are "in short, the forms by means of which a community establishes itself and maintains its existence." Gehlen developed this idea further in a manner true to the times: "For a people, as history has shown us, the primary purpose of life is to maintain its existence."

This particular part of the book was thoroughly revised after World War II. In the 1950 edition, chapter 44, "The Exposition of Several Problems Relating to the Mind," referred to institutions that hold fast to and "crystallize" "objective, overlapping expediencies." Gehlen's theory of institutions and the "directing ideas embodied in them" was further elaborated in his book *Urmensch und Spätkultur,* published in 1956. In this book as well, Gehlen begins with action and the effect on the social structure of the use of tools, which served as a means of shaping action; he then argues that man's actions involving things take on a dynamic and validity of their own from which in turn certain obligations ensue. Imputing values creates order and at the same time establishes the "objectivity" of institutions. This line of reasoning invites a sociological approach and opens up the possibility of integrating this line of inquiry with social and cultural anthropology. One of the functions Gehlen's theories served after the war was to demonstrate in the framework of sociology the links possible between different disciplines and to reintroduce Anglo-American traditions of thought and research directions.

VIII

Gehlen's theories have been subject to criticism from the outset. He accepted many of the individual objections and, in revising the present book in 1950, he discussed in depth some of the critical arguments raised against him. For example, he believed in retrospect that he had indeed overestimated the dearth of instincts in the human being; in revising his position on this, he referred most often to Konrad Lorenz, who argued that, even in human behavior, a not insignificant number of innate mechanisms (as for example in expressive gestures) could be identified.

Gehlen further came to believe that he had made a fundamental error in setting up the basic categories of his theory of action by neglecting the interactive mediation between the world and the self. Toward the end of his life, he admitted that he had left out an entire anthropological dimension. Gehlen's discussion of human interaction with things in the world is to the point, as, for example, when he describes how a child learns through its contact with the things in its world and then analyzes the child's emerging sensitive ability to manipulate things. In his analysis, however, he sees the human being as confronting the world of things, the real contents of his surroundings, in a manner that is too direct. For human interaction with objects, the very process whereby we "get a grip on" things, takes place in stages of learning; our perspectives toward and expectations of things and events are socially conditioned. Even Gehlen's presentation of some of the most important ideas of G. H. Mead (which were not familiar to most Germans at this time) cannot compensate for this conceptual weakness. Gehlen himself ultimately does not deny that any further work on an "elementary" anthropology would have to address these problems and he came to believe that the two-sided relationship between human beings and things should be conceived of more as a "triangular relationship," in which the reciprocal relationships between subject and object could be represented along with the partners in interaction who influence and define these relationships.

Gehlen did not change his standpoint on those points that were the most frequent targets of his critics, such as, in particular, his rejection of metaphysics, his theory of language and its relation to action (which was seen as overly instrumentalistic), and his theory of humans as "deficient" beings. His stance is articulated most clearly in his response to the accusation of "biologism" levied at him—an accusation that stems from the criticisms of his theory of language and that agrees to some extent with the objecting views holding that the program of an "empirical philosophy" cannot possibly be carried out and is in fact without foundation.

Gehlen also remained firm in his rejection of all philosophical theories that propose a stratified structure in the world, even though he does, for example, draw liberally from N. Hartmann's theory of the hierarchy of ontological strata in his argument. After the first edition of the present book appeared, Hartmann wrote an enthusiastic review in which, after a favorable discussion of the work, he went on to list a series of objections, most of which he refuted himself. He then, however, addressed Gehlen's rejection of the model of the stratified structure of the world, criticizing it in great detail and pointing out the basic irreconcilability of his and Gehlen's approaches.

Gehlen also maintained a firm stance against those of his critics who argued that his views on evolution, particularly his rejection of the Darwinian theory of evolution, were unfounded. Critics argued, for example, that Gehlen's theory of evolution, which was based on only a few principal sources, relied heavily on "outsiders in biological research." This particular line of criticism is closely related to the rejection of Gehlen's narrow notion of the "deficient" being.

Gehlen defended himself most strongly against the "philosophical objections" raised against him. He was accused, for example, of deriving his concept of action from the morphological characteristics of the human being without any philosophical basis. Furthermore, it was argued that, in his theory of language, Gehlen incorrectly assessed the primordial nature of language and thus failed to grasp its "essence," because he viewed language solely as a relieved mode of action, thus, as a form of instrumental interaction with the world. Habermas's "theory of communicative action," to cite one example, takes issue with Gehlen's views; he assesses and explains the forms of knowledge and rationality in terms of linguistic structures. Then, however, language would become a guide for reason, by which the irrationality of the suppression of arguments and, similarly, the possibilities for action, could be measured. To insights such as these, which came about in part as a result of the critical reception of his work, Gehlen has basically closed his mind.

IX

As far as philosophy is concerned, Gehlen's book shifts often in its "standpoint of reflection," but certain fundamental themes can be seen to run through the background. From an early interest in existential phenomenology (1931), Gehlen went on to embrace the traditions of German idealism (1933) and finally came to formulate his "philosophical anthropology," which established the methods of his thought and which was then developed further into a sociologically oriented study of modern industrial societies, as well as, for example, of aesthetics (1960), of the problems of "cultural crystallization." Gehlen himself believed at one time that this development followed the "course of Comte's law," that is, it was aimed at providing an empirical foundation for knowledge. In all these works, however, the basic convictions were already firmly established, just as specific sources of Gehlen's thought were also inevitably present: Fichte, Schopenhauer, and Nietzsche, the French moralists, the keen reflection of idealist philosophy without, however, the constraints of its system.

When invited to write a "methodological self-portrait" for the English journal *The Human Context* ("An Anthropological Model," *The Human Context* (1968–1969). 1: 11–20), Gehlen described the development of his thought in great detail. He pointed out that anyone interested in philosophy in Germany in 1935 might still harbor the desire to formulate a grand system or might still have "metaphysical ambitions." Gehlen did not believe the reason for this lay in the fact that the majority of German professors of philosophy belonged to the idealist tradition; he cited instead the repercussions of Nietzsche's thought, the ontology of Nicolai Hartmann, and— somewhat curiously—the later work of Henri Bergson, who had moved away from metaphysics, albeit, as Gehlen believed, in pursuit of a new form of mysticism. At the same time, however, it was clear that such a traditional philosophical position had become quite tenuous—in particular, the belief that a philosophical system must never "lose contact with the sciences," although it had become increasingly difficult to form a comprehensive view of these sciences. Thus, "it had become perfectly obvious that philosophy had surrendered up a large part of its jurisdiction, the most important areas involved being the natural sciences and politics." Husserl's phenomenology and Max Scheler's analytical study of possible experiences modeled thereon gave back to "many young thinkers"—Gehlen himself included—"a sense of immediacy and the ingenuousness to adopt a direct approach to philosophical problems" and the urgently needed opportunity for a new beginning.

Gehlen retained this aspect of the phenomenological approach, although not in the sense that he pursued a continuation of a "fundamental analysis," as Husserl did, but rather in the sense that his vision is based on experience and directed toward parts of objects, made into the focus for philosophical and scientific reflection, which remained as the foundation for his search for "categories." Gehlen therefore responded to this call for a new beginning by turning toward an "empirical philosophy." It is the exact and concrete observations that make up the underpinnings of his philosophy which also make his books read like literary essays. The walls that already separated "science" from "literature," with its great range of opportunities for communication (ranging from the aphorism to the analytical breadth of the novel), were ignored; this can be seen, for example, in the fact that Gehlen profited greatly from the "keen reflection" he found in the novels of Thomas Mann, Franz Kafka, and Robert Musil, as well as the work of Gottfried Benn and others.

X

Arnold Gehlen was born on January 29, 1904 in Leipzig, the son of Dr. Max Gehlen, the publisher. From 1914 to 1923, he attended the well-known Thomas-Gymnasium in Leipzig. From 1923 until the summer of 1925 (when he spent a semester in Cologne, studying primarily with Scheler and Hartmann), and again in 1926 and 1927, Gehlen studied philosophy in Leipzig,

also attending courses in German, art history, physics, and zoology. He was awarded a Ph.D. on November 5, 1927 for his dissertation, which is still relevant, on Hans Driesch, his instructor in philosophy, entitled "Zur Theorie der Setzung und des setzungshaften Wissens," a work that he later said was intended only to fulfill the academic requirement for the degree. However, even here we can detect an interest, perhaps awakened by Nicolai Hartmann, in the critique and study of categories.

On July 17, 1930, Gehlen advanced to the rank of university professor in philosophy *(Privatdozent)* with a work entitled "Real and Unreal Mind." During the summer semester of 1933, he took over the academic chair of Paul Tillich in Frankfurt, who had been removed from his post by the national socialists and forced into exile.

Somewhat later, on November 1, 1934, the thirty-year-old Gehlen succeeded Hans Driesch as professor of philosophy at the University of Leipzig. Because Hans Driesch was labeled a "pacifist" by the government in Dresden and was forced into early retirement, it is possible that Gehlen's appointment was related to an action of the national socialist government. It is not clear exactly who urged that Gehlen be given the vacant post, but, in his inaugural lecture on "The State and Philosophy," Gehlen clearly expressed his indebtedness to the fascist regime. One could interpret the basic thrust of this lecture as right-Hegelian, as an affirmation of the government's unification efforts. In this lecture, he argued that philosophy was an intellectual effort that could "not be unpolitical today" and that it should be directed toward orienting the "concrete existence" of the German people, to whom "the national socialist movement [had given] a new drive for life and new structures for existence."

Gehlen's academic career has not usually been viewed solely as the product of political opportunism, because several sources make it clear that, quite independently of his avowal of the German strain of fascism, he was lauded as one of the most promising philosophical minds of his generation—even by those who clearly opposed his political leanings or even his philosophy. Nonetheless, even if expectations of Gehlen's contributions to philosophy did figure in some way into his university appointment—and perhaps even gave the initial impetus for it—his university career cannot be viewed independently of Hitler's rise to power. At the very least, he gained certain advantages from the new political constellation of power in Germany after 1933; at the very least, he behaved opportunistically. It is more likely, however, that he entered the NSDAP (National Socialist German Workers' Party) in May of 1933 because of personal convictions, for until 1935, it appears that Gehlen sympathized to a considerable degree with the regime.

It is difficult to assess this question nowadays, in part because the accounts of contemporaries are so contradictory. Nonetheless, it is worth noting that while pupils and colleagues of Gehlen's identify in retrospect different reasons for his entry into the national socialist party, they do all agree unanimously that he never appeared publicly as a Nazi, never in uniform, for example. He did serve, however, as the head of the league of university lecturers at the University of Leipzig for two semesters; in other words, he represented the national socialist university teachers. As letters written by Gehlen to Nicolai Hartmann attest, Gehlen began to draw away from the NSDAP in the early 1940s at the latest; one can detect a growing conflict with the party, in particular, in the organization of the German Philosophical

Society, which Gehlen headed in 1942. His split with the national socialists might perhaps be related to the acclaim that his principal work of anthropology had found. Here one must keep in mind that this book, even in its first edition and despite its several allusions to the "world-view" of national socialism, was strictly nonracist. On the issue of racism, we can agree with the philosopher Wolfgang Harich, who said in an interview in 1976 intended as an obituary for Gehlen: "Although [Gehlen] was a Nazi at that time—not for opportunistic reasons, but rather because of his nationalistic, conservative beliefs—he essentially destroyed all theoretical foundations for racism in his major work.... The book is clearly opposed to any form of "biologism," . . . and it necessarily also calls into question the 'blond beast' which was then in fashion."

We should realize that the fascism of the upper classes and the conservative intellectuals was "nobler," sometimes even supported by fascinating insights; it was more abstract and at times more refined than the primitive party ideology, but it was nonetheless just as blind and dangerous. Some conservatives did take part in an opposition against Hitler, many at least kept a passive distance, and indeed the majority opposed Hitler's conduct of the war, branding it as "dilettantism" which would inevitably lead to military and political disaster. Nonetheless, conservatism created many of the necessary prerequisites for a broadly based fascist movement, which could then be consolidated—at least on the emotional level—and exploited by the National Socialists. Their grand personal distance, their arrogance toward the "brown shirts," often served to conceal their own interests and dispel any feelings of guilt or responsibility they might have had; these attitudes were certainly typical of the times and the social rank of many individuals who could afford to keep such distance because they were the privileged and enjoyed the benefits of a good education and good social position. The importance Gehlen accorded to human decision, to acts of will (*dezisionistisches Pathos*), his appeal to order, his formalism, his pessimistic pronouncements made from an elite position, his aversion to any efforts for social emancipation consequently appear more significant than his allusions to Alfred Rosenberg in the first versions of this book.

One reason it is important to establish the proper context for evaluating Gehlen's life and work is that his appeal for "responsibility" and "duty" necessarily implies that those who enjoy privileges and occupy exalted positions bear special responsibility and guilt. To Gehlen, this did not mean open complicity of participation in carrying out the crimes of the regime, but referred instead to a "relieved" degree of involvement, in the sphere of validity of words and norms.

In 1938, Gehlen was appointed to the department of philosophy at the University of Königsberg—a position once occupied by Immanuel Kant. In 1940, he transferred to the University of Vienna. After the end of the fascist dictatorship in Germany, Gehlen—like all German national professors in Austria—was in turn removed from his post, although at the same time— and many have attempted to see herein the proof that he never appeared in Vienna as an active National Socialist—he was made a member of the Austrian Academy of Sciences. In 1947, he became professor of sociology at the College for Administrative Sciences in Speyer, newly founded by the French military regime. In this new post, Gehlen turned his attention to analyzing the machinery of the social welfare systems of care in industrial societies and the consequences of bureaucratization—topics that, although by no means unpolitical in nature, nonetheless created a sort of neutral space in which open political debate could be suspended. Only much later did Gehlen turn once more to political issues, this time in an explicit and polemical form, as a response to the student movement and the social democratic and liberal reform politics of the late sixties and early seventies.

Gehlen's break with philosophy became apparent after 1945 and was even expressed in certain changes in his teaching contract. He had come to believe that philosophy could function only as historical dogma and that the problem areas that had been developed through the philosophical tradition now demanded a more scientific approach. Thus, after the war, Gehlen developed his anthropological model principally in the form of a theory

of institutions, and he also published social psychological studies of industrial society (*Man in the Age of Technology,* trans. by P. Lipscomb, New York Columbia University Press, 1980). The monographs he published during this time include *Urmensch und Spätkultur* (1956), his essays on the sociology and aesthetics of modern art (*Zeit-bilder,* 1960), and his final book, *Moral und Hypermoral* (1969), in which he intended to present a "theory of social regulations." Interspersed with these are various essays on cultural and contemporary topics as well as his many lectures and articles promoting his conservative beliefs.

Many of the major universities in the Federal Republic of Germany (Göttingen, Heidelberg, and Tübingen, for example) debated whether or not to appoint Gehlen to a chair in philosophy or sociology; however, time and time again, political considerations proved insurmountable obstacles. In 1961, he was given a position in the sociology department of the Aachen

Technical University; he taught there until his retirement in 1969. Arnold Gehlen died on January 30, 1976.

XI

At the beginning of this introduction, we posed the question of the "relevance" of Gehlen's work today. In the course of presenting the most important theses of his "elementary anthropology," along with the various critical responses to these, it became evident that Gehlen's theories inevitably have a "political" aspect, one that is responsible for their ideological effectiveness as well as for their limitations described here. It should be stressed that Gehlen's theories do not represent the isolated vision of one individual. There were in fact many other efforts pursuing a similar course; indeed, even as early as 1934, one spoke of the "anthropological bent" in German philosophy and social science. Parallel to the development of existential philosophy, and hence also under the influence of Soren Kierkegaard and, at least as far as the formulation of problems was concerned, parallel as well to Martin Heidegger's philosophy of being (whose philosophical solutions were strange to Gehlen), the human being was rediscovered. The first book to give this new philosophical-anthropological perspective was probably *The Riddle of Mankind* (*Das Menschheitsrätsel,* 1922) by Paul Alsberg, with its anti-Darwinist and anti-zoological leanings. However, the first work to present this new direction of thought in depth was Max Scheler's *Man's Place in Nature* (English edition, 1961; German edition published in 1928).

Helmuth Plessner, one of the major proponents of "philosophical anthropology," recognized early on that this philosophical "parallel-action" was motivated in part by ideology and world-view. In 1936, in his inaugural lecture at Groningen, Plessner discussed how the "task of philosophical anthropology" related to a society suffering a crisis of orientation: "In the movement of the Hegelian left, anthropology entered the scene for the first time as philosophy, that is, as the opponent of and heir to all open and camouflaged theology. This trend then led to Marx and Stirner and thus also to the self-destruction of anthropology in the philosophical sense. Under the pressures of industrial development, which both encouraged an extreme division of labor in research and split the interests into bourgeois and proletarian, idealism was revitalized on the bourgeois side while, on the opposite side, Marxism was preserved. This situation, which had existed in Germany since the 1870s, fell apart after the war. A new state of social affairs came to light. As the world shaped by Christianity and antiquity dissolves, the human being, whom God has completely abandoned, faces the threat of sinking back into bestiality and so poses once again the question of the purpose and meaning of human existence."

This turning back to the structural elements in the existence of the human being as a natural species took the form of a philosophy of life. Based on the understanding that life is the category that binds together body and mind, nature and culture, the attempt was made to sidestep the division created between the natural and cultural sciences. It was not solely the heuristic talents of a few theoreticians that led to proposing the concept of life as the central category of anthropological study; there was also a political motivation related to world-view for this development. Thus, the very foundations of man's vital drives and abilities became the subject of study of a philosophy in which an underlying need for stability served as the backdrop. It was hoped that two contradictory and yet curiously complementary fears could be thereby conquered: on the one hand, the fear that the excessive nature of man's vital powers might destroy the basis for his existence, that they might plunge him into a chaos of drives and urges; and on the other hand, the fear that reflection, thought divorced from deed, could threaten life and inhibit vital impulses. From a sociology of knowledge perspective, one could probably argue that, because the vital nature of the human being has become problematic in this dual fashion, here problems having to do with the realization of life were being formulated from the perspective of bourgeois elites—by persons who basically opposed the masses' pursuit of happiness, which was legitimated, and indeed even made inevitable, by the rise of consumerism sparked by capitalism. Often enough, this threat against one's own exclusivity was interpreted as a danger to "culture." On the other hand, however, these intellectuals and specialists in culture found themselves in a position in which their own options for action were limited; that is, they enjoyed a wide space for reflection, which was completely out of proportion to their real chances of intervening in the relations controlled by "real" powers—especially as the adventurous businessman and entrepreneur were still referred to, now as before, as the personifications of bourgeois ethics and freedom to act.

"Philosophical anthropology" therefore has a very clear relationship to the political conditions at the beginning of this century, even if it did not explicitly discuss its relationship to the epochal crisis, to the acutely felt loss of certainty and order which was augmented after the defeat in the war and the collapse of the Kaiser's government. Philosophical anthropology transformed these burning questions of the times, the great uncertainty and consequent need for world-view, on the abstract level of a science of foundations.

All this is particularly clear in Gehlen. The revamping of the social and political system following the end of Kaiser Wilhelm's era, the class conflicts which came to light in the struggle for a new form of government, exacerbated the already tense situation in Germany. After the fundamental religious and metaphysical certainties (but first the more short-winded political ones) were undermined, the resulting insecurity was so great that a flood of charismatic leaders came forth, proposing different solutions for the crises. In this time of ingenious adhoc proposals, Gehlen recognized clearly that any ideas that one "key" could be found to solve everything, any such closed views of the world, had now become anachronistic—these had perhaps been possible for the last time with Nietzsche, on whom so many (Gehlen himself included) had preyed. Gehlen did not want to rely on the contingency of a dogma of salvation, nor did he wish to found his theory of the fluctuating conditions for human survival which demand cultural stabilization and discipline on a few single ideas. For these reasons, he based these stabilization interests on much deeper "truths"—truths that were carefully thought out on a philosophical level and at the same time ascertained empirically and scientifically (that is, by drawing on the findings of biology, psychology, ethnology, and sociology).

This is clear at many points throughout the book, even where Gehlen does not specifically treat social orders. For example, it surfaces as an unvoiced secondary meaning of the concept of relief, which provides legitimation from an anthropological perspective for these forms of "relief," as they have developed historically in systems of government and in the division of labor. For, in the sublimated forms of interaction with things, in the "suspension" of direct manual activity made possible through sight, in the linguistic, and ultimately intellectual, methods of responding to the world— as well as in all the higher levels of "work" (that is, all planning, organizing, and symbolic activity)—one finds ways of dealing with the world that are particular to the human being. In contrast to these, there is the other sort of difficult and usually physical labor, which affords only a small degree of relief, which demands great efforts, and which to this extent, from the anthropological view, carries the stigma of "inhuman." This line of reasoning could certainly be used more critically, but, when interpreted from a conservative standpoint, it leads instead to the theory that such hierarchical differences cannot be overcome and are in fact necessary. The theory which others besides Gehlen have espoused that great cultures arise only where domination and oppression exist is a good illustration of this.

Related to the concept of relief is another equally effective theme. Habit and tradition—in other words, all forms of habitualizing behavior—are interpreted by Gehlen as modes of relief. In contrast, reflective consciousness, which "renders uncertain" and "inquires after," can, as has already been suggested, actually endanger man's very survival. It then becomes easy to build an argument for the prohibition of reflection, and consequently of criticism as well, and base this on the nature of the human constitution.

One final example of how Gehlen's theory of anthropological foundations relates to the political order involves his intricate and insightful descriptions of man's interaction with things, which we have already discussed. I remarked earlier that an intermediary element is missing in this scheme, not because Gehlen believed it to be superfluous, but because he chose to leave it out of this book. This weak point in the "elementary anthropology" argument provides the basis for an important ideological shortcut in Gehlen's social theory—namely, his belief that the "pressures of facts" (*Sachzwänge*), which we have created and which threaten to control us (the nature of which may change in the course of history, as Gehlen does not deny) are directly related to the organic deficiencies peculiar to the human being. Thus, the human being's lack of organic specialization and consequent need for stabilization lead directly to an affirmation of institutions, which Gehlen understands as that form of "alienation" that first makes freedom possible. At one time, in a candid revelation of his keen analytical abilities as well as of all the disadvantages such an affirmation of institutions entails, Gehlen summed up as follows: "It would be just as false to reckon directly with the smallness of the human beings as with their greatness, or their pettiness, or with the fact that each is carved from warped wood. The direct playing out of subjectivity is therefore always false and, ultimately, it is the same as in the relationship between the sexes: between man and woman, the most passionate, the richest, and most stimulating relationship can be maintained directly only as spiritual pathos [*Seelisches Pathos*], under the rarest of conditions; on it alone, nothing can be founded. Biological and economic considerations, the coming generation, hunger, and urgent needs are all stronger, and the relationship must be objectified, it must be generalized beyond the exclusivity of these individuals. In a word, precisely if these human beings are not to lose each other and become strangers to each other, their relationship must be alienated as the institution of marriage. The human being can maintain a lasting relationship toward himself and his peers only indirectly, he must find himself via a detour, parting from himself, and here is where institutions come in. Indeed, as Marx correctly surmised, these are forms created by the human being, in which the spiritual, an intangible substance for all its richness and pathos (*Pathos*), is objectified, interwoven with the course of things, and only in this way made permanent. At least now human beings are burned and consumed by their own creations, and not by brutal nature, as the animals are. The institutions are the great orders that preserve and destroy us, that outlast us, they are our destinies upon which we human beings hurl ourselves with our eyes wide open, with what is to someone who judges such things a perhaps higher form of freedom."

I do not believe that Gehlen's vision of the human being, who on the motor level is so inventive and versatile, must necessarily lead to a conservative theory of stabilization, as Gehlen has compellingly advanced. Gehlen was able to do this only because of the one-sided nature of his own premises and findings, for, based on the anthropological theses developed here, one could also identify possibilities for the emancipation of the human being. This would not of course signify a liberation from the anthropological facts, but would instead focus on the versatility, the openness, and "non-determined" nature of the human species. Thus, it is also possible to develop ways of obtaining "relief" from these oppressive burdens which would not link a stabilized existence for man so rigidly to the forms of relief represented by government and privileged monopolies. These thoughts—which are quite contrary to Gehlen's own—I have interpolated here to make clear that Arnold Gehlen's "philosophical anthropology" is of course never completely separate from his own conservative values but yet it is not totally subsumed by these either. To put this another way, one does not have to understand Gehlen's anthropology solely from the perspective of his own social theory of political order. To be sure, one cannot read his anthropology without this frame of reference and, if need be, even in opposition to it.

Introduction

1. Man as a Special Biological Problem

The need felt by reflective persons for an interpretation of human existence is not simply a theoretical need. Depending on the decisions that such an interpretation entails, certain concerns become evident while others are concealed. Whether man sees himself as a creature of God or as a highly evolved ape will make a distinct difference in his attitude toward concrete facts; in each case as well, he will respond to very different inner callings.

Of course, religions, world views, and the sciences are not exclusively devoted to answering the question of man's nature. They do, however, tend to offer some answers or at least points of view from which an answer may be drawn. There is no guarantee of finding an agreement among these, however, because, as is the case above, the answers may be mutually exclusive.

Precisely these circumstances should be considered in determining the nature of the human being; that is to say, there is a living being, one of whose most significant characteristics is the need for self-explanation, for which an "image," an interpretative formula, is necessary. This self-explanation must include not only the individual's own perceived motivations and characteristics, but also those of other humans, since treatment of others will depend on how the individual views them and how he views himself. However, it is not as easy to explain what it means to say that man *must* interpret his existence and, based on this interpretation, must actively formulate opinions about himself and others.

Nonetheless, an answer is necessary because one could otherwise mistakenly assume that it is possible to remain neutral in this issue and refrain from choosing one of the conflicting interpretations of the meaning of man's existence.

The first of these interpretations sees man as descended from God, the second from animals. The first is not a scientific approach and the second, as we shall see, is scientifically ambiguous. It is striking that both points of view do share one common assumption—that man cannot be understood in and of himself but that it is necessary to employ categories above and beyond man to describe and explain him. It is here that the particular interest of this book comes into focus, for I contend that this assumption is *not* necessary, but instead, that it is possible to develop an understanding of man's nature that would make use of very specific concepts, applicable only to the subject of man. This line of examination opens up when one considers the following question: What does man's need to interpret his existence mean?

We could answer this question if we viewed man as a being whose very nature and existence poses a problem, which man must seek to understand and clarify through his self-interpretation. It all depends on whether or not it is possible to develop this point of view within a scientific, that is to say empirical, analysis of man. Man would be, according to this understanding, not only a being who must, for a variety of peculiarly human reasons, seek explanations, but also, in a certain sense, would be unequipped to do so. In other words, man is a being whose very existence poses problems for which no ready solutions are provided. If this view is correct, then man has to develop an understanding of himself, for he can make something of himself only after he has formed a self-concept. The problems man faces must indeed be a part of his very existence and must, therefore, lie in the very fact of his identity as "man." Nietzsche recognized precisely this at one point when he referred to man as "the not yet determined animal."[1] The phrase "not yet determined" is apt and has two meanings. First, it is as yet undetermined exactly what man is; second, the human being is some-how "unfinished," not firmly established. We can accept both statements as true.

The above discussion has given a preliminary indication of the contents of this book. These will be elaborated upon further in the following pages.

This work is a philosophical and scientific one. It will remain firmly within the bounds of experience, of analysis of facts or processes that are accessible to or verifiable for everyone.

In view of the advances in modern technology, metaphysical statements possess only a very limited persuasive power and, above all, little true ability to motivate and influence the actions of real people. Lofty statements formulated as abstract truths can hardly hold their own against the broad range of attainable factual knowledge, which is indeed often subject to internal contradictions. Such statements necessarily prompt the further question: What internal and external experiences are they based upon and therefore limited by, and in what traditions or revolutions do they appear logical? Empirical-analytical science, on the other hand, does have the advantage that it can rely upon a consciousness that is, even today, self-evident and self-sufficient, but it pays for this advantage with its fragmentary statements. Even the presentation in this book may be one-sided, at best many-sided, and in any event in need of critique or, better yet, elaboration. In any case, it is apparent that the facts described here can be realized only with the precondition of a technical abstention from metaphysics. Man is an area of research in which, even today, an indefinite number of unseen and unnamed phenomena exist.

The first topic that calls for a metaphysical explanation is that of the "mind." The problems attendant to taking a stance on this subject are so complex, many-layered, and difficult that any simplified position necessarily appears naïve. Who are to be convinced by global theses about the mind, which may, for example, ignore the problem of ideology or of relativism? These great questions are not directly a concern of this book so I will reserve them for later examination. The final section of this book will be devoted to an exposition of these fundamental questions to the extent that I am able to undertake at this time.

To turn back now to the original theme of this introduction, we are attempting to describe the "special place" of man. It would be advantageous if, in the course of this discussion, the general, popular view that characterizes everything that is not man, from a worm to a chimpanzee, as "animal" and thereby sets it apart from man, could be upheld. But what truth is there in this distinction, and is it possible to maintain this view when one takes into account the basic principles of evolutionary theory?

Just as anatomy is a general science of the structure of the human body, so must a comprehensive theory of man be possible. Since we are never in doubt as to whether or not a being is a man and since, furthermore, man does actually constitute a true species, we are justified in our expectation that a general anthropology should have a clear, well-defined subject. Logically, such an anthropology would be ranked above every specialized anthropology, certainly above a theory of races, but also above psychology, as well as any other science that focuses on a particular aspect of man. It would therefore not expressly treat the problems of these specialized disciplines, just as general anatomy does not treat particular anatomical features of race.

When one speaks of the special position of man, one must first make clear from what man is being distinguished. For this reason, no small amount of space has been devoted to comparing human characteristics and abilities with those of animals. It is only in recent times, however, that these comparisons have been carried out with the preconceived purpose of tracing the descent of man from animals by using the every-handy concept of "development," which all too easily grows from a hypothetical construct to a metaphysical one. Quasi-empirical concepts, too, which were originally developed in opposition to metaphysical ones, such as creation, may become "metaphysical" if they take on the latter's functions. The derivation of human traits from those of animals succeeds perhaps in cases of individual characteristics or complexes of characteristics, but not when "the whole man" is taken into account; the problem of explaining man is very difficult—often attempted but not yet achieved.

This challenge has not been met for several reasons. The main reason is that the "external" and the "internal" have not been brought together; morphology and psychology, body and soul, have always been treated as separate worlds. In addition, the general claim that man is a unity of body, soul, and mind must necessarily remain abstract. This claim is no doubt correct, but logically speaking it is a negation because a rejection of abstract dualism is expressed therein. Nothing is said, on the other hand, of the positive side of this claim. As does every universal statement it remains abstract—too true to be correct—and can offer no answers to concrete questions. To use concepts from Nicolai Hartmann's new ontology, it is up to us, in spite of the admitted impossibility of deriving "mind" from "life," to find those categories that are common to both and that therefore make their coexistence possible.

A further reason for the failure of universal anthropological theories of man is that in any such effort several single scientific disciplines must be combined: biology, psychology, cognitive theory, linguistics, physiology, sociology, and so forth. Simply becoming oriented in such widely different disciplines would not be easy; even more questionable is the possibility of forming a point of view from which all these sciences could be applied to *one* subject. The boundaries between these sciences would have to be torn down, but in a productive way. Out of this destruction, material for the creation of a new single science must be obtained. I wish to propose such a unifying point of view, which cannot be derived from any one of the single disciplines involved, but which is instead a philosophical one. This book will detail the application of this one fundamental thought, this one simple viewpoint.

Until now, the development of a philosophical anthropology was prevented by the following difficulty: Although individual distinguishing features or characteristics were identified in man, none of these was found to be uniquely human. Human beings do indeed have a very unusual physical structure but the anthropoids (great apes) have one quite similar. In addition, there are many animals, from ants to beavers, that form living quarters or artificial dwellings or that are social. Like man, elephants are also clever, and acoustical communication similar to our language definitely exists in many species. Later, we will take a look in greater detail at Köhler's interesting studies of intelligence in chimpanzees. If, in addition to such specific observations, we add into account evolutionary theory, then anthropology would seem at best to be the last chapter in zoology. As long as there is no universal theory of man, we must be content with simply considering and comparing individual features. As long as this is the case, there will be no truly independent anthropology because there is no independent being "man."

If one wishes to adhere to the latter view, one must acknowledge the "totality" of man. The theory of the unity of body and soul does not, however, actually overcome the dualism of body and soul, of the "external" and "internal." It only avoids the problems contained within it. Why did it occur to Nature to fashion a being who, by reason of his consciousness, so often falls prey to error and disturbance? Why, instead of "soul" and "mind," did she not supply him with a few unerring instincts? Furthermore, if such a unity does exist, where then are the concepts and philosophical categories necessary for understanding the "soul" and the "mind" in terms of the "body," or for understanding the "body" in terms of the "soul" and "mind," which should theoretically be possible if such a unity does exist? No answer has been provided to this question and therefore the right to try anew is incontestable.

It could be that there is a hitherto unrecognized connection between all external and internal human traits and capabilities which becomes clear only from *one* particular point of view. While this train of thought might necessitate choosing concepts that would be directly opposed to those prevalent in zoology and animal psychology, this would help solve the anthropological problem of defining man and thereby contribute to an understanding of man's special place in nature and to the formulation of a universal theory of man. This single point of view would have to be a central one or, in any case, make it impossible to declare any one distinguishing characteristic of man—such as his intelligence, upright gait, use of hands, language, or anything else—to be the "whole." Such an approach never succeeds, for any one of these isolated characteristics can be found somewhere in the animal kingdom and hence, if taken on its own, becomes ambiguous.

Strictly speaking, I am proposing only an *elementary anthropology*, but one that, as far as man is concerned, is far-reaching and probably even unlimited in its implications. For this purpose, many facts from various scientific disciplines must become easily accessible; to accomplish this by employing a universal theory is the real philosophical challenge. Philosophy is concerned with specific existing facts and objects (even when these are processes, such as actions) and thus "man" is a theme of philosophy. None of the single sciences that are also concerned with man—morphology, psychology, linguistics, etc. —has "man" as its principal subject; however, there can be no science of man that does not take into consideration findings from these various disciplines.

This book takes issue with another view as well—the widespread "naturalistic" and so-called "biological" interpretation of man as descended from animals, whether it be in the form of the classical—or, as one may also call it, naïve—theory of evolution, or in any other approach that claims to be "biological" and reduces everything to physiology. I will evaluate these approaches from a scientific perspective in the body of this work and would like just to foreshadow my argument here: I assert that it is precisely this type of approach that is *not* biological when it is applied to man and, further, that it discredits biological thought. I claim in addition to have developed a biological approach to man that contradicts almost all current views. If one were to accept the hypothesis, which will be supported throughout this work, that in man there is a unique, unprecedented, all-encompassing plan of Nature, then any direct derivation of man from animal—that is from the great apes, chimpanzees, etc.—would immediately rule out this line of inquiry. In fact, even an attempt to seek such a derivation would scatter all kernels of truly anthropological thought. Thus, an important dialectic becomes evident in what we call "biological thought."

If one considers man from an external perspective—in terms of his physical structure—and if one is well-versed in the history of zoological development, and perhaps also in fossils, then a definite theory will present itself, particularly if one yields to the intellectual instinct to simplify and unify—the theory of man's evolution from the anthropoids. This theory claims to be a biological approach because it proceeds from the corporal, from physical structure, from the laws of development of organic life. Precisely for this reason it never touches upon the "inner side" of man at all, and thus has to place great importance on Köhler's experiments with chimpanzees, according to which anthropoid apes also possess intelligence, even creative intelligence. Thus, a schema for a general theory of man does exist, and it is currently dominant; but this has resulted in the quite inconsiderate neglect of the inner life of man or at best in rather child-like representations of the nature of this inner life. What is language? What is imagination? What is will? Is there such a thing as cognition? And, if so, what is perceived and what is not? Why one and not the other? What are "morals" and why do they exist? With the concepts of the theory of evolution, these questions cannot even be posed, let alone answered.

I would like to argue that one can come closer to answering these questions by examining the possibility of impartial, purely descriptive concept formation. The difficulty here lies primarily in the casting aside of stubborn habits of thought. If man does indeed represent a "special plan" of Nature, then any nonspecific consideration of him necessarily falls short. I will prove, on the contrary, that there is an "anthropobiological" view that brings together the peculiar physical structure of man and his complex and complicated inner life. This is accomplished by means of special fundamental concepts that can yield insights even where the nexus of body and soul is probably permanently obscured from direct observation.

An objective analysis of a living being from a biological perspective is possible only if it treats the spiritual and intellectual aspects of life as facts in relation to other facts. Such an approach should not be restricted to an examination of the somatic or to a comparison of certain of man's intellectual or physical achievements with those of animals. A biological approach can succeed only if it can discover specifically human laws, which can be documented in all areas of the human constitution. It thus makes sense for now to turn away from all current theories, to "bracket" them, even the theory of man's direct descent from the anthropoids. It is also necessary to bracket the belief that there are "transitions" from animal to human intelligence or language, from animal societies or symbiotic arrangements to human institutions. This holds true as well for many familiar psychological concepts. This bracketing is by no means an unreasonable suggestion since these theories have in any case not yet succeeded in coming up with a satisfactory universal theory of man, even within the boundaries of what can be achieved. A new approach is needed.

As far as man is concerned, any biological consideration should not confine itself to the somatic or physical. What then constitutes the anthropobiological approach? It consists of answering the question of what are the necessary conditions for man's existence. Let us consider this strange and incomparable being who lacks the conditions for survival which animals possess and ask ourselves what problems does such a being face in simply staying alive and surviving. It will soon become apparent from our study of this difficult question that what is clearly at stake here is nothing less than the whole spectrum of man's inner life—his thought and language, imagination, unique structure of drives, unique motor skills, and mobility. Each of these features will be considered in turn and will serve to shed light on and clarify the others. A highly complex, marvelous array of skills is necessary for a being with this particular physical constitution to survive until tomorrow, next week, and next year. This is what a biological approach to man should involve.

.   It was stated above that man is the "not yet determined animal"; he is somehow not "firmly established." I also claimed that he finds his existence a challenge and therefore needs to develop an interpretation of himself—a matter that has always been of crucial importance. We can now expand upon these statements: Nature has accorded a special position to man, or—to put it differently—in man she has pursued a unique, hitherto untrodden path of development; she has created a new organizational principle. A consequence of this principle is that man's existence poses a difficult problem; his survival becomes his greatest challenge and greatest accomplishment. Quite simply, it is a considerable feat for man to survive from one year to the next, and all his abilities are employed toward this end. To say that man is not "firmly established" means that he draws upon his own aptitudes and talents to survive; of necessity, he relates to himself in a way that no animal does. I would say that he does not so much *live* as *lead* his life. He does this not for reasons of enjoyment, not for the luxury of contemplation, but out of sheer desperation.

There must be a good reason for Nature to expose a being to all the dangers of disturbance and aberration that are intrinsic to man's existence as an "undetermined" being, to his compulsion to understand himself and exercise control over his life. The reason can be found in the risks posed by a physical structure that contradicts the organic laws in strong evidence among animals. If any approach can be called biological, then it is the following one: to ask by what means a given being is able to exist. By adopting this approach, the ground work is laid for a new science—a universal science of man. We will learn that man's unique biological—indeed anatomical,—structure makes his particular form of intelligence necessary.

We will also see how language is an extension of a system of deeply rooted interrelationships of movement and sensation, hôw thought and imagination are developed, and how man's perceptual world harmonizes with all this. An unprecedented structure of drives, unknown among animal species, is also evident in man. Finally, there is one system of thought that can enable us to organize the wealth of factual knowledge we have accumulated about man. We would like to create a system of relationships encompassing all the essential features of man, from his upright gait to his morals. These features do form a system, because each presupposes the other; a single error, a deviation in one point would render the whole system incapable of life. It is impossible to identify "causes" here because there are no causal relationships between these features; intelligence did not bring about language, an erect posture did not "cause" intelligence, and so on. Precisely these characteristics in precisely this system of interrelationships permit man to exist. In part I, I will demonstrate that this special position of man poses an insoluble problem for the classical theory of evolution and I will draw on other theories to document this.

Again, in terms of methodology, it is necessary to keep in mind here that the notion of "cause" should be discarded. This concept has a meaning only in those cases in which single relationships can be isolated—that is, only within the bounds of experimental science. Otherwise, it is of limited value and usually indicates that one feature has been isolated from an entire system and designated as the "cause" of that very system. Examples of this include the claim that the use of the hands caused strong brain development which, in turn, led to the emergence of man or the argument that the disappearance of the jungles during the late Tertiary Period caused the famous descent from the trees which then caused man to walk upright, and so forth.

Another approach exists which avoids the pitfalls of such questions of cause and which is firmly in keeping with our biological orientation. This involves determining the relationship between conditions and can be formulated as follows: without A there is no B; without B, no C; without C, no D; and so on. If this sequence ultimately circles back upon itself—without N, no A—then we will have arrived at a total understanding of the system in question without having to resort to the metaphysics of a single cause.

It should be immediately clear that this method alone is appropriate for investigating the "totality" of man, if such does indeed exist. Conversely, this totality can be proven only if this method, which we will adopt, is successful.

The fundamental theses that I have been emphasizing in an unchanged

form since the first edition have not protected this book from misunderstandings; these have usually stemmed from a narrow, popular understanding of the term "biological." I have become sensitized to this term because
it is so frequently misused. It is difficult, however, to come up with a
satisfactory alternative. I wish, therefore, to stress again that I am not
proposing to derive consciousness, imagination, and language from bodily
processes nor am I claiming that art, religion, and law should be understood
as mere outgrowths of organic life. Instead, the method of observation I
have chosen and termed biological consists of examining in process the
higher functions of imagination, language, thought, and so forth. Parallel
to this, I will document the unique position of man from a morphological
or, in a narrower sense, biological, perspective. At this point, the question
arises: how can such a vulnerable, needy, exposed being possibly manage
to survive? The answer then suggests itself that the higher functions must
be necessary for survival, that they are necessary determinants of man's
unique morphological position. Both lines of inquiry share the important
concept of *action*, a close empirical analysis of which reveals true structures
or categories, which express the relationship between the physical and spiritual and limit this relationship to certain areas of concentration. This relationship itself transcends our understanding. As Heisenberg wrote: "As
we perceive it, reality is separated into distinct layers which, as it were, are
only united in an abstract space behind phenomena" so that "all knowledge
is, in a certain sense, suspended over a bottomless abyss."[2] On the other
hand, this relationship between mind and body is, of course, continually
expressed in every voluntary arm movement and is therefore a fact and an
experience. An analysis of man's actions as they are carried out might
possibly shed some light, however slight, on this darkest of all "abstract
spaces."

Here I would like to give an example involving the fundamental category
of "relief" *(Entlastung)*. Thought, representation, and imagination rest—
as will become apparent—upon a broad base of "sensorimotor" functions
expressed through the hands, eyes, and in language. It would, however, be
an inexcusable simplification to attempt to attribute the former to the latter
or to claim one evolved from the other. On the other hand, there can be
no doubt that the former are based upon the latter. The category of relief
employed in this discussion means that the functions of thought and imagination have achieved their level of versatility through primary visual and
tactile experiences interwoven with language, that they develop the experiences gained through sight and touch in an easier, or freer, form. Further,

certain structures in both areas can be proven to be identical. These higher functions can, as Hartmann explained in his review of this book, "surpass and leave behind the speech apparatus but could also for this very reason first gain their range of freedom through it."[3] In Bergson, there is a tendency in a similar direction, also employing the category of relief: "In man . . . the motor habit can hold other motor habits in check, and thereby, in overcoming automatism, set consciousness free."[4] According to this scheme, then, the problems of thought and language, of language and action, are formulated in such a way as to leave them open for analytical study as long as such study retains *action* as its focal point.

To return to the more general issues at hand, the higher functions are understood here as belonging to the conditions that enable a vulnerable being such as man to survive. Although this "biological" viewpoint is elementary, few objections can be raised against it. As one cannot treat all problems at the same time, we shall later see how this viewpoint must be modified when it is applied to the intellectual superstructure of an entire society. Even now it should be apparent that our viewpoint is actually the opposite of one that seeks to explain the intellectual and spiritual aspects through the organic. Indeed, it becomes obvious again and again that what is commonly attributed and relegated solely to the area of intellectual achievement is often actually already presaged in the vital functions. The vegetative, sensory, and motor functions apparently work more ingeniously than Idealism has been willing to or than Materialism was able to admit. Precisely for this reason, one cannot conceive of those higher functions as existing in an arbitrarily structured organism and they will never be clearly understood if they are not seen in relation to the organically unique position of man.

If, in comparison to animals, man appears as a "deficient being," then this designation expresses a comparative relationship and is therefore of limited value and not a concept of real substance. In this respect, this concept attempts precisely what H. Freyer criticizes it for: "One envisions man fictitiously as animal only to discover that he makes an imperfect and indeed impossible animal."[5] The designation "deficient being" is intended to convey the following: From a biological point of view, in comparison to animals, the structure of the human body appears to be a paradox and stands out sharply. This designation does not, of course, completely define man but it does serve to point out his special position from a morphological perspective.

2. A Critique of the Hierarchical Scheme

It seems advisable to provide a preliminary overview of the ensuing discussion. Before I outline the anthropological scheme, which constitutes the principal basis for all later examinations, I wish first to dispense with a prejudice that crops up almost as a matter of course wherever the relationship between man and animal is concerned.

This prejudice surfaces in Scheler's well-known book, *Man's Place in Nature (Die Stellung des Menschen im Kosmos)*,[6] in which he puts forth the following ideas: habitual as well as intelligent behavior arises from instinctive behavior, an efficient, nonacquired and species-serving behavior that unfolds in a definite rhythm. Habitual behavior is evidenced in any living being that slowly and steadily modifies its behavior in a self-serving and expedient way based on its previous experience and independently of the number of attempts and trial efforts. When an animal retains and employs successful trial and error efforts, they become habit; in like manner, associative memory is also formed. The imitation of actions and movements plays a crucial role in this process. Without resorting to unreliable categories, it can be said in general that any behavior in which practice, habit, imitation, and memory can be observed is quite distinct from more primitive instinctive behavior as well as from intelligent behavior. When Nature permitted this new psychical form to emerge, she also provided it with a means (practical intelligence and judgment) for dealing with any attendant new dangers. A being behaves intelligently if, without any trial attempts, it carries out an appropriate behavior in new situations, unfamiliar to the species or to the individual, or if it suddenly solves an instinctively interesting problem. Involved here is a sudden understanding of an entirely new set of circumstances, which is facilitated by anticipation and prior experience of similar situations. This experience is then promptly transformed into creative action. If one assumes the higher apes possess this ability, which can hardly be doubted, then the question arises as to whether a fundamental difference actually exists between man and animals.

Scheler responds affirmatively to this question by proposing that the new principle that makes a being human is set against all life, is far removed from anything that we could call life: it is the mind. The essential character of the mind, according to Scheler, is its existential detachment, its independence from the organic. An intelligent being is no longer bound to its drives and its environment, but rather is independent of these, or "world-open" *(weltoffen)*. It is able to elevate the centers of opposition originally present in the environment to the status of objects and can carry out the process of ideation—it can make the fundamental distinction between existence *(Dasein)* and essence *(Wesen)*.

In Scheler's view, man is able to suspend his impression of the reality of the world through an ascetic act of inhibiting his own instinctive inclinations and is able thereby to sense the pure essence of things while disregarding their existence; indeed, he may even allow himself to be determined by this insight into the pure essence of things. The *existence* of things is conveyed through our experience of their resistance to our strivings and instinctive urges; in relation to these urges, the world appears primarily as a resisting force or irritation. Man is capable of rendering these urges powerless and can then sublimate this repressed instinctive energy into an unending development of the intellectual acts whereby the pure essence and nature of things are perceived. This means that the mind lives on strengths that are not transformed in the world but rather are drawn from it; the mind moves outside of life and, indeed, at the expense of life. I quote Scheler: "Man alone ... is able to go beyond himself as an organism and to transform, from a center beyond the spatiotemporal world, everything, himself included, into an object of knowledge. . . . The center, however, from which man performs the acts by means of which he objectifies body, psyche, and world in its spatial and temporal abundance, cannot itself be part of this world."[7]

In my view, anthropology has not really progressed beyond the teachings just cited; even the programmatic theory of the unity of body, mind, and soul only modifies Scheler's view by refusing to accept the extra-worldliness of the mind.

All this is intended as an introduction. There is also a generally held prejudice in Scheler's teaching: a hierarchical scheme, composed of the stages of instinct, habit, practical intelligence, and human intelligence. This ranking is deceptive and should not be relied upon, for it can lead to only two possibilities. One possibility is that there is merely a gradual distinction between the practical intelligence possessed by animals and human intelligence—a continuous transition from animal to man such that man is defined merely by a greater concentration, degree of refinement, or increased complexity of animal "characteristics," as the classical theory of evolution holds. The other possibility is that the difference between man and animal—that which is essentially human—is to be sought in the particular characteristic of *intelligence,* in the special quality of "the mind." It then follows that the mind would have to be contrasted with all preceding skills, up to and including practical intelligence and, as is readily apparent, it would be "denatured" thereby. The claim (Scheler, Klages) that the mind is "outside of" of "beyond" life then has nothing new to contribute besides making clear that its proponents arrived at it because they were bound to this rigid scheme.

Through adherence to this hierarchical scheme, another real possibility is neglected—that man's difference from animals may lie in an all-pervasive structural law; in other words, the "style" or form of his movements, actions, sound articulation, intelligence, drives might be fundamentally different from those of animals. I intend here to pursue this line of reasoning, which will prove to be impossible to refute if a structural law can be identified that governs *all* human functions from the physical to the intellectual. The difference can no longer be seen as resting solely with the mind but instead is equally evident in the forms of physical movements. For now, as an initial definition, we will define man as an "acting being" *(handelndes Wesen).* Our earlier characterization of man as a being who seeks explanations, who is undetermined, who seeks to exercise control over things and over himself, now receives further, important clarification. In addition, it is clear that this definition cannot possibly appear within the hierarchical scheme and that it is totally beyond the question of whether the mind should be added to animal characteristics in order to define man. I intend to show that man's disposition toward action is the fundamental structural law behind all human functions and skills, and that this essential feature clearly results from his physical design. A being with such a physical constitution is viable only as an acting being. With these statements, we have formulated the structural law of *all* human processes, from the somatic to the intellectual.

What should be dismissed is the age-old conception (evident even in the background of Scheler's thought) that a hierarchy of life forms is united in man. This idea expresses the belief that in Nature there exist primitive instinctual beings, slightly more advanced animals with habit and memory, and still more advanced animals with practical intelligence, and that all these worlds are united in man, a microcosm, who crowns them with his human intellect. Aristotle reasoned along similar lines. This scheme must be recognized and refuted because it casts the relationship between man and animal in a false light.

There are two basic misconceptions in Scheler's scheme. First is the misconception that a developmental order of skills exists, ranging from instinct to the human mind; second, that this ranking of skills moves from the lower to higher animals and culminates with man. We must refute each of these theses separately.

The new animal psychology, of which Konrad Lorenz in particular is a proponent,[8] dispensed with the belief held by Spencer, Lloyd Morgan, and others that "instinct" was the ontogenetic and phylogenetic "first step" toward the higher intellectual capabilities. To begin with, as careful experiments have shown, there are two fundamentally different types of innate, species-preserving movements: orientation responses evoked by external stimuli and instinctive movements. For example, when a frog, before snapping at a fly, positions itself symmetrically toward it, first just with its eyes and then with its entire body, it is carrying out an orientation response (Taxis). When a fish directs both its eyes toward a mosquito larva and swims toward it while circumventing a water plant in its path, it has thus solved a problem of space; it has taken a detour, without any prior trial and error attempts. There is a fluid transition from the simple mechanisms of orientation to insightful behavior and intelligence. When the Blenny is fleeing from an enemy and can simultaneously keep in view the direction from which the enemy is coming as well as the location of its place of refuge, then its behavior appears "intelligent." Orientation responses are most likely the phylogenetic roots of complex, *variable* modes of behavior, sharing a common origin with true instincts, but not attributable to these—that is, totally distinct from them.

True instincts, on the other hand, are movements or, better yet, precise configurations of movement of a very specific type, which are carried out according to innate automatism and which result from *internal* endogenous stimuli. Prompted by such an internal "re-tuning," birds begin their instinctive nest-building activities, gathering material which has no significance for them before and after this period. Similarly, many animal species perform rhythmical, very precise patterns of movement when courting and mating. That these innate patterns of movement are evoked by internal stimuli can be proven by presenting an intense stimulus—for example, hunger—and seeing that if the desired object is lacking, these movements will still take place "in a void" so to speak. Lorenz observed this phenomenon in a young starling that carried out all the appropriate movements for trapping prey, including pursuing the nonexistent quarry with its eyes and head, swooping down, snapping, and swallowing—all this without an actual object. A budgerigar, raised in isolation, that displays courting behavior before a totally limbless dummy, seems to be hallucinating the body of an actual female budgerigar because he directs distinct movements toward the spot where the female's head (which he has never seen) would normally be.

Instinctive movements, that is, innate, species-specific behavior patterns, are of course normally triggered by the appropriate object (another animal, sexual partner, prey, enemy, etc.) which the animal encounters in its environment. To put it more accurately, these patterns are not triggered by the objects themselves, but rather by highly specific, perceivable "signals" from them which are called releasers. A female mallard raised exclusively among pin-tailed ducks had never exhibited sexual response toward a pin-tailed drake. But when she by chance spied a mallard drake through a tiny gap in the fence, she responded to the sight of its characteristic plumage by breaking into all forms of mating behavior typical to its species. The releaser for the instinctive flight response in mountain hens is the precise, symmetrical outline of a soaring sparrow hawk. A dummy made of pasteboard with the same outline evoked intense, instinctive movements in animals only twenty days old: the sole cockerel spread his wings in a defensive posture while the hens fled for cover. Chemical signals, such as smells, often function as releasers, as when many animals smell the enemy or the prey; often acoustic signals (for example, warning calls) or visual signs, such as striking, bright colors or regular or symmetrical forms, also take on this function; in still other cases, "signal movements," that is, unusual, precise, and rhythmical patterns of movement, may play the same role. As Lorenz observed, "We find in octopi, spiders, bony fishes, reptiles, and many birds certain organs which can be spread like a fan to reveal a colorful pattern. These are organs of display behavior (as Heinroth termed it), by means of which a male is recognizable both to another male and to a female. An orientation response has the result that the entire surface of the displayed organ, for example, a peacock's tail, is perpendicular to the line of vision of the other animal."[9]

In each case, the releasers are so precise and specific that researchers have been able to duplicate them with dummies and elicit and study the instinctive behavior in experiments. Tinbergen was able to lure stickleback females toward the nest, using crude dummies in which only the red color of the male and the specific movements of the "zigzag dance" were imitated. There is a complex, reciprocal staggering of specific instinctive movements between two members of the same species which builds in intensity as Seitz, for example, has documented in the fish *Astatotilapia*.[10]

These studies,—carried out primarily by Lorenz, Seitz, Tinbergen,[11] Heinroth, and others—have totally revolutionized the prevalent views of animal instincts and surpassed the existing literature on the subject; they have also opened up an experimental science with a solid conceptual basis. However, the attempts, in particular by Lorenz, to apply this concept of instinct to man have been unusually feeble and disappointing, as we shall later see. A significant characteristic of man, as Lorenz himself recognizes,[12] is a *reduction of instincts,* an apparently phylogenetic severing of almost all the firmly established connections between "releasers" and innate, specialized patterns of movement. This is so much the case that very often purely affective "emotional storms" may occur, unaccompanied by any actions, or sometimes by highly variable and unpredictable actions, in response to equally unpredictable stimuli that surface in the greatly restructured perceptual world of man.

For our purposes we can safely say that a hierarchical relationship definitely does not exist between intelligent and instinctive behavior; instead, as Bergson realized, there is a tendency for these to be mutually exclusive. Even in the numerous cases in which orientation responses *(taxis),* conditioned reflexes, or self-training appear in conjunction with instinctive behavior, one is still able to distinguish analytically between them. The remarkable, "capricious" instinctive movements are based upon internal cumulative processes of reaction-specific energies which function like hormones and compel the organism to act. This situation results when the appropriate releaser—affecting the centers of perception—shuts down the central inhibitions. Physiologically, these processes are apparently completely different from orientation responses as well as from all self-instilled behavior, learning processes, and "insights" which make variations in behavior possible depending on the specific circumstances. Instinctive behavior originated at the same point as these other behaviors and is not a preliminary stage to them.

Scheler's second thesis is also unfounded. No parallel can be drawn between a structural order of skills and the systematic representation of higher and lower animals such that an empty niche at the top is accorded to man. Closely related animals with almost identical instinctive behavior patterns show remarkable differences in their abilities to learn. Jackdaws and ravens both hide leftover food with the same instinctive movements, but the raven has learned that this behavior is successful only if it goes unobserved. In investigating skills, one is operating outside the boundaries of zoological categorization; the order of skills does not correspond to zoological genera. Buytendijk has proven this beyond doubt in several articles.[13] He writes: "The Darwinistic interpretation that the increase in learning ability in vertebrates runs parallel to zoological development and reaches its zenith in man's ability to learn contradicts the facts." Such arboreal animals as monkeys, squirrels, and parrots often demonstrate the same habits and all show a highly developed learning ability; squirrels, for example, locate their hidden nuts by remembering visual clues. According to Köhler, this characteristic, along with the ability to use detours to reach a goal, belongs to the most sophisticated achievements of the higher apes.

The intelligence of animals, if considered in and of itself, in no way corresponds to their ranking in the zoological system. Such predatory insects as praying mantises and dragonflies, which can focus on their prey by turning their heads toward it while other orientation responses occur without interruption, seem much more intelligent than their close relatives who lack this ability. In this respect they resemble Köhler's apes, who "reveal by their gaze that they are actually taking stock of a situation." This skill, as Buytendijk has pointed out, is not confined to higher animals, but rather is a characteristic of many predatory and arboreal species.[14] Cats, apes, and birds all possess the ability to orient themselves visually in a strange space but dogs do not. Conversely, zoologically closely related species, such as frogs and toads, may show entirely different behaviors; frogs wait in ambush while toads actively hunt for prey.

On the other hand, the simple instinctive response is not confined to the lower animals. "In particular, social instinctive actions in birds are very often triggered exclusively by innate schemes of high specialization," writes Lorenz.[15] Coupled with this, however, birds learn to limit instinctive actions to very specific objects. "Thus, for example, the defensive response of a mallard directly after the birth of her young occurs in response to the distress call of any duckling; but after a few weeks this reaction will occur only in response to her own ducklings which she now knows."[16]

These few examples, more of which are available in the works cited, suffice for our purposes. My intention here is to refute the hierarchical scheme that has accorded one specific niche to man. One must above all refrain either from assuming that there is only a gradual differentiation between man and animal or from claiming that man is distinguished from animals through his mind alone. Anthropology can come into its own only when these prejudices have been set aside; it must establish a special structural law to explain all human peculiarities which must be understood from the perspective of man as an acting being.

It is possible to formulate several laws that govern animal skills and set the limits to these capabilities. These are as follows:

1. In general, animals do learn; that is, they capitalize on previous successful experiences by adopting a smoother, more expedient course if these experiences are repeated under the influence of vitally important stimuli or shocks. Precisely this is the basis for the mechanism of the "conditioned reflex." If an animal is given a biologically meaningless stimulus several times and this is then followed by a more meaningful stimulus which triggers an innate instinctive response, then the animal will, after awhile, respond to the initial stimulus as if it were a preliminary step to the biologically meaningful event that follows. As Lorenz[17] and Guillaume[18] assert, the substitute stimulus begins to function as a signal for the ensuing, biologically significant one. One should, however, be careful here to avoid the word "meaning" because the *meaning* of the signal comes to be only through the act of differentiating it from *what* it means; at this point, the signal becomes a symbol—that is, it is accorded a certain value in social intercourse.

2. As far as animals are concerned, then, a gain in skill can be achieved only in concrete, immediate situations, which in the final analysis must indeed be instinctually relevant. This can also be expressed as follows: Learning capabilities lie somewhere on the path toward a final phase of instinctive behavior, a consummatory action. Hence, they are thus frequently connected to *appetitive behavior*—that is, a mode of behavior that shows adaptive flexibility while maintaining a constant goal. This constant goal is an instinctive consummatory action. As Lorenz himself emphasized[19] the "appetite" for a certain instinctive action is capable of "instilling in the animal a specific, noninherited way of behaving, just as a circus lion's appetite for a piece of meat trains him in such a behavior." Moreover, this self-training can be incorporated into the consummatory actions themselves, as, for example, when young chicks quickly stop pecking at stones or when a young red-backed shrike learns about thorns by trial and error.

In contrast to the above, the possibility of relieving behavior is specifically human. This can take the form of relieving an intellectual or practical activity of its function of fulfilling instinctive drives and thereby provides an opportunity for learning without the presence of a biologically unusual situation. In other words, the ability of a free (for example, experimental) activity to become detached from biological needs on the one hand, and from the pressures of a reward situation on the other, makes it possible to carry out such a behavior independently of a stimulus. What an animal learns, however, can be manifested only in the specific situation that triggers it. It is wrong to ascribe this astonishing human ability solely to man's intelligence, because it is based on a deep-lying substructure. This is what Storch[20] described as a "disengaging" of the sensory organs from their ties to functions—a view that happily corresponds to my own. Similarly, another element in this substructure is the reduction of instincts; because of this, most human behavior cannot be described as instinctive or appetitive behavior. It is of the utmost importance that any true use of symbols—as, for example, in language—is based on this ability to detach the behavior from the context of the present situation; it is in the very nature of symbols to point to something that is not given and that cannot be deduced from the context.

3. Konrad Lorenz polemicized against my argument,[21] making the claim that certain curious animals, such as ravens, actively seek out new learning situations, that they "carry out exploration for its own sake," and therefore, "by virtue of their method of controlling their environment, are much more closely akin to man than is, for example, the chimpanzee as an expert climber." That such animals positively turn toward any unfamiliar external stimulus, in order "through systematic examination of all stimuli, to react to the one that is biologically most relevant" closes the enormous gap between man and animal as little as does the word "curiosity," or the impassioned fondness of this excellent researcher for his experimental animals. In this manner, Lorenz eventually comes to propose the thesis that the essential cultural achievements of man "are exclusively founded on achievements of exploration which, exactly as is the case with a curious, playful young animal, are carried out purely for their own sake." Not much in the way of knowledge is gained through these animal feats of exploration. When a raven examines a rag tossed to him, and possibly uses it later to carry out his instinctive drive to hide remains of his food, this behavior appears extraordinarily intelligent to us, and one only misses hearing the words "well, then, let's just take this for the time being." We are indebted to Lorenz elsewhere for pointing out that "it can be shown that the raven does not possess insight into the meaning of 'hiding' in the sense of rendering that which is hidden invisible."[22] According to my understanding, human curiosity is the highly intellectual faculty of satisfying an interest with definite instinctive roots in a thing by gaining knowledge of it. In contrast, the even more highly developed intellectual character of research consists of seeking

out the true laws governing objective facts, in order to put them in a meaningful context with other facts. The precondition for research is that the instinctive, first-hand orientation toward the first set of facts be bracketed (as an anatomist does with his fear of a corpse) or sublimated to an extent so that a purely rational approach is possible. The history of science is a history of laborious inner acts of ascetism, of artificially cultivated acts of renunciation of instinctive conditioned "prejudices." I would not label this interest in research as curiosity and would further clearly distinguish between these two and Lorenz's active appetitive behavior toward unspecific new stimuli.

3. A Preliminary Definition of Man

The laws formulated in the last section appear to be applications of that truly biological approach which first came into its own with Johannes v. Uexküll. Later on, in our discussion of man's "world-openness" *(Weltof-fenheit),* we will examine in greater detail environmental theory. For now, it is sufficient to remind ourselves that almost all animals show evidence of strong ties to specific environments and of "adaptation" to these environments. Therefore, by looking closely at an animal's organic structure, its sensory organs, its means of defense and attack, its organs of nourishment, and so on, we can draw conclusions about its way of life and the type of environment it inhabits. An animal like the deer, an almost totally defenseless herbivore and inhabitant of great expanses of forest, survives because of its highly specialized build for running, its sensitive organs for perceiving danger, and so on. Instincts are important in this context but it would be difficult to design experiments in which these could be identified. In every instance, however, the instinct is a specific type of movement unique to a species and to its particular environment.

I will now present an overview of the anthropological scheme that I will set forth in this book.

Man is an acting being. In a narrower sense, he is also "undetermined"— he presents a challenge to himself. One might also say that he is a being who must form attitudes. Actions are the expression of man's need to develop an attitude toward the outside world. To the extent that he presents a problem to himself, he must also develop an attitude toward himself and make something of himself. This process is not a luxury which man could forego; rather, his "unfinishedness" is a basic part of his physical condition, of his very nature. In this sense man must become a being of discipline: self-discipline, training, self-correction in order to achieve a certain state of being and maintain it are necessary to the survival of an "undetermined" being.

Because man, dependent on his own initiative, may fail to meet this vital challenge, he is an endangered being facing a real chance of perishing. Man is ultimately an *anticipatory (vorsehend)* being. Like Prometheus, he must direct his energies toward what is removed, what is not present in time and space. Unlike animals, he lives for the future and not in the present. This disposition is one of the preconditions for an acting existence, and human consciousness must be understood from this point of view. Indeed, all the aspects of man, which should be kept in mind through the ensuing discussion, are actually elaborations of the basic defining characteristic of man— action. We shall see that many of the isolated statements about man are really developments of one basic point of view—that man represents Nature's experiment with an acting being.

In Germany, I believe it was in the classical period that a tendency in this direction of thought was first proposed, although not ardently pursued. Evidence of this tendency can be found in the works of Schiller and Herder. In his essay "On Grace and Dignity" Schiller writes: "With the animal and plant, Nature did not only specify their dispositions but she also carried these out herself. With man, however, she merely provided the disposition and left its execution up to him. . . . Among all known beings, man alone as a person has the privilege of breaking the bonds of necessity, to which all creatures of nature are subject, with his will and can begin in himself a completely new series of phenomena. (This is a Kantian definition of Freedom.) The act, through which he accomplishes this, is called an *action*."[23] Herder, whom I will discuss in greater depth in later chapters, writes, "no longer an infallible machine in the hands of Nature, [man] himself becomes a purpose and an objective of his own efforts."[24] These are valuable insights into the problem of the undetermined animal, of the being who is its own challenge, but these thoughts were not developed further in the philosophy of the times, because the prevailing philosophical orientation then favored the old understanding of man as an intellectual being—a view that was too narrow to permit consideration of the abovementioned ideas.

This characterization of man, somewhat sketchily described for now, permits us to account for his special morphological position. This is of great importance, for only by pursuing this concept of an acting, undertermined being can man's peculiar physical constitution be explained. The definition of man as an intellectual being does not in itself bring to light the relationship between the peculiar human bodily structure and the human mind. In terms of morphology, man is, in contrast to all other higher mammals, primarily characterized by deficiencies, which, in an exact, biological sense, qualify as lack of adaptation, lack of specialization, primitive states, and failure to develop, and which are therefore essentially negative features. Humans have no natural protection against inclement weather; we have no natural organs for defense and attack but yet neither are our bodies designed for flight. Most animals surpass man as far as acuity of the senses is concerned. Man has what could even be termed a dangerous lack of true instincts and needs an unusually long period of protection and care during his infancy and childhood. In other words, under natural conditions, among dangerous predators, man would long ago have died out.

The tendency in natural development is for organically highly specialized forms to adapt to their specific environments, for the infinitely diverse "milieus" in nature to serve as living spaces for creatures adapted to survive in them. The shallow shores of tropical waters as well as the depths of the oceans, the bare precipices of the northern Alps as well as the underbrush of a forest are all equally specific environments for specialized animals that are capable of surviving only in them. The skin of warm-blooded animals serves the same function for parasites; countless examples are possible. Man, however, from a morphological point of view, has practically no specializations. He exhibits an absence of specialization that appears primitive from a developmental, biological stand-point. His bite, for example, shows a primitive lack of gaps between the teeth and an undetermined structure, making him neither a herbivore nor a carnivore. Compared to the great apes—highly specialized arboreal animals with overdeveloped arms for swinging, feet designed for climbing, body hair, and powerful canine teeth—man appears hopelessly unadapted. Man is characterized by a singular lack of biological means—a fact that we will examine more closely in part 1. He compensates for this deficiency with his ability to work and his disposition toward action, that is, with his hands and intelligence; precisely for this reason, he stands erect, has circumspect vision, and a free use of his hands.

Again, as I will go into later, it was Herder who first put forth this idea, though, because of the limited knowledge available in his time, he was able to do so only with a certain vagueness. Kant, too, expressed a similar intuition in 1784 in his paper "Idee zu einer allgemeinen Geschichte in weltbürgerlicher Absicht."[5] He wrote that nothing in Nature is superfluous and that while she gave man reason and freedom of will, she denied him instinct and the means of looking after himself through "ready knowledge." "Instead, man must obtain all that he needs from himself. Everything, food, shelter, security, and self-defense (for which she did not provide him with the horns of a bull or the claws of a lion, or the fangs of a dog but rather only with two hands), all the pleasures to make his life comfortable, even his power of insight, his cleverness, and his good disposition were all left up to him. Nature seems to have been pleased with her extreme economy here and to have measured her supply of animals exactly so as to meet the great needs of a new existence. It is almost as if once man had managed to pull himself up from a crude existence to the greatest level of skill, to inner perfection of thought and, as much as is possible on earth, to happiness, Nature wanted him to receive all the credit for this achievement and owe it all to his own efforts."[25] In these important sentences, Kant has brilliantly characterized man as lacking the organic means and instincts, as dependent upon himself to develop his potential, and as facing the challenge of interpreting his own existence. Kant's insight is a product of his times only in that he narrows man's challenge to the "acquisition of rational morality."[26]

Recent biological findings have allowed us to place the exposed and vulnerable human constitution in a larger context. For most animals, particularly for the higher mammals, the environment is an unchanging milieu to which the specialized organ structure of the animal is adapted and within which equally specific, innate, instinctive behavior is carried out. Specialized organic structure and environment are mutually dependent concepts. Man's "world," in which the perceivable is clearly not limited to what is necessary for basic survival, may at first seem to be a disadvantage. To say that man is "world-open" means that he foregoes an animal adaptation to a specific environment. Man's unusual receptivity to perceptions that do not have an innate function as signals definitely constitutes a great burden to him which he must overcome in special ways. The lack of physical specialization, his vulnerability, as well as his astonishing lack of true instincts together form a coherent whole which is manifested in his "world-openness" (Scheler) or, what amounts to the same thing, in his lack of ties to a specific environment. In animals, organ specialization, the repertory of instincts, and the ties of the environment correspond to each other. This is an important point. We have now formulated a structural definition of man, which does not rely solely on the characteristic of reason or the mind. We can move beyond the alternatives mentioned above of assuming a gradual differentiation of man from the higher animals or of arguing that the basic difference lies with the mind. We have proposed that man is organically a deficient being and is for this reason world-open; in other words, his survival is not strictly dependent upon a specific environment. It is now clear in what sense man is "undetermined" and a "challenge" to himself. The survival of such a being is highly questionable; simply getting by poses great problems which he must face alone and solve through his own efforts. He is therefore an acting being. Since man is obviously able to survive, it logically follows that the necessary conditions for solving his problems must lie within himself; if existence alone is a serious problem and man's greatest achievement, than this must be evidenced throughout his entire structure. All special human capabilities must be examined in light of the question: How is such a strange being able to survive? Our biological approach is hereby justified. It does not consist of comparing man's physique to that of chimpanzees, but rather rests in the answer to the question of how the being, essentially incomparable with any other animal, is viable.

In light of the above, man's world-openness might appear to be a great burden. He is flooded with stimulation, with an abundance of impressions, which he somehow must learn to cope with. He cannot rely upon instincts for understanding his environment. He is confronted with a "world" that is surprising and unpredictable in its structure and that must be worked through with care and foresight, must be experienced. By relying on his own means and efforts, man must find *relief* from the burden of over-whelming stimulation; he must transform his deficiencies into opportunities for survival.

At this point, the deeper, scientific problem surfaces which this book will address. We could continue to orient ourselves in the scheme described by touching on various researchers, but real proof of the validity of this scheme, including the particulars of the interrelationships between human functions, has never been provided. This is so because the principle of relief has not been recognized. This principle is the key to understanding the structural law governing the development of all human skills; the second and third parts of this book are devoted to substantiating this. The underlying thesis is that all the deficiencies in the human constitution, which under natural conditions would constitute grave handicaps to survival, become for man, through his own initiative and action, the very means of his survival; this is the foundation for man's character as an acting being and for his unique place in the world.

The acts through which man meets the challenge of survival should always be considered from two angles: They are *productive* acts of overcoming the deficiencies and obtaining relief, on the one hand, and, on the other, they are completely new means for conducting life drawn from within man himself.

All human actions are twofold: First, man actively masters the world around him by transforming it to serve his purposes. Second, to accomplish this, he draws upon a highly complex hierarchy of skills and establishes within himself a developmental order of abilities; this order is based on potential usefulness of the skills and must be constructed singlehandedly by man, sometimes overcoming internal resistance to do so. Thus, the essence of human skills, from the most elementary to the most sophisticated, is their development by man through a process of coming to terms with the world, the purpose of which is to set up a ranking order of skills in which a true ability to survive is achieved only after a long time. Later sections of this book will go into the particulars of this process so for now I will try to make it clear by focusing on a few special points.

Man is incapable of surviving in truly natural and primitive conditions because of his organic primitiveness and lack of natural means. He must make up for this loss of means on his own by actively transforming the world to suit his own ends. He must create weapons for defense and attack to compensate for those that have been denied him; he must obtain food that is not readily available to him. To this end, he develops through experience techniques of objective ways of coping with particular situations. He must devise his own shelter against the weather, care for and raise his offspring during their abnormally long period of dependence; to accomplish these things, he needs to learn to cooperate and communicate with others. In order to survive, he must master and re-create nature, and for this reason must *experience* the world. He acts because he is unspecialized and deprived of a natural environment to which he is adapted. The epitome of nature restructured to serve his needs is called *culture* and the culture world is the human world. There are no "natural men" in a strict sense—that is, no human society without weapons, without fire, without prepared, artificial food, without shelter, and without systems of cooperation. Culture is therefore the "second nature"—man's restructured nature, within which he can survive. "Unnatural" culture is the product of a unique being, itself of an "unnatural" construction in comparison to animals. The cultural world exists for man in exactly the same way in which the environment exists for an animal. For this reason alone, it is wrong to speak of an environment, in a strictly biological sense, for man. His world-openness is directly related to his unspecialized structure; similarly, his lack of physical means corresponds directly to his self-created "second nature." Furthermore, this explains why man, in contrast to almost all animal species, does not have natural, geographically defined territories. Almost every animal species is adapted to a specific milieu with a consistent climate and ecology. Man alone is capable of existing anywhere on earth, from the polar to equatorial regions, on water and on land, in forests, swamps, on mountains and plains. He is able to survive in these places if he can create the possibilities for constructing a second nature in which he can live.

The cultural realm of man, that is, of any particular group or community of man, contains the conditions necessary for his existence such as weapons and agricultural tools. In contrast to this, the conditions necessary for animals to survive are already given in the environment to which they are adapted. The difference between cultural men and natural men can easily be understood. No human population can exist in real wilderness; every society has some form of hunting techniques, weapons, fire, tools. Accordingly, I do not agree with the familiar distinction between culture and civilization. In my understanding, culture is the epitome of natural conditions actively mastered, reworked, and used by man and it includes the more qualified, *relieved* skills and abilities which become possible only with this foundation.

Now that this has been established, one of the most important aspects of the above mentioned principle comes to light—namely, man's "world-openness," his exposure, foreign to animal species, to an overwhelming abundance of perceptions and impressions which he is not organically equipped to handle; this first poses a tremendous burden, but is also a necessary condition for man's survival, providing, of course, that he can successfully come to terms with this openness. The abundance and diversity of the world accessible to man and streaming in upon him harbor the possibility of unexpected and unpredictable experiences which man may possibly be able to use in his struggle for survival, in taking the next step to secure his existence. To put this another way, the world-openness of man is so limitless and undifferentiated in its variety precisely because man must choose from this chaos those experiences that he can use to his own advantage, as a tool to survive. This immediate handicap is thus productively turned into an opportunity for prolonging existence. We will see in detail how the process of coping with the abundance of impressions is always simultaneously a process of obtaining relief, a way of reducing immediate contact with the world; we will learn how man is thereby able to orient himself, to order his impressions, to understand them, and above all to gain control of them. As we are now touching on an area in which little research has been conducted, I should provide a certain preparatory and orienting introduction.

In the first place, it should be noted that the perceivable world around us is undeniably the result of human activity. From a purely visual point of view, this world is highly symbolic, that is, a realm of *suggested experiences* which conveys to us the nature and usefulness of the objects around us. Exposure to an unchecked flood of impressions presents man, even at the earliest age, with the problem of coping with it, of relieving himself of this burden, of taking action against the world sensuously impinging upon him. This action consists of *communicative,* manipulative activities involving experiencing objects and then setting them aside and these activities have no immediate value for gratifying drives. The world is thereby "processed" in communicative, relieved movements; its open abundance is experienced, "realized," and subsequently absorbed. This process, which occupies the majority of childhood, results in our perceptual world in which symbols convey the potential usefulness of objects. A superficial visual impression gives us symbols which impart the utility and specific properties of an object (its form, weight, texture, hardness, density, etc.). The profound cooperation between eye and hand and the communicative, manipulative activities culminate in the achievement that the eye alone oversees a world teaming with symbols of experienced objects always readily available to man. The existence of such a system in which certain skills are dominant and others subordinate, in which hand and body movements gradually disassociate themselves from the task of initiating experiences and thereby become free for other tasks—namely, planned work—while the eye alone is able to undertake "trial experiences," provides further substantiation for the law of the development and relief of human skills. A variety of functions come into play here: the senses of near and far (which to some extent regulate each other), language, thought, imagination, and highly complex "deferred" needs, oriented toward potential, not given, situations. All of these react to each other and occupy varying positions of dominance and subordination within the system.

4. Continuation of the Same Approach

Man's world-openness is actually expedient in the sense that it provides him with a truly infinite range of real and possible experiences, a realm of creativity in which there is such great diversity that, no matter what the circumstances may be, man is always able to find and employ some means of effecting changes that will enable him to survive; thus he is able to compensate in some manner for the deficiencies in his organic structure. By his own efforts, he transforms what was a handicap into something productive.

In general, these efforts consist of the "movements" that occupy man's childhood, movements through which man gradually experiences the world around him. In this process, objects are seen, touched, moved, handled in communicative movements of interaction, which we will study more closely. This process involves the coordination of all types of movement, particularly between the hand and the senses (above all, the eyes). As a result, the world is "worked through" with an eye toward its potential availability and usefulness to man. In succession, objects are experienced by man and then set aside; the objects are thereby unwittingly endowed with a high degree of symbolism such that, eventually, the eye alone (an effortless sense) can take them in and quickly assess their potential usefulness and value. The problem of orientation in the face of a deluge of stimulation is thus solved in that man is both able to manipulate objects and also to put them aside and dispense with them until the irrational abundance of impressions is finally reduced to a series of easily manageable centers (things). Each of these centers holds suggestions for potentially fruitful interaction, for changes that might be effected and for potential usefulness. When described in this manner, the relief that these processes provide is readily apparent. Man can, while immobile, look around him and oversee a wide range of highly symbolic visual suggestions of the ends to which certain things and situations may be used. He has achieved this through his own initiative alone, through a laborious process of actively accumulating experiences. Clearly, only a being who is not adapted to a specific environment, a being who is "unspecialized," would have to resort to this behavior. Furthermore, only such a being would have to rely on its own initiative, finding itself confronted with a flood of stimulation amidst which it must try to orient itself. This process of self-orientation thus entails a reduction of the incoming impressions to certain productive centers, thereby providing relief from the pressure of the direct flood of impressions. Whereas an animal is subject to the pressures of an immediate situation and changes in that situation, man is able to draw back and establish distance.

Directly involved in this process of orientation is another series of problems posed by the immaturity of a child's motor skills. As is well known, animals gain command of their range of movement after only a few hours or days and this range is then set. Human movements, on the other hand, are characterized by an enormous potential diversity, by a wealth of possible combinations that exceeds imagination. One need only consider the number of precise movements used in one single motion of the hands, not to mention what is involved in the complexity of an entire industrial system. Movements are, therefore, incredibly "plastic," that is, able to be coordinated and combined in an unlimited variety of ways. Each new combination of movements is self-directed, developed on the basis of a more or less conscious plan of coordination. Consider the difficult changes in movement necessary when learning a new sport. Remarkably, this incredible abundance of possible movements (used by artists, athletes, and all the numerous professions) and of arbitrary combinations of movements has rarely been seen in contrast to the monotony of animal forms of movement.

If we ask ourselves why man has available to him such a wide diversity of movements, then the answer can only be because his range of movement is unspecialized. The unlimited plasticity of human movement and action can thus only be understood in view of the similarly unlimited abundance of facts that confronts such a world-open being from which it must select and utilize certain ones.

The immaturity of a child's motor skills is a handicap, when compared to the situation with animals. It is also a challenge, a challenge to develop possibilities for movement through one's own efforts, through a difficult learning process involving failure, inner resistance, and self-mastery. The immature motor skills are qualitatively different from those of animals, which are established very early but then become monotonous and purely self-serving. Human movements are undeveloped because they contain an infinite number of possible variations, which the human being must work through in his interaction with his surroundings. He does this in such a way that each experience of movement opens up new combinations of imagined movements, so that ultimately man has at his disposal an infinite number of possible movements and variations involving the dominance of certain movements, coordination of movements, reversals, etc. This range of motor skills differs from that of animals in two additional respects:

1. It can be developed only through the same process of interaction with the surroundings that we described above from another angle. The experiences of movement in the unlimited, open sphere in which man must orient himself are at the same time solutions to the problem of developing a broad and refined range of motor skills equal to the infinite range of situations man might encounter in life. A being with such unnatural conditions for survival needs to be able to vary his movements in accordance with the demands of each particular situation because it must change an unanticipated situation to meet its needs. To accomplish this, *controlled variations in movement* are necessary. They are developed in the same actions through which man orients himself in the world. Thus, these two achievements, orientation and controlled variations in movement, can be described as follows.

A defenseless being, overcome by stimulation and incapable of movement, transforms this double handicap into the basis for an existence totally foreign to the animal kingdom. The world is mastered and ordered through communicative actions unrelated to the gratification of needs. Only in a controllable, manageable world can incentives be found to enact those changes which will help an organically defenseless being survive. Through this same process, a wealth of experienced, controlled, and variable actions is developed to form initially immature movements, by carefully honing the ability to cope with unpredictable, changeable circumstances. From a philosophical perspective, it is vitally important to expose *the common root of knowledge and action,* for orientation in the world and the control of actions are the primary laws of human life. The immaturity of motor skills leads to a personal experience of the ability to move, and this in turn provides an incentive for the further development of the potentially unlimited diversity of movement.

2. An important factor in the development of these skills is the great sensitivity toward things and toward oneself in human actions. Human motor skills involve an acute tactile sensitivity; in addition, the actions

themselves are seen as they are carried out along with the changes they effect. It is exceedingly important, as we shall see, that all movements be re-experienced through visual and tactile sensations, so that the movements are not engaged solely in responding to new impressions from the surroundings, but can also react *to themselves* and *to each other*. We shall later learn that this is a prerequisite for developing the ability to imagine movements. All human sensorimotor skills are *self-perceived*, that is, capable of reacting to themselves and to each other. This facilitates the forming of an "inner world," composed of imagined interactions and movements, ideas of possible outcomes, and anticipated impressions. This world can be constructed and developed *independently of the actual situation* and represents a high, but by no means the ultimate, level of relief. In relation to man's ability to observe his own movements and re-experience them through touch and sight, one must also consider his erect posture, the variety of perceptual axes, and his hairlessness (which makes the entire body a sensory surface).

To sum all this up in a few words: The existence of an unspecialized, world-open being depends upon action, upon anticipatory practical changes in things in order to use them as means. Making sense of the reality streaming in upon him and developing an unlimited, variable ability to act comes about through special, relieved, communicative processes of experience and interaction which are not in evidence among animals; above all, this is achieved through cooperation between the hands, eyes, and the sense of touch. Hand and arm movements, with their visible relation to the behavior of things, permit the broadest range of variation; given man's orientation toward the future, these may also appear as imagined movements, as images of outcome of actions, and as expectations (see part 2).

Adolph Portman[27] has studied man's unique position from an ontogenetic viewpoint. Such lower mammals as many insect eaters, rodents, and martens, with their short gestation periods and high number of young, come into the world as "nestlings"—that is, in a completely helpless condition, hairless, and with sensory organs not yet functioning. In contrast, among the higher mammals, a much greater degree of differentiation is achieved in order to form a central organ that to some extent, as far as its functions are concerned, corresponds to a mature state. Among these species we find a marked reduction in the number of young (usually limited to one or two) and a lengthening of the gestation period, during which time the embryo/fetus undergoes a functionally meaningless phase of closing the eyelids, organs of hearing, and so forth, which are then reopened right before birth.

The young thus pass through a stage in the womb that corresponds in form to the condition at birth of a nestling, such that their development at birth is already comparable in many respects to the mature form. They can command the species-specific patterns of movement and means of communication—in a sense, they have already left the nest.

Human ontogenesis, however, is unique among vertebrates. Man's brain at birth weighs approximately three times more than that of newborn anthropoids, and man also has a correspondingly higher body weight at birth (roughly 3200 grams compared to 100 grams among orangutans). The characteristic erect posture and the rudiments of communication (words) are usually established a year after birth. "After one year, man has achieved a level of development which a true mammal must effect at birth. For man's situation to correspond to that of true mammals, pregnancy would have to continue a year longer than it actually does; it would have to last approximately 21 months."[28]

The newborn is thus a type of "physiological," or normalized, premature infant, a "secondary nestling," and is the only example of this category among vertebrates." The great increase in length and mass during the first year has long been recognized as having a fetal character.[29] This "extra-uterine year" has a fundamental significance: in it, processes of maturation, which as such would also be fostered inside the uterus, are combined with experiences of countless sources of stimulation; in the course of working through these experiences, the processes of maturation, as well as the acquisition of an erect posture and of the rudiments of language and movement, first get underway.

"Thus, natural processes take place in man in the first year of life under unique conditions instead of under the generally favorable conditions within the mother's body," or "it is man's lot to go through critical phases in his behavioral and physical development in a close reciprocal relationship with psychic and corporal events outside the mother's body."[30] The special status of human ontogenesis, with its marked morphological peculiarities (high birth weight and brain weight, high sensory receptivity coupled with immature motor skills, and an unusually late development of mature physical proportions) can therefore be understood only in relation to the "world-open behavior of the mature form," which again is directly connected to the "early contact with the richness of the world, accorded to man alone."[31] To put this in another way, the mode of existence and laws of behavior of the mature form are prefigured in the embryology of man. Consequently, "a series of ontogenetic peculiarities, such as the duration of gestation, the early physical growth, the level of development at birth, can only be under-stood in relation to the manner in which our social behavior is formed."[32]

"To clarify this astonishing fact, it is useful to draw a comparison with the condition of a nestling from the group of higher birds. In these groups (as Portmann has shown)[33] a longer period of dependency is necessary because of the great degree of differentiation needed for the development of the central nerve organs; this is then compensated for by involving the older birds in the process of development. "The older bird becomes an obligatory component in the entire ontogenesis," and the "staggered pro-cess" between the older and younger birds, in particular, of course, the coordination of their instincts (feeding, on the one hand, and opening the jaws on the other) is one of the laws of the ontogenesis of the nestling. If we agree with Portmann's description of man as a "secondary nestling," then we must further say that not only maternal care, but also communi-cative contact with other humans, and indeed, even the indefinite open stimulation from the surroundings, all become "obligatory functions of the entire ontogenesis."

5. Action and Language

By now a framework has been established within which the uniqueness of the human constitution is represented in man's achievements. These achievements arise from man's active attempts to solve the problem of orientation in the world in order to make it accessible to him and bring it under his control. Man obtains relief and thereby breaks the spell of immediacy under which animals remain captive because of their direct sensory suggestiveness and immediate responses. The human being singlehandedly creates an "empty space" around him, a world that he can oversee, that is readily available for his use, and that contains a wealth of suggestions for ways in which it can be used. He creates this in the course of his experiences and movements, in which, without the pressure of fulfilling drives, but instead in more of a playful manner, the things around him are experienced, communicatively explored, and then set aside, until eventually the eye alone reigns over an ordered, neutralized world. Through these laborious, self-experienced processes, in which man also discovers the impetus for further variations, he matures and develops a faculty for action which, in its controlled flexibility, reflects the diversity of his world. Because man has refined and developed these movements on his own, he is able to build up a rich reserve of variable movements that can then be called into play whenever the eye spots a promising possibility for their use. Here we are not speaking of some sudden impression that calls forth an immediate response, as, for example, an unfamiliar stimulus would provoke flight in an animal; instead, by his own doing, man has reduced *the points of contact with an immediate situation* to a minimum, as far as his senses and motor skills are concerned.

It is precisely in the context of this development, interwoven with these processes, that *language* evolves. Language springs from several roots which at first function independently of each other; as part 2 will examine this more closely, I will not treat it in depth here. It can be established here, however, that the following are developed to a high degree in language: communicative, interactive behavior; the creation of "indicators," or symbols; self-perceived activity reexperienced through the senses; and, finally, reduced, relieved contact with the world. These are not, however, solely confined to language; indeed, they are, as has been stated previously, features of man's relieved existence in general and are already present in prelinguistic behavior.

If these statements hold up under closer scrutiny, as I intend to demonstrate, then it will be clear that the fundamental law of the structure of human sensorimotor behavior is continued in language and that it ultimately explains the uniqueness of human intelligence. In other words, the task man faces of transforming his basic handicaps into means of securing his survival result from his morphology. To meet this challenge, man creates a surveyable perceptual world and orients himself within it, in the process of which objects become accessible to him. Man also develops a highly flexible ability to act. The *direction* of these sensorimotor processes is clearly taken over by language and there perfected. It is here that the transition to "thought" can be located. This anthropological model is distinguished from others by the fact that it can, by using the concept of a structure of skills, find the level on which a transition from the "physical" to the "intellectual" can be carried out, reconstructed, and understood. Under the pressure of a vital challenge, a hierarchy of skills is developed throughout which a single law can be documented.

In order to show how language continues the described law of the structure of skills, I would like to raise the following points for consideration:

Even among animals, there exists the "primal phenomenal" *(urphanomenal)* ability of *intention,* which cannot be further reduced. This is an active self-orientation by means of a perceived signal toward a "whole" that is manifested therein. The development of a "conditioned reflex," in particular, means that an entire situation has been restructured in perception such that a precise initial signal is confirmed in behavior through the subsequent development of the situation. *Symbols,* on the other hand, are essentially formed through communicative interaction. The symbols of the infinitely open world in which man exists were created in the course of his interaction with his surroundings. If, for example, the front of an object, its shadows, and its highlights are sufficient to suggest to us a heavy, metallic, round object, then behind this highly concentrated symbolic structure lies a long period of practice, of manipulation of objects, and of learning. The self-developed symbolism of things around us creates a world of implications of availability even when automatic gestalt-psychological processes are also involved. The laws of the forms of perception, which are aimed at establishing an overview of a situation and at facilitating classification, formation of points of emphasis, and the transposability of forms, are designed to make "changes" and "interventions" possible. These processes are involved in creating the symbolic structure of things, which is developed in the course of our interaction with our surroundings and which culminates in an implied world of potential availability.

Analogous to tactile movements, movements of sound articulation have the extraordinary quality of being reexperienced—in this case, through the sense of hearing. A sound is, for the time being, to be considered simply as a movement, and belongs in the category of movements that are reexperienced. Such movements play an important role for man because, above all, they make possible the experience of movement and thus promote self-directed, self-controlled improvements in skills.

Within the realm of communicative, sensitive movements of interaction, "movements of sound" arise from several roots; the "heard" aspect of these movements is experienced as a sensation, as originating from the outside world. The articulation of the sound resounds back from the world to the ear. When specifically these sound movements are employed in ways which I will detail later as means of communicating with seen things, it then becomes possible to direct oneself toward something in a specific, free, and effortless movement; in other words, man is able simultaneously to intend the movement and to perceive it. This unusual ability represents a very high degree of relief. This intention, that is, directing oneself in a communicative manner toward things, is the vital basis for thought.

In language (as will be more closely analyzed in part 2), we again find sensorimotor communication within an unrestricted sphere which culminates in the active development of concentrated symbols and in the ready availability of these symbols (or what they represent). The act of intending, as it occurs within movements of sound articulation, directly creates a symbol, the heard sound, which it receives from a thing in the course of interaction. This intention simultaneously perceives itself and hears the sound. This type of communication is highly creative, because it actually *increases* what can be perceived in the world; it is also the most effortless, most relieved form of communication. The perceivable abundance of the world is actively increased through this communication, only then to be condensed and concentrated in specific, easily used symbols which are themselves actions. This is the masterpiece of human skill: the maximal ability to orient oneself and create symbols with the freest access to what is perceived—a process that, through words, is involved in man's self-awareness of his own actions.

It is perhaps already apparent from what has been said that the process just described logically carries the anthropological challenge to the furthest extreme. This should become even clearer if the following points are considered:

1. It is possible to concentrate in symbols even that which is removed from direct experience and thereby gain an overview of it. Man's ability to organize his world and create symbols extends as far as his eye can see.

2. Now a form of active behavior becomes possible that extends beyond direct interaction with the surroundings. This does not actually change objects, but in fact leaves them untouched. As far as the infinite range of the perceivable is concerned, there is a type of communication, experienced only in itself, that effects no actual changes in the world. This is, of course, the basis for all *theoretical behavior* which, however, invariably remains oriented toward things so that it may, at any time, through a simple inner transformation of the form of movement, become practical behavior. Between perception and the active treatment of what is perceived, there is positioned an intermediate phase of interaction with things which brings about no changes (planning).

3. All movements of sound are readily available and reproducible. Thus, to the extent that these sound movements can express an intention toward things, such intentions may be *independent from the actual presence* of the things or situations represented through symbols. The sound symbol perceived from a thing is distinct from the thing itself. It thereby represents the thing even in absentia. This is the basis for imagination. It is thereby possible to direct oneself beyond the actual situation toward circumstances and realities that are not given. As Schopenhauer once said, through language, man acquires an overview of the past and future as well as of that which is absent. The biological necessity of this skill is clear for man. If man were restricted to the here and now, as animals are, he would not be able to survive. Man must possess the ability to break through the boundaries of an immediate situation, to direct himself toward the future and what is not present and to act accordingly, as well as to turn then back to the present, employing its resources as means for coping with future circumstances. Man thereby becomes "Prometheus," simultaneously planning ahead and taking action.

4. Because sounds may also symbolize actions in general and even one's

own actions (as in verbs), any movement or action can be intended through language along with the subject it concerns, and can accordingly be represented through symbols and communicated independently of the actual situation.

5. The importance of this fact for man's particular challenge in life hardly needs clarification, as is also true of this final point: language allows man to *communicate* intentions, whereby he is directly *freed from his own realm of experiences* and becomes able to act based on *those of others*.

To summarize all this: Language leads and closes the entire structural order of human sensorimotor functions in its incomparable, unique structure. In language, man's progress toward obtaining relief from the pressure of responding to the immediate present reaches completion. The experiential processes of communication reach their peak in language, man's world-openness is productively mastered, and an infinite number of models for action and plans become possible. Language facilitates agreement between men toward the direction of common activity, a common world, and a common future.

6. Action and Impulses

The basic challenges man faces are liberating himself in order to pursue circumspect and anticipatory activities and obtaining relief from the pressures of the immediate present. To meet these challenges, he perfects difficult skills through a lengthy, laborious process of coming to terms with the world and with himself. In view of man's deficiencies, it is clear that he must perceive in order to act and must act in order to survive. This simple formula becomes more complicated, however, once one sees that this perception is itself very limited. At first, nothing can be perceived amidst the chaos of overwhelming stimulation; only with the gradual mastering of this chaos through interaction with the surroundings and accumulation of experiences do the comprehensive symbols evolve that make what we call knowledge possible. Immediate perceptions are always just the beginning of the process through which man acquires an overview of a situation and becomes able to take advantage of whatever it may offer. Language grows from this structure of achievements and is employed within it; and accurate memory and keen foresight are bound up with language for, without these, there can be no planned, directed activity, as well as no possibility of communication or understanding. Again, it is easy to see how, the problem of survival for man is such that an individual can never solve it alone.

In contrast, an animal exists in the here and now and hence does not encounter the problems man faces. An order and harmony (expressed by the concept of biocenosis) of which it is not aware and which it cannot influence in any way ensures that the means for its survival are accessible to the animal. For example, the restlessness accompanying hunger results in searching movements and, guided by a highly specialized sense of smell, permits the animal to find its prey. An animal lives *with* time. Man, whom "even future hunger makes hungry"[34] has "no time"—unless he prepares for tomorrow, he will not be able to survive. Because of this, man has knowledge of time. It is important for him to remember and to anticipate, while remaining active in a state of suspenseful alertness.

In part 3 of this book, we will examine the question of the nature of the needs and drives of such a being as man. The answer, in brief, is quite simple: it is crucial for man's survival that his needs and impulses function in the direction of action, knowledge, and anticipation. It would present an untenable situation if man's impulses were concerned simply with the here and now, directed only toward what is perceived, and running their course within the confines of the immediate situation while his consciousness and actions were oriented beyond the immediate toward the future. Human needs must become objectified and long-term; they must become removed interests in specific, experienced things and related specific activities. The hunger drive must smoothly lead into the need to search for food in, for example, a certain place proven successful earlier and the need to exercise those practical skills necessary to reach this end. To put it another way, the basic, minimal needs for relieving physical distress must be able to be augmented to include needs for the means of satisfaction and the means of obtaining these means; that is, the needs must become clear, specific interests, which must arise from actions and encompass the activities necessary for their gratification.

Many peculiarities in man's system of impulses can be explained from this point of view, including, above all, his awareness of his own impulses. Not without good reason would Nature have made man aware of his own motivational life, thereby exposing him to possible disturbance of it. Man must be conscious of his impulse; they must incorporate images of goals, of situations in which fulfillment was achieved, and the specific steps for obtaining gratification. They must also allow even the most indirect actions toward the desired end. The boundary must therefore be fluid between basic, short-term drives, such as hunger and sex, and the more sophisticated interests in concrete, objective situations and activities in order to obtain lasting and successful fulfillment. For this reason, I always propose the formula of "needs and interests," because interests are conscious, long-term needs that have been *adapted to action*. Clearly, two unique aspects of human motivation come to light here: the ability to *inhibit* and the ability to *defer* gratification of needs and interests. Again, inhibition and deferment can only be possible when needs and interests are conscious. Man must be able to inhibit spontaneous instinctive actions in the immediate present whenever long-term interests are vital to his survival. Long-term interests can surface only when immediate needs have been suppressed. For example, if a child were unable to suppress his occasionally strong destructive urges, he could not develop an objective interest in the properties of things, which is a necessary prerequisite to the ability to manipulate objects. A need, in addition to being conscious, can also be suppressed or deferred; this even holds true for hunger. The ability to defer gratification of needs is, of course, necessary if these needs are to become substantial and goal-oriented. The needs must be able to vary along with any changes in external conditions or new constellations of facts. This is possible only if the needs are conscious, that is, imbued with mental images of content.

In an acting being, therefore, impulses present a unique structure. Above all, they can be oriented—that is, they can encompass not only certain vital needs but also the particular steps necessary to satisfying them. In addition, because the means of attaining gratification are so changeable, the impulses can vary accordingly. Awareness of the nature of the impulses, mental images of the situation of gratification, and the necessary procedures for achieving gratification guarantee the proper orientation. Deferment of gratification is therefore of the utmost importance and must extend so far that even the most qualified and inconvenient actions can have a motivational interest; otherwise, one would not bother with such actions or would carry them out haphazardly. Thus, the key to understanding the structure of human impulses is *action*.

Man's *lack of instincts,* often remarked upon and bemoaned, does have a positive side and brings up a fact of great significance. Between elemental needs and their external gratification (which varies according to unpredictable and random circumstances) is interpolated the entire system of world orientation and action; that is, the intermediate world of conscious praxis and objective experience, which is conveyed through the hands, eyes, sense of touch, and language. Finally, the entire social context inserts itself between first-hand needs of the individual and their gratification, thereby connecting these. It is this reduction of instincts which, on the one hand, dismantles the direct automatism that, given sufficient internal stimulus, will evoke an innate response if the appropriate releaser appears, and which, on the other hand, establishes a new system of behavior, relieved of the pressure of instincts. This new system is the one I have just described, in which perception, language, thought, and variable action patterns (not innate but learned), can respond to variations in the *external world,* in the behavior of *other people,* and, importantly, can even react to *each other.* To express this differently, man's actions and his perceiving and thinking consciousness are to a great extent independent of his own elemental needs and drives. Man has the ability to disjoin or "unhinge" these aspects from each other and thereby create a "hiatus."

This behavior, which is not manifested by animals, can definitely not be categorized as "appetitive behavior," if one understands thereby a behavior that can vary while maintaining a constant goal or consummatory action. Ever since Tolman, however, animal psychology has held fast to this notion of purposeful behavior, of behavior directed toward a goal. In fact, as far as man is concerned, it is this hiatus that opens up the extraordinary possibility of a *change in the direction of the drive*. Although our rational behavior naturally includes the goal of procuring daily sustenance, it can, at times, ignore this altogether and bring about a *purely subjective state* on this side of the hiatus. For example, all primitive cultures possess some means of inducing a state of intoxication, trance, rapture, or ecstasy usually achieved through drugs. This is on the whole a collective process: through feasting, music, and dancing, man becomes transported beyond himself; these are social intoxications which, biologically speaking, are just as irrational as the self-mutilation and asceticism (asceticism as a stimulus, not as a discipline or sacrifice) often accompanying them. In many cases, the acts that usually appear as the final phase or consummatory action (such as eating, drinking, or sexual intercourse) take place on the same level where otherwise the rational, expedient behavior would occur; that is, they are used as the *means* of symbolically expressing an inner, ecstatic relationship among men. One finds this in numerous cults. This "change in the direction of the impulse" can be understood as a progressive increase in the ability to contain one's drives. Indeed, in the advanced forms of asceticism, it can be viewed as a continuation of instinct reduction itself, that is, of the process of becoming human.

I would like to clarify the independence of actions from impulses or the ability to "unhinge" these and create a hiatus. The cycle of action—that is, the cooperation of action, perception, thought, etc.—in changing a situation, can, now that it is relieved, function alone and develop its own motives and goals. It is obliged to follow the laws of objective reality, to investigate facts, and to develop them. On the other hand, objectivity of behavior toward random facts encourages the suppression of needs—these needs must be set aside or deferred, must be prevented from prematurely disrupting invention or orientation, particularly when such activity is designed to serve *future* needs. The ability to contain impulses, to vary behavior independently of them, first creates an "inner life." This hiatus is, to be exact, the vital basis for the phenomenon of the soul. The containment of impulses is infinitely important for man's existence and is impressed upon even the smallest child, in that the immaturity of his movements and actions, as total inhibitions of his needs, cause his needs to be dammed up and hence perceivable.

If, as I have proposed, elemental needs are not adapted to established releasers but rather have a looser relationship to the objects of gratification, it then becomes obvious why it is necessary to *orient* these needs to experience, to "imprint" them in their initially formless openness, to give them substance. The ability to inhibit impulses, to give them substance, and to defer gratification as well as the plasticity of impulses are all aspects of the same thing; we commonly call that level of impulses that manifests itself in images and ideas, that level of conscious needs and of oriented interests, the "soul." Only in this hiatus can needs and actions continuously be oriented to each other; needs must be formed, must be tempered by experience, and must become subject to differentiated expectations, in order to remain equal to the widening range of man's activity in the world, which is constantly increased and "opened up" through his knowledge and action. Finally, man can entertain a specific "objective interest" in, even a need for, a specific activity while the image of and the motivation toward the goal of this activity lie in his soul and outlast any immediate changes. This is precisely the purpose of such a structure of drives.

Human impulses should thus be considered from the point of view of their role in the context of action; one can then identify a series of clearly related characteristics. I would like to propose the following series of schematic statements that encompasses the general structure of man's drives and within which other special features function which still remain to be considered:

1. Impulses can be inhibited and contained, thereby creating a "hiatus" between them and action.
2. They are first formed through the accumulation of experiences, thus are systematically developed through experience.
3. They can be invested with mental images and "memories" of their content and nature. If suppressed, they then become conscious along with these images as specific needs and interests.
4. They are plastic and variable, can adjust to changes in experience and circumstance, can grow from actions.
5. For this reason, there is no sharp boundary between elemental needs and qualified interests.
6. Higher needs can grow from inhibited ones; these "enduring interests" sustain action into the future and, in contrast to the changeable needs of the present,

remain internalized. They are always the subjective correlates of objective institutions.

7. All needs and interests, as soon as they are awakened by experience and thereby given substance, are also the *object* toward which other virtual interests are directed and may then be put aside or deemphasized.

The teleology of this arrangement is clear for a being who acts in anticipation of the future, governed by internal impulses as well as by the changing demands of a changing world. On the one hand, it is vital that man's needs, which can be acute because of his lack of organ specialization, remain world-open, that they be developed in a close relationship with active experience, and that they become, without sharp demarcation, interests in specific situations and activities. The changes that such a vulnerable being must effect in the world in order to survive are themselves, however qualified and complex they may be, important for his basic drives. For this reason, all intermediate activities to accomplish these changes also turn into needs—perception, language, variations in movement, instrumental actions. On the other hand, enduring interests must also be cultivated, oriented, and retained and must remain conscious as inner invariants which control and outlast any changes in activities and circumstances of the present. Organizing this architectonic and well-oriented system of impulses is one of the problems man faces, perhaps even the most difficult one. Testament to this is provided by the often very limited stability of *institutions,* only through which or beyond which can this organization be carried out.

The approach, developed from the study of animals, which seeks to attribute all human behavior to instincts (McDougall's method, for instance) shows as little regard for the special conditions of man as does the abstract view that considers his inner life without regard to action and that has fostered the chaos in the various branches of psychology.

7. The Excessive Nature of Impulses and Their Control

We can now take a closer look at the structure of human impulses. The prevailing view would indicate that human impulses are excessive in nature. Alfred Seydel was probably the first to introduce the important concept of the "excess of drives" *(Triebüberschuss)*; later, Scheler described man as a being whose unsatisfied drives always exceed his satisfied ones.[35] One should be careful, however, not to confuse the constitutional excess of impulses in human beings with the disintegration that occurs in the culturally highly cultivated divisions of impulses when the institutions to which these are bound break down; the result then is that unsatisfied social needs overburden the primitive ones, particularly sexual ones. The modern concept of a free-floating, unrestrained libidinal excess of impulses has as its sociological background the disintegration of institutions in large cities.

The *constitutional* excess of impulses, on the other hand, can probably be understood only as the internal aspect of an unspecialized, organically helpless being who suffers chronic pressure from internal and external stresses. The excessive impulses are thus a reflection of man's chronic state of need, and for the moment can be described as those impulses that are not exhausted in the satisfaction of basic needs such as hunger and sex.

In this respect, the difference between man and animals is extraordinary. An animal's instincts are the instincts of its organs, through which it has adapted to its environment; thus, these instincts follow the great rhythm of Nature. At certain times, when the appropriate conditions are present, the migratory urge, the sex drive, the nest-building instinct, or the urge to hibernate are awakened. In contrast to this, it is vital for man that he weather any changes in external and internal conditions in order to cultivate long-term drives that will not disappear but that instead will cause him to resume an activity the following day, to take up again the daily Sisyphean chore of survival. The energy for impulses appears to be tailored to the unpredictable, sometimes even extraordinary, feats that adverse circumstances demand of man, and this energy, of unbelievable strength, is rarely truly exhausted. Though it is impossible to measure it, one suspects, as we take a closer look at this difficult problem, that man's potential energy for drives, in pure quantitative terms, would surpass that of any animal of comparable size.

A second aspect arises from man's chronic state of need. This state is manifest physically in his deficient organic makeup and, intellectually, in the wide range of stimuli and motives available to him which he must master. As far as human impulses are concerned, however, this state manifests itself in the *nonperiodic*, or *chronic* nature of the impulses themselves. First, the sexual instinct is not bound to periodicity, and the duration of sexual fertility in man is abnormal when compared to any animal's; that children have an unusually long childhood already suggests a biological context which must have its similarly chronic instinctual correlate. Further, if one assumes that a herding instinct, initially only slightly differentiated, arose from the sexual instinct and was directed toward smaller groups at that point when economic necessity forced a differentiation of the ever-increasing herd into cooperative groups, then here, too, a synthesis of social and economic long-term needs, as a substratum, must be assumed. In other words, with the steady progression of the generative process, with the intact, enduring context of a growing society, and with the constant pressure to operate economically (because future hunger already makes man hungry), objective, nonperiodic factors appeared that only enduring excessive drives could master. A partial instinctual rhythm would be a disturbing disharmony in a being continually under stress. Moreover, in certain events in the natural cycle, adaptive instincts pause in accordance with the rhythm of the cycle. However, favorable—that is, adaptive—natural conditions simply do not exist for man whose challenges are therefore just as "chronic" as they are "undeterminable."

Only a being who continually experiences acute urges and thus has excessive impulses that extend beyond any short-term gratification can then transform his world-openness into something productive. The motivations for his actions come from outside himself. From the generative, social, and economic context, he creates more sophisticated tasks, which are then reflected objectively in the various social orders.

We can view these excessive impulses from yet another angle. Man is characterized by an abnormally long period of development, in comparison to animals, by an unusual length of time until he becomes independent. His motor skills, even more so his sexuality, remain immature for a long time;

his ability to participate in the common struggle for survival is formed very late. Throughout this time, man is already suffering from excessive impulses which he cannot, however, yet put to use in solving serious problems—in primitive societies, this is hardly possible before the age of fourteen. The excessive impulses are channeled into "unburdened," playful, and unstable activities for a long period, allowing man to build up a structure of skills for use in communicating with the world. It is only after he has oriented himself in the world, has acquired language, motor skills, thought, manual dexterity, and skills of all kinds, that his sexuality awakens. Only at this point is he ready and able to struggle for his own survival. The excessive impulses are thus a priori and compel man right from the start to cope with them somehow. Once again, it is extremely expedient that the *inhibitions* within the structure of impulses themselves are both the necessary means of managing the excessive impulses, and also the preconditions for developing needs that can be gratified through action and that are socially acceptable. In other words, because of his excessive impulses, man experiences a "pressure to form" *(Formierungszwang)* which is the prerequisite to developing drives appropriate for an acting, anticipatory being. Man's conscious, oriented interests are asserted over other, equally possible ones and are established, perhaps under an external influence, by inhibiting these other interests. This does not happen by chance, but rather is due directly to the pressure to form arising from the excessive impulses, and these are thereby to some extent dealt with and controlled.

The pressure to form runs very deep. Even the basic drives of hunger and sexuality adhere to the laws of higher interests: they too can be inhibited, can be diverted to some extent, and sometimes can even be overcome so that other interests may be pursued (as in asceticism, hunger strikes, etc.). A man who, for pathological reasons, cannot form needs and interests that are appropriate for his world and enduring in nature, degenerates under the overwhelming pressure of his excessive drives and falls into self-destructive mania. Channeling this energy into activities is even a precondition of the vegetative order—the vegetative functions of man are coordinated with it.

To summarize the discussion thus far, the excessive impulses appear to be correlated with the chronic neediness of a vulnerable being whose energies are similarly chronically employed. The "damming up" of energies during the abnormally slow and drawn-out period of development is probably of another origin as far as hormones are concerned, as a superaddition, however, it has a similar effect. Furthermore, one should realize that the reduction of instincts in man, which we have already discussed, does not in any way point to a dynamic weakness, but instead indicates a release of quantities of energies for impulses from their ties to specific organs and specific environment so that they are no longer concentrated in an organic mold. This befits an "embryonic" being who retains the essential characteristics of fetalization for its entire life (see below, chapter 11). It suggests a certain failure to differentiate of the instinct residues, along the lines of what Jung's concept of the libido, properly understood, means; this, in turn, is coupled with a suspension of the rhythmic activation of the hormonal system of drives. The consequence of both these influences is a very striking feature of human impulses which cannot be explained by theories of "domestication": this is not only the "constant, enduring sexualization of all human systems of drives," but also, "the significant pervasiveness of other effective motives for human behavior in sexual activity."[36]

By viewing the excessive impulses as a reflection of man's physical vulnerability and also, in a sense, as the strength which makes this vulnerability tolerable, we can finally gain an understanding of the great, puzzling phenomenon, the key to so many creative "answers" to the "challenges" (Toynbee's term) in the world—namely, the phenomenon of that passion for risking one's own life, of "biological hardiness,"[37] which arises from an "excess of energy." The reduction of physical risks, which can be accomplished by adapting to the environment as completely as possible—in other words, by specializing—was *not* the developmental path that lead to man. It is also not the developmental path *of* man, that is, of his culture; our culture is not based on a conservative retention of known certainties and balances but rather appears to be founded upon great spurts of energy which are fueled and fired by physical risk-taking. Man often seeks and finds opportunities for endangering himself, for consciously creating risks. From this point of view, there is essentially no difference between the mammoth hunters, the Polynesians who used the high sea winds to power their crafts, and the first men to fly. A biological theory of man should be able to account for this biologically paradoxical behavior.

Man's excessive impulses are thus one of his most salient features. They lie at the heart of his grandest creations through which he has subdued Nature; they are also responsible for the disciplined, enduring structure of his impulses, which, in essence, constitute what we call character. Thus, it is possible to define man as a being of discipline. This definition encompasses everything that can be placed under the heading of *morals* in an *anthropological* respect: the need for discipline—the pressure to form which an "undetermined animal" experiences. Education, self-discipline, and the imprinting through institutions in which the problems of life are mastered—are only the most conspicuous stages in this process. Because man presents a great problem to himself (one that he can attempt to solve only through action in conjunction with the problem of his survival), because he must develop a hierarchy of needs and interests, and, finally, because he must establish himself within a system of oriented will, all "harmonic" views of man, which ignore this incredible inner tension, are false. A community of a people, of a race, and, above all, of a small group thus have a meaning that defies comparison to animal "states."

First of all, the human child, because of his singularly drawn-out period of growth, demands continual protection which can be provided only by an institution. Moreover, the higher sensorimotor and ideosensory processes, beginning with walking and speaking, are, from a structural point of view, the communication processes of a relieved being, free from the pressures of instincts; in the course of these processes, reexperienced sensations help develop skills. These processes could occur without external interference and guidance but would then demand very long and great expenditures of energy and therefore would not yield a habitualized substructure of higher, relieved skills. Community is as essential to an individual's development as oxygen. Finally, the strength to lead one's own life is first imparted at an age in which neither an understanding of the purposes of such education nor any sort of ability to achieve it on one's own exist. The condition for the development of this vitally important ability to assume a controlled, self-initiated stance toward the external and internal world is the influence and constant presence of society.

8. The Law of Relief: The Role of Consciousness

The concept of relief, which I have referred to several times already, has proven itself to be an essential category for anthropology.

It is clear that human consciousness (and animal consciousness as well) can only be understood in relation to *behavior,* such that it may be defined as a *phase of action.* This basic tenet of pragmatism, founded by Peirce and James, is doubtlessly correct. Sorel has argued that even Kant could be viewed as a "pre-pragmatist."[38] Human cognition and thought are, to the extent that it can be conveyed in language, actually or virtually directed toward the external. This process originates with perception, and a study of the structure of skills reveals that these inevitably involve an integration of perception and action to form an *ability.* Under certain social conditions, the action aspect may be abbreviated to symbols. However, even a contemplative charismatic like Buddha seeks not only revelation but also another form of *living;* he does not renounce communication, even if it is only of a nonverbal, symbolic nature, and he requires two things from the society of which he is a part; first, that society support such behavior as a higher ability, and second that society absolve such mystics from doing basic work by taking it on itself.

To return to our discussion of the principle of relief, the following aspect comes first to mind. Man's special biological conditions make it necessary that he sever his ties to the world from the immediate present. For this reason, he must experience life on his own, laboriously and actively, so that he can avail himself of these experiences by means of his highly developed abilities which can adjust to any nuances in a situation. The end result of this process is that man creates great symbol fields in vision, language, and imagination which provide him with indications as to how to behave most effectively. Furthermore, the motor functions are relieved and put at rest but they can easily be reemployed toward any desired end if the course of action man decides to pursue requires this. Man is capable, using a minimal expenditure of energy and drawing on his most sophisticated, freest—that is, most relieved—skills, of anticipating himself, falling back upon himself, of adjusting and reversing his movements, and of planning; he can put these skills to use in directed acts to perform work. We can see how vital this process is if we consider that man's unusual physical constitution, his un-specialization and world-openness, places the incredible burden on him of singlehandedly creating his own opportunities for survival. Simply staying alive is man's ultimate challenge—there is no greater problem for a human community, a people, than to maintain its existence. History reveals how difficult such a challenge is—what has happened to the Carthagians and Burgundians, once such powerful peoples?

Thus we find the first evidence of the principle of *relief*. Man transforms his fundamental handicaps into opportunities for survival; his sensorimotor and intellectual skills (fostered by language) propel each other to higher levels, until a point is reached where circumspect control of action becomes possible. We could better understand these highly complex processes of relief and control if the science of neurology was able to tell us something definitive about sensorimotor processes and the nervous system because these processes illustrate, in some way, the laws of human achievement. Unfortunately, this is not the case, so we must attempt a direct reconstruction of the developmental order of human behavior.

To clarify further the concept of relief, one must trace it into the depths of our physical organization and show how man's special "technique" of staying alive is evident even in the structure of his sensorimotor life. This brings up first the relationship between suggestion and overview in the visual field: we do not perceive things in their entirety but instead the perceptual field becomes symbolic to a great degree in the course of our development of movement. For example, when we look at an object such as a cup, we tend to overlook its highlights and shadows as well as any ornamentation. In part, our eyes tend to use these things as indications of the cup's space and form to help recognize the object, whereby the far sides and the portions averted from us are indirectly "experienced." Any overlapping portions are assessed similarly. In contrast, the material structure (in this case, "thin porcelain") and the weight of the object are seen, but in a different, more "predicative" way than the character of the container (its hollows and curves) which stands out in the foreground. Similarly, certain visual data—for example, the handle or the "wieldable" point on the total form—suggest ways of manipulating the object. The eye can take in all this information at one glance. One could say that our eye, while quite indifferent toward the actual amount that can be perceived, is very sensitive to highly complex suggestions.

In terms of the concept of relief, it is the final stage of this process that is of particular interest here. The directness of the impression and influence of the abundance of stimulation is broken, the points of contact with it are reduced to a minimum, but this minimum holds great potential for development. The order of perception thus corresponds in the same way to man's indirect, future-oriented behavior as it, in turn, arose from unadapted, unspecific "trial and error" behavior. The prerequisite to the development of this vitally important structure of perception is man's confrontation with unadapted, unsorted masses of stimuli. Only with the aid of this structure of perception can impressions be "laden" or endowed with symbols and the visual field ordered and classified in the course of man's interaction with his surroundings, so that an overseeable world finally results. Man has clearly achieved some distance, has broken the spell of immediacy, and has made possible a future-oriented behavior, anticipating future impressions and exercising a great degree of control over his world. Thus, man takes the means of survival from his abnormal conditions; I characterize this by no means simple relationship with the term "relief."

This concept is further intended to signify another aspect of the same phenomenon—the *progressive indirectness* of human behavior—that is, the increasingly reduced but at the same time more refined, freer, and more variable contact with the world. Intermediate steps are placed between an action and its ultimate goal and these, in turn, may become the objects of a diverted and detoured interest. By human action, we understand not the chance use of a tool that happened to be present, but rather the creation of a tool for a not immediately evident purpose. Thus, what may appear superficially to be indirect, variable behavior is actually planned, anticipatory behavior directed by higher centers of control.

In this respect, the concept of relief takes on yet another meaning. In order for the lower functions to be directed and utilized, the higher ones must take over certain tasks which were previously the province of the lower functions. Above all, these are the variation and combination of movements. The higher functions, however, do this in a suggested, predominantly symbolic form. They are therefore conscious. This mechanism is, in fact, the basis for categorizing the functions as lower or higher ones.

The simplest example of this is a *planned* movement. At first, movements of the arms and hands are occupied with the problems of locomotion but become free of this once an upright stance has been achieved. Through the great variety of movements of play, of manipulation of objects, of touching and grasping, a great store of combinations and variations in movement involving direct contact with the things themselves is explored. But no real action in a true sense, no planned task has been accomplished. Only once a range of projection has been developed in the imagination can all the variations and combinations of movement be planned anew in the imagination, in the ability to imagine movements and situations; the real movement then becomes a controlled usable work movement. The problems of movement variation and coordination, which occupy a small child for years, are thus later assumed by the "virtual" (virtuell) movements and the real movement is simply carried out and may even become automatic to a degree. A planned movement is only touched upon; it is a virtual and thus also simultaneously an anticipatory movement, one which is merely possible but nonetheless, given its future orientation, is definitely experienced as possible.

Relief allows human behavior to concentrate increasingly on the "highest," the most effortless, purely suggestive functions, that is, on the conscious or intellectual functions. Thus, relief is a key concept for anthropology, for it teaches us to view man's greatest achievements in relation to his physical structure and his basic requirements for survival.

We can now appreciate what an extraordinary role habit plays. Habit relieves, first of all in the sense that, in a habitual behavior, the expenditure in motivation and control, the efforts to correct the action and the emotional investment in it are not necessary. "In daily life," writes Guillaume, "habitual actions are conditioned by the perception of certain objects to which we automatically react."[39] A behavior which thus becomes habit also becomes stabilized by forgoing the intervention of consciousness; it resists correction, is immune to objection, and forms a basis from which a higher, variable behavior can grow. For example, only once a person is already familiar with the common vocabulary and syntax of a foreign language can he then begin to work on its finer points. One can identify even in conditioned reflexes the process of relief, by which a habit becomes the basis for a higher behavior. In a conditioned reflex, a reaction, coupled with an immediate stimulus (such as salivating at the sight of food) is triggered by a random stimulus, such as the ringing of a bell, which regularly precedes the other. Doubtlessly, in this instance, the initial instinctive response is akin in its structure to a habit, for automatism is linked to a situation that regularly repeats itself, whereby any otherwise insignificant stimuli, as long as they are regular, take on the power to trigger the response. Thus, we can already see here how the formation of habit functions as a basis: this process establishes a level of behavior toward a stimulus from which point new things can be experienced and utilized. A reflex conditioned in this manner signifies a broadening of the mastered environment from its initial basis. Pavlov observed that the value acquired by one signal can be transferred to another. If the sound of a metronome, which announces the appearance of food, already provokes salivation, then a light signal preceding the metronome will ultimately have the same effect. This is a broadening of the range of stimuli based on an acquired habit.

All of man's higher functions in every realm of intellectual and moral life, as well as of refinement of movement and action, are developed because the formation of a base of habits *relieves and shifts upward* the energy for motivation, experimentation, and control previously expended in the habitual action. For example, let us consider how the organization of a society provides for the somewhat regular and habitual, long-term gratification of basic biological needs. Since the Neolithic era, man has used the growing surpluses of agriculture and livestock to build up reserves, to provide for the habitual, long-term gratification of the need for food. Those persons not directly involved in the production of food are thus freed in all their higher intellectual and practical functions for modes of behavior that can no longer properly be termed "appetitive behavior;" they may, for example, create things that are useless but beautiful, or they may devote themselves to the development and enrichment of arts, crafts, and rituals. Furthermore, all the energy and emotion liberated by the trivialization of the habitual gratification of biological needs are now directed toward these cultural achievements. How else can we explain the great passion in all early cultures for the construction of artificial forms as, for example, in rituals of magic, despite the obviously doubtful rate of empirical success? Clearly, these are so stubbornly retained because they have a higher gratification value for great amounts of energy, which are freed by the habitualization and trivialization of basic need gratification and can then be channeled into the *liberated* intellectual and motor functions.

I wish to close this section with a few general philosophical remarks. Hartmann's theory of ontological categories has shown that, in the stratification of the world, the categories of the lower strata, such as the inorganic, are the stronger; in other words, these are indifferent to the existence of higher strata and define the framework within which the higher strata can exist. By the same token, the higher categories are the dependent ones, just as a spiritual life presupposes an organic and an organic an inorganic one.

However, they are also richer: each higher stratum contains a "categorical novum," that is, new structures and phenomena, which cannot be derived from the lower strata. The higher categories are, of course, "weaker" in the sense that they are dependent upon the existence of lower strata, but, compared to them, they are free or autonomous.

I believe that anthropology can contribute a series of special categories, some of which are of great interest because they cut across several strata. With the aid of the category of "relief," we can describe one of the fundamental laws of sensory and motor life which defines the latitude within which our thinking consciousness can emerge. We can identify this category of relief even in intellectual activity itself, namely, in the development of language (see chapter 33). We can trace it downward toward the biological level, to "conditioned reflexes," and we only lose it once we go beyond habit to the obscure region of the vegetative. Of course, no theory can explain how the organic evolves from the inorganic and the spiritual and intellectual, in turn, from the organic. The concept of "development" should replace that of "creation" only in the sense of a quasi-automatic emergence of the new, but it does not account for the creative aspect of this process. Hartmann writes: "The appearance of life in the universe is bound to certain conditions, which it is easy to see could exist only as rare exceptions in the cosmic relationships." I would like to expand this thought into a hypothesis: it appears that *improbable conditions* in each lower stratum had to be met before the phenomenon of the higher stratum could emerge. Thus, the *special place of man* has an ontological dignity. It is a biological improbability; the exceptional human physical organization must have been achieved before the higher categories could manifest themselves in a way that they cannot be derived from the lower ones. Furthermore, it is likely that the variety and diversity of human drives would, on the whole, produce unstable social structures, so that the preconditions for higher cultural achievements would be an improbable balance among many instabilities. This accounts for the surprisingly short flowering of cultures—Toynbee, for example, posits the decline of the Egyptian culture quite early, after the construction of the pyramids, in the old kingdom.

I would like to raise one final point concerning consciousness. Consciousness apparently emerges from perception, in the sense of a guiding and "meting out" of behavior toward removed sources of stimulation. The theory of J. M. Baldwin, Bergson, Dewey and others on the relationship of consciousness to the *inhibited* life process rests on several facts. For one thing, the perception of moving beings involves a "deferring" of the response to a distant thing, not yet close enough to collide with or to pose a threat. This leads to the second point, that any kind of process that is unconsciously automatized and unerring in its function becomes conscious only if it is somehow disrupted. Finally, one can easily determine that unexpected inhibitions of our actions prompts a reflexive response: "la reflexion apparait comme le choc en retour du reflexe brusquement inhibé" [Thought comes as a shock as a result of the suddenly inhibited reflex] writes Pradines.[40] Hartmann argues that the emergence of consciousness cannot be explained solely by the inhibition of immediate reactions, but more likely by the diversity of creative achievements that fill the resulting gap.[41]

At this point, the pertinent views of Pradines should be raised, which he has put forth in the above-quoted work as well as earlier in his "Philosophie de la sensation." He has connected perceptual consciousness to two basic life functions—"need" and "defense." The stimulation of needs is related to the anticipated absence of the object of gratification, the presence, possession, or consumption of which satisfies the need; Pradines assigns to this function of need the "need senses" of smell and taste, whereby he overlooks the fact that in many animals the triggering of instinctive behavior to satisfy elemental needs is connected to the sense of distance. Defensive responses are primarily triggered by the direct effect of existing objects upon the organism, the removal of which then frees the organism. Pradines proposes an *irritation originelle* as the fundamental event in this process, that is, a defensive reaction of the irritated life process. To it, he assigns the sense of touch and the higher senses.

We come now to the heart of the theory, which is significant because it combines the view of the emergence of consciousness from the inhibited life process with that of sensory perception as "relief." The original irritation differentiates itself first in the direction of perception and then in the direction of the ability to feel pain, which are described as distinct, successive modalities of the *same* activity. He assumes that the ability to feel pain emerged indirectly as a repercussion of the sensory differentiation to the original irritation and presupposes intelligence in the lowest levels of perception. Pradines expresses this as follows: "The actual means which intelligence needed to develop perception from the direct irritation was to sensitize the being to irritations of decreasing emotional value, a sensitization that was no longer related to the effect of an aggressive influence, but rather to its increasingly removed threat."[42]

Pain is thus not a function of need; desire is a more likely one. Pain is not tied to the need sense of taste and smell. Its actual domain is the sense of touch; it is excluded from visual and auditory perceptions because these are bound up with the vibrations of a medium that communicates to us potential sensations of touch in an immaterial and intangible form that cannot injure us. Perception at a distance, we could say, relieves the organism of the necessity of direct, possibly painful, contact. Pain, however, is not a tactile sensation that increases by degrees, even though the basis for tactile perception is the anticipation of pain through the sense of touch. Tactile sensitivity is apparent in the ability to register the gradual approach of an intruding irritation in a painless increasing in intensity, until the archaic, "expulsive," or "aversive" activity is triggered at the point where pain is felt. The quality of pain itself, as we said, is a reaction of sensitization: "Nature could not bring the biologically insignificant forerunners of the irritating stimulus to consciousness, without increasing the awareness of the stimulus itself, when it was given, to the point where it becomes pain."[43] Thus, an intimate and profound relationship exists between intelligence and pain. "For this is intelligence itself, when it descends to the root of the irritation, the result of the light with which intelligence illuminates it, by rendering the weakest irritations expressive, conscious, and transparent." This is Pradines' view.

If consciousness is essentially, given its origin, oriented toward the external world, then, by the same token, all life processes must be essentially unconscious; they take place in the darkness of the unconscious and the "how" of the processes remains completely hidden from us. We know as little about how we breathe and digest, how we see and think, as we do about how we lift our arms.

We have no knowledge of the incredible complexity and perfection of the vegetative and motor processes; consciousness is apparently not able to inform us about these.

Kant, in his Critique of Judgement,[44] of which Schelling rightly said that perhaps never in so few pages have so many profound insights been concentrated, argued that according to the *unique design of our cognitive faculties,* which are divided into sensory perception and discursive thought, the "explanation of the possibility of a product of Nature" is not given to us, only its "discussion" is permitted. At this point he proposes the idea of a higher cognitive faculty, not our own, the "intellectus archetypus," a productive reason that sees the emergence of its products in their genesis, which we would have to possess in order to comprehend the inner expediency of an organism.

This reminds one of a theory of Nietzsche's. When he spoke of the great reason of the body, the tool of which is the lesser reason, the mind, he was also proclaiming the perfection of the organic process which is inaccessible to consciousness and incommensurable. "All perfect acts are unconscious and no longer subject to will. . . . A degree of consciousness makes perfection impossible."[45] "Consciousness is only a tool of life, and not even the most necessary one, when one considers how many great things are accomplished without it"—a closing remark which is, by the way, incorrect from an anthropological point of view; the following thesis is much more accurate: "Consciousness—beginning quite externally as coordination and becoming conscious of "impressions"—at first, at the furthest distance from the biological center of the individual, but a process that deepens and intensifies itself, and continually draws nearer to that center."[46]

The general formulation of this process is as follows: consciousness, directed toward the external world, is an aid in the service of achieving perfection of the organic process and thus is essentially not capable of and also not designed for perceiving this process. It was actually Schopenhauer who proposed this view.[47]

At a certain level of complexity of the life process—at the point where moving beings exist—consciousness originates from the total organic conditions, at first as perception, and is thus, essentially, underivable. Its achievement obviously lies in its concern with the course of complex life processes which take place under difficult conditions. If we recall our discussion of the law of relief, then we realize that the higher symbolic skills of consciousness are also used in order to make possible higher vital processes of control, subordination, and coordination. *Only so much is illuminated, as can be used for a more complex, more refined, and "better" cessation and initiation of functions in the darkness.*

In man, because of the extraordinary burden of his requirements for survival, the processes of relief, control, and guidance are especially complicated and variable; accordingly, the functions of consciousness, incorporated into these processes, are unusually diverse. However, once we can explain how man could survive based on his unusual physical constitution, then we will have a direct way to answer the questions: Why is there language, why imagination, inner life, memory? We will discover that, indeed, each of these questions is overdetermined because it can be answered from any achieved perspective.

Thus, our consciousness, oriented toward the external world, predisposed toward experience and communication with others, cannot provide us with knowledge of the great expediency of organic events. We can only conjecture that, merely by existing, a "problem" has been solved, with a perfection that surpasses comprehension. In any respect, it appears that great store is set by life itself and that an existence amidst the fullness of the world is itself a value, perhaps the greatest value, as is expressed by the worldwide propagation of the belief in life after death, or by the fact that religions exist which hold the ritual duty of sparing life, of killing nothing, as one of the highest duties.

We can identify only the circumstances in which man exists, as well as the means available to him—within himself and outside of himself—for mastering these circumstances; we cannot identify the "how" of existence and of mastery of the world, the fact that we *are* and we *act*. Thus, once we have acknowledged that existence cannot be measured empirically, then it is not possible to say that life is "meaningless" or to claim that there is something in our experiencing and thinking consciousness that must be "realized" in order for it to have a meaning. It is quite likely that simply by solving the problems of daily existence, something else of great importance is also being accomplished. Nietzsche once asked "whether all conscious willing, all conscious purposes, all evaluations are not perhaps only means through which something essentially different from what appears in consciousness is to be achieved," that everything "could be a means by which we have to achieve something that lies beyond our consciousness."[48]

The view of life presented here as transcending empirical existence leads to the idea of an "unspecified obligation." By "simply existing," we could be achieving something of infinite importance, the purpose of which is essentially indecipherable to us because we *are* this purpose and is only suggested symbolically. Nietzsche's concepts of the superman (never properly understood), of the eternal return, the will to power, thus find their place. Taken literally, they make little sense and are only extensions of Schopenhauerian metaphysics or of Darwinism. For Nietzsche, however, these were symbols that were intended to identify a way of "getting more from life" *(Mehr an Leben)* and to define more exactly the "unspecified obligation." As such, these concepts are positivistic and undialectical but, even though not Christian, they are not unreligious by any means. For it can be shown (as I will do later) that the "unspecified obligation" is one of the fundamental categories of archaic (protomagic) religious behavior.[49]

Every definition of the "unspecified obligation" in religious, political, judicial, and civil life has its historical and social backgrounds and limitations. These will not be discussed in this book but the view I wish to develop here of the "undetermined being" necessarily ties in with this concept.

Theodor Ballauf[50] aptly summarized this point: "It is not being as 'will' " that becomes apparent here but rather being in its original structure of relative indeterminateness, which it principally consists of and which appears specifically at the edge of Nature and, for this reason, compels that it be carried out as 'will.' "

9. Animals and Their Environment: Herder's Contribution

In my essay, "Die Resultate Schopenhauers," mentioned above, I wrote that Schopenhauer first proposed the general scheme for the modern view of a harmonic relationship between animals and their environments.[51] He describes the perfect harmony in every animal species between the will, character—thus, between the system of drives and instincts—and the organic specialization and life circumstances. He speaks of the "striking suitability, right down to the finest detail, of an animal to its way of life, to its external means of survival." He goes on to say that "every part of the animal corresponds specifically to its way of life; the claws, for example, are always adept at grasping prey, which the teeth are designed to tear apart and the intestines able to digest, and the limbs are skilled at transporting the animal towards its prey and no organ remains unused."

"Consider the numerous types of animals, and how each is, without exception, only the image of its will, the visible expression of the strivings of its will, which make up its character."

By the same token, the structure of an animal is completely suited to its environment: "If it (the will) wishes to climb in the trees as an ape then it reaches with both arms for the branches, thereby extending the ulna and radius, while simultaneously lengthening the os coccygis into a prehensile tail, in order to hang by it from the branches and swing from one to another."

Independently of Schopenhauer (but not, by his own admission, of Kant), J. von Uexküll, in his well-known works[52] has examined the relationship between the structure of an animal's organs and its environment. He pays particular attention to the question of what sensory stimuli could be given to an animal based on its particular type of sensory organs alone; and he rejects the naïve view that ascribes our world to animals as their own, whereas, in fact, each species has its own unique environment which it experiences and masters through its own system of specialized organs. If we know the sensory organs and skills of an animal, we can reconstruct its environment. I would like to mention here only a few of Uexküll's best known examples. The tick waits in the branches of a bush to drop onto warm-blooded animals or to be brushed off by them. Though it is eyeless, it possesses a general sense of light in its skin, apparently to orient it as it climbs upward to its waiting point. The approach of the prey is sensed by the blind and deaf animal through its sense of smell and this sense is attuned solely to the single odor which all mammals give off—butyric acid. At this signal, the tick drops, and if it falls on something warm and reaches its prey then it follows its sense of touch and temperature to the spot with the least amount of hair, where it then bores into the skin and pumps itself full of blood.

The "world" of the tick thus consists solely of sensations of light and warmth and of a single quality of smell. It has been proven that it has no sense of taste. Once its first and last meal is over, it falls to the ground, lays its eggs, and dies.

Its chances are, of course, slight. In order to ensure the continuation of the species, a great number of these animals wait in their bushes, where they are able to go for long periods without nourishment: In the Zoological Institute at Rostock there are ticks which have gone hungry for eighteen years. Their way of life is perfectly illustrated in the structure of their organs: the sperm cells, which the female tick shelters during her waiting period, remain in sperm capsules until the mammal's blood reaches the tick's stomach; then they are freed and fertilize the eggs in the ovaries.

This example offers striking proof of the harmony between the organic structure of an animal, that is, its particular type of organs, its environment (the impressions of the external world available to it), and its way of life.

Let us consider some other examples. Some sea urchins respond to all darkenings within their sense of light with a defensive movement of their spines—no matter whether the darkness is caused by a fish swimming by, the shadow of a boat, or even clouds obscuring the sun; their sense of light is poor but nonetheless expedient. This part of their environment knows neither color nor form, but only shadows. The most dangerous enemy of the scallop is the starfish *Asterias*. As long as the starfish is immobile, it has no effect on the scallop. Its characteristic shape does not signify anything to the scallop. As soon as the starfish begins to move, however, the scallop responds by sticking out its long tentacles which function as organs of smell. The tentacles approach the starfish and take in the new stimulus, whereupon the scallop swims away. It makes no difference what shape or color a moving object is. It appears in the scallop's environment only if its movements are as slow as those of a starfish. The scallop's eyes are not oriented toward shape or color, but only toward the slow tempo of movement of its enemy. If the additional feature of smell is also present, flight results.

Similarly, in the environment of bees, only broken-up forms, such as stars or crosses, have significance, not closed ones such as circles or squares. This is because only those blossoms which have the former type of shape (as opposed to buds, which are still closed) are of vital interest to the bees. The high-frequency sounds a bat emits affect moths in the same way as does an imitation of these tones produced by rubbing a glass stopper in a bottle. It is the signal of the enemy. Moths are able to perceive only these high tones; they are otherwise totally deaf. Those moths whose light coloring make them easily visible fly away when they hear the high tones, whereas other species with protective coloring alight at the same tones. Of course, no moth has ever seen its own color. Here, too, the perceptual world of the animal is exactly and reciprocally adapted to its vital interests, and both again, to its biological structure. (All examples are drawn from Uexküll.)

This same approach can be applied to the higher animals. If we look upon an ape's snout as an antechamber of its respiratory organs, we can draw conclusions about its life circumstances. Baboons—ground-dwellers residing in dry, dusty climates—have a characteristically long snout which functions as an air filter and humidifier; tree-dwelling primates have receding ones. The gorilla, more adapted to ground life than the chimpanzee and orangutan, has a more developed external snout. One can even infer from the shape of the snout that some species of macaques resemble the ground-dwelling apes in their style of life, for the snout protrudes far forward, forming narrow ducts for the air passage.

This approach is also valid for fossil study. F. H. Osborn[53] has shown that fossil elephants' molars harmonized completely with their environment. In terms of dental structure, there are complete transitions between part grass-eating, part leaf-eating, or exclusively leaf-eating (mastodon) forms. Osborn says that the proboscidians' ability to adapt to extraordinary conditions and their plasticity can be compared only to the adaptation man has achieved through his intelligence.

Buytendijk[54] gives a good example of the specialization in acoustic perception in lizards and frogs: they cannot be trained to respond to a tone even when coupled with an electrical shock. However, a lizard in a terrarium will immediately react to a light scratching on the ground, similar to the sound of a moving insect. It is specialized toward only this perception.

The following law, for example, holds true: certain primarily visually oriented animals, such as birds and apes, who feed on immobile things, respond predominantly to visual impressions, particularly to forms and colors; predatory animals, on the other hand, respond to *moving* stimuli. It is clear that a very specialized perception of great significance to the species must be followed by a definite behavior; the more specialized the animal is, the more "reactive" the behavior will be. To put this another way: perception acts "as a suggestion" and automatically shifts abruptly into a reaction. Specialized senses are not interchangeable.

The inability of chickens or apes to rely on other sensory impressions, taste and hearing, is striking, as is the significance that visual impressions have for them. A chicken will stop pecking at grain when the light begins to gradually dim, even if grains are covering its feet, even if it is hungry, and even if one imitates the noise that falling grain makes; the chicken remains still and falls asleep.[55] The inevitability of the reaction to a specific visual impression is expressed in the following example: A group of higher apes (baboons, mandrills, chimpanzees) were shown a dummy orange; they immediately reached for it in great excitement and greed, without being affected by the absence of smell or by different tactile sensations. When a hole was made in the dummy, this discordant visual impression irritated them; they calmed down, however, once the dummy was turned, in front of their eyes, so that the hole was on the side facing away from them ("alors, les mains revenaient instantanement)."

This aptly illustrates the irresistibility of the visually specialized perception. Buytendijk demonstrated how surprisingly little a mandrill relies on touch, smell, and taste. When the dummy was torn into pieces, the mandrill immediately stuck a piece in its mouth, took it out, "examined it carefully," smelled it, put it back in its mouth, and only threw it away after several such attempts. It took that long for the powerful suggestion of the visual impression to be overcome. Hereafter, no doubt can remain as to the specialization and unilateralness of the perceptual world of apes.

Uexküll compares the certainty with which an animal moves in its environment to that of a man in his own house. In its house, the animal finds familiar objects around it, "signifiers" *(Bedeutungsträger)* specific to its species: its food, its pathways, its mate, its enemy. Many animals perceive only a few forms, colors, odors, and sounds from the vast richness of the world—only those that are connected with their special agents of meaning. "Since, in order for an animal to be affected by stimuli, the appropriate sensory organs must be present, Nature is being quite radical in giving an animal no sensory organs besides those that are absolutely necessary."[56]

This approach falls short only in special cases. It does not work for house pets, the domestication of which has greatly changed their original behavior. Furthermore, some other ordinary but versatile species with high rates of population growth (rats, sparrows) have attained a considerable degree of neutrality toward their environment. The highest mammals, however—elephants, anthropoids, large cats—are very specialized and, in the wild, strictly bound to their environments. The structure of an animal must thus be studied in connection with its environment. Its organs of nourishment, movement, and reproduction, as well as its sensory organs, bodily covering, defenses, and so on, each have a specific function and together form a very distinct, unique context: a system. This system is adapted to a strict, species-specific environment: a specific way of life, a mode of reproduction and eating, a "home" with familiar pathways and haunts, specific types of prey or food, of enemies, symbionts, specific climate, etc. The totality of this system is called a *biocenosis* and can, in certain interesting cases, have many members. Woltereck[57] describes such a biocenosis of algae, small crabs, and fish that are part of a food chain. The unprotected crabs live in the same months (June, July) and in the same water depths as the fish who, after this time period, feed on the sediment and plants of the shore zone. In early summer, however, these fish eat countless numbers of the plankton crabs. Some individual crabs produce eggs as early as June which then take months to develop; the majority, however, bear live young and are eaten along with their young. Crabs later grow from the eggs once the fish, now fully grown, refuse to eat them (by the way, this should, according to natural selection, have lead to a preference for the protected individuals; this is, however, not the case). The indices of population growth correspond with the number eaten. The fish statistically consume nineteen of the crab's approximately twenty offspring and the mother, but never eat the twentieth one; thus the crab species does not die out, the crab's over production of offspring does not increase to thirty or forty but rather equals the number destroyed. Despite these great losses, a balance in the system as a whole is maintained. The subject of the process is thus neither the individual nor the species, but rather a relationship between species and environment, or, better yet, a structure of species and environment.

Uexküll's theory of the environment was a spark of genius and convinces us that the world of animals is not our own. The theory is incomplete, however; Uexküll declines to bring in the concept of instinct, probably because of the uncertainty of contemporary, pre-Lorenz opinion toward this topic. Since then, in addition to the organ specialization in the environment of animals, there are the equally specific instinctive patterns of movement which can definitely be considered as organs—inded, which can be used, as with these, for systematic classification. Furthermore, it has been noted that Uexküll's theory led to a narrowing of his approach to the "world of perception" (Merkwelt) and the "world of action" (Wirkwelt), thus relating it strictly to the Sensorimotor nervous system. The tendency at this time was increasingly toward studying the unique environments of animals; the actually quite productive behavioral research receded while the Kantian substructure of theory prevailed ("All reality is subjective appearance," Uexküll and the school later even worked with the idea of Leibniz's monads. Hermann Weber, on the other hand, correctly points out that numerous environmental factors, such as temperature, air pressure, radiation, bacteria, and so on, cannot be included in a subjective concept of the environment and yet are nonetheless highly influential environmental factors.[58]

Another, equally significant fault in Uexküll's theory is that he attempted to apply it to man; for example, he presented the well-known idea that a forest means something different to a poet, hunter, lumberjack, lost person, etc. In his work, Niegeschaute Welten, with the characteristic subtitle "The environments of my friends," he described a number of his old acquaintances and assorted characters and, based on this, proceeded to distinguish two types of people—"perceivers" (Merklinge) and "actors" (Wirklinge)—corresponding to his differentiation of Merkwelt and Wirkwelt.[59]

In doing this, a distinction of great importance is lost. The original, truly instinctive behavior patterns of animals, which are tied to specific natural environments, are confused with an acquired specialization of behavior in man which is his response to a finely structured cultural sphere. The question fundamental to theory and practice then arises: How does man, given his world-openness and reduction of instincts, with all his great plasticity and instability, actually manage to achieve a predictable, regular behavior, which can be evoked under certain conditions with some degree of certainty? Such a behavior, which could be termed quasi-instinctive or quasi-automatic, in man takes the place of a truly instinctive behavior and apparently first defines a stable social context.

To ask this question is to bring up the problem of institutions. One can even say that just as animal groups and symbioses are held together by releasers and instinctive movements, so are the human groups held together by institutions and quasi-automatic habits of thought, feelings, judgment, and action, which first establish themselves therein and become one-sided, habitualized, and thus stabilized. In this manner, behavior patterns become habitual, and, to some extent, reliable or predictable. If institutions are destroyed, then we would immediately witness a great degree of unpredictability and uncertainty, a lack of protection in behavior against stimulation that could then properly be characterized as instinctive. Furthermore, one of the most shocking sights is when virtues, after the collapse of institutions in which they developed themselves in characteristic narrowness, fall back on the individual and are manifested as confusion and helplessness. The highly cultivated and irreversible attitudes that Uexküll describes can exist only within a firmly institutionalized cultural system; and then the concept of "environment" is totally unbiological and can only mean something along the lines of a highly civilized individual milieu.

The clearly defined, biologically precise concept of the environment is thus not applicable to man, for what "environment" is to animals, "the second nature," or culture, is to man; culture has its own particular problems and concept formations which cannot be explained by the concept of environment but instead are only further obscured by it.

These claims are not intended to provoke a battle over terminology. Weber has proposed what I feel to be the best definition of the biological concept of environment: "By 'environment' should be understood the totality of conditions contained in an entire complex of surroundings which permit a certain organism, by virtue of its specific organization, to survive."[60] For all highly specialized animal species (the overwhelming majority), one can identify the complex of species-specific external conditions that must be met in order for the species to survive and reproduce. I cannot find such a complex of preexisting natural conditions for man, apart from those universal ones that pertain equally to any organism (i.e., atmosphere, certain air pressure levels, etc.). "Man" does not live in a state of organic or instinctive adaptation to a set of definite, specifiable external conditions, but instead, his constitution necessitates intelligent, planning activity which permits him to create the techniques and means of survival by changing random constellations of natural circumstances. For this reason, man is able to live anywhere, in strong contrast to the geographically strictly defined territories of all specialized animals. Human beings live in deserts and polar regions, among antelopes and polar bears, in high mountains, steppes, and jungles, in swampy areas, on the water, and in all climates; above all, they live nowadays in cities. A specific arrangement of environmental components, in the sense of the above definition, which would be valid for the entire species of man and which would have to be present for man to survive, simply cannot be identified.

Man is able to accomplish all this because he creates his cultural sphere from the existing conditions, whatever they may be, by effecting planning and anticipatory changes; this cultural sphere is his "environment" and belongs, indeed, to the *natural* requirements for life of this unspecialized, organically helpless being. "Culture" is hence an anthrobiological concept and man is a cultural being. An Australian aborigine possesses approximately 200 instruments and techniques which he uses to survive in his unfriendly surroundings. Culture is thus firstly the totality of physical and intellectual means and techniques including institutions by which a specific society "maintains itself;" secondly, it is the totality of all resulting institutions based on it.

Adaptations to climate, present in individual races but not in man as a species, are probably secondary. The ancestors of Indians, Negroes, etc., lived in totally different climates under very different conditions and must also have looked quite different. The Pleistocene Epoch and Holocene Epoch were a time of great unrest and displacement among the hominids, and the present-day North American Indians probably received their strongly caucasian and mongolian features from their original north asiatic homeland.[61] The skulls discovered in east Africa, especially in Olduvai, show quite striking caucasian resemblances.

That human societies do "change their environments"—a concept unknown in zoology—can be documented in historical times. Great migrations to new living spaces demand a revolution in culture, a complete change in survival techniques and means of thought—a change that often affects religions as well. The Teutons' reception of Christianity was one such stage in a migratory movement. The Germanic religion, with its heavenly bands of warriors,[62] its minor cult development ("sacrifiis non student," Caesar, *The Gallic Wars*) must have been the religion of a migrating people, and it was impossible from this basis to conquer a far superior civilization, such as the late Roman. Even more impressive examples of sudden cultural changes can be taken from other continents. According to Eickstedt,[63] the territory of the Sioux and Fox around 1700 was the wild-rice region of Minnesota. This indicates a society based on hunting and gathering and the use of canoes. Driven out by the Ojibway, who possessed firearms, they then moved to the prairies and acquired horses from Europeans. "A few years later, the whole people could ride and thereby a giant living space in the high prairie was suddenly open to them."

Every man on any cultural level experiences himself, his society, his cultural milieu and its background, his particular natural surroundings, as parts of the "world." Even Australian aborigines conceive of their homeland as part of one giant whole that stretches out indefinitely, and man's orientation in and interpretation of the world expands to encompass this whole. Our senses, of course, can experience only a part of the world, as is also true for animals' perceptual organs. We know this because we can expand this limited view through the use of microscopes and telescopes. Primitive people know this in a religious sense from their uncertainty toward what is given. We all conceive of the visible world as a portion of a not-given world, and it is immaterial whether the latter consists of electrons and bacteria or of demons and spirits. Man, in general, reads into what is perceived that which *can* be perceived and into what can be perceived that which cannot; above all, his *behavior* is geared toward all these areas. For a squirrel, the ants on the same tree do not exist. For man, not only do all these exist, but so do the far mountains and the distant stars, the perception of which is biologically superfluous, and beyond what can be perceived exist the gods with whom man interacts through rituals and cults. Lorenz's statement that "the entire sociology of higher animals is founded upon releasers and innate schema" expresses a rejection of the concept of environment for man. When observing a Chinese peasant or a European factory worker, one cannot find any innate patterns of movement that are related to a species-specific order of environmental components that function as releasers. This is so because man's survival depends on a variable, consciously controlled behavior which is first established through social interaction, then regularized, and, if need be, habitualized, while still remaining open for new, additional motivations and further development. First and foremost, man has to create the conditions necessary for his basic physical existence from the infinite diversity of the world. Even the North Star, as a means of orientation, is useful toward this end.

I cannot fail to mention that Herder pursued a similar line of thought in his *Essay on the Origin of Language,* which I will now discuss. Herder attempts an interesting differentiation between man and animal based on several points. He writes: "It seems assured that man is by far inferior to the animals in the intensity and reliability of his instincts and indeed that he does not have at all what in many animal species we regard as innate artifactive skills and drives."[64] Beyond this, he brilliantly introduces a new point of view which is essentially that of the environment; he terms this the "sphere of animals."

Every animal, according to Herder, has its own sphere within which it is born, lives, and dies. "It is a remarkable fact that the keener the senses of the animals and the more wonderful their artifacts, the narrower is their sphere; the more uniform is their artifact." [65] Herder states that he has been pondering this relationship for a long time and has discovered that a striking inverse proportion exists between the inferior nature of an animal's movements, its diet, means of self-preservation, mating habits, rearing of young, society, and its drives and abilities. The narrower its sphere, maintains Herder, the more certain and perfect are its abilities. "When infinitely fine senses are concentrated in a narrow sphere on the same kind of object while all the rest of the world means nothing to them, how they must penetrate!" Conversely: "The more varied the activities and the tasks of an animal, the more diffuse its attention and the more numerous the objects of it, the more unsteady its way of life, in short, the wider and the more varied its sphere, the more we note that the power of its senses is dispersed and weakened."[66]

Thus, Herder assumes the following: "The sensitivity, the skills, and the artifactive drives of the animals increase in strength and intensity in inverse proportion to the magnitude and multifariousness of their sphere of activity."[67] An animal's senses, argues Herder, are cultivated through its drives. Although Herder does not have a clear concept of organ specialization and devotes more attention to sensation, perception, and "artifactive drives," and although his theory is too strongly oriented toward insects, he nonetheless was the first to recognize and express that animals' abilities, their actions as well as their perceptions and instincts, are adapted to a limited portion of the world—i.e., to their environment.

With the same certainty, he describes man in a way that is fundamentally correct. He speaks of the unique character of mankind with whose appearance everything changed. Furthermore, he defines man as a deficient being! The newborn child "expresses neither conceptions nor instinctive drives through sounds as any animal does in accordance with its species. And placed among animals alone, the infant is the most orphaned child of nature. Naked and bare, weak and in need, shy and unarmed, and—to make the sum of its misery complete—deprived of all guides of life. Born as it is with so dispersed, so weakened a sensuousness, with such indefinite, dormant abilities, with such divided and tired drives, clearly dependent upon a thousand needs, destined to belong to a great circle...No! Such a contradiction is not nature's way."[68]

According to Herder, then, man can only be characterized negatively in comparison with animals. "His senses and his organization are not focused on one object: He has senses for all things and hence naturally weaker and duller senses for each one. The powers of his soul are spread over the world; there is no orientation of his conceptions toward one single object and hence no artifactive drive, no artifactive skill" (no instincts). Therefore, he also has no environment. "Man has no such uniform and narrow sphere where only one performance is expected of him: A whole world of ventures and tasks is lying about him." He has "dispersed appetites, divided attention ...obtusely sensing senses."[69]

It is admirable that Herder recognizes the inner relationship between man's biological helplessness, his world-openness, and the absent-minded nature of his desires. He then comes to the question of compensation for these deficiencies and at this point proposes that language arises from this new-found "character of mankind," as a substitute originating "precisely [from] the area of these wants—at the bottom of his great deprivation of artifactive drives."[70]

Nothing more fitting can be said about the relationship between man and animal than that the difference is not "one of degree nor one of a supplementary endowment with powers; it lies in a totally distinct orientation and evolution of all powers." Thus, man's reason is not based upon his animal organization; it is rather "the total arrangement of all human forces, the total economy of his sensuous and cognitive, of his cognitive and volitional nature...[that] is called reason in man as in the animal it turns into an artifactive skill; [that] in man is called freedom and turns in the animal into instinct." Nature thus takes a new direction with man. Herder achieved what every philosophical anthropology, even those which are founded on a theological conception of man, is dedicated to achieve—to view man's intelligence in the context of his biological nature, the structure of his perception, action, and needs, that is, to view "the overall determination of his powers of thought within the total complex of his senses and of his drives." Human consciousness presupposes a unique morphological design, a unique mobility, unique perceptual skills, and a unique structure of drives, a "totally distinct orientation and evolution of all powers."[71] Philosophical anthropology has not progressed significantly since Herder. His is in essence the same approach I wish to develop using the tools of modern science.

Indeed, philosophical anthropology does not need to progress any further, for this is the truth.

Note: I am indebted since the appearance of the first edition (1940) to Nicolai Hartmann ("Neue Anthropologie in Deutschland,") *Blätter für deutsche Philosophie,* 1941 Vol. 15) and Hermann Amman ("Sprache und Gemeinschaft," *Die Tatwelt,* 1941 Vol. 17) for their important comments which I hope I have taken into consideration here. Extensive and frequent discussions with Konrad Lorenz, Hans Bürger-Prinz, and Helmut Schelsky have also been incorporated in many formulations. O. Storch's paper, "Die Sonderstellung des Menschen in Lebensabspiel und Vererbung," Vienna, 1948, helped broaden the biological foundations of basic insights which proved to be common. The essay "Tier und Mensch" *(Die Neue Rundschau,* October, 1938), which appeared under Buytendijk's name, and of which I said in earlier editions that he agrees with the theory put forth here in its crucial points and that this agreement is important in theses arrived at independently, rose, as H. Plessner has since informed me, from a collaboration with him.

PART I

The special morphological place of man

10. The Primitive Nature of Human Organs

Our next task is to document man's special place from the point of view of morphology. As we have already indicated, man is characterized by a pervasive absence of highly specialized organs which are adapted to a specific environment; this is in keeping with his nature as an acting, world-open being who has to rely on his own initiative for survival.

The deficiencies and peculiarities in the human organs should be understood as evidence of man's failure to specialize; they are primitive in an ontogenetic sense (that is, man has retained fetal states into adulthood) or phylogenetic sense (studies in comparative anatomy have shown that, from the point of view of evolution, the human organ is primitive or "geologically old"). Although some organs may qualify as primitive from both these points of view, this is not always the case; I am indebted to Mijsberg for emphasizing that this distinction is necessary.[1] Specialized states, in contrast, refer to the final phases of development. Hence, to propose that primitive organs could have developed from already specialized ones contradicts all that biological science has taught us.

In this discussion, we must define our terms carefully. The concept "primitive" is synonymous here with "unspecialized" and is never intended to connote "inferior": for example, one might call an Australian aboriginal skull primitive in comparison to a European one. Moreover, for our purposes, unspecialized means prototypical (*ursprünglich*) in an ontogenetic (embryonic) or phylogenetic sense. By the term specialization, I understand a *loss* of the wealth of possibilities for development that are present in an unspecialized organ, with the result that some of these possibilities are pursued while others are not. Any regressive developments are always part of a process of specialization; this is true, for example, of the anthropoid's thumb, the penguin's flippers, or, in many parasites, of the disappearance of superfluous intestines.[2] Dollo's law states that functions once lost cannot be regained. Since regressive developments such as we have described are part of a specialization process, this would mean that specializations are essentially irreversible.

Specialization is the ultimate goal of all organ development and has been achieved by all mammals with the exception of man. From a biological perspective, it is inconceivable that specialized organs could develop into unspecialized ones and thereby regain a wealth of possible directions for development. If it can be proven that the basic human organs are unspecialized (that is, embryonic or archaic), then this will pose a fundamental problem for the doctrine of human evolution. Given the obvious absence of specialization in human organs (which I will document later), any theory that claims that man is *directly* descended from animals and that does not resort to a special supplemental hypothesis to account for this particular issue necessarily confronts the insurmountable problem of deriving primitive forms from developed ones. Indeed, the great apes, given primary consideration in such theories, are unusually highly specialized. This, then, is the fundamental difficulty with the theory of evolution when applied to man; it is further compounded by the fact that there is obviously a close kinship between man and ape. I cannot emphasize too strongly that any theory that fails to acknowledge this problem cannot possibly have a true understanding of its difficulty. Whereas it is reasonable to argue that birds are descended from Permian reptiles (as types), the situation with man is far more complex.

To my mind, there are two types of doctrines of human development. The first type, with which we are in agreement, takes the above-mentioned problem into account: either man is understood as a highly archaic being who has avoided the path of specialization in the course of his evolution or a supplemental hypothesis is proposed to make it possible to trace man's ancestry from a primate branch. In both cases, the special place (*Sonderstellung*) of the human being is clearly acknowledged. Although the supplemental hypothesis may take very different forms, it in essence always makes the point that the emergence of man can be understood within the framework of the known laws of development only if a *special law* is introduced that can account for his unique position.

The other type of evolutionary theory is the classical one that derives man directly from the highly specialized great apes. This theory does not deal with the problem discussed above. In seeking to derive man directly from the great apes, it has to assume the existence of a "missing link." This presents an insoluble problem; if man's special place is accepted as fact, then it is necessary to assume that this missing link must have possessed *conflicting* characteristics common to both man and animal. This produces such a fantastic, wondrous being that we then must accord the missing link itself (instead of man) a unique place in the entire animal kingdom. Thus, the proof for our theory has been unwillingly furnished by its opponents.

In this chapter, we will first concentrate on the special features of the human head, after which a short presentation of the important problems posed by the human hand and foot will follow. In chapter 11, I will discuss the remaining primitive human traits in the context of the complementary theories of Bolk and Schindewolf. The problem of evolution will be treated in chapter 12.

Let us now turn to a consideration of the primitive or unspecialized traits evident in the human head and particularly in the teeth and jaw.

In the majority of mammals, the cranial and facial portions of the skull stand in inverse proportion to each other. In apes (anthropoids, anthropomorphs), the snout is unusually well developed and protrudes, with the result that the cranial portion is proportionately reduced. In man, on the other hand, the nose has almost completely disappeared under the calvarium.

The further back we go toward the embryonic stage in all vertebrates (particularly in mammals) the more similar is the shape of the head: the head, in relation to the rest of the body, is large and round, with the nose hardly protruding at all from underneath the calvarium. According to Bolk, the position of the teeth is perpendicular to the jaw—"orthodont"—in all mammals.

Thus, in all animals including the anthropoids, the base of the skull has grown far forward in relation to the cranial vault; the nose protrudes, and the bridge of the nose together with the receding forehead form a continuous, oblique, and often almost horizontal surface. The nose has therefore developed at the expense of the brain. In man, however, one could argue that the embryonic structure has been *retained*. As Westenhöfer has pointed out, the development of a massive, lengthened jaw causes the teeth to become angled forward (as in the horse, chimpanzee); in a small, round jaw, however, the teeth are positioned perpendicularly. Westenhöfer quotes a relevant remark Ludwig Fick made on this topic in 1853: "If skulls are measured before development is complete, the results seem to indicate a higher organization than is the case if they are measured after completed development. This is only natural since it is a universal law of development for the vertebrates that the system formed by the cerebrospinal complex and the specific sensory organs increases only slightly in mass from birth to full development whereas the opposite is true for jaw development."[3]

For anthropology, this issue becomes most significant when we compare anthropoid and human skulls. The anthropoid's skull bears a marked resemblance to man's in the embryonic and infantile stages; only later does the imposing snout of the great apes develop. Naef, in several important papers, described the horseshoe shape of the human (and half-ape) jaw and contrasted it with the subsequent lengthening of the jaw which occurs in the great apes in order to accommodate their more massive bite: "This change takes place in all the pongids in the course of later development but proceeds from an early form that is quite human."[4] He argues that in the embryonic stage there are great similarities among all mammalian skulls, which are even more pronounced among the simians; these are subsequently lost to the degree that the individual forms undergo further development and specialization. One skull shape is typical of the mature simian embryo: the calvarium is relatively large compared with that of other mammals and the jaw proportionately reduced; further, the orbital cavities are directed forward (stereoscopic vision!) and are separated from the temporal fossa by a joining of the frontal and zygomatic. In the anthropoids (including the gibbons), we find the same combination of features in a slightly intensified form. The same holds for the true anthropomorphs* (hominidae, pongidae, and *Australopithecus*) [technically, hominoids—trans.]; here, however, the proportions have become definitely human. Among all the simiae, the skull retains much of its predisposition toward humanness and in the true anthropomorphs the infant always has a clear, free human forehead. As the animals mature, however, they diverge from one another and what had been common among the various groups diminishes. The unique, specialized character of the species develops from an inherited, prototypical foundation. I will not take time to recapitulate here Naef's subsequent reconstruction of *Propliopithecus* (middle Tertiary Period) and his attempted proof of a direct, simple development from it through *Pithecanthropus* to Neanderthal Man and *Homo sapiens;* I wish only to make the point here that, according to Naef, specialization in the anthropoids (or pongids, in a narrower sense) took the form of an increase in physical strength, agility, and natural defenses while the basis for developing higher capabilities was not retained. The

---

* As the use of terms varies in the literature, I would like to define my use of them. *Anthropoidae:* chimpanzees, orangutans, gorillas, gibbons. *Anthropomorphs:* this group plus man. *Pongidae:* a special term for the group chimpanzee, orangutan, gorilla.

young pongids are, without question, far more intelligent than the older ones. Thus, we could say that the problem the human being faced in terms of development was to conserve the body-to-brain ratio and corresponding cranial vault characteristic of the embryonic and fetal stages of the simians and particularly of the pongids. 'As far as the skulls of the pongids are concerned, historical evidence indicates that the pongids deserted their original developmental path, which was human in character and which individuals still pursue for some years; even the prototype of the family more greatly resembles man than do its modern representatives. This prototype however, must have existed very long ago, at least as far back as the middle of the Miocene. By the upper Miocene, the present-day specialized character had already been established."

Elsewhere, Naef discusses *Australopithecus africanus*.[5] From certain anatomical features (absence of brow ridges, vertical incisors, weak canines, prominent chin, etc.), he identifies it as an anthropoid whose brain continued to develop along human lines in childhood longer than is the case with the present-day pongids. Its profile is strikingly reminiscent of the infant pongid. Like Raymond Dart, Naef also claims that the spinal column was vertical, which indicates a more or less upright posture.

Naef concludes that *Australopithecus* "more closely resembles the presumed common ancestors of man and early hominids *(Menschenaffen)* than do the pongidae." This view "is all the more natural since the structure and development of the anthropoids prove that—compared to man—they once stood much taller than today; certain paleontological facts support this. The eldest of their representatives have deviated the least, the youngest the most from the human norm." The group must at least have had the *potential* to retain these early definitely human states for a much longer period of time than do the modern pongids. "Even if adult early man in the late Tertiary Period still possessed many ape-like characteristics which have been lost today, he must still have had plenty of freedom to adapt, must have been primitive, childlike, and, for this very reason, human."

In sum, man alone has conserved this form (cranial vault, minor development of a recessed bite, and orthodonture) which appears in the fetal stage in mammals, particularly in the anthropomorphs. This is certainly primitive in an ontogenetic sense and most likely in a phylogenetic sense as well; it is evidence of man's failure to specialize. The later development of a powerful facial structure in the great apes in doubtlessly a highly expedient specialization; it integrates the functions of biting, eating, and smelling and is also in keeping with the physical structure of quadrupedal animals, in which the snout is the most anterior part of the body. The baboons, as pure (secondary) ground-dwellers, have developed even more strongly) along these lines while the true hominids (Menschenaffen) have done so to a lesser extent.

I have not introduced any startling new theories into this discussion but have simply rediscovered earlier ones. Even Kollman remarked upon the similarity between the skull of the young ape and the human skull and concluded, on a biogenetic basis, that the apes must be descended from more human-like forms.[6] Man therefore could not have evolved from forms comparable to present-day anthropoids but rather from "fetal forms," whose skull shape he preserved. Kollmann believed that the anthropoids of the Tertiary period did not possess skulls shaped like those of apes today but had instead round heads such as anthropoid fetuses still have. This theory is similar in many respects to Schindewolf's, which we will discuss later.

Even before Kollmann advanced this theory, however, Ranke had thought along similar lines: Specifically, the skull of a mammal initially manifests a shape similar to the human one with the characteristically human predominance of the brain over the autonomic organs. The animal skull shape developed from this human shape. The process is therefore precisely the reverse of what the current theory of development holds, not ascending from the lower to the higher, but rather descending from the higher to the lower. The highest form of skull development—namely, the human—is the common point of departure for skull development in all mammals."[7] Ranke's extension of the problem to all mammals is superfluous and his use of the terms "higher" and "lower" is questionable; it is correct, however, that the skulls of the apes develop toward a specialized final form while those of man, in contrast, appear to have retained their primitive (fetal) and archaic (in the sense of the fundamental biogenetic law) state. Kollman also adhered to the view that the undifferentiated, nonspecialized forms are to be considered as the prototypes and he thereby excludes the anthropoids from man's evolutionary history. As I understand from Kohlbrugge, Aby came to similar conclusions in 1867.[8]

Another related primitive feature of the human skull is the extremely primitive dentition. Klaatsch has stated in this regard that no definite evidence of adaptation can be found in human teeth. Man's teeth appear to be a "very marked continuation of that primitive state from which the teeth of other mammals have developed. Consequently, as far as his teeth are concerned, man has remained extraordinarily 'primitive.' "[9]

Man's teeth are primitive primarily because of the absence of a gap (diastema) between the canines and premolars. This gap is necessary when the canines have become specialized into powerful fangs, as in the anthropoids. The development of powerful canines is absent in all present-day and fossil humans, as well as in *Sinanthropus* and *Homo heidelbergensis*.

Adloff has pointed out that the premolars, located behind the canines, are monocuspid in all anthropoids, following their pattern of specialization, but are bicuspid in man, that is, similar to molars. Adloff emphasizes "that the human canine tooth has a primitive form which is manifested primarily in the formation of a tuberosity on the lingual aspect which is also present in the incisors, whereas in the anthropoids, the canines have lost this original form through specialization. It is therefore totally inconceivable that man ever possessed canine teeth similar to those of anthropoids."[10]

Werth argues along similar lines concerning the absence of developed canines in man: "Here, too, without question, we have a phylogenetically primitive, geologically old feature. The absence of a canine tooth that protrudes clearly or even only slightly from the row of teeth is a standard trait today even in the most primitive placental mammals, the insectivores. Furthermore, we also find this condition in an entire order of early Tertiary mammals."[11]

Adloff discussess other primitive characteristics of human teeth, among them,

1. The very primitive lower milk molar, in comparison to the single-pointed shape of the milk molars in anthropoids. (Thesis: the milk teeth of recent forms resemble the permanent teeth of their fossil ancestors more than their actual successors.)
2. The perpendicular position of human teeth, particularly of the incisors, in contrast to the teeth of anthropoids, with their incisors angled forward.[12]

It is indisputable that, in the vast majority of mammals, the teeth are perpendicular to the jaw in the embryonic stage. In apes, particularly in the anthropoids, the teeth remain perpendicular to the jaw until eruption; correspondingly, there is only a moderate degree of prognathism because the mid-face region is almost vertical. Only once the teeth begin to erupt does the characteristic prognathism appear in the anthropoids; in humans, the perpendicular placement of the teeth with an over- or underbite is retained.

The significance of these findings becomes clear when one considers that a change in dental development cannot be due to functional adaptation, because the teeth are developed inside the jaw and are therefore immune to external influences.

S. Frechkop comes to the similar conclusion that the individual types of teeth (molars, premolars, canines, and incisors) resemble most a prototype that must have served as the point of departure for development and differentiation in the various primate species; they therefore represent a relatively primitive state.[13]

It is now apparent that human teeth could not have evolved from the much more specialized anthropoid teeth, for man's teeth are more primitive than those of all recent anthropoids. We must exclude from man's ancestral line all those forms that could be classed with living anthropoids in general, including, first and foremost, *Dryopithecus* (in contrast to the views of Weinert, v. Eickstedt, and others) who was a true Tertiary chimpanzee.

For several reasons, the problem of dentition is of great importance and cannot be treated separately from hypotheses of evolutionary theory. First of all, fossil discoveries are very often limited to bits of skulls, jaws, and teeth. Secondly, the teeth are unsually hardy and impervious to external forces—of selection as well as of adaptation. Thirdly, the teeth stand in an important harmonic relationship with the entire skull structure. The fact that human teeth remained at an undifferentiated stage of development and that the canines did not become specialized must be correlated with the development of the brain for, in addition to these, man also failed to develop the powerful chewing and neck musculature of the anthropoids along with their ridges of bone and sagittal crests. Furthermore, the widened, almost parabolic curve of the rows of teeth in man (as opposed to the parallel rows in anthropoids) called for a roomy oral cavity with a larger tongue and thereby also brought about a lengthening of the distance between the mandibular condyles and a broadening of the skull.

In his later works, Adloff formulated his views on man's developmental history as follows: "Hereafter, the hominids formed an independent group which can have evolved only from a primate form probably very unlike modern man in its external habitus, but which must have been predisposed toward a specifically human character and which never passed through an anthropoid stage. Similarly, the anthropoids were also an independent branch which was originally closely related to the hominids; their development was basically parallel, with divergence only in certain characteristics. Finally, hominids and anthropoids could possibly be descended from a common ancestor, but it must have branched off early on and pursued its own path of development by forfeiting, as a result of its one-sided specialization, its original predisposition towards the specifically human characteristics."[14]

According to this last possibility, then, one would expect that the oldest fossil anthropoids would possess relatively primitive, that is, more human-like features than the present-day ones. This is, in fact, the case. Robert Broom's discoveries in South Africa from 1937 on *(Paranthropus* and *Pleis-anthropus),* which date from the lower Pleistocene, had small canines without the diastema and first lower premolars similar to the hominids; thus they had an omnivorous dentition of an unspecialized form. The diluvial *Australopithecus africanus,* discovered by Raymond Dart, has dentition quite similar to the hominids. The related specializations had therefore not yet occurred; development had been arrested at a primitive stage. Adloff agrees with Klaatsch that man has his own genealogical line dating back to the Tertiary period.[15] Primitive forms possessed the basic structures for the specifically human characteristics, developed these, and gradually evolved into man. The other primates were probably descended from the same root, but could not pursue this development; they remained behind and, sooner or later, took other paths which removed them further from the human line. Thus, to put it bluntly, man did not descend from the apes; the apes descended from man.

Under the forcefulness of Adloff's argument, Weidenreich, who had earlier been a determined adherent of the "reduction theory," now proposed a new theory. Adloff explains it as follows: according to this new theory, the hominids are descended from unknown anthropoids who divided into two branches before *Dryopithecus; Dryopithecus,* judging from his teeth, was already a definite anthropoid with highly specialized canines. The branch with teeth similar to the hominids' (to which group *Australopithecus* also belongs) led to the hominids, the other led to *Dryopithecus* and its descendants, the modern anthropoids. This anthropoid-like ancestor is supposed to have been neither a chimpanzee nor gorilla, but instead a sort of bull-nosed figure that retained some of its specifically hominid traits with astonishing tenacity. At this point, Adloff aptly points out that this form, which was *similiar* to the anthropoids but possessed specifically hominid traits, could indeed equally correctly be termed a hominid![16]

There is no point in carrying this dispute further here; it is purely academic, a matter of definition. In conceding this much, however, the classical theory has already conceded the principal point: "Specialized forms, such as the fossil and recent anthropoids, are not part of the ancestral line of the hominids."[17] Also, according to Weidenreich, the hominids must have branched off from these unknown anthropoids at a time when the specialization of the canine teeth had not yet taken place. In other words, the anthropoids' teeth developed from a state similar to that of the hominids.

Human teeth must thus have retained primitive forms and developed directly to their present state. It is inconceivable that man could have developed in the directions of the anthropoids only then, through "reduction," to take the opposite course.

Now that we have examined the evidence of primitiveness in the human head and teeth, let us turn to the equally important matter of the hand and foot.

As is well-known, Klaatsch argued that all the other mammals became trapped in dead ends because of their specialization and were unable to turn back, whereas man alone, by virtue of his primitiveness, still possesses a great potential for development.

Klaatsch believed that the similarities between apes and men are reminders of their common evolution from a primitive type that was more akin to man than ape; he claimed that the anthropoids diverged only secondarily from the human route. The anthropoid hand was altered by regressive development of the thumb; however, Klaatsch argues that the prehensile foot of the apes was the point of departure for the development of the human foot.[18]

The almost universally accepted view that man's foot developed from the anthropoid's follows inevitably from the assumption that man's ancestors were anthropoids; Klaatsch would not find this view uncontested today.

In the context of this issue, I would like to discuss the theories of Osborn and Frechkop which, although they differ in many respects, nonetheless agree in emphasizing that the human extremities are primitive, unspecialized, and could not have evolved from anthropoid ones.

Osborn put forth his views in a series of essays.[19] He proceeds from the very plausible thesis that one cannot consider the morphology of organs separately from their functions. There is a clear development in the anthropoids toward a "highly specialized arboreal type known as limb-swinging or brachiating." The following adaptations are part of this specialization:

1. Forelimb elongated in direct ratio to acquisition of hyper-arboreal habit.
2. Hind limb reduced in the same ratio.
3. Four digits of the hand directly elongated, appressed, with conjoined movement, i.e., syndactyly.
4. Thumb actually and relatively abbreviated, with loss of grasping function.
5. Consequent final transformation of the hand into a hook, i.e., angulodactyly.
6. Transformation of the foot into a hand by moderate elongation of the four main digits, and strong separation, development, and grasping power of the big toe.[20]

As is evident from the above, the anthropoids were not originally quadrupedal; rather, their hands have changed because of the loss of their true function, while their feet, in losing their "feet-like" function, have become more like hands.

Because Osborn accepts Dollo's law, according to which development is irreversible and organs once lost cannot be regained, he considers it inconceivable that the anthropoids could have reversed the entire direction of their development, regain their lost functions or rudimentary organs, and pursue the totally new developmental path leading to man.

Embryological studies corroborate Osborn's theory: the hand of the human fetus bears no resemblance to the long and hooked fingers of the anthropoids: the fingers are short and spread apart, and the thumb does not appear to be descended from the rudimentary anthropoid thumb. If man were actually the descendant of an arboreal being, then human fetus would show evidence of this.

In other papers, Osborn justifies why he has discarded the ape-man theory.[21] He no longer believes that comparative anatomy studies alone are sufficient for answering the question of evolution. This problem should be investigated jointly by a number of sciences—geology, zoology, paleontology, comparative anatomy, embryology, ethnology, botany, paleobotany, as well as psychology and behavioral science.

Osborn sets up a juxtaposition of the following characteristics:

Hominidae	*Simiidae*
1. Progressive intelligence, rapid development of the forebrain.	1. Arrested intelligence and brain size.
2. Ground-living, bipedal habit—cursorial, adapted to rapid travel and migration over open country.	2. Arboreal to hyper-arboreal quadrumanual habit—living chiefly in trees.
3. Bipedal habit and development of the walking and running type of foot and big toe.	3. Quadrupedal habit when on the ground.
4. Shortening arms and lengthening legs.	4. Lengthening arms and diminishing legs.
5. Development of the tool-making thumb.	5. Loss of the thumb and absence of tool-making power.
6. Walking and running power of the foot enhanced by enlargement of the big toe.	6. Grasping power of the big toe for climbing purposes, modified when walking.

"In brief, man has a bipedal, dexterous, wide-roaming psychology; the ape has a quadrupedal, brachiating, tree-living psychology.... In the life

and conduct of the pro-ape was the potency of the super-apes living today
... but in the Dawn of Man was the potency of modern civilization."[22]

From a similar juxtaposition;

1. Use of the arms and tools in offense, defense, and all arts of life.	1. Use of the arms chiefly for tree-climbing purposes; secondarily for the prehension of food and grasping of the toe.
2. Use of the legs for walking, running, travel, and escape from enemies.	2. Use of the legs in tree-climbing and limb-grasping.
3. Escape from enemies by vigilance, flight, and concealment.	3. Escape from enemies by retreat through branches of trees.

On the basis of these juxtapositions, Osborn argues: "Between man
and the ape—not only the hands and feet of the ape, but the ape as a whole,
including its psychology—you will find more differences than
resemblances."[23]

Osborne operates with the idea of an independent ancestral human lineage
descending from a neutral, common ancestor in the Oligocene. The ape-
branch diverged and led via *Dryopithecus* to the specialized arboreal types.
The neutral original form should not be thought of as man or ape (Adloff).
Instead, it was truly a "neutral form," living on the ground as well as in
the trees, possessing the "alertness" of the lower apes, with its fingers broad
and separated, a well-developed thumb and a "slightly separated" big toe—
thus, more human than ape. Osborn writes: "I view the ape-man theory as
totally false and misleading. It should disappear from our thoughts and
works, for purely scientific reasons."[24]

Osborn is reckoning with extraordinary periods of time. He does *not*
count the fossil types of Neanderthal, Heidelberg, Krapina, and so on as
the ancestors of modern races but rather views these as the last representatives of a secondary branch. The views of this first paleontological and
geological expert are set forth in his paper "Is the Ape-Man a Myth?"[25]

In this regard, I would also like to refer to the views of Frechkop who
agreed with Westenhöfer's probably unverifiable theory that the ancestors
of the mammals were bipedal.[26] Frechkop also addressed the question of
whether the structure of the human foot indicates that man passed through
an anthropoid stage in the course of his phylogenetic development. The
opposability of the big toe of the ape's foot should be understood as an
adaptation to its arboreal existence. If we consider the series man-gorilla-
chimpanzee-gibbon-orangutan in terms of foot structure, we will find an
increase in opposition of the big toe and a tendency toward its regressive

development. "The purpose of the development of the anthropoid foot is that the big toe becomes capable of moving independently of the other toes; furthermore, the foot takes on a prehensile form with an opposed big toe and thus resembles a hand. As the outer phalanges (toes 2–5) become adept at closing around a tree branch, the digits become longer and more curved (curvature of the phalanges in orangutans) and the big toe shorter."[27] The heel is also involved in this opposition and functions as another phalanx. The greatest specialization of this type has been achieved by the sloth; its first toe has disappeared altogether and the skeletal parts of the heel, which is rounded like a pincer, are used for grasping along with the other four toes.

If one wished to argue that the human foot developed from the anthropoid one, it would be necessary to assume a double reverse in the specialized development: first because the anthropoid foot shows opposition of the big toe, in man, this toe would have had to revert to become like the other toes; secondly, the clear specialization in the brachiating apes, which is manifested in their long arms and shortened legs, would also have to have been reversed so that the physical proportions common to most of the lower apes could be reestablished. Bipedal posture appears to be correlated with a plantigrade gait.

"Nous croyons pouvoir dire que l'évolution du pied de l'homme n'a jamais passé par un stade de pied d'anthropoides" (we can safely say that in its evolution the human foot never passed through a stage of the anthropoid foot). The human foot "n'est pas d'origine arboricole" (is not of an arboreal origin).[28] Anthropoid-like forms should therefore not be counted among the ancestors of man.

Finally, as far as the hand is concerned, there can be no doubt as to its primitiveness compared with the prehensile hand of the anthropoids with its long, curved fingers and regressive development of the thumb; that the hand of the anthropoids could have developed into the human one appears impossible. The opposition of the human thumb is a specialization but apparently of very recent date. Hancar reports on the discovery of a Neanderthal type in Russia, specifically in Tesik-Tash in Central Asia and in Kiik Koba (Crimea). Hand bones were unearthed which permit for the first time a reconstruction of the hand of stone-age man. This hand was short, broad, massive, and straight-fingered; in short, it does not resemble the anthropoid shape in the least. It does, however, resemble the hand of an anthropoid embryo. "On the one hand, this rules out the possibility that a "descent from the trees" immediately preceded anthropogenesis; on the other hand, in terms of development, this indicates that the apes became specialized to arboreal life in the tropical jungle more or less parallel to anthropogenesis; if we consider this specialization from the standpoint of its potential for leading to man, it appears that it led the anthropoids into a dead-end and neither primitive man nor early man had anything to do with this."[29] The most interesting feature of the Kiik-Koba hand is that in place of the thumb joint, which is a free-moving ball-and-socket joint, there is a joint with a cylindrical articular surface. This, although it allows lateral movement of the thumb, permits opposition only to a very limited degree. Opposition of the thumb would therefore qualify as a striking new development; indeed, because it lacks this specialization, the Kiik-Koba hand is exceedingly primitive. The low-ranking insectivores of the species *Tupaja* have a five-fingered hand with a divergent—but not opposed—thumb. Schwalbe and Gregory have (incorrectly) identified these as proto-primates.[30]

11. Bolk's Theory and Other Related Theories

The research we have described thus far has pointed out a number of primitive and unspecialized traits in man and rendered highly unlikely the possibility that these traits could have developed regressively from anthropoid states. Indeed, from a morphological point of view, the reverse process appears more likely. It should be immediately apparent that the primitive traits we have discussed—the vault of the cranium, orthodontism, the exposed hand, and plantigrade foot—are actually closely related; together they constitute what we call erect posture. Thus, once man's primitive, archaic anatomy has been recognized, his special place is quite obvious.

We have by no means exhausted the area of primitive traits in man. However, I do not wish to introduce further examples without first presenting Bolk's systematic theory, because his theory, along with Schindewolf's, provides a new scheme for understanding the problem of evolution; specifically, they lend support to the argument that man is descended from the anthropoids by proposing a special *supplemental hypothesis* which suggests that an unprecedented developmental process occurred in man and is responsible for his special position.

The Dutch anatomist Louis Bolk set down his views in two lengthy pieces.[31] Here he integrated morphological study and interpretative theory so closely that we must discuss his views in a step-by-step fashion. Bolk readily acknowledges the close kinship between the anthropoids and man; indeed, he believes that man is descended from ape-like ancestors. However, he stresses that man himself must be taken as the point of departure for investigating this problem. He formulates the question as follows: "What is essential in man as organism and what is essential in man as form?"

To answer this question, Bolk makes a distinction between "primary" and "consecutive" traits. Man's upright posture and its consequences are said to be a consecutive phenomenon. Bolk writes: "The path was not prepared for anthropogenesis because the body became upright but rather, the body became upright because the form became more human."

Bolk identifies the following as primary traits that are responsible for man's special place: orthognathism, (the jaws aligned beneath the brain with the lower jaw neither projecting nor receding); the lack of hair; loss of pigment in the skin, hair, and eyes; the shape of the auricle; the mongolian eyefold; the central position of the *foramen magnum;* high brain weight; persistence of the cranial sutures; the *labia majora* in females; the structure of the hand and foot; the form of the pelvis; the ventrally-directed position of the vagina.

All these characteristics are primitive in a special sense: *they are fetal states or proportions which have become permanent.* In other words, "Characteristics or proportions of form that are transitory in the fetus of other primates have been stabilized in man."

Thus, in Bolk's view, these are not newly acquired traits; instead, transitory states common to all primates, and succeeded by particular specializations in the fetal development of apes, have been retained or "stabilized" in man. This theory clearly shows that man is unspecialized; to explain this, Bolk proposes the thesis that although man is closely related to the anthropoids, his development has been retarded.

The human constitution is thus essentially fetal in character. Because the distinguishing physical traits that define a human being are all unspecialized, primitive, and are embryonic features that have been conserved, Bolk assumes that there must have been an internal cause for this; he believes that the factors that brought about the emergence of man were internal rather than external. The human being is the product of a specific transformation that is responsible for the typically human characteristics. Bolk argues that human development was delayed *(Verzögerung)* or retarded *(Retardation)*. This theory accounts for the one human characteristic we have not yet mentioned and which has not been sufficiently explained by other theories— man's abnormally slow rate of growth. The tempo of a human life is unusually slow, from the prolonged childhood to man's long, purely somatic life after reproductive functions have ceased. The law of retardation *(Retardationsgesetz)* provides an explanation for these facts; we should take care, however, not to equate this retardation with any reduction in life intensity. The following table illustrates man's slow rate of growth:

	Birth Weight	Time Required for To Double (days)
Pig	2.0	14
Cow	40.0	47
Horse	45.0	60
Man	3.5	180

If we believe that a distinguishing characteristic of man's development is that it has been slowed down, this would mean that the ancestors of modern man must have developed at a faster rate. Bolk believes he can document this, at least as far as one specific feature is concerned. By referring to the child's jawbone discovered at Ehringsdorf and to some of the discoveries at Krapina, he claims man's dentition then developed at roughly the same rate as the anthropoids'; in modern man, however, the eruption sequence has been retarded and takes place at a slower tempo. Bolk also gives delayed development as the reason behind modern man's chin. If we imagine that this sort of delay occurred in the organism's development as a whole and that the organ systems responded more or less independently to it, then we can understand why there would be certain disharmonies between the physical and functional development in the individual organ systems, particularly between the "germinal" and "somatic" parts of the human organism (see below).

A closer look at this retardation, which appears to affect each phase of human life, indicates that it must be caused by a specific peculiarity in the endocrine system. "It is known that the acceleration and deceleration of growth in certain lower parts and areas of the body is caused by an alteration in the function of these organs." If we assume that retardation is a universal anthropological law and that it involves an action in the endocrine system which impedes and delays growth, then we would logically expect that if this growth-retarding factor were absent for some reason, malformations and progressive developments would result: body hair would begin to grow again, cranial sutures would close prematurely, the jaws would increase in size, etc. "You will note that a number of the so-called pithecoid characteristics are present in our organism in a latent state and it only takes a weakening in the retarding forces for them to become active once more."

The pathological growth phenomena that stem from malfunctions in the endocrine system lead us to conclude that physical growth must also be controlled in some manner by glandular secretion. "The retardation in individual development which has come about gradually in the course of the long evolution of the human race and has established a new norm for the course of man's life can be attributed only to an action of the endocrine system."

Bolk's theory is particularly useful for explaining man's abnormally slow development, his prolonged childhood, his extremely long life span given his size, his long old age after reproductive ability has ceased, etc. To my knowledge, Bolk is the only one who has provided an explanation of these striking and anthropologically significant data.

Let us now consider how retardation is manifested in the individual organ systems, first of all, in human dentition. In apes, the milk teeth emerge almost immediately at birth; usually, the shedding of milk teeth and growth of permanent teeth occur simultaneously. Shortly after the second milk molar has appeared, the first permanent one breaks through and the process of deciduous dentition gets underway. The milk incisors and other teeth are shed while new ones come in so that (as I gather from the article on this topic by the same author), the jaw must continually grow to keep pace with the increase in teeth.[3]

In human beings, on the other hand, retardation has resulted in two pauses in the dentition process. The milk teeth have all broken through by the end of the second year, at which point there is a pause until the sixth year, then the first permanent molar appears. After another period of time, which varies from individual to individual, the changing process begins and only once this is finished does the second permanent molar break through. The third may not even appear at all, which testifies to the great variation in this retardation among individuals, which sometimes results in complete elimination of the feature.

Bolk's theory also sheds light on an otherwise puzzling area—puberty. If we assume that somatic and germ cells are affected differently by retardation (with germ cells being more resistant to its influence), then we would consequently expect to find that the female ovary would mature long before the organism is physically ready for pregnancy. At four years, the ovary is already 27 mm long and 12 mm wide; at 14 years, it is the same length and width. Thus, the female ovary is basically mature by age 4 or 5. Around the fifth year, there is a pause in development; the function must not yet begin because the body is not prepared for the consequence of this function— conception. Here, retardation has not slowed down growth, but has simply postponed maturation. This inhibition is then relaxed at a certain age which varies depending on the individual. In our latitudes, sexual maturity is usually reached in the 11th or 12th year. A girl who begins to menstruate at this age is, however, actually a biological anomaly, an organism with a basic error in function. In the human being, sexual maturity does not represent the final stage of development, as is the case among the higher mammals. Development is usually completed around the 18th year, although the *potential* maturity is actually present at age 5, and puberty normally occurs in the 11th year. With the onset of puberty, a growth spurt sets in that signifies a further relaxation of the retardation factor.

Retardation therefore refers to the overall delay in the rate of development. However, the true value of this theory lies in the explanation it provides for man's special morphological features. Bolk writes: "What is essential to the human form is a result of fetalization, what is essential to man's life course is a consequence of retardation. These features are causally related, for fetalization of the form is the inevitable consequence of retardation in morphogenesis.[33]

We must now ask ourselves how a delay in development could have been responsible for man's specific physical traits. Because the individual organ systems vary in their responses to the influence of retardation, it can happen that, although the organism as a whole has reached the endpoint of its development, one or another of these features will not yet have reached its normal stage of development and will consequently manifest an infantile character; if the delay is even greater, it will have a fetal one. If retardation continues further, development may be halted altogether and the morphological feature may not appear at all. "Progressive retardation" leads to infantilism and fetalization and culminates in the omission of the feature entirely.

The inevitable consequence of retardation is thus that *the body takes on a fetal character to an increasing degree;* conditions that were once transitional have become permanent. All the primitive human traits discussed thus far by various authors, along with the new ones contributed by Bolk, can be clearly explained: they are fetal stages that have become permanent.

To the best of my knowledge, Bolk does not discuss the human hand and foot but chooses to concentrate instead on the following features:

First, he discusses body hair. The nakedness of the human torso and limbs is the result of a process that did not begin with man. Man has preserved a state that is present only briefly in the anthropoids—it occurs toward the end of their fetal life and shortly after birth. We cannot attribute the loss of hair to an external factor that acted on the mature human body. It is instead an example of how progressive retardation can cause a characteristic not to appear at all, although the predisposition toward it is retained; we know this because a thick growth of hair, sometimes covering the entire body, may come about as a result of glandular disturbances.

We can set up a hierarchy based on this particular characteristic as follows:

a. The Lower apes: Hair growth appears simultaneously over the entire fetal body; the newborn ape has a complete coat of hair.
b. Gibbons: At first, only the head of the fetus is covered with hair; just before birth, however, it grows on the back of the body as well. In this state, with naked ventral surfaces, the young gibbon enters the world; the coat of hair is complete soon after birth.
c. Anthropoids: Again, the head hair grows first. In chimpanzees and gorillas, the fetus is born naked, apart from its long head hair. Body hair grows approximately two months after birth.
d. Hominids: The obvious progression here provides striking proof that a fetal state has become permanent in man. I would like also to add a fact that Bolk does not mention, namely, that man keeps his very light coat of hair over most of his body until death; in this, he is unique not only in the order of primates, but in the entire animal kingdom. There is yet another unique feature of the human skin which is appropriate to bring up in this context—it has avoided any sort of specialization, in terms of self-protection (against the weather, for example), of self-defense (armor, spines, fur), or of attack (horns, hooves). Man's skin is the least specialized of all; we could say that it is a giant sensory surface.

To return to Bolk, he offers another example of how man has preserved embryonic forms: he retains the curvatures in the fetal body axis whereas in quadrupedal animals these are straightened out.

In the higher mammals, the curvature of the embryo's body is initially very symmetrical; this gradually changes, however, as the middle segment is lengthened so that the cranial and caudal segments become two independent curves in the body axis. Let us first examine the cranial segment of the axis as Bolk sees it. If one examines a cross-section of the head of a dog embryo, and compares it with a human embryo one would find that both are 20 mm long. Man, however, has retained the fetal curvature. Bolk terms the three ventral bends in the axis the occipital, intrasphenoidal, and rhinal; in the last of these bends, the cerebral and rhinocephalic segments are almost perpendicular to each other, so that the latter runs almost parallel to the neck. Significant changes occur in the axis during development. The occipital angle is still present, but it may disappear while the animal is running; in fact, it has totally disappeared in other mammals (moles, hedgehogs). The second angle has totally vanished and a secondary bend in the axis opening toward the back has appeared so that the rhinocephalic axis is actually an extension of the basal. In this manner, the prognathism of the mammals is formed. In man, however, the fetal axial angles remain unchanged. All ape skulls, by the way, show a retention of the rhinocephalic bend, as does man. The prognathism of apes (and more primitive races of man) is otherwise not comparable to that of mammals because it is created by an elongation of the base of the nose toward the front without the twist in the axis which is present in dogs. The proportions of the concave bend in the caudal segment of the fetal body axis do not deviate obviously from those of anthropoid embryos. Man preserves the ventrally curved fetal body axis and this accounts for the unusual anatomy of the female sex organs. In chimpanzees, the axis has been straightened out, so that the anus opens toward the back. The topographical and anatomical proportions in this area of a chimpanzee's body correspond exactly to those of apes with tails.[34]

Bolk argues that the pelvic morphology is due primarily to a retention of the fetal body axis; the human pelvis has remained at the stage of embryonic development which follows the cartilaginous stage.[35]

I am discussing Bolk's views in detail here because, curiously, they have been almost completely forgotten. Lobosch, who believed Bolk's theory was persuasive and productive, has not had his expectations fulfilled. He wrote, "These thoughts should not disappear again from debates over anthropogenesis because they are incredibly useful and help clarify many issues."[36]

As with any hypothesis, the worth of Bolk's hypothesis can be judged only by what it accomplishes; this can be summed up in the following points:

1. All the typically human traits that are examples of man's failure to specialize can be explained by this one principle—retardation.
2. Retardation also accounts for other peculiarities in man, such as his slow rate of development and related factors such as puberty and the biological necessity of enduring families.
3. In addition, Bolk's understanding of anthropogenesis offers an internal cause for this process—endocrine glands; this allows us to avoid the shortcomings of Lamarckian theories of adaptation (such as the famous descent from the trees).
4. The principle of retardation was not invented ad hoc; it is a biological process, even though it appears elsewhere in the animal kingdom only in rare cases. Only in man has it unexpectedly manifested itself to a very great degree. The Batrachian Axolotl becomes sexually mature in its normal environment while it is a gill-breathing tadpole; it develops into a lung-breathing form only as an exception. The cave salamander no longer even achieves a land form. These animals, with their unusual patterns of development: sparrows and rats, with their "environmental neutrality"; and chimpanzees, with their intellectual feats, can all be compared to man in terms of isolated characteristics. Man's special place does not

mean that he cannot be compared to other animals as far as individual characteristics are concerned. However, from the point of view of Bolk's theory, man
is the only "embryonic higher mammal" *(embryonische höhere Säuger)*.

5. Further support for Bolk's theory is furnished by certain pathological phenomena
in man. When normal hormone function is impaired, the retardation effect is
reduced with the result that once latent characteristics now surface or functions
that had been slowed down now proceed at an accelerated rate (see examples
given above). The late fusion of the cranial sutures may be attributed to the
retardation principle; a malfunction in this process would cause these to close
prematurely, as happens in the anthropoids. If the retardation of sexual development is impaired, we would see "the picture of a five- or six-year-old sexually
mature girl." The list of the malformations that can result from disruptions in
the retardation process is long indeed.

6. Bolk's theory has very interesting implications for the problem of race. Several
researchers have already argued that certain racial features stem from differences
in the hormonal balances. Bolk declares himself to be a "convinced believer in
the inequality of races." He argues that the Mongolian race has kept a typically
fetal physical appearance while the nordic race has not, although the latter's
embryos do exhibit this same complex of characteristics (sunken roots of the
nose, protrusio bulbi, and the mongolian eyefold).[37] The striking differences
among races in pigmentation, hirsutism, prognathism, as well as in rate of development (faster physical development, shorter prime, and faster decline in the
Negro race), can also be understood from this same point of view. For example,
the Negro child bears a greater resemblance to a European than does the adult
Negro (E. Fischer); this may be paralleled with the fact that young anthropoids
resemble humans more than adult anthropoids do. As Bolk says, "Not all races
progressed equally along the path to anthropogenesis." Bolk did not discuss fossil
remains, but he would probably have agreed with the view that certain characteristics of fossil and living man (in the aborigine skull, for example), such as the
absence of a chin, brow ridges, and prognathism, should be interpreted as racially
specific developments which are similar to the specializations in animals. Thus,
in Bolk's terms, these represent cases where retardation was incomplete.

7. Bolk's theory still allows the claim that man is descended (even in a direct line)
from the anthropoids, although this is possible only with the aid of his supplemental hypothesis which explains man's unique place by proposing a biological
law that applies only to man. Bolk's theory also assumes that new forms cannot
arise from already specialized adult states but instead can evolve only through a
"retuning" *(Umstimmung)* of the organism at the embryonic stages. In identifying
these stages as the site of anthropogenesis Bolk has gone far beyond all theories
of adaptation or "reduction." Furthermore, the remarkable and incontestable,
albeit temporary, similarity between young anthropoids and humans (even in
their common tendency toward an upright posture) indicates that a process of
fetalization or a degree of retardation is in effect in the anthropoids. The ape,
however, loses these fetal characteristics soon after birth whereas man retains
them. This suggests that the process of anthropogenesis takes place twice: as a
suggested process in the primates and an actual one in man. This also helps

account for the obvious distinction that separates the anthropoids in turn from other mammals and lower primates, since they can be classified either as bipedal or quadrupedal.

Versluys integrated Bolk's theory with research that Dubois carried out.[38] Dubois compared the ratio of brain size to body weight among closely-related mammals and found that, in general, the brain weighed five ninths of the total body weight. Dubois assumed that the ratio of cerebrum size to body size differs from genus to genus and he called this the "cephali-zation" factor.

If we take mammals of different sizes, and figure the brain weight they would have if they were the same size, we can determine the differences in cephalization. In many cases, particularly when animals of the same order are involved (both living and fossil forms), the weight of the cerebrum increases dramatically by *double* in each instance. If cephalization (the ratio of cerebrum size to body size, calculated by using equal body sizes) is then used, with the primitive mammals of the lower Tertiary being 1 or base level, we find that shrew mice have remained at this level while the over-whelming majority of living mammals have achieved a higher cephaliza-tion—one, twice, four times, eight times as great. Apes have a cephalization that is 16 times that of the base level; in man, it is 64 times greater—thus four times again as great as the apes (approximately 14 billion neurons compared to approximately 3.5 billion). This dramatic increase can be ex-plained only by a mutative doubling in each case of the number of nerve cells.[39]

The Versluys-Bolk theory accounts for a great number of anthropological phenomena. Two of these deserve our particular attention: First of all, man's highly developed brain and his embryonic, primitive physique did not come about through the "struggle for survival" or a process of selection, but from direct, internal causes. This "retuning" in man is so radical that it signifies a completely new mode of existence.

Secondly, theories of anthropogenesis tend to assume a gradual increase in brain development and intellectual ability fostered by the "struggle for survival." Opponents of our theory have claimed that man, too, is special-ized, in that he has a specialized brain. Nonetheless, any theory that proposes a highly developed brain with an arbitrary "substructure" is false. The brain is the organ that makes any specialization in organ development unneces-sary. From the point of view of behavior, the brain is the organ of plasticity, versatility, and adaptability; however, it must always be viewed in con-junction with the unique human constitution—its vulnerability, mobility, and openness to stimuli, as well as its failure to specialize (which may be regulated hormonally by the brain); the human constitution first makes such a brain possible. The "struggle for survival" really began only with anthropogenesis, beyond the confines of the cycle of eating and being eaten, of adaptation and flawed development; it became a struggle for the very foundations of life, for the possibility of surviving until the next day.

These are the reasons why I believe Bolk's work to be so valuable. It is therefore a welcome task for me now to discuss Schindewolf's theory, which agrees with Bolk's in certain crucial points although it was developed independently of his.[40]

Schindewolf's research was limited to the skull. As his starting point, he used a fact I have mentioned before; all the characteristics that distinguish the human skull from all other mammalian skulls are not only present in the human embryo and child but in fact appear there in a purer, intensified form and are thus in a sense almost superhuman. Schindewolf, along with the other theorists discussed above, sees this as a clear indication that man could not be descended from apes of a species like or comparable to the present-day anthropoids. He rejects the classical theory that derives man from fossil types of the chimpanzee-gorilla family and argues instead, as did Naef, Kollmann, and others, that the skull of the ape embryo and infant has certain human characteristics of form which are lost in the course of life to the extent that the original proportions are reversed. These characteristics are: the dominance of the strongly arched cranium, displacement of the facial portion to below the skullcap, marked curvature of the frontal, central position of the foramen magnum, closure of the orbital fossa against the temporal fossa, the forward direction of the orbital cavities. Schindewolf claims that man has retained this form which is exhibited by all ape embryos and young apes (Bolk). As the apes mature, the snout lengthens (as in carnivores and brain size is reduced. The ratio of brain to the facial portion of the skull is reversed and, thereby, the human-like characteristics of the young ape skull are lost. The *foramen magnum* moves backward, the temporal lines become pronounced, the forehead recedes, the ramus of the lower jaw becomes steep, the teeth develop (including the canines), the brow ridges are formed. In this manner, the typical "carnivore skull" of the apes is formed.

Unlike Kollmann, Schindewolf does not conclude from this that, according to the fundamental biogenetic law, the anthropoids must be descended from more human-like forms while man preserved the prototypical form. Instead, he brings to bear here a phenomenon (also in evidence among invertebrates) he terms "proterogenesis." He puts forth the theory that the biogenetic law is not valid for the apes or rather, that it functions in this case in reverse in that it is in the adult, not the juvenile, stages that earlier phylogenetic phases are recapitulated. The adult states manifest the characteristics of ancestors; new complexes of characteristics are acquired suddenly, and without any preceding phylogenetic stages, in the earliest ontogenetic stages of the apes. The youth forms take on new characters. In man, this development is *progressive,* either in the sense that the juvenile characteristics migrate to the adult stages or that these features "persist." In the apes, the characteristics of the juvenile states are regressively broken down; they are not shifted to later stages of growth but are instead pushed back toward earlier stages as the inherited phylogenetic structure asserts itself.

"In our view, the transformation of the proto-apes into true apes occurred as human-like characteristics of form were acquired in the early ontogenesis of the fossil types at the beginnings of the apes' ancestral lineage." From *Propliopithecus* (Oligocene) on, in the hominids, the proterogenetic development of the human complex of characteristics (only in the skull) took a strongly progressive course; in the pongids, however, it came to a standstill and then regressed. Schindewolf believes the "reduction theory," which holds that the human teeth evolved from the highly specialized anthropoid teeth, is untenable; he argues that "the wide-spread view of man's descendance from fossil anthropoids cannot be upheld at least as long as we mean forms that are specialized along the lines of the modern apes, in terms of the specific characteristics (the embryonic and unspecialized ones) described above."

According to Schindewolf, then, two laws are in evidence in man—proterogenesis and the biogenetic law. He points to the indications (which later disappear) of earlier phylogenetic stages which the biogenetic law would lead us to expect: embryonic tail; the structures for several milk glands or nipples; the structure for palatal folds; the inner nose. Originally, these were even more pronounced, as is the case with the lower mammals.

Schindewolf's theory would predict that the oldest representatives of the human race were more apelike in certain respects since in them the progressive development of proterogenesis, the "persistence" of embryonic features, would not have extended as far as it does in modern man. By the same token, the oldest ape species should show a greater resemblance to man than present-day ones. Proof of this is in fact furnished by the well-known hominid fossils and by Dart's discovery of *Australopithecus afri-*

canus. Like Osborn and Adloff, Schindewolf excludes *Dryopithecus* from the direct ancestral line of man. Despite the strong human resemblance in the molars, the apelike specialization had progressed quite far in *Dryopithecus*. On the other hand, *Australopithecus* resembles man more than any other known fossil or living great ape because of its strongly-arched cranium, the relatively small facial portion of the skull which is developed downward and protrudes only slightly from beneath a prominent but receding forehead, the absence of brow ridges, the large wing of the sphenoid bone joined to the parietal bone, the vertical position of the incisors, and the relatively small canines.

Schindewolf believes the hominids emerged in the early Miocene. He rejects the notion that man could have descended from already specialized apes, or that the apes and other mammals could be descended from man (as Dacqué, Westenhöfer, Kollmann, and others believe).

To my surprise, he also rejects Bolk. I can, however, see no essential difference between their hypotheses except that Schindewolf treats only a small part of the problem defined by Bolk. In the following main points, however, both authors are in agreement and, what is more significant, they have arrived at their theories independently:

1. The persistence of fetal characteristics is the fundamental distinguishing feature of man, that is, of his skull.
2. Man is a descendant of the primates, but is subject to a special law as far as his ontogenesis is concerned.
3. This special law appears as a supplemental hypothesis which Bolk calls "retardation" and Schindewolf "proterogenesis."
4. A preliminary manifestation of this special law occurs in the early ontogenetic stages of the primates or anthropoids and thus constitutes a preliminary "anthropogenesis."
5. This preliminary anthropogenesis does not progress further; it is "outgrown."

I believe these are the most important points in the two theories and I am greatly pleased to find so little difference between them.

Schindewolf's rejection of Bolk is partially intuitive, as he himself has admitted—a fact that I, as a third party, can easily overlook. Schindewolf also chooses to reduce Bolk's theory to simplistic statements, such as the contention that man has not progressed beyond the developmental stage of a primate fetus. Bolk did indeed employ such formulations, as well as the misleading catchphrase that man is "a sexually mature ape embryo" *(geschlechtsreif gewordener Affenembryo);* this sort of thing most likely prompted Schindewolf's intuitive rejection. However, in research it is often necessary to summarize an entire, complex theory in one sentence; this is particularly customary in anthropology. The "missing link," for example, is a theory that has been condensed into a catchword. When Bolk so often says that in man certain fetal characteristics that are also common to anthropoids have been stabilized *(stabilisiert)*, he is not ruling out the possibility that further development or growth might take place; he is simply proposing a unique mode of development for the human organism. In fact, he often speaks of "conservative" as opposed to "propulsive" development, which refers to the transition from fetal forms to specialized adult forms. This special developmental law that applies to man is retardation and it is defined as follows: "Although the organism as a whole has reached the final stage of its development and its growth is complete, one or another of the particular physical characteristics has not yet achieved the degree of development which was originally appropriate for it. This characteristic then becomes fixed at what we may call an incomplete stage and this incompleteness manifests an infantile character.... The necessary consequence of retardation is thus that the body takes on a fetal character to an increasing degree."[41]

Schindewolf describes precisely this same special mode of development: the "persistence" of embryonic features in man until they ultimately become stabilized. We are justified in emphasizing the common ground between these two theories, although their hypothetical explanatory principles (retardation and proterogenesis) represent a definite difference in interpretation.

Because Bolk and Schindewolf both stress the primitiveness of man, their theories are superior to the classical theory that works with the scheme of functional adaptation in the adult forms. It is quite improbable that a transformation in the species could originate in the adult stage; Schwalbe believed that primitive man lost his canines because he no longer had need of them since he already had weapons!

It is inconceivable that the human embryonic characteristics could have evolved from the specialized simian features. However, if we imagine a "retuning" *(Umstimmung)* of the organism in its early ontogenetic stages, it is possible that this could be expressed primarily as a retention *(festhalten)* of embryonic characteristics. It is quite interesting that the classical theory has had to resort to Lamarckian concepts because it must explain the "regressive development" from the specialized apes to man, and since these developments represent a *loss*, they could not have come about as the result of natural selection. This is an interesting problem. It means that no objection can be made to the curious but necessary assumption of the "primitivists" that man evolved directly from a proto-primate *(Urprimat)* while avoiding specialization or that retardation must have been established in anthropoid-like ancestors in an unusually favorable environment *(optimale Zufallsumwelt)*. The classical theory itself demands such an assumption: I will return to this important issue later in the book. The famous descent from the trees, no matter how gradual it is supposed to have been, could have taken place only if no tigers happened to be strolling by underneath. For precisely this reason, the orangutan remained aloft.

In this context, it is appropriate to bring up another important issue, that of the evidence of *domestication* in the human being. Eugen Fischer pointed out morphological similarities between man and domesticated animals, thereby touching on a very profound question. Fischer understood domestication to be "the arbitrary influencing of diet and conditions of reproduction" and found that it led to great variations especially in terms of size, integumental organs (hair, pigmentation), and appendages (tails, ears, cockscombs, etc.). He then proceeded in a casuistic fashion to liken man to his domesticated animals; Fischer argued, for example, that white skin color as well as the partial loss of pigment, which is responsible for green and blue eyes, represented "domestication albinism." He went on to point out that "no mammal existing in the wild has a distribution of pigment in the eye comparable to that of a European; by the same token, among almost all domesticated species, there are individuals or breeds with eye color identical to a European's."[42]

Albinism is a Mendelian trait. Fischer views the true dwarf races (East African pgymies, with an average height of 141cm[4.6ft]) from the same perspective: "Domesticated forms, including man, have a pronounced tendency to vary in size..., and in domestication, size is usually hereditary." Fischer similarly felt that a reduction in the facial portion of the skull and a weakening of the teeth are also signs of domestication.

Hilzheimer related this issue to Bolk's theory.[43] Independently of Bolk, Hilzheimer had come to view domestic animals as juvenilizations *(Verjugendlichungen)* which came about as a result of domestication; for example, lap dog is the juvenile stage of a full-grown dog, which has now become permanent. Similarly, Hilzheimer believed that the shape of the human skull is due to arrested development at an early stage. He attempted to draw parallels between the massive jaw and small teeth in the Mauer mandible [a jawbone discovered near Heidelberg in 1907–trans.] and similar features in domestic animals to support his argument that these represent characteristic variations which result from a domestication process.[44]

Konrad Lorenz explored domestication in great depth.[45] His thesis that domestication played a crucial role in the evolution of man has been widely accepted.[46] Although he declares categorically that man is beyond doubt a "domesticated" being, he errs by confusing domestication with retardation and this mistake detracts from the theories of this distinguished researcher. Evidence of domestication in animals can be found in external and internal characteristics: among the former are the tendency toward short legs, adiposis, brachycephaly, myasthenia, variations in size, albinism, and others. The latter include disruptions in drives—increased appetite, increased and indiscriminate sexuality, breakdown in instincts. "The brood hen of the wild jungle fowl (the ancestor of all our domestic chicken breeds) will attend only to chicks of the same species that make certain characteristic sounds and have certain markings on their heads and backs which function as releasers for the hen. Our common chickens usually show no reaction at all to the coloring of their chicks. In the heavier breeds, such as Plymouth, Rhode Island, and others, the sounds of the brood have also ceased to matter; these birds will even care for young mammals."[47]

Doubtlessly, the characteristics listed here as signs of domestication are present in many humans, but they should more properly be classed as the "ravages of civilization" *(Zivilisationsschäden)*. Lorenz is wrong to interpret the constitutive human characteristics, as Bolk has described them, as consequences of domestication. The infantilism of the big cities is quite different from the constitutional juvenilization of *homo sapiens*. Above all, however, one of Lorenz's principal examples—the cave bear—is not valid. The bear has practically all the earmarks of domestication that we can identify today on dog skeletons—gigantic as well as dwarf forms; brachycephaly; short, crooked dachshund legs; etc. Lorenz believes that this is an example of self-domestication and that we can explain these features in the same way as we explain man's. Like man, the bear lived in caves and was therefore well-protected from the influences of the climate; the process of selection through predation was halted and thus the bear was well on the way toward domestication. "Without any doubt, the first processes of domestication occurred in the caves of the cave bear and then somewhat later in those of man at the anthropus stage."[48]

Yet doubts do remain strong. "The vast majority of the European and Mediterranean cave dwellings existed in the Würm glacial period (the last) but some also date from the preceding interglacial period"[49] There is, for example, the "Dragon Hole" near Vättis (2445m above sea level) which was sought out during the Riss-Würm interglacial for the purposes of hunting cave bears and was apparently inhabited for periods of time each year. Furthermore, "all discoveries which date from the Riss glacial (apart from Castillo) and from the earlier periods in the Ice Age in Europe, the Near East and Africa came from open air encampments."[50] This clearly refutes Lorenz's empirical proof. In addition, as Portmann has pointed out, the theory of self-domestication would have to explain why man does not exhibit the principal characteristic of domestication—a reduction in or even complete halt to brain development.[51] In fact, in man's case, the opposite has occurred. Similarly, another sign of domestication in animals, early sexual maturity, is not present in man.

Consequently, there is no reason to deviate from the main tenets of Bolk's theory. Retardation or juvenilization and domestication are heterogeneous processes. Bolk's theory is not complete, however. It has difficulty accounting for some facts: Schultz for instance, claims that mature apes retain the fetal body proportions more than man does while man's pattern of growth deviates significantly from that of apes in that he reaches physical maturity long after birth.[52] Portmann greatly improved upon Bolk's simplified concept of delayed development. Human development begins with a rapid increase in growth that continues until the end of the first year; then there is another late growth spurt at puberty which is without parallel in the animal kingdom. In between, there is a period of very slow growth during which motor skills, language, and behavior are developed through interaction with the social surroundings. "Slowness of development does not appear to be simply a fundamental somatic situation; it seems to be related to the world-open nature of man's existence."[53] This represents a very significant extension of Bolk's theory and makes it truly suitable for serving as the basis for a universal anthropology.

I believe that man is a "cultural being by nature" (von Natur ein Kulturwesen). This means that while a unique law of development, such as retardation or proterogenesis, may form the basis for an unspecialized, acting, and undetermined being, the principal orientation must be toward behavior, toward actions designed to change the world; the very existence of such a being depends on the changes it can effect. Behavior and the effects it has on man's self-created conditions for survival then further encourage this unique law of development so that the typically human characteristics are continually *reinforced* by the repercussions of man's own behavior.

Mutations such as those in the endocrine system that were responsible for ushering in anthropogenesis would be favored over others. For these reasons, the characteristic features of fetalization and those of domestication may be difficult to distinguish from one another.

We have now outlined the principal problem posed by the morphology of the human being. I have attempted to organize the scattered material in the literature under one point of view because the insight that man is unspecialized and unadapted to a natural environment and is a "deficient being" in a morphological sense is of great significance for anthropology. Once this viewpoint has been adopted, the question logically arises as to the viability of such a being. The theory that *action* forms the center of human existence provides an answer to this question. The concept of action also gains us an understanding of the biological function of consciousness. To put this another way, is it not time to admit that, based on comparative anatomy alone, the question of the origin of man cannot be resolved? For, before we can begin to ask after the origin of something, we need a firm idea of what it is that has evolved.

This book will present the scientific, analytical foundations for defining the human being. One advantage to this goal is that developmental issues are only of secondary importance. We will be primarily concerned with documenting man's special position and proposing a general theory of man which will account for numerous facts and details; our interpretation will be necessarily rudimentary, however: it must exclude the immense realm of cultural-anthropological and socioanthropological questions, but it will nonetheless serve to relate the internal and external aspects of man to each other in an understandable fashion based on the concept of action without having to raise insoluble metaphysical problems such as that of the body and soul. For this reason, the categories we will employ, of relief, communication, retardation (juvenilization), and so forth, may be "psychophysically neutral," as Scheler says, in that each aspect of consciousness here is correlated with a drive and has a morphological counterpart. However, this has the advantage of enabling us to avoid the body-soul problem as long as we confine our examination strictly to the phenomena themselves. The insight that man is primitive and unspecialized from a morphological point of view is a key factor in our interpretation and had to be clearly documented. However, morphological problems are necessarily always related to evolution and hence the following chapter will examine evolutionary hypotheses.

12. The Problem of Evolution

The fact that man is unspecialized is the touchstone of any theory of evolution. Any theory that fails to grant this issue a central place has overlooked the difficulty and seriousness of this problem. The classical Darwinian theory makes precisely this error by claiming that man, in a direct and uninterrupted development, passed through an anthropoid stage. Rensch also believes firmly in the hypotheses of mutation and selection.[54] Scholars such as Weinert, Weidenreich, v. Eickstedt—despite differences in their assumptions— all basically agree that man is directly descended from the anthropoids of the Tertiary period, which are closely related to the present-day great apes in the most important characteristics. *Dryopithecus,* a Tertiary chimpanzee with large canines, is most frequently cited as this first ancestor.[55]

As we mentioned above, Rensch proceeds from the standpoint of a rational theory of descent and argues that, given the appropriate blueprints, higher development could be seen as the inevitable consequence of natural selection. He objects to the contention of Bolk, Dubois, and Versluys that retardation could not have come about as a result of selection. Rensch writes: "The prolonged childhood with its accompanying dramatic increase in a versatile, plastic ability to act would constitute a clear advantage in selection and must have produced favorable results in any competition." He argues further that "with the development of language and of a speech center," it is probable that an entirely new form of universal conceptualization became possible. "Thus, modern man thinks in words; this is the basis for his facility for complex concept formations, for imagination and speculation, for abstract thought. Here, too, this ability posed a definite advantage in natural selection for the imagination allowed man to visualize future situations."

At this point the theory becomes self-fulfilling. Of course, every human ability serves some sort of function which may be viewed in in terms of its usefulness. However, it must be proven that this usefulness figured into the selection process; the mere fact that a function functions and does so in a useful way cannot serve as proof that it did not come about through autonomous evolutionary forces instead of through a process of selection. Based on the usefulness of a particular function, one attempts to determine its value for selection. From this knowledge, the process of selection, the necessary mutation, as well as the origin of the function or its organic substratum (for example, the speech center), is then deduced. In the course of doing this, however, the "competition" to which primitive man was supposedly exposed, and which he survived by virtue of his advantageous mutations, becomes purely fictitious. With what kind of being is he supposed to have been competing and for what living spaces? There is no evidence to refute the other possibility, that an autonomous evolutionary development opened up totally new opportunities for survival for primitive man so that he could leave the trees to the apes where they still live today. It is not clear that language and thought offered man a selective advantage over the anthropoids in the competition for survival in the jungle. Similarly, we must ask ourselves: In what sort of competitive struggle, and with whom, could man's lengthy, unprotected childhood have figured as an advantage in selection instead of a life-threatening disadvantage?

To present a concrete description of an anthropoid from whom man could have evolved directly is an insoluble problem, as Weinert's attempt demonstrates.[56] He claims that *Dryopithecus germanicus* is the direct ancestor of man and the recent anthropoids. *Dryopithecus,* who lived in the Miocene epoch, was an anthropoid with large canines and a specialized third premolar—a true primitive chimpanzee. *Dryopithecus* is believed to have ushered in the first phases of anthropogenesis in central Europe. Weinert believes it is possible that a group of chimpanzee-like hominids acquired the use of fire by chance and gradually became accustomed to it, unlike the unsuccessful candidates for anthropogenesis, who "sat at the first fire as unthinking participants" and then "sank back down into the animal kingdom."[57] In part 2, I will undertake an analysis of anthropoid intelligence which will prove that this is completely impossible: maintaining an accidental fire requires a level of abstract thought that is not possible without language. We know very well that this is far beyond the intellectual capabilities of the anthropoid apes. Moreover, every animal possesses an unconquerable, instinctive fear of fire.

Because the first discoveries of true hominids were made on Java, Weinert assumes that his creature migrated from central Europe to Java. Beyond any doubt, any such journey, in view of the numerous changes in climate and terrain, from plains to forests and high mountains, would be impossible for any animal and contradicts all our knowledge of the strictly regional ties in all animal species. However, Weinert's assumption is the logical consequence of his premise. Thus, he writes: "Dryopithecus no longer had feet which in true simian fashion were also suited for grasping."[58]

We are thus asked to imagine a chimpanzee that could use fire and walk on human feet and further, to believe that it was a desire for knowledge that compelled it to forsake its home territory.[59] We know, however, that the intellectual abilities of the anthropoids are strongly connected to their eating and play interests and that such concepts as the perception of objective things are totally foreign to them. We will see that the specifically human structure of sensorimotor functions as well as intelligence are all involved in the apprehension of objective things (chapter 16).

If, as Weinert has attempted, one really wants to construct a "missing link" between the anthropoids and man and not simply claim that some fossil remains represent this missing link, then one would have to assume that it possessed the basic human characteristics: bipedal gait, possession of fire, beginnings of language, upright posture. This results in such a fantastic animal—beyond all known biological categories—that we would have to grant this being a special place in all of Nature.

It is impossible to construct such a being because in even the most basic human skills (for example, handling an object and experiencing it) all the essentially human characteristics are involved: the upright stance, the free use of the hands, reexperienced and versatile movements, the unique structure of impulses, symbolic vision, a vertically oriented perceptual space, and abstract "perception" (Merken). If we single out any one of these human characteristics and transplant it to an animal, we have disregarded all that biology has taught us about the relationship between environment, the perceptual world, specialized organs, and the structure of animal drives. The unique construction that man represents would then be partially based on an animal and as such would be beyond the limits of our biological knowledge; indeed, it would be a legendary creature like the salamander, which is also said to be unafraid of fire. I cannot imagine a creature that would have a "standard of life that, apart from the possession of fire, was not essentially different from that of the anthropoids." It is not the case, as one sometimes hears, that, as far as the evolution of man is concerned, modern theory has abandoned the classical view of evolution through mutation and selection. However, the hypotheses discussed above have arisen to compete with it; they attempt to justify man's special position and take his absence of specialization as the focal point of their approach. If we take these into account, then three and only three possible solutions to the problem of man's evolution present themselves:

1. The argument that man evolved from his own line. This hypothesis takes two forms:

1a. Man has his own ancestral line extending back earlier than the mammals; a "special branch" with a distinctly hominid character existed as early as the pre-mammal times. Attempts have also been made to trace human ascendancy directly from primitive mammals, bypassing the apes entirely. Adherents to this theory 1a are, among others, Klaatsch,[60] Westenhöfer,[61] Dacqué,[62] F. Samberger,[63] and Frechkop.[64]

1b. Man and the anthropoids developed parallel to each other, and share a very distant common ancestor. Since it then becomes necessary to assume that this common ancestor possessed the basic structures or prerequisites for anthropogenesis, the development from it to man must have been direct, while a secondary branch must then have led to the anthropoids and their specialization. This proto-primate could be classified as either a hominid or an anthropoid with equal justification and must have possessed at least the basic characteristics which today define man's special position. According to this hypothesis, one would expect that the fossil anthropoids would resemble man more than the present-day anthropoids which is, in fact, the case. Such types as *Australopithecus* or *Paranthropus* might then be late examples of a very early side branch of this primitive primate (Adloff, Osborn).

2. It can also be argued that man is descended from relatively unspecialized anthropoids, but it is then necessary to add a supplemental hypothesis or rule of exception to account for man. This is where Bolk's retardation and Schindewolf's proterogenesis fit in. It is, incidentally, of no consequence whether this special law appears elsewhere in the animal kingdom, it would still have to be the determining factor behind those traits that are specifically human.

As it is virtually impossible to come up with evidence to support 1a we may rule it out. As far as 1b and 2 are concerned, I believe no real choice can be made until new material is found to support one or the other. Nonetheless, we can say that the Bolk-Versluys theory, with the inclusion of Portmann's findings, accounts for the greater number of facts and traits. It expressly considers the basic facts of man's archaism, primitiveness, and lack of specialization, and furthermore provides a biological framework for understanding the phenomenon of consciousness. Moreover, this theory assumes that, during the actual time of anthropogenesis, a particularly favorable, optimal random environment must have existed—a "paradise," because an unspecialized being who had not yet developed tools must have been totally unadapted and unprotected and thus could only have survived in the "bosom of Nature." Klaatsch came earlier to this same remarkable conclusion. He correctly understood man's lack of specialization as "the clear rejection of all elements useful in the struggle for survival" and explained this by "the assumption that in the early history of man there were long periods in which the struggle for survival substantially abated, in which unusually favorable conditions permitted the race of the pro-anthropes to undergo transformations which would otherwise have been impractical, even dangerous, in the struggle for survival."[65]

As far as the fossil discoveries are concerned, *Sinanthropus,* Neanderthal man (including Heidelberg man), and modern man may be placed in a progression. This does not mean that there is an actual genetic relationship between these, but even if one is assumed, the question still remains completely open as to whether or not a special autonomous evolutionary law came into play. *Sinanthropus* is estimated to be at least 400,000 years old. Remains have been found of approximately 40 individuals, revealing an astonishing variation "which ranges from very primitive states to kinship with Neanderthal."[66] *Sinanthropus* had the use of fire and simple tools. Neanderthal man was unusually tall and massive; his brain was larger than that of the average modern man. It is therefore not certain that he belongs in the ancestral line of modern man, who might have simply passed him by.[67]

Dubois' famous discovery of *Pithecanthropus* [now Homoerectus—trans.] at Trinil in 1891, which Virchow declared to be a giant gibbon, has been augmented by a further discovery of von Koenigswald's in 1937 at Sangiran, central Java. This type shows a mixture of human and ape characteristics; among the latter are a constriction behind the eyes and a bend in the occipital. Then, in 1939, an upper jaw was added to these finds which had the definitely simian feature of a diastema, into which the large canine tooth must have fit, and a poorly preserved cranium. The upper jaw is remarkable because, until then, the absence of a diastema had been taken as a typically human primitive trait. In 1939, because of the advanced specialization the large canines indicated, von Koenigswald claimed that *Dryopithecus* could not be directly related to man; the same must apply to this upper jaw. On the other hand, a lower jaw fragment, also discovered at Trinil, seems to indicate that the canine tooth and adjacent premolar were small. Since there are no cultural relics of Pithecanthropus and no complete, well-preserved skull, the question again arises of whether it was in fact a hominid,—all the more so since Dubois, before his death in 1940, adopted the view of his old adversary, Virchow, and declared his *own* world-famous discovery of 1891 to be simply a gibbon. Most likely, the relationship between *Sinanthropus* and *Pithecanthropus* is not as close as one believes, even though they may well have been contemporaries.

The *Australopithecus* group—with its astonishingly human, unspecialized set of teeth, its remarkable vaulted cranium, and the absence of brow ridges—appears to be more closely related to man than recent anthropoids, but also more so than *Pithecanthropus*, if we assume the latter had well-developed canine teeth. Following Raymond Dart's discovery (1924) of the skull of a primate infant in Taung, which he called *Australopithecus africanus*, Broom found skull fragments near Sterkfontein which are similar to this type and which he called *Pleisianthropus*. In 1939, discoveries near Komdraai turned up *Paranthropus*, and today all of these and other apparently related types are grouped together as *Australopithecinae*. At present the remains of more than a hundred individuals have been discovered. The brain volume appears to surpass that of modern great apes. The structure and function of the bite and teeth are unmistakably hominid and the pelvic bones indicate an upright gait, especially since the *foramen magnum* was positioned much further forward than in the anthropoid apes.

In the caves of Makapansgat and Sterkfontein, some tools of a pebble-tool industry have come to light. Primitive techniques of stone-working are indicated: the stones were struck at an oblique angle, thereby forming a cutting edge.[68] Dart even found bone splinters jammed into antelope bones to be used as a tearing instrument.[69] Leakey's discovery in 1959 at Olduvai of the skull of Zinjanthropus [now assigned to *Australopithecus*.—trans.] from the same family and stone tools most likely dates from the Pleistocene; this is perhaps the oldest hominid yet discovered.

My suspicion (suggested by Adloff) that we should seek man's ancestors in the *Australopithecus* line seems confirmed. "It is quite possible that we have been walking upright for millions of years and, with head erect have been following a prescribed course of development wherever it may lead."[70]

We will now resume the primary course of our investigations. The next problem, to be treated in the following chapters of Part 2, is to describe the sensorimotor processes by which man constructs his perceptual world and develops and controls his versatile ability for movement. Once this has been accomplished, man has found relief and he becomes able to reduce and condense the world into perceptual symbols which provide him with an overview of the world and make it accessible to him. At the same time, he also acquires mastery of his infinitely diverse and variable movements, syntheses of movements, and suggestions of movement until, ultimately, these form the substructure for the development of language and give us a glimpse into the profound connection between cognition and action.

PART II

Perception, Movement, and Language

13. Fundamental Circular Processes in Interaction

Now that we have established man's special morphological position based on the primitive and unspecialized nature of his constitution, we can clearly see that man himself has to create the conditions necessary for his own survival. Because man is unspecialized, there is no environment to which he is naturally adapted, with which he can live in a biological balance; further, his lack of *specialization means that he must* use his own initiative to ensure the survival of his vulnerable, organically helpless, and unprotected being. Thus, it is through his efficient and controlled actions that man makes his physical existence possible.

This situation results in two related series of tasks. The first consists of appropriating the open abundance of the world—a world which is not an environment tailored to the human being, sparing in its stimuli, and accessible to him through his instincts, as is true of the environments of animals. The world is instead a field of surprises *(Überraschungsfeld)* in which man must first orient himself. This orientation is accomplished not on a "theoretical" level but on a practical one, through movements that are designed to open up the world to man, allow him to experience it and then set the experience aside until he needs to make use of it. These movements primarily involve the senses of sight and touch. We call these communicative movements. We will study their uniquely human structure and process as well as what they effect—the construction of the interpreted and controlled visual world that we adults believe we possess directly. This world has been reduced to clear, potentially productive centers which we oversee, which we know intimately, and which provide us with suggestions for how they might be used; in other words, the world is reduced to the familiar things we know. This is a process of relief: the field of surprises is transformed through action into an accessible, manageable world in which impressions and outcomes can be anticipated. In this part of the book, we will also examine the way in which language originates in the course of this process and directly continues the development it set in motion. Our discussion will further elucidate the process of relief or withdrawal from the direct pressure of the present and the liberation and development of increasingly sophisticated and effortless abilities that facilitate a turning back to the world in order to achieve mastery over it and make use of it.

The second series of tasks can be grouped under the heading of "the development of the control of movement." These tasks are closely related to the processes described above; they are, in fact, met through an ongoing counter-process. Much too little attention has been given to the ability of the human being to enjoy a wide range of possibilities for movement, unknown among animal species. The combinations of voluntary possible movements available to man are literally inexhaustible, the delicate coordinations of movements unlimited. We are not only able to touch any part of our bodies but we can also coordinate any movement with any other and transpose a movement from one limb to another. The anatomical basis for this is man's erect posture; the nature of his sensory organs; the mobility of the head, back, etc.; the versatility of his joints (such as the hand and arm); and finally the fact that human skin is one giant sensory surface. Our ability to imagine movements and to carry out symbolic, suggested movements is also important because it allows us to transpose movements, arrange them in sequence, and intend one movement with another. Only then can we exercise a controlled ability to act of almost absolute plasticity and variability which is equal to the indescribable diversity of the world.

Our faculty for action is also fostered by our independent activities, by those *same* processes that allow us to experience and work through the wealth of impressions. The newborn child is as defenseless against stimuli and lacking in orientation as it is incapable of movement. All animals can master their necessary range of movement after only a short period. Human movements, on the other hand, are predisposed toward self-direction and highly variable and controlled coordinations which are employed in our direct experience of the world and things. Human movements are plastic and sensitive. We can integrate imagined movements with images of their outcomes and the changes they might effect. Human movements are so very immature at birth because their development is based on self-perceived efforts; at the same time, they remain adaptive and can grow only through interaction and communication with the things in our surroundings. These two related series of tasks thus clearly express the necessity of human action in an appropriated and familiar world. The human being masters the world through communicative actions, which take place without the pressures of instincts; he experiences the open abundance of the world because he can find the means to his survival only through efficient, directed, goal-conscious actions. The plasticity of human movements is essential for survival, for it represents the ability to adapt to any situation and to anticipate its potential usefulness. From a philosophical perspective, it is of the greatest significance here that knowledge *(Erkenntnis)* and action share a common root, that orientation in the world and the control of actions are *one* process; it will be important to keep this in mind later when the two draw apart from each other.

Man enters the world in such a helpless state that at first he is disturbed by most stimuli and reacts adversely. Nature comes to his aid by allowing him to screen out the overwhelming stimuli until he can better cope with them. An infant learns in the second month to tolerate a stimulus, such as an acoustic one, without discomfort and by the third month has taken the important step to becoming indifferent to it, which is only possible given the protected situation of the human infant. One study recorded that in the eighth month, 2.5 percent of the stimuli was negative, 92.5 percent neutral, and 5 percent positive (that is, attracted the infant's attention). In the sixth month, 5 percent of the stimuli was negative, 67.5 percent neutral, and 27.5 percent positive: thus, through "habituation," the delicate organism learns to tolerate its own vulnerability to stimulation. The percent of neutral stimuli increases initially before the ability to deal with it has begun to develop; at around the tenth month, however, the child obviously turns eagerly to experiencing and exploring the external world in detail. (These examples were drawn from a number of current texts on child psychology.)

After several months, once the child has learned to control its movements to some degree, one observes the interesting phenomenon of the child's joyful repetition and untiring reproduction of movements. In the second half of the first year, the child begins to be more active: it learns to manipulate objects, to crawl, stand up, and move its limbs independently. Let us begin our examination of the development of motor skills with an example (from Guernsey) which we will return to several times: a child, eleven months old, falls down in bed, striking its forehead. It cries for several minutes. Then, it suddenly stops, gets back up, and carefully proceeds to hit its forehead several dozen times, again and again, in precisely the same manner. How can this be explained? What is involved here is the anticipated return of the original stimulus—the sensation of pain at a certain place; the movement is repeated along with its "sensory outcome"—the pain of impact.

One could explain this as self-imitation, but this does not adequately answer the following question: What pleasurable feeling can be so strong as to tolerate the recurrence of the pain? I believe that we are dealing with a fundamental human phenomenon here. Man's motor skills, which are characterized by plasticity and self-direction, must draw the motivation for their development from within themselves; the *awareness of one's own activity* is the source of pleasure in these movements. I do not mean to say that an intellectual understanding of movement is already present at this age; it is a fact, however, that random movements and their sensory outcomes can be *appropriated* and then *controlled* and *used*. I wish to avoid the statement that the child can behave "objectively" toward its own movements; however, a *detached self-awareness of his own movements (entfremdetes Selbstgefühl der eigenen Bewegungen)* is conveyed to the child by the sensations that accompany his movements; this discovery is new and exciting and is immediately repeated. Any unintentional or involuntary movement can thus act as a stimulus and evoke a special awareness, a detached awareness of the movement which can then be adopted, used, and developed further. It is this detached awareness of one's own activity that directs the further development of the activity itself.

The development of the range of adaptable and plastic human movements depends on the following: the movement must be reexperienced through the senses in order for it to become conscious and usable; it must gain a "detached awareness of self" within a shell of real or anticipated sensations. We discover and experience the perceptual world only through our movements within it; by the same token, all perceptions suggest productive or useful directions for our movement to take. For example, I only need to see a bird's-eye view of a house to determine what views I would find if I walked around it. We will go into more detail about this later.

For the moment, let us ask ourselves if there are not certain distinct systems of movement in which sensory outcome is linked in a special way to the actual motor process. This would be the case if there are sensorimotor processes in which the motor portion has a direct and regular sensory effect such that the movement itself provides the *stimulus for its own continuation*. Such sequences of movement could then easily become automatic. In fact, it appears that walking is one of these. Baldwin recounts that he held his nine-month-old child in such a way that its bare feet barely brushed a smooth table; he observed the child perform four well-controlled, consecutive, alternating movements of the legs that would have carried the child backwards.[1] Here, a movement of the legs produced a particular sensation in the soles of the feet which then functioned as the stimulus for a continuation of the movement: the movement furnished the incentive for its own repetition.

The most important example of this involves the audiolingual system. As is well known, babbling, the production of meaningless sounds, is one of the skills of a two- or three-month-old infant, who thereby develops an ability to produce sounds which he only later learns to use properly. The basic fact behind this audiolingual system is the *dual reality* of the sound: it is a motor process involving the speech mechanism as well as being a self-perceived, echoed tone. We behave actively toward a self-produced sound by articulating it and passively in that the product of our activity is effortlessly perceived by the ear. Here, our ability to develop a "detached self-awareness" is striking and is analogous to what takes place in the tactile sensations in the hand. Here, too, the active-passive dual reality comes into play, for as the hand moves, sensations of touch are continually produced. In both these circular systems, the movements are directly reflected in the senses; they promote a detached self-awareness of the activity which is motivated to continue by the sensations it evokes. Once the hand has become freely mobile, it is an almost independent mechanism, for every tactile sensation encourages a "follow up" whereby new tactile sensations are developed. With its meaningless babbling, the child practices its audial and linguistic skills; hearing and imitating the sounds it produces, indulging in the inevitable variations in articulation and tone quality—these are important aspects of the child's self-concept and awareness of his own activities which he develops and explores himself.

Guernsey's example is very significant. For one thing, it indicates a certain "purposelessness" of action, indeed, even a grave inexpediency: pain is "freely" repeated. Movement is perceived through its effect on the senses. It is checked suddenly, stopped short; it is experienced because of the peculiar fact that something has interfered with it. It is not the abstract re-sensation that propels the movement further but rather the *communication* with an external thing incorporated into the movement. In this example, the inhibition produces the sensation of pain. Nonetheless it constitutes a new way of interacting with things and is consequently excitedly taken up and carried further or repeated. An interrupted movement is conscious only in a passive way, but because it affects the world in some fashion, it is also communicative and *usable*. It occurs, of course, by accident. A controlled movement is one that has become independent or "detached," one in which part of the world is also moved.

Guernsey's example is not yet fully explained by categorizing it as sensorimotor "communication games." The remarkable "theoretical" character of the action has not been sufficiently accounted for. The movement Guernsey describes is not purposeful in any way, it is not innate, not instinctive, not a "reflex," and its outcome does not make sense from a biological standpoint. Even so, if one wishes to use this term for what has been described, it is "intelligent."

My thesis that the difference between the human and animal constitution is already in evidence in the structure of movement has encountered opposition. Nonetheless, this example serves to strengthen my claim further and proves even more besides. I do not adhere to the trend in recent psychology to reject completely the concept of "sensation" or to use it as a purely hypothetical construct. One can debate this point in the context of the sense of sight, but not the sense of touch: in the latter, there is an "extinguishing" of sensation in the experience of the properties of a thing (such as coarseness or hardness). By the same token, a very definite experience of sensation as the objective "possessing" of a subjective state exists. The subjective state thus sensed and "theoretically" possessed is, in Guernsey's case, precisely the point of the process: the movement is directed toward this end. This process involves not only the pleasure in communicative movement that Köhler's chimpanzees, just like any athlete, experienced in their play with a vaulting pole. In addition, the movement culminates in an "experience of ascertainment"—in this case, the ascertainment of pain, which becomes, in turn, the impetus for new executions of the movement.

Sensorimotor circular processes are of particular interest when the formation of a habit with its accompanying effect of relief has been incorporated into them (see above, Chapter 8). In his commendable studies, Baldwin identified the ninth month as the age at which the child imitates seen movements with its hand. When an older child, of 26 months or so, traces a pattern it sees with its hand, its eyes guide motions of the drawing hand on the pattern and the tracing. The drawing movements are initially uncertain and inexact and the drawing is consequently usually distorted. The child learns to transpose a design into a parallel pattern, thereby perfecting fluid, fine movements. Once this has been mastered, the visual control of the act of copying is relieved and the eyes can be directed toward the next pattern shape. (A similar process is involved in learning to write.) The manner in which the relieved eyes direct the sequence of movements by anticipating and no longer directly controlling them is quite clear. The intermediate stages of the sensorimotor processes are dropped because they have become automatic. Ultimately, the original pattern is no longer necessary and the idea of the shape directs its reproduction in writing or drawing. In this example, we can see the extraordinary internal complexity of skills which on the surface appear quite simple. As Baldwin has stated, development is not only evolution but also involution, in that its elements are disguised in the complex forms that they create. Furthermore, these coordinated movements are guided as much by unsuccessful experiences as by successful ones; a child will stare at his fingers in astonishment when it reaches for an object too far away to be grasped and the expected tactile sensation does *not* occur. Here we have a "theoretical" behavior in the sensorimotor process similar to that in Guernsey's example.

There can be no doubt that through this cooperation between sight and touch, we experience the objective existence of the things in our world as well as their value for interaction (that is, their appearance in relation to our movements). We can therefore state that the *"objectivity" of the world of things becomes a reality only in relation to this structure of "reflected" movement.* The expression "detached self-awareness" of one's own movements should be understood in this sense. As we have discussed, in the sensorimotor circular processes, interaction with a part of the world provides the impetus for its continuation; the movement takes on a value of its own that spurs its further development and finds gratification in its own vitality. This circle may be broken at any point, however, as soon as the feeling of detachment sets in. In other words, the subjective aspect of the tactile sensation as such (thus in an objective sense) or the visual perception of a thing becomes a datum and can set the process operating in reverse: the movement is initiated in order to evoke a particular sensation (as is the case with Guernsey's child) or a particular perception of the form of a thing or even the image of one's own limbs.

This topic is by no means a simple one; but then neither is the structure of human movements. One could agree with Diderot[2] and call man a "système agissant à rebours" (a system operating in reverse) but this would serve only to characterize the intelligent nature of the form of his movement, indeed, of *all* human movements, for they are all sensitive to tactile sensation. The human skin is one extensive sensory surface; because of our extreme flexibility, we can touch almost any part of our bodies with any other part.

Our movements are not only able to respond to things but also to each other. A *controlled* movement can reach an object but it can also reach itself; it can be redirected or "reversed" toward the "subjective datum"; we see this in young children when they experiment with the most unusual means of locomotion, delighting in their ability, their control, and their awareness of the strangeness of their physical sensations. This experimentation becomes immediately practical whenever unusual coordinations of movement need to be learned—in rowing, swimming, in every sport, and in the operation of machines. It is crucial that such "experimentation" or practice be part of a child's natural development of his abilities and that a child explore his great degree of versatility in movement as well as the "intelligence" of his movements, the ability to redirect movement, to become detached from himself, and thus the possibility for a movement to culminate in a "theoretical datum" of the sense of sight or touch.

Because of the unique human constitution, we enjoy an unusual degree of mobility of the extremities and head—those organs that are primarily involved in these circular processes, among which, as noted before, those conveyed through the hands, eyes, and language, are dominant. These organs can be moved voluntarily and also independently of each other and thus can respond to and conflict with each other. The digestive and circulatory systems, on the other hand, are dependent upon each other and thus not subject to voluntary control. The external organs are open to our control; they function independently and even in opposition to each other. They are also susceptible to fatigue and need occasional rest periods. Bichat based his distinction between the *vie animale* and the *vie organique* on this most significant fact. He writes: "L'intermittence de la vie animale est tantôt partielle, tantôt générale: elle est partielle quand un organe isolé a été longtemps en exercice, les autres restant inactifs. Alors, cet organe se relache; il dort tandis que les autres veillent. Voilà sans doute pourquoi chacque fonction animale n'est pas dans une dépendance immediate des autres, comme nous l'avons observé dans la vie organique."[3] The intermittence in the animal life is sometimes partial and sometimes general: it is partial when a single organ has been exercised for a long time while the others have remained inactive. Then, this organ relaxes; it sleeps while the others wake. Here, without doubt, we see why every animal function is not directly dependent upon others as we have seen with organic life.

Because these organs can operate independently of each other, they may at times work against each other. We shall soon see how important this fact is to the careful development of the proper cooperation between hand and eye, to our ability to touch our own bodies, to the process of learning to distinguish between our own bodies and the external world. At an age at which a child does not even have words or thoughts, it is already developing flexible hierarchies of dominant and subordinate skills. We can observe this when a child discovers the "topography of his own body" or learns to keep his eye on an object toward which his hand is reaching without being distracted by the sight of his own moving hand. Communicative movements are always involved in such cases; following his own sensitivity and intelligence, a child experiences the world by selecting and adopting new movements, which he then learns to control and use. A movement is voluntary when, based on previous experience, it anticipates its result; it is thereby greatly enriched but also becomes vulnerable to a great degree and open to further refinement or adjustment. The particular movement is chosen from an array of many equally possible movements. When a random movement is learned and adopted, the child becomes aware simultaneously of his motor ability and of the ready availability of this motor skill.

The decision not to analyze these fundamental facts further is one of the problems of, but also one of the conditions for success of, a prudent study. We might also describe the process as follows: A child becomes aware of its movements and their consequences, "associates" the two, and by "imagining" the result in the future, its "will" is able to carry out the appropriate movement. However, this explanation only increases the number of unknown factors and is bound up with certain theories that further study could never really sort out. Furthermore, in its particular choice of words, it opens up the gulf between the "physical" and the "psychical." On the other hand, the concepts I have chosen (such as "availability," "appropriation," "detached self-awareness") are neutral as far as the distinction between the physical and psychical is concerned.

Bostroem counts as "ideomotor" (that is, sensorimotor) movements those involved in for example, walking, bicycling, and playing the piano.[4] This is quite correct. However, it is the relationship between relief and control, so important for cultural anthropology, that is in evidence here. When a pianist in a recital plays from sight, his eyes, which when he was learning to play had been needed to control the finger placement, now anticipate the coming measures, which are translated directly from the written score into movements. As another example, the ear does not keep track of one's own sounds but is instead attuned to those of other people. These examples illustrate the manner in which relieved abilities are freed for other uses and the complexity of human achievements is greatly increased by incorporating automatic movements. Whenever I speak of communicative movements, sensorimotor circular processes, or detached self-awareness, we must keep in mind the intelligent nature of the structure of human movement, as described in this chapter. By "intelligent nature" I mean the reciprocal way human senses relieve one another and the uniquely human ability to use an isolated subjective datum (and not instincts, indeed, even in opposition to instincts as when pain is involved) as the basis for directing a movement.

Once the hands, eyes, and speech all cooperate, our ability to experience the world through communicative interaction is greatly increased. Circular processes operate in this higher system and incorporate everything else. All the human achievements from motor skills to truly intelligent feats converge in this system, as we shall see. As the dominant field, it controls the integration of all motor and intelligent experiences.

The following fact will make my point clearer. The system involving the hands and that of language are similar, and not only because both systems can function independently to a great extent of the state of overall movement. More than this, their similarity is based on the fact that *only* in these two areas is our activity actually creative, in the sense of serving to increase what we can perceive of the world. Our language makes a mute world a resonant one; our hands, by manipulating, destroying, or creating things, elicit new tactile and visual sensations. When our activity is truly productive and increases the wealth and attractions of the world, we are once again faced with the task of mastering this new wealth. Our language and our hands are continually concerned with coping with these newly created experiences that confront and overwhelm us. Thus, they are sources of a highly concentrated, communicative, sensorimotor life process into which our imagination also flows. Speech and imagined speech, the work of our hands and its imaginative variations, are original forces that spring from these points of concentration of intelligent sensorimotor life processes.

14. The Further Development of Circular Processes

At this point it is appropriate to introduce into our discussion the *first root of language:* the purely communicative, as yet unthinking and open "life of the sound" *(Leben des Lautes)*. An articulated sound, which also qualifies as a movement, is perceived by the ear; this is one of those actions that provides the impetus for its own continuation. For the time being, we should shy away from discussing the "meaning" of a sound, but we may nevertheless assert that a small child holds babbling "conversations" with itself; it immediately hears the sounds it produces and tries to repeat these. This process is quite similar to the development of a detached self-awareness of movement which was discussed in the preceding chapter. By re-creating and embellishing upon what it has just heard, the child also practices its sensitivity to acoustic form and impression and its ability to articulate. Because the sound echoes back from the world, it makes no difference in this game whether the heard sound originates from the child or from others speaking to the child. The incentive is still there to imitate heard sounds, which leads to a clear effort to use the heard sound as the *motivation* for a movement directed toward reproducing it. An adult says the sound sequence "re re re" to a child; the child listens, its face becomes strained, it cries out abruptly and breaks into tears. Then, suddenly and quietly, while smiling but with obvious effort, it produces the sounds "re re re" (two months, eighteen days).

Thus, in this fashion, a purely sensory communication evolves which consists of hearing, imitating, hearing again, and modifying sounds produced by oneself or others—a process that teaches a child to articulate sounds properly. This process, which I call the "life of the sound," is based on this form of sensory communication and involves the self-development of language ability. The only parallel to this can be found in the area of tactile sensations, which also involve self-perpetuating processes whereby the external world is fused with one's own activity—there, too, sensory communication is possible. For Helen Keller, blind, deaf, and mute, this was the only form of communication.

Let me explain this sensory communication exactly. Whenever I articulate a sound, hear it and then repeat it, whenever it passively enters my ear and I then imitate it, I am developing a sense for the double-sided nature of sound. The same also holds true, to an extent, for a blind child. Our imagination leads us to expect to hear an articulated sound repeated and echoed from the outside world. If this expectation is not met, if a response is not forthcoming, the life of the sound is cut short, and our expectation remains unfulfilled.

Every communicative process involves experiences of failure and success which in turn encourage further experiences. The dynamic, communicative sound that is echoed back and carried further is very different from a sound that slowly dies away, meeting with no response. In the former instance, communication is fostered. This provides evidence of a general law of progression through abandonment or selection. All human capabilities, including motor skills, are increased and developed to extraordinary perfection; if they are restricted in some manner, they will cast off certain possibilities for development and will consequently become "specialized." A very significant feature of language, indeed, of any intellectual experience in general, comes to light in the process whereby certain sounds are selected over others, based on which prove most successful in establishing communication. Because language (and any further development of man's inner life) grows from interaction, because the foreign sound, penetrating from the external world, becomes, through its reproduction, part of one's own activity and thus part of one's awareness of that activity, *all* subsequent resources in the world that are affected by language are *drawn into our consciousness as something we know intimately and have ready access to*. In language, "signs" are not simply pasted onto things. Things are drawn into interaction with us; they become intimate participants in our lives. Humboldt recognized this, as the following passage reveals: "For, as living sound, [the voice] proceeds, as does respiration itself, from the breast; it accompanies—even without speech—pain and joy, aversion and avidity, breathing life from which it streams forth into the mind which receives it. In this respect, it resembles language. The latter reproduces the evoked sensation simultaneously with the object represented. Thus, it connects man with the universe or, to express it differently, associates his independent activity with his sensory receptivity."[5]

We are not dealing with truly meaningful speech here, but are rather still concerned with sensorimotor processes, with movements. Nonetheless, the "intelligence" of these processes must be stressed. Once these movements have been broadened through experience of the world, once they have become communicative, we do not simply live them, but live *in* them. We can now use these movements, develop them further, and profit from any failures as well as from successful experiences.

This brings us to the topic of the imagination of movement *(Bewegungs-phantasie)* which we will soon consider more closely. For now, I wish to treat it in conjunction with the imagination of sensations *(Empfindungs-phantasie)*. First and foremost, we must take note of the fact that every movement, insofar as it communicates something—that is, insofar as it is concerned with relating to the external world—has, right from the very beginning, certain expectations. In the initial phases of a movement, its later phases are as undetermined as are the future reactions of things and the changes brought about in the things encountered. Even a sound already contains the expectation of being repeated; this is its "intention" of finding fulfillment. "Intention" here means the expectations in every controlled movement of a certain outcome or response. It is a very grave mistake to relegate intention solely to the spiritual or intellectual realm. Any controlled movement intends in its initial phases to be continued and to have a certain result. The anticipation contained within a sound of finding fulfillment through other, responding sounds is, of course, of particular significance: it is the *vital basis of thought,* of the "intention of something" expressed in a sound; it is self-aware, directed, and hence freely available.

The question of whether animals, when they give warning calls, "mean" a definite danger and thus possess "language" is usually taken too seriously. I believe it is thoroughly possible that animals use a true warning call that contains an "intention" to convey danger. Nonetheless, this does not mean that they have language. Three additional essential qualities are necessary for language: (1) the expectation in a sound of finding fulfillment in *other* sounds, (2) the strict assignment of precise types of sound to equally precise things, and (3) the *independence* of the availability of a true language from the context of the immediate situation. No animal would give a warning cry in a nonthreatening situation. The animal is not relieved of the pressures of the immediate situation, and therefore its sounds are not freely available to it at any time but are instead forced upon it.

We can detect an important capacity for development, which is fostered by the restrictions placed upon it and the pressure to appropriate successful sounds. This is because self-motivated activity and receptivity, one's own activities, and animating, stimulating interaction are all closely interconnected. Happiness or pleasure lies in the unhampered continuation of activity in which any obstacles are incorporated into the movement. No explanation is really necessary for the different forms our actions take as we communicate with other people and with the things in our world.

The American Pragmatists, (in particular Dewey), but also Nietzsche and Bergson, proposed the idea that consciousness originated from the inhibited life process; in a general sense this is certainly correct in that consciousness, movement, resistance, and sensation are all interrelated. The pragmatists made the significant contribution of understanding consciousness in relation to action. I do not believe, however, that Dewey's theory of the episodic character of consciousness is valid; it means only that disjointed movements are made fluid once more by recombining the obstacles in order to sink back again into a smooth, simple, and habitual mode of operation—an episodic turning back in order to eliminate the difficulties in the essentially unthinking action. I believe, in contrast, that in the human being, there is no unconscious existence but rather only one that has become unconscious— habits formed despite resistance now take on the entirely new function of acting as the *basis* for *relieved* higher and conscious behavior. The actual foundation of life is not, as Dewey believes, everyday existence. Instead, we live in the everyday with a constant view towards the *future*. Consciousness determines our everyday actions over and beyond habit based on what the future might hold.

Let us now return to our examination of sensorimotor, communicative self-development. Another example, much more complex, is that of dance. In a free-form dance, our movements communicate with the music. In a good dance, music is not simply accompaniment but insteads seems to continue the inner music of the movements themselves into the audible sphere; the movement seems to draw the music, which is essentially beyond space, into itself and concentrate it at a visible spot.

The circular processes involved in sensory responses are rhythmic or capable of becoming rhythmic. Rhythm appears to be the original form for the development of such movements. As in taking deep breaths, the feeling of vitality is continually renewed through the movement our senses reexperience, a movement which runs its course with a certain rhythm while experiencing a detached and yet intimate knowledge of the world.

There is another aspect of these processes in which our actions find the incentives for their continued development. The abilities we develop become "free" or independent. They distance themselves from their original impetus and are exercised in increasing independence from the original situation that motivated them. A specific, single factor may serve as the initial impetus; however, once set in motion, these circular processes actually become caught up in themselves. As we manipulate objects, we broaden our range of movement and our movements become in turn more "receptive" to new tasks that arise. We can observe children manipulating things and see how they become absorbed in exploring their properties. Thus, the process of discovering these properties is the same one in which the child develops its skills and abilities. The ties to the original situation are severed and the movements become caught up in themselves. Our awareness and exploitation of the potential of these processes are very important in the development of language.

The structure of human communicative movements is highly significant, for it is the foundation for any *objectivity* of behavior. Small children construct many arbitrary and strictly defined areas of habitual actions which focus on specific things—this is an important aspect of play. Only after the surrounding objects become interesting in themselves can their individual properties be discovered. As this happens, the tension becomes greater between the "objective" and the "subjective" poles, between the *outcome* of an action and the *awareness* of the ability to perform the action. The more precise and striking the outcome of an action is, or the greater its distance is from the initial cause, then the stronger is our awareness of the activity: for example, the loud sound of the rattle serves to encourage the child to shake its hand.

Thus, to develop objectivity or an awareness of what movements are appropriate in which situations, things must be removed from their surroundings so that we may explore them in communicative movements and develop a sensitive ability to manipulate them and to anticipate the consequences of our movements. At first, a child's scribbling or block building is not intended to "mean" anything; these creations arise because the child is deeply involved and immersed in sensorimotor activities which are self-contained and independent of the immediate situation. Similarly, babbling and meaningless singing signify a liberation of function; this occurs before content and thought can be liberated from the concrete stimuli in the existing situation—a fact that is of great importance for language. I believe it is possible that the systems formed by speech and hearing and hand movements have somehow, in terms of the physiology of the brain, become independent; this is certainly true of the visual system (see below). These processes provide relief from the surroundings and freedom from the pressures of the immediate situation; at the same time, they represent the path to "objectivity" and to that intimate level of appropriate behavior that we can develop only through independent interaction and communicative movements.

It is in this light that we must understand the unusually long period of immaturity of the child's movements and its general state of helplessness. The length of time it takes for a child to master simple motor skills is striking compared to animals, who gain control of their movements shortly after birth. I have observed how an elephant only a few days old was pressed and prodded by his mother into running because he could not be allowed to delay the progress of the herd. Human movements are not developed as quickly because they are not adapted to a specific environment; instead, they must acquire a degree of adaptability unknown among animals. They develop a much higher level of integration of movement. Perhaps no other example conveys so clearly how human beings are predisposed in their very physiology to action and not to adapted response.

It is not because animals lack the necessary intelligence or language that they do not possess this ability to develop their own patterns of movement; the reason lies instead in the fact that they lack the plasticity and sensitivity of human movements, the "intelligence of movement." This fact should be kept in mind in our later discussion of "willed actions."

There are two situations in which our actions show a characteristic change: if movements are interrupted and attempt to prevail over resistance and if an accidental movement produces a result that is seized upon and later "intended" or used in repeated, controlled movements. The same phenomenon can be observed in animals. In both cases, behavior is adjusted accordingly in the sense that it "concentrates" on a particular task; one would be justified in employing here the special concept of will, even when the behavior is still "appetitive" and oriented toward goals that have an instinctive value.

Since, in this case, it is difficult to draw the line between "voluntary" and "instinctive" behavior, we may speak of a willed action in a narrower sense if the result of an action becomes the motivation for repeating the action. Here, too, there are transitional forms. When a child sees an object it played with the previous day, it will move toward it; as the movement is begun, the child's memory will awaken and form an "expectation." This expectation determines the child's actions, which now have a "motive" and are therefore willed. The same process might take place in higher animals as well: chimpanzees, for instance, can search for familiar boxes and sticks to help them reach something they want.

However, another interpretation is also possible: it could be that an "expansion of the complex" *(Komplexergänzung)* is involved such that one part or component in an entire situation triggers the sequences of movement necessary for coping with the existing stimuli. To exclude this possible interpretation, we must come up with an even narrower concept of willed action. It may be that a given sequence of movements is aimed at a specific result; this result is an isolated and independent part of the situation as a whole and has no instinctive value. The result (if it is a sensation) then most likely becomes the motivation for the movement. For example: "While babbling, a child suddenly produces new sounds. It stops abruptly, takes on an astonished, expectant expression, lies there briefly with its mouth open and its eyes large and dreamy, and then slowly and carefully articulates a few of the same sounds (such as g, w, and b). Its entire body is caught up in movement as it produces these new sounds" (5 months, 19 days).

This is an example of a willed movement, in the sense of the above definition, and it would be theoretical hair-splitting to contest that the child "wants" to repeat this unintentional result. It is also clear that the removal of the result from the situation that originally produced it, its independence as the motivation for the movement, and its subsequent adoption for future use occur earlier in the area of the manipulation of things. For example, it is not until the end of the first year that the child becomes aware of its random scribblings and attempts to reproduce them.

We have defined a special class of actions that is uniquely human. All motor, intellectual, emotional, etc., processes may be "willed achievements," which indicates that a particular ability is controlled and directed toward an intended result, and this takes place independently of the context of the given situation. For this to happen, the following conditions must be met:

1. The manner in which the movement is used is determined by its expected result.
2. The result is anticipated, planned, or
3. the particular action is neutral toward or carried out independently of the context of the situation as a whole.
4. The ability is therefore spurred by an independent isolated motivation.
5. Any obstacles to the movement or action are overcome by making the action more forceful, by taking detours, etc.

The concept of "will" is an abstraction based on the important fact that the relationship between our actions and the reactions of things may itself become the object of our interest. The "cycle of action" is spurred further as things respond in the way we expected them to. The motivation for actions may be drawn from our interaction with things; there is gratification here because a result and a series of actions reinforce each other, regardless of what meaning or interest this may hold for another, more vital drive. Any arbitrary situation may serve to gratify drives because it is seen as the result of an action directed toward it. All hypothetical, trial-and-error, or experimental behavior is determined by the thing it concerns and is gratifying in itself; this type of behavior is willed. It may in turn be set off and become the object of a need, in which case Wordsworth's statement would apply, "the mechanism furnishes his own drive" (1918). The human being finds gratification in action and the positive, affirming response of things to his actions—not in the type of gratification the situation he created may offer to some other drive.

Because of the sensitive nature of human behavior, our interaction with things may consist solely of experiencing the results of a movement. The example of the child who "wants" to pronounce b, w, g, is instructive in this regard. There is no necessity for and no real interest in this achievement; in a few months, the child will have acquired these sounds by imitating others. What is striking in this pattern of movement, however—as was also true in Guernsey's example—is the "matter of factness" with which the child strives to achieve this in the realm of the perceivable, the clear, willed nature of the behavior which is reflected within itself. Communicative movements develop themselves and foster the development of the will in which the activity itself is increasingly separated from the impressions of the external world because the movement itself determines the nature of our activities.

15. The Limits to Animals' Achievements

For reasons we can easily understand, the study of animal psychology has until now been almost exclusively concerned with finding the "bridge" from animal to human intelligence and thus has arrived at the idea that a quantitative, not qualitative, difference exists between the two. Given the importance that terminology had in this process, it is probable that dogmatic, rather than purely objective, needs played a role here. A recent study describes how a chimpanzee infant pushed a chair over to a door in order to open it. Because the door was locked, it had no success and then proceeded to get more chairs. The researcher called this, along with W. Köhler, a "good mistake"; he could just as easily, however, have termed it a "foolish repetition," but the former expression serves a dogmatic purpose when agreement is being sought.

One reason behind these attempts to find similarities between animal and human behavior is that before we can develop a feeling for what the animal *cannot* do, we must first research and form an idea of what it *can* do, whereby opportunities arise for drawing parallels to man. The systematic investigation of the limits to what animals can do has only just begun. To substantiate my own view that there is a qualitative difference in capabilities between animal and man, we will examine the best example of research of this type—the work of W. Köhler.[6] I believe that the *limits* to what an anthropoid ape can achieve are determined not only by the inferiority of its intelligence (whereby "intelligence" means something along the lines of insight into new situations) but *equally* by its specific structure of impulses, its type of sensory organs, and the nature of its sensorimotor capabilities. These limits are thus set by the animal's constitution and are therefore qualitative. This means that a simply gradual increase in the anthropoid ape's intelligence, unaccompanied by any changes in its constitution as a whole, could not constitute a "transition" to man.

In Köhler's studies, the truly remarkable feats of Köhler's chimpanzees invariably took place in plain view of instinctively desirable objects—such as bananas, oranges, and so forth—and thus were directly related to a strong attraction in an artificial setting. The animals behaved as one would expect: they learned only when the presence of a strong, instinctive stimulus compelled them to do so, and only within "striking distance" of the desired object could an increase in skill be witnessed. Thus, what these animals lack is the development of a skill independent of need gratification (such as we can observe in children's games), based purely on the discovered properties of a thing that has no value as far as instincts are concerned.

Köhler's experiments showed that these animals orient their behavior by visual cues, but in characteristic fashion soon reach their limits. When the cleverest animal, Sultan, noticed a rope, from one end of which the fruit was suspended while the other end was fastened by means of a ring to a nail, the animal recognized the visual connection between rope and object and attempted to get it by pulling on the rope; however, he failed to take the rope from the nail. When several ropes apparently led to the desired object (which, however, was attached to only one), the animal would at first pull the shortest rope regardless of whether it was attached to the object or not. The animals attempted to use a ladder to reach a suspended object in the following manner: they would opt for the visually most appealing, but statically most unstable, position of the ladder; that is, they would attempt to "glue" the ladder to the wall. When the experiment called for using a stick to bat at the object, if the stick was too short, the animal would place it next to another one so that visually the two would seem to make a stick of twice the length; but its hands had to hold the two parts together and thus, what seemed to be an improvement from a visual perspective, proved to be of no practical use. Later on, Sultan was able to stick two pipes together and work with this longer instrument; however, he discovered this solution only by chance in play and then used this random result—an often noted achievement in the animals. For example, in play, they would dig with a stick in the ground, turn up edible roots in the process, and then excitedly dig further. Furthermore, in terms of the visual orientation of their behavior, it is of note that when they had to place one box on top of another to reach a suspended object, they would visually "lengthen" the top one and place it closer to the goal by setting it on one corner. Even once the animals had learned to connect two sticks together, they became confused if the sticks by chance lay almost parallel in their hands; they then appeared not to be "attachable." It should also be mentioned here that they attempted to use sticks to bat at the object only if the sticks appeared in the same visual field as the object or were easily drawn into it—a stick propped against the opposite wall of the cage was not noticed or used. On the other hand, they tried to use anything that *appeared* to be portable and long, such as towels, pieces of wire, branches, blankets, etc., despite the actual inappropriateness of these things.

These findings reveal that the behavior of these animals is guided primarily by visual cues, although they have only a limited ability to make fine distinctions in visual data. Furthermore, static values hold no meaning for the animals, as Köhler himself emphatically indicated.

The animals never learned to place one box on top of another in a secure and stable way. One animal, standing on top of two boxes, attempted to pull out the lower one in order to place it on top and was greatly surprised when the whole structure collapsed. The chimps would "glue" the boxes at eye level on the walls in order to put them visually closer to the desired object. They never managed to place the ladder in a normal fashion, which had the least visual appeal but was the most stable.

Thus, we have defined the boundaries within which intelligent achievements in the sense of true insights appear. We may conclude from the preceding discussion that a chimpanzee's visual field is structured differently from that of man. The chimpanzees are primarily visual animals, but the things in their visual world, unlike those in man's, do not have the static values of weight, density, stability, and so forth. In addition, they seem unable to comprehend the vertical as the line of gravitation; given their arboreal existence, with its continually shifting perceptual axes, this is not surprising. The "fine structure" of man's visual field is primarily due, as we will soon see, to the cooperation between sight and touch, by means of which man explores the wealth of objective properties of things. I do not see how one can avoid the conclusion that animals lack the necessary structure of movement because they do not need it. When a child plays, it will use anything within reach. Its play is independent of the pressure of instincts; it does not represent "appetitive behavior" as do the actions of the animals that Köhler studied. Above all, however, when a child plays, it reveals the intelligence of its movements *(Bewegungsintelligenz)* which means that it can refine and improve its movements not only when this appears necessary on a practical level but also when its sensory impressions dictate, such as when the expected coincidence of visual and tactile sensations does not occur. A child would not use a cloth as a stick because, as a result of its experience in interaction with the cloth, he recognizes that certain tactile sensations that he would experience with a rigid object are absent; hence, he knows that the cloth is not rigid and accordingly expects that it would be unsuccessful for this use. An ape can manipulate objects, but does not rely on its past experience and expectations to do so. Its hands and eyes do not cooperate in a "relationship for its own sake." The independent vitality and "intelligence" of man's communicative movements, the objectivity created from visual and tactile impressions and their interrelationship, is a crucial aspect of the total problem of "man." The cooperation between the hands, eyes, and language is independent of the gratification of basic organic needs. To a great extent, this system draws its substance, impetus, activity, fulfillment, and improvement from within itself; this is of fundamental importance for the structure and development of human impulses, indeed, for the entire problem of man's "inner life." Human actions are concerned with objective situations and are carried out *independently* of needs; this creates a "hiatus" wherein lies the key to the problem of the "soul." This hiatus first opens up the inner life of our impulses and explains our awareness of and the plasticity of human impulses which are formed in accordance with the objective conditions necessary for their fulfillment through action. Part 3 treats the area of human impulses in greater depth.

Given the above, one would expect that the chimpanzees would be further restricted in what they can achieve in those instances in which they must act against or even only "bracket" their own instinctive urges, or where the appropriate behavior would be possible only within such a bracket. The animals knew how to take detours to achieve a desired goal—their arboreal existence often demands this. They could also use a short stick to get a longer one and then use this to get the fruit. But they failed when it was necessary to "think away" or ignore an existing situation in order to reach their desired object. In this type of situation, it is necessary to shut down the instinctive impulse and allow the behavior to be prescribed by the presence of the obstacle. After the animals had learned to bring over empty boxes to reach suspended objects, the most intelligent ones were later able to remove heavy stones from the boxes so that they could carry them. However, when stones or cans on the ground directly beneath the goal made it impossible to place the box securely, not even Sultan made an attempt to clear the stones away; none of them even glanced at the obstacle.

Instead of removing a stone lying before a door they wished to open, they cooperated, like the Gothamites, in trying to lift the door over the stone! One of Buytendijk's experiments is relevant in this context: an ape *(Cercopithecus)* learned to open the simple latch of a box in which there was an apple. However, if a wooden block was placed under the latch, making it impossible to open, the ape was not able to recognize the block as an obstacle and to remove it. Beyond any doubt, obstacles and overcoming them are obviously not part of the environment and related abilities of apes.

It is also practically impossible for apes to act against the immediate direction of their impulses. A series of experiments revealed this. In one, fruit was placed in a device shaped like a drawer which was attached to the front of the cage. The side facing away from the animal was missing. To solve the problem, the animal had to push the fruit away from itself with a stick towards the open side of the box and then had to move it out of the area of the box and finally draw it close.

The animals failed in this experiment because of their inability to understand, indeed even to perceive, a thing as itself. At first, the desire to pull the fruit toward them totally prevented any recognition of the open side of the box and its significance for their actions, because the opening lay in the opposite direction to the instinctive direction of movement. Even the most intelligent animal, Sultan, had to witness a random movement of the fruit toward the opening four times before he could envision how to successfully extract it. Two animals even hastily retrieved the fruit when it was near the edge. When one ape was startled by a noise while pushing the fruit toward the open side, he looked away and his careful progess was lost. The direction was abruptly changed and he began again to pull the fruit toward himself.

The susceptibility of the apes' actions to disturbance is striking. They simply do not act independently of the total situation, so that any new stimulus changes the total picture and any gains are lost. Only the strong pressure of a present, instinctual stimulus promotes the learning process. The animals' actions are not independent and hence are unobjective. The animals do not possess a "detached self-awareness" of their own activity; their interaction with things is not based on a "fine sense" for their properties.

Another example: A stick that the animals needed was attached to a rope, the other end of which was tied by a ring to a nail. It could be freed simply by lifting it off the nail. The apes tore and bit at the rope, even tried to bite off the nail or break it. They discovered the solution only after they noticed the movements of the ring on the nail. They were unable to identify the pivotal points of the total situation and direct their actions accordingly.

By the same token, the attempts they did make were senseless. If a stick could not reach the object because it was too short, they turned it around or tried using a green branch, which was even shorter. Surprisingly, it turned out that they often gave up on useful methods after chance failures because they had no real insight into the situation, no detached and objectified experience of movement of a discriminating nature. Similarly, the chimpanzees would immediately and "unthinkingly" resort to experimental attempts, whereas man turns to trial and error experimentation only after his expectations prove of no use. What chimpanzees lack is thus not an intelligence comparable to man's, in place of which they have "chimpanzee-intelligence"; rather, they lack the structure of communicative and independent actions. They are slaves to their instincts. For example, in one experiment, it was necessary to climb on a box to get a stick to reach the fruit. Koko dragged the box toward the stick placed high up on the wall. But when he passed by a spot where, outside the cage, fruit lay on the ground, he could not resist the sight; he changed his direction and tried to use the box as a stick to fish for the fruit. In another example, the animal headed toward the stick but left the box in its place. Later, it even senselessly climbed up on the box, remembering totally different experiments.

Sometimes, randomly occurring glances and head or body movements proved successful and led to the discovery of suitable aids. These movements were then appropriated and employed, but, again, only under instinctive pressure. The animal did "search." This alleviated the difficulties originally posed by the visual separation of goal and tool (see above), when distant tools were not even noticed by the animal. It is important, however, that they were not able to make their searching independent; they had no objective image of what they were searching for because they do not on the whole possess an objective view of the situation, relieved from immediate needs, which would enable them to turn away from an insoluble problem and search for practical means of solving it. The searching remains anchored to instincts in the immediate vicinity of the desired object; the animals stubbornly stick to the area of the desired object and do not, for example, turn back to the open corridor to search for appropriate tools. Even when Sultan was led out into the corridor and passed the tool he needed, he did not take it. It is also worth noting that the animals only realized the inappropriateness of the tools they brought (for example, a box that was too low to allow them to stand on it and reach the goal) once they were in direct view of the goal, in the "critical proximity." For example, when one ape, Grande, went to get a second box, the first box was secretly removed. Grande placed the second box underneath the goal, climbed up and when she was still not able to reach it, "she looked all around with an expression of astonishment and finally turned whining toward the observer."

We have considered these experiments from a point of view totally different from Köhler's. In all these cases (as in the total confusion that affects the animals if their practiced habits are interfered with), it is apparent that these animals are incapable of developing and employing abilities independently of the pressure of the immediate situation, not to mention devising a scheme of orientation using imagination and planning. This is only possible with language.

Furthermore, the motivations of these animals did not arise from their actions and to be subsequently adopted. Under favorable conditions, in clear view of the desired object, it is possible for a result of an action to serve as the motivation for it. However, they were not successful in isolating the results of their actions from the "here and now" and establishing them as the *independent* motivation for repeating the action. Köhler describes the apes playing with white chalk and writes that they "looked at their creations with interest." I maintain, however, that if they were led back the next day to their paintings, one would never see them then persistently search for chalk in order to draw again. Apes have no "objective" relationship to things, independent of their functional value for satisfying instincts. This does not represent simply a lack of "intelligence" but actually goes much deeper. The structure of sensorimotor movement and the nature of the chimpanzees' impulses are essentially not those of man; indeed, their obvious intelligence is related to their constitution, their "arboreal, quadrumanual habit" (Osborn).

The striking indifference of these animals toward anything that does not directly address their instincts, toward whatever does not fit into their species-specific environment, can be attributed to the monotony and "lack of ability" of their senses *and* movements. This indifference is distinctly different from the *acquired* indifference of man, which is manifested after he has appropriated and worked through all of the knowable world and has then set these experiences aside for later use. The acquired neutrality and occasional indifference toward our surroundings result after we have already experienced the world in minute detail, primarily through language. We will return to this topic later on.

In sum, it is only possible to identify the difference between man and animals if man is understood as an acting being, with all the ramifications this view entails. The difference is based on the dual nature of human actions and stresses the uniqueness of these even on their simplest level, that of communicative interaction.

It is thoroughly incorrect to attempt to identify "intelligence" as the essential difference between man and animal: The difference actually lies in anatomy, in the sensorimotor system, and—as we shall now see—in the physiology of the senses. Since we cannot peer into the inner life of animals, we cannot cite "reason" as a criterion. The Indian belief that apes are extraordinarily wise and much more clever than man because they do not speak cannot be refuted.

Man is characterized by his sensorimotor movements, which are integrated with sensations of sight and touch; these are circular processes, which furnish the impetus for their own perpetuation. They take place "independently of instinctive desires" and have no direct value for satisfying drives. They are communicative, focusing on any objects drawn into the movements. They are carried out with a "detached self-awareness"—they are experienced on the same level as things, just as these things are involved in the awareness of the activity. These processes become further developed and diversified as new combinations of movement are experimented with and new impressions or sensations are evoked which further stimulate us to interact with the world. This productive type of interaction is at the same time practical because new movements teach us new ways of dealing with changes in our world; because of our ability to imagine, any of the phases in this process may serve as the motivation for an action. These processes run their course in an "indifference" or independence from other nonsignificant aspects of a situation and are thus self-sufficient. All this can be summed up in the phrase "the experience of things through the practice of movement" *(Sacherfahrung in der Bewegungsübung)*. It is not basic physical needs that spur these actions but other interests related to communication and play, which do not, however, simply serve to "practice" later instinctive activities (such as a cat's "play" does).

It is important to stress here that the "objectivity" of behavior, its concern with exploring the properties of things, is inseparable from our "need-free" interaction, through movement and the senses, with things. Chimpanzees manifest occasional "islands" of objective behavior, but only under artificial laboratory conditions and then only under the strong pull of visible instinctive goals. These "traces" of human-like behavior do not represent *beginnings* but, on the contrary, the highest limits to what they can achieve.

In the above discussion of human processes we have not considered those actions that constitute the step from objectivity to "neutralization" or indifference ("higher objectivity"). We will examine these in conjunction with self-developed symbolism.

16. Visual Forms and Symbols

Our next task is to examine human perception and its symbolic structure, which is based upon sensorimotor processes. Clarification of this should provide us with a deeper understanding of language.

If we initially confine our examination to visual perception, we can determine that our senses organize and shape what we see into "forms" (*Gestalten*). Insects do not have a diffuse, complex perception; instead clearly defined groups of stimuli stand out for them from diffuse total perceptions.[7] Bees orient themselves by path markers, and if these are displaced they will go astray. Similarly, a dog can easily learn to pick out the shape of a triangle from a series of figures, no matter what its size.

The signal apparatus of visual releasers (as described by Lorenz), which trigger instinctive movements, usually consists of conspicuous forms or of rhythmic, precise patterns of movement, the intensity of which is often increased by brilliant colors. Hence, the sight of the drake's green head evokes mating behavior in the mallard. Heinroth found that Nile geese would follow Turkish ducks which, although not zoologically closely related to them, have identical markings on their wingtips. In another experiment, a female budgerigar chose a male whose yellow "beard," decorated with blue spots, had then been "corrected" with artificial colors. A particularly simple form guides the behavior of the young of the fish species *Haplochromis multicolor*. In times of danger, the young slip into the ready mouth of their mother. By using parafin dummies with dark glass beads as eyes, experimenters determined that it is the precisely symmetrical and horizontal position of the mother's eyespots that functions as a releaser and means of orientation. Any change in the symmetrical position of the eyes diminishes the response of the young.

All these forms are precise (*prägnant*). The Gestalt theory, even in its most recent and distinguished formulation by Metzger,[8] cannot explain exactly what the "preciseness" of a form is. Metzger called structures "precise," if they were the pure embodiment of a being and if they presented a distinct and consequently stable order. These are, however, circular definitions, for precision is already implied in the very concepts "pure" and "distinct." Among the infinite number of quadrangles, the square is distinct, and among the infinite curves, the conic section or the sine curve stands out. Everything that language designates with the words imperfect, exaggerated, crooked, impure, coarse, fragmentary, deformed, and so on, is imprecise compared to its opposite. Furthermore, in perception there is a tendency toward precision, so that lines that are almost parallel or figures that are almost symmetrical are perceived as being completely so; angles of 87° or 93° are perceived as right angles; conversely, it is impossible to comprehend a right angle as one of not quite 93°. The preference in our perception for precise forms may well have very deep roots and extend to the instinctive level. Lorenz had the brilliant insight that the universal characteristic of the releasing signal is its *improbability*.[9] This holds true for the chemical signals of smell as well as for acoustical (such as the cock's crowing) and visual ones, in which regular, symmetrical figures, rhythmic patterns of movement, and colors play a crucial role. All of these precise signals are improbable in the sense that they stand out from the confusion of the background of total perception as being *conspicuous*. By the same token, the protective coloring of many animals, by means of which they render themselves inconspicuous, means that they relegate themselves to an average status or zero level in their surroundings; pale or spotted patterns along with grey, brownish, and muted tones predominate while colors of the spectrum are avoided. One can ultimately explain the preference for symmetrical figures only by their improbability.

All these forms have two very important characteristics which are already predisposed in the sensory realm: these are *constancy* and *transposability*. Constancy is the visual stability of the form as such despite changes in the surroundings. For example, a chair has the same "form" visually, no matter from which angle, or perspective, or under what lighting conditions it is viewed. In spite of any changes in the "nuances" *(Abschattungen,* Husserl's term) of merging perspectives which a box I hold and turn in my hand presents, it form remains the same. The transposability of a form means that it can be removed from the sensory context in which it appears and transferred as itself to something else. For example, a melody can be transposed into another key. Transposability and constancy, taken together, are the basis for man's ability to understand similar things as representatives of the same type. Everyone understands two circles as "two of the same thing" (transposability) even if one circle appears foreshortened (constancy of form).

In the higher animals at least, these two laws of form are definitely already in effect in the senses such that there is in the senses a type of direct general conception. This is what Buytendijk's concept of the *formation d'invariantes* means. For example, a trained dog can form an idea of the general shape of a triangle which is independent of the triangle's size, the direction from which it is viewed and, indeed, even of the size of its angles. "L'animal est en état d'appendre á reconnaître l'invariable, le commun dans une série de perceptions" (The animal is in a position to learn to recognize what is invariable in, or common to, in a series of perceptions.—trans.). Köhler's apes attempted to use long cloths, pieces of wire, etc., as sticks to get the fruit; thus, they transposed the form properties of "long" and "movable." This ability is, of course, the sensory-physiological prerequisite to concept formation.

Form constancy incorporates two parallel laws. First and foremost is size and color constancy. It cannot be determined whether these exist for animals. Size constancy refers to the fact that when a thing we see is moved away from us, its visible size is not reduced to the same degree that would correspond to the geometric laws of representation on the retina. Within a certain "orthoscopic" range, we see things as the same size; we not only know that the thing drawing away from us remains in reality the same size but we also see in this way for a disproportionately long time. Constancy of color or light refers to the fact that what we see seems to retain its color or brightness despite changes in the color of illumination (for example, the reddish light of dusk) or in the strength of light. (According to physical light values, a piece of chalk on an overcast day should show the same color as a piece of coal in the sun.) The cooperation of these abilities allows our senses to perceive the flux of stimuli in our surroundings as real objects. The ways in which perception draws on the laws of constancy and interprets the fluctuating array of stimuli in the world may in fact coincide with reality in which there often are real, constant objects. Therefore, Metzger has a good reason for his repeated emphasis on the objectivity of the form process.

Lorenz realized that there is a system that runs counter to that of perception of form—the "quality of the complex" *(Komplexqualität)*. This means that behavior is bound to a visible complex of conditions such that a change in any one of the conditions disturbs the entire complex. The biological reason for this arrangement doubtlessly lies in the fact that *one* sequence of behavior is linked to one and the same complex of data, which as a rule does not change. The great degree to which the behavior even of higher animals is bound to the qualities of a complex in the environment is illustrated by the following observation of Lorenz: "During the first lesson I gave to a young female dog in lying down, she tended to see the total situation as triggering the trained behavior. In this situation, apart from the stimulus of the command word, an indefinite number of stimuli data of a determining quality were involved which initially could not be disregarded without destroying the releasing quality of the training situation. The first lesson took place on a level, narrow pass leading uphill and in the company of an acquaintance who, by chance, stood behind the dog during its first attempts. I let the leash hang on the dog's collar. The training went well in the described situation but fell apart when any one of the above-mentioned details were changed. For example, the dog leapt up and came towards me when I (1) removed myself from the path; (2) when the path took a sharp turn so that the dog's nose was no longer pointing straight at me; (3) when my acquaintance no longer stood behind the dog; (4) when I removed the leash; and (5) when we turned around and repeated the experiment going down the mountain."[10]

From this example it is apparent that the binding of behavior to the qualities of a complex is *acquired* and can no longer be distinguished from habit formation. In the wild, away from training situations, such an arrangement makes sense if there are stationary structures of data in the organism's surroundings to the totality of which a behavior sequence can be tied. Thus, behavior is bound to what remains the same or regularly reappears—in other words, to the *probable*. Lorenz points out how the uncommonly sensitive responses of many animals to slight changes in their familar habitats explains their fine ability to avoid traps—an ability we usually interpret as cleverness. The qualities of a complex are not transposable, but rather strictly individual; the perception of form, however, as we saw earlier, allows visual generalization because of the transposability of form.

We have not yet completely exhausted the perceptual capabilities of animals. It is crucial to any learning process, and to any training, as well as to the more important exercise of self-discipline, that certain elements be isolated from the total qualities in a complex as *forms*, against which the rest then recede to build the *background*. The dog's training, for example, progressed as follows: Initially, it is the situation as a whole that triggers the behavior; later one single precise feature—a word, a gesture—is singled out and the animal then orients itself by this one feature, disregarding the background. Thus, because of the transposability of form, the same behavior can take place in other situations with different backgrounds. This process may occur spontaneously. One study, for example, revealed that, from the situation as a whole, sea lions single out, as a releasing signal, the cap of their attendant or their feeding pail.

The mechanism just described should be understood as a process of relief: the quality of the complex recedes to form the background, and consequently random changes which previously could have disturbed the behavior no longer affect it; thereby, an individual form is singled out as the "signal." When the signal appears, the response follows quickly in anticipation of what usually comes next. At the signal of the attendant's cap, the sea lions leap in the water to receive their fish. The "background" may vary at will, but it will not affect the behavior. What is apparently involved here is a mechanism that allows the animal to orient itself to the if-then sequence in the external world, disregarding any changes in the details of the situation as a whole. This mechanism has also been designated a "conditioned reflex" (with great overestimation of the implications of the concept). The well-known experiments with rats in mazes have shown that these animals do not navigate the maze by learning the details of the paths. Instead, the general direction of the goal is first determined from the confusing overall situation and, based on this orientation, certain corridors are accorded a specific vector, so to speak, while others recede into the role of "background." Guillaume determined this in his analyses of the experiments of Warden, Dashiell, and others.[11]

This is a fitting opportunity to remark that the attempts of the behaviorist school (by Shaffer, for example[12] to explain all human behavior as conditioned reflexes is reminiscent of the similarly exaggerated claims of associational psychology in Hume's time. Bertrand Russell made the following astute comment about Watson's claim that the principle of the conditioned reflex could account for everything: "Until he has explained why the word 'pepper' does not make you sneeze, his system must be regarded as uncompleted."[13] In fact, it cannot even account for very basic facts: the idea that all the abilities of the central nervous system exhaust themselves in responding to external stimulation is contradicted by the fact that "dammed-up" instinctive responses place an organism in a state of unrest and "drive" it to search actively for the situation that will provide gratification. Here, the stimulus is of an internal origin, as from hormones.[14]

To return to the topic of perception, one must then assume that for higher animals the visual forms possess a "visual absoluteness" when they set themselves off from the background in the manner described. This applies not only to the feature of precision and stability or constancy against a fluctuating background but also to the paradoxical fact, studied by Gestalt theorists, of the apparent disregard of the relative nature of all properties. Considered objectively, all perceivable data are definitely relative: all colors are relative in terms of light; size is relative depending on the standard of measurement (usually, one's own size), and this holds true for all other qualities as well, such as above, below, fast, slow, loud, soft, and so forth. On the other hand, to our eyes, these qualities appear absolute; any relationship of size, distance, brightness, and so on appears to be the result of the size, distance, brightness that each object possesses *for itself*. The color of a thing is apparently part of the thing itself; it is not experienced as being relative to light, which in reality is the case. The *system of reference*, (the background of a form, the light of day for the colors, and so forth) is inconspicuous to our eyes, while the qualities that are actually relative, stand on their own and are absolute.[15]

The average, the moderate, and, again the probable have the tendency to function as the zero level in the system of reference. The brightness of daylight is the standard by which we measure bright and dim lighting; a moderate degree of diligence or propriety is the basis from which deviations in both directions appear as absolutes. Similarly, if one has become accustomed to a monotonous noise, then it becomes the zero level for external noises so that a sudden silence becomes the absolute. Thus, against an indifferent and variable background, the form stands out not only as constant and precise, but also as absolute. The background is a special case in the system of reference.

Finally, animals possess an even more sophisticated ability: they can respond to *individual* organisms or individual familiar objects. When a young mallard instinctively responds to the call of its mother, this is an instinctive reaction to an acoustic releasing stimulus. It learns in the space of one day to recognize its mother from among other calling ducks—a feat that represents the embodiment of the qualities of the complex *in a thing* integrated with its form. For example, one can represent a human face with a few strokes, as Wilhelm Busch has done. A portraitist, on the other hand, must discover the shadows, color values, subtle moldings, and light values that taken together become a complex of qualities that determines the total individual impression, which cannot be rendered in words. Since many captive animals "know" their caretakers, one may assume that they develop this ability toward a *few* beings or things. In contrast, the apparent *objectivity* that *all* the things in man's experience possess is not part of an animal's environment; this came across clearly in the above-described failure of the chimpanzees to recognize things which they already knew.

There are other factors which contribute to this general objectivity and we will now turn to these. In our discussion thus far, we have said little about the special structure of the human perceptual world, apart from the fact that a small child's visual world does not remain chaotic for long but rather soon evidences some classification. Any consideration of the nature of human perception must begin with the specific conditions and tasks that occupy man at the earliest age. The main thrust of the following examination will be to demonstrate how man *alone* independently constructs his perceptual world.

When we open our eyes, we cannot think away the memories and traces of earlier activities from what exists in our visual world. This poses a special and most important problem: the role of action in the development of human perception will be studied in conjunction with what we already know about the structure of human action. It is worth noting that many higher animals (chickens and horses, for example) can orient themselves even in strange surroundings without being able to scan things with converging eyes and without being able to feel with their limbs.[16] It has been shown that it is easy for the animals to convince themselves of limitations to their freedom of movement purely on the basis of visual perception. When a crow was put into a nearby cage for the first time, it was completely oriented and tame because it had seen it before. However, it responded to any disturbance in the familiar qualities of the complex with fear or flight.

As is well known, the almost totally helpless newborn child must learn on its own to move, gain control of its limbs, and assimilate the resulting experiences. As we discussed earlier and will study more closely, the child's movements are designed to be communicative; they are not directly adaptive. The child must experience the world and assimilate these experiences as intelligence of movement; it must develop a complex hierarchy of dominant and subordinate abilities in order to be able to deal with future problems. For this reason, the child's movements are necessarily immature and versatile and require a long period of practice. In addition, however, the nature of the child's senses leaves it open to a barrage of impressions which he must then cope with as he develops his movements. Thus, man has to sift through a chaos of sensory stimulation if he is to develop a plasticity of motor skills. And furthermore, human senses become increasingly acute with each new sensation.

As one can see, man's task is twofold: precisely because he is "world-open," he must discover, appropriate, and work through the uncommon fullness of the world with no help from instincts. And in this task, he meets another: to make himself ready, since he is unready, to gain control of himself and develop a whole range of controlled abilities. *These problems can only be solved in conjunction with each other.*

The primitive morphology of man, which was the subject of part 1, should be seen in light of the absence of a specific, natural environment to which man is adapted. Man is compelled to transform reality through action and planning to serve his purposes; this is the principal function of action. Thus, patterns of human movement are to a great extent unadapted but yet capable of adapting—unspecialized as well as plastic. By plastic I mean that man is able to develop certain abilities through his self-initiated interaction with things, and he can then set up a flexible hierarchy of these abilities. Even when we later encounter this plasticity—for example, in human impulses—it still refers to man's self-mediated selection and development of certain abilities, the creation of an architectonic system (that is, one of flexible relationships of dominance and subordination), and the ability to adapt to almost any situation. Man's appropriation of the world is always simultaneously an appropriation of himself; his attitude toward the external world is always also an attitude toward the internal one. The problem inherent in man's constitution is also a practical problem, to be mastered in terms of the external world, as well as in terms of himself. Man does not *live,* but rather *leads* a life, as can be seen on the lowest level, in the context of movement and perception which the human being develops on his own and by means of which he orients himself in the world. We will come across this phenomenon again and again in this book, even in our discussion of language, in which man's interpretation of the world and his self-awareness are always developed in concert. We will use it to explain the otherwise puzzling structure of human impulses, at which point it will become apparent that an impulse directed toward the external world is simultaneously an attitude directed toward, and an attempt to control, the inner world. Only in this form does this impulse then figure into the creation of *institutions* in which our individual needs are intertwined with the universal practical necessities society demands.

The fundamental thesis, without which human experience remains incomprehensible on the whole, is that this experience has a *communicative character*. By this term, we understand that our sensory experience of the external world grows from our *practical* interaction with it which is *relieved* of pressing instincts and predetermined adaptations and is a type of sensorimotor "conversation" with things. The expression of this "conversation," as we shall see, is its symbol-saturated objectivity, which is part of any thing we see. Dewey, in particular, adhered to the theory that all psychical (we would say vitally psychical) processes have a communicative character.[17] Even before language is acquired, human actions have a dual nature and are unique in this sense. In psychical processes, a dialogue always takes place. Experience is not a "lonely" process, because an action directed toward a "you" forms the basic structure of all psychical processes. Any thing can assume the role of this "you," if we involve it in our experience.

There are two laws in particular that operate jointly here but that should be analyzed separately. The first is that our own movements, tactile sensations, and sounds are reexperienced; they have a dual validity which makes it possible for them to be interpreted passively as well as actively and subjectively as well as objectively. In chapter 4, we discussed the extreme sensitivity of human actions toward things as well as toward themselves. In chapters 13 and 14, we spoke of our ability to want to reproduce physical sensations and illustrated this with the example of Guernsey's child who hit his forehead repeatedly. Hence, Schopenhauer made a great discovery when he described the body as a "subject-object," as something originating simultaneously from the external and the internal world, which can conceive of itself as acting in reference to the external world and, as a part of the content of this external world, reacting to itself as if to external things.

The second law states that any "determination" of what is real is effected at the intersection of two heterogeneous senses. Roughly, this may be formulated as follows: touch and sight cooperate at close distances; sight and language cooperate at long distances. At their point of intersection, a special *detached intimacy (entfremdete Intimität)* is created which is responsible for the objectivity of the things in our world. What is to qualify as reality must fulfill two conditions: it must be established via two heterogeneous pathways and it must be reflected, even if only through language, in our ability to sense ourselves. If this is correct, then it follows that those animals that orient themselves solely by visual means can have no "objective" things in their environment, although these things may have a precise form and individual value.

Hartmann identified this law as a principle of cognitive theory and formulated it as follows: "A single attestation of an object can, taken for itself, *be* true or untrue, but, as such, it can have no criterion for its truth or untruth in itself. This only becomes possible when two attestations of the same object from different directions can be made and can be compared to each other within *one* consciousness."[18] This "Two Path Principle" *(Zwei-Wege-Prinzip),* as it could perhaps be called, apparently has a universal anthropological validity, even within each of the two "dynamic senses," touch and language, where experiences in movement and sensation constitute the two heterogeneous ways. The sequence of tactile sensations (or the self-perceived sounds of words) is correlated with the sequence of tactile movements (or sound movements) and these provide the two attestations that confirm each other as takes place in the world of the blind).

Palagyi did us the great service of stressing that experiences in movement and in sensation, especially tactile sensation, are essentially incomparable.[19] One cannot, as psychology once attempted to do, break up the active experience of one's own movements into passive sensations, and the sensations in the skin, muscles, and touch which arise when a limb is moved are *not* the movement itself experienced from within. Schopenhauer clearly expressed this same idea: he made a strict distinction between the experience of turning a willed resolve into a movement and the perception ("idea" *[Vorstellung]*) of that same movement from the external perspective. He wrote: "Every true act of his will is also at once and without exception a movement of his body. The act of will and the movement of the body... are one and the same, but they are given in entirely different ways."[20]

Palagyi rendered the communicative character of simple tactile experiences with his term "passive-active double sensations." Whenever I touch my own body with my hand, the movement is primarily experienced by the hand and, in the course of the movement, tactile sensations are produced in the touched limb (B) as well as in the touching limb (A). At first, sensation B in the passive limb monopolizes the attention, while sensation A in the active limb is drowned out, in a manner of speaking. Because the moved limb B is also movable, however, this relationship may immediately be reversed: the sensation in A can be expressed, if this limb becomes passive and is touched in an active way by limb B. In that A and B are active alternately, the double sensation separates itself out; in each case, the sensation aroused in the passive limb drowns out the other. However, this still does not fully explain this set of experiences. Because the touching limb encounters something else in the course of its movement and this something else then initiates a countermovement, active and passive sensations arise in both limbs in the exchange of the movement. So do feelings of pressure and counterpressure, of resistance and yielding, of direction, counterdirection, and change in direction. Each movement is continually in transition from action to reaction and back, and is thus continually reproduced, a process that is successive and simultaneous.

Palagyi also employs the expression "self-alienation" *(Selbstentfremdung)* in describing the experiences of interaction.[21] The structural similarity of these experiences with those described above (chapter 14) of the "life of the sound" is striking. In both cases, we may witness an "exchange of roles" whereby the experience focuses on the sensory, reexperienced result and from this point the circle then runs in reverse. The touched limb is itself movable and thus, at one point is both the object of the tactile experience and a countermovement.

In the same manner, sound movements, reexperienced by our ears, adopt the foreign sound as a stimulus and incorporate it into the self-experienced sensorimotor event. The only difference between a tactile sensation of external origin imposed onto our bodies and one caused by ourselves is that the experiences of moving our own limbs, which usually precede and lead up to the sensation, are absent. The same thing occurs when a sound, repeated by someone else, is picked up by our ears in the same way as our own sounds are without, however, the reexperience of our own articulated sounds. Therefore, a tactile sensation originating from the outside is, in a manner of speaking, only half a sensation; it is not a communicative experience, in which our own movements are involved, but only the passive reception of a sensation. A blind child learns that there are moving external things which can touch him when he feels the touched place on his body, so that the self-initiated sensation coincides with the one of external origin. Thus, the child travels on its own the path that something else must travel in order to evoke the same sensation.

The child's own behavior is transferred into the behavior of that external thing; it "takes the role of the other," exactly as the child does who repeats a sound it has heard. G. H. Mead stresses the fundamental significance of "taking the role of the other" in his philosophy of language.[22] The same applies to tactile experiences. The "exchange of roles" is fundamental to all communicative experiences.

In an isolated tactile experience or in the "life of the sound," we can witness the two-path principle in the form of a reciprocal affirmation in which movements are reflected as sensations and sensations trigger movements. To use a simple example, whenever we touch or hold in our hands an object that we see, complex processes of interaction develop. The motion of turning something in our hands has the same form as the seen rotation of the thing; our fingers, when they are turned away from view, are then part of the "back side" of the object. Finger tips moving over the object experience perceptions that are qualitatively different from those that arise when we touch ourselves; these include the wide range of the properties of the object that can be experienced through touch—its coarseness, coldness, elasticity, etc.—properties that the eye also perceives, though it uses completely different data to do so. If we cover a seen spot A with a tiny movement of our fingers, we will then see ourselves at the same place but will have a tactile sensation of the object. If the object falls from my hand, then my eye, following it, will see it land on the floor, and it can be disputed whether my movement of bending over to retrieve it retraces the "role" of the falling object or repeats the downward movement of the eye. Every movement of the fingers reveals new properties of the object; these correspond to the visible "nuances" *(Abschattungen)* merging into one another which then stimulate movements in response.

Thus, both senses continually find new points of intersection, whereby the stimulus to continue the behavior arises alternately from the object or from the continuing movement. The opposition between movable and immovable things in the external world, which is very drastic in visual perception, is duplicated in tactile sensations. Evasive objects draw back from the tactile experience by letting it end in emptiness so that only a real or imagined extension of our grasping movements can draw them in again by judging the space for the object's own movements. When immovable masses, on the other hand, are touched, the process of communication cannot become an exchange; it is cut off and in this sense is similar to what occurs when the life of a sound is cut off because the produced sound is not returned. In this case, there is only the experience of the unyielding resistance of the object, which will not give to the strongest pressure, and the tactile properties that the hand picks up as it passes over the object.

In the manner just described, we amass a wealth of nonverbal experiences about changes we can and cannot effect in the world and about the expenditures of energy and adjustments to our movements necessary to effect these changes. Things we see, on the other hand, show us at a glance the properties that they would prove to have if we handled them: their weight, hardness, softness, substance, wetness, dryness, and so forth.

In the perception of larger or distant objects, the tactile movement is replaced by the total movement of the body or of the head. Our visual impressions change radically in the course of these movements; turning the head or even closing the eyes removes what was just seen from sight. These processes are also communicative in structure, for what is involved here (as was the case in the example of the object turned in the hand) is a process of differentiation between the change in the perceptual content that *responds to* or *follows* our own movements and the change *to which* our own movements respond or that *causes* these movements to follow. In the first group belongs, for example, the increase in size and clarity of an object as we approach it. Small, distant, unclear, and immobile things gradually become larger, more defined, and moving; similarly, the overlapping between objects, the screening of one object by another, and the continuing new views of the object become visible in relation to our movements. We must first see and become accustomed to these closely related views of objects, to the new perspectives presented when objects emerge to block each other, concealing some parts while revealing others; we must then learn to overlook them.

The things we see vary greatly depending on our movements and the individual systematic representation that becomes visible in this exchange. Helmholtz contributes the following example: when we move around a table, the changes in our view of it, the "nuances," are clearly related to our movement around the table; but the image, which in each case corresponds to *one* of our successive, momentary placements, is, by nature, independent of us and "given." Hence, the law that defines the relationship among all these views—the manner in which they merge with each other in accordance with our course of movement—seems to be independent of us although it actually only becomes apparent through our movement. Duret did the best study of these important processes and gives a further instructive example: If I approach a person who is standing between me and a building and go around him, then the image of the person will change in the course of my movements in such a way that new profiles, views, and overlapping perspectives will continue to appear while others will disappear. The relationships between the perceived views change in a regular and obvious manner. From a visual perspective, this change is completely different from the simultaneously occurring visible changes in the appearance of the house behind the person, the parts of which are abruptly concealed by the person between and then uncovered again in the course of my movements.[23]

These changes in our visual world are quite distinct from those that originate from the movements of the thing itself and that cause our own movements. For example, a bird might suddenly take flight in a landscape in which I am walking and I might then follow it with my eyes. Or a distant object that I wish to reach becomes smaller, which means it is moving more quickly and I must run to get it.

It is clear that communicative experiences are involved in visual perception as well. We undertake *response movements* as a result of changes in the visual world and the responses of the things we see to our movements, which here take the place of tactile movements.

Finally, the structure of our visual world is thoroughly *symbolic* because it is developed through these communication processes. This parallelogram signifies a book because it can become part of a set of habits—that is, leafed through and read. That rectangle identifies a house because as I approach it, I experience the behavior and impressions that correspond to a house: one can enter it, etc.

The thoroughly symbolic structure of the human perceptual world thus has an extensive physiological and visual basis and does not first originate through "abstraction" or similar processes. There is a certain "automatism" in visual perception which Brunswik has likened to instinct.[24] Perception follows fixed, stereotypical individual laws in the same way that instinct, in a superficial manner, takes signs as the thing itself; furthermore, perception, as we know from optical illusions, remains essentially "unteachable." However, we should not overlook those symbolic values that are reflected in the existence of things as a result of our interaction with them; I believe that the Gestalt theory, with the aid of its "virtuoso little figure" (Pötzl's expression), has isolated the visual sector and has overburdened it with claims of what it can achieve.

We orient ourselves in the sensory world through certain minimal optical, acoustical, tactile, etc. symbols. From a biological perspective, this is highly expedient: it saves us from getting caught up in the profuse abundance of things; furthermore, the greatest possible degree of receptivity to stimuli in an organism is not the purpose of perception. Our visual perceptions give us "symbols"—of outcomes and reactions we can expect, of resistance we might encounter. With the aid of these symbols, we can initiate and regulate movements, even *before* success or failure has occurred. Here we again encounter the essential category of relief, which is of great importance to anthropology. It is clear that man needs relief from the overwhelming stimulation he experiences as an infant. It is quite puzzling that little attention has been devoted to this biologically important aspect of symbolism; certain intellectual prejudices have caused symbolism to be looked at from the point of view of "opinion" or "meaning." To my knowledge, Dewey alone suspected and investigated this phenomenon: "Ability to frame hypotheses is the means by which man is liberated from submergence in the existences that surround him and that play upon him physically and sensibly."[25]

Our sensory world is therefore symbolic: certain visual suggestions, foreshortened perspectives, frontal views, overlapping images, shadows, highlights, striking colors, or forms are *sufficient* for indicating the real mass of an object. As we have already indicated, this is biologically expedient both because relief and quick response thereby become possible, and because symbols allow us to "overlook" *(übersehen)* a situation. Only then can we achieve an overview *(Übersicht)* of even larger areas: perception, relieved of the necessity of occupation with individual masses, becomes free to be used in the pursuit of higher, more circumspect skills. Overlook has a deep double meaning here: only by overlooking countless possible perceptions can we achieve an overview of a situation. From a biological perspective, the perception of individual things and details is of only secondary importance. What is most important is the perception of *situations*, whole fields of environmental data. Language is actually the ultimate organ that breaks situations down into their individual components. Moreover, it also makes use of symbolic fields: "sentences" are the contextual fields of acoustical symbols; the person hearing a sentence only takes in acoustical samples from it, and through this process of relief is able to develop a context for forming these "samples" into a sentence.

Once language has been learned and mastered, then its words, taken as patterns of sound, are only acoustical "samples," which must suffice for us to recognize the sounds; no one fully articulates a word nor is this expected. Only a *few* of the elements in a word carry the burden of meaning; they are, so to speak, the "front sides" of the total word. In this sense, Bühler speaks of "diacritical relevance," by which he means that in every spoken word there are a number of sound markers responsible for the differentiation and comprehension of words.[26] Bühler calls these symbols "phonemes," and defines them as "the natural markers, whereby, in the flow of sounds in speech, the semantically important units in this stream of sounds are recognized and distinguished from each other."[27]

The unit of meaning, the word, confronts us as little with the entire range of its concrete properties as does the thing we see; instead, certain stressed accents are sufficient for us to differentiate words and thereby meanings. A

---

*The German word übersehen has two meaning (to survey; to fail to notice) which Gehlen obviously intends to bring across here. We translate it as "survey" or "overlook" depending on the context, but the dual meaning of this word should always be kept in mind. Übersicht has been rendered as "overview."—Trans.

subtle difference in sound can indicate a great difference in meaning while other sounds tolerate very significant differences in the preciseness of articulation. In English, for example, there are many word pairs in which the only difference is that the final consonant is voiced or unvoiced, for which reason p and b, t and d, k and g must be clearly differentiated. Corresponding to this on the motor level of speech is the impossibility of stressing *all* elements of a word in its articulation: we downplay, neglect, or slur over certain elements in order to articulate cleanly those most important for the word's meaning. As we will see, this parallel process of "motor symbolism" lies in the nature of "perfected" motor processes. To return to visual perception, we found in our study of the structure of perceived things that these are endowed with visual indications for movement. Even as they are perceived, they give indications to us of their potential value in interaction, of their weight, their general properties, their surface composition; they also suggest how they may be expediently and productively handled. Thus, they either meet or fail to meet the expectations we form through our imagined interaction; any changes in these would result as consequences of specific changes in our behavior.

The series of conditions that must be met for this to be achieved is astonishing. As long as our eye cannot overlook the images of our own movements, we naturally are not able to distinguish between the self-caused changes in images and the externally caused ones which adhere to their own laws. Furthermore, until this happens, the movement itself is not certain of its goal and not truly able to adjust when necessary. Perhaps even more difficult than this is learning to differentiate and overlook the changes in the merging images of the external world which accompany our movements and to figure out what visible external changes (for example, in the relationship of background to foreground) are brought about by the movements of individual things. After this is achieved, tactile perception involving experiences of touching oneself and other things must be developed and integrated with these other processes: in this manner, we become able to overlook the subjective aspect of a tactile sensation in the objective act of touching. Without all this, a sure direction of action based on anticipated results (an act of will) is not possible. Intermediate stages in this process include overcoming obstacles, adopting and utilizing variations in movements and results, gradually enriching our imagination of movement, and so forth.

Let us now direct our attention to the principal result of these movements—the self-developed and concentrated symbolism of objects. Relief definitely figures here: Man solves the problem posed by the overwhelming stimulation on the sensorimotor level by experiencing and manipulating things and then setting them aside and disregarding them. This point has been reached when a mere glance suffices to announce to us what things are and what we would have to do if we wished to handle them. Ultimately, the eye accomplishes this alone. In this fashion, the field of surprises of the world is reduced to a number of "overlooked" centers, or things, each of which contains a set of indications (easily discernible by sight) of ways to experience it and of its possible "response"; objects thus remain for us in a state of "undecided availability." This process makes sense only for a being who is *not oriented toward or adapted to typical environmental processes;* it is continued in language. It represents the culmination of human abilities involving the direct sensorimotor orientation and experience of the world.

The following example illustrates how it is possible to overlook phenomena, in the sense of not getting caught up in them, but allowing the eyes instead to survey entire visual fields. The shadows, highlights, and color reflections of a thing are usually not noticed; otherwise, the works of the Impressionists would not have called forth such astonishment. In general, our eyes pass over these things to take in the spatial configurations along with the circumference, depth, and relative distance. The finely graded shadows on the surface of things do not conceal their true colors, even in tinted lighting or when they themselves are colors; on the contrary, they also even indicate the topography, the forms, and distances. This is possible because of our innate, biologically based interest in the constancy of things and not solely, as is true of many animals, in their mobility.

The structure of our perception and movement is already uniquely human, even without bringing into consideration the higher intellectual skills. No animal possesses the plasticity of human movement, the sensitive nature of our movements, the cooperation between hand and eye, or the unrestricted world-openness of the human senses. The animal is stubbornly indifferent toward all possible perceptions that are not of vital importance or instinctive interest to it; it has an "environment," not a world (see part 1).

These human capabilities are thus not necessary for the animal. *It cannot achieve what man can in terms of perception and action; that is, to build up and develop movements through the process of interacting with things, thereby involving these things in his activities and progressing toward a state of familiarity with them.* This does not occur in the gratification of immediate physical needs, but rather in relieved communicative circular processes. Indeed, even the *structure* of the behavior that facilitates *objective* experience is definitely beyond animals. Though this is not "thinking" behavior, it is essentially "intelligent." The "inner intelligence," so difficult to grasp, of man's perceptual and motor skills is illustrated here.

We experience reality only by coming to terms with it on a practical level and by experiencing it through our senses, (touching and feeling what we see) and ultimately addressing it. When we do so, we initiate a third type of purely human activity. We confront the things we see with a form (a word) we have created or another means of mastering them, which allows us to draw them from one sphere into another, to manipulate them, address them, regard them, and comprehend them. In brief, we explore their ambiguity and become familiar with them. At this point, we become aware of our own abilities and their potential through our comprehension of the thing and develop them further through newer, vigorous impressions and impulses, through the great fullness of the vital realm of mental images, imagined movements, sensations, anticipated emotions, etc. We do not "possess" the things themselves, but rather we assimilate and appropriate them, integrate them into our activities wherein we touch what we see, express what we expect, "understand" what we remember and handle what is graspable.[28] *Through this process, things become for us what they in fact are; their practical objectivity is their quality of being "undecided"* whereby they indicate possible ways of handling them and making use of their properties. Even the highest animals, as can be proved, have no "objective" things around them because they lack the specific structure of human senses and movements.

Let us consider this objectivity more closely. To be exact, at the end of the development described, man finds himself within a familiar but "undecided" *(dahingestellt)* world. He has experienced and come to know things; their properties in interaction are visible to him along with indications for manipulating them, which were formed in the course of his interaction with them. However, their "disposition" remains open; when our action no longer directly involves them, they remain "potentially" available and our eye alone, glancing over them, takes them in.

The things in our world thus have the essentially human character of *acquired neutrality.* This is not the indifference toward anything that does not appeal directly to instincts, as is the case in the environments of the higher animals. In contrast, the things around us are thoroughly known and "worked through," but remain "undecided" for the most part, available for interaction at any time. This is how man masters the overwhelming barrage of impressions, this is how he obtains relief: *He actively "check-mates" the forcefulness of the world's impressions, making the world potentially available at any time,* placing it under the control and supervision of the most effortless sense, the sense of sight. Things reveal their *potential* value in interaction and their usefulness to our eyes. We move from reality to possibility. Furthermore, man develops an unerring ability to interact and control, to carry out movements with a foreknowledge of their outcomes. This ability is also available at any time. A temporary, complete shutdown of the organism in the middle of a familiar world is possible. Man can rest, whereas an animal is either occupied with immediate interests or is sleeping. When we sit quietly, a world is still visible to us in which we are completely at home, in which, at any time in any manner, we can initiate actions, confident of their results. This is what I mean by *intimacy* with the world, encompassing the three distinct aspects of familiarity, neutrality toward things, and relief. From now on, I will characterize this with the expression "the availability of things" *(Verfügbarkeit der Dinge).* We will soon see how language continues this process which determines the perceivable *objectivity* of things.

Relief manifests itself simply in the fact that *one* sense is enough to take control of the broad experiences of sight, touch, and movement. After many experiences, our "glance" alone will suffice in future to make these available to us, to allow us to use them or disregard them. Sight provides us with a wealth of symbolic experiences which we may disregard if we choose; it saves us from repeating these experiences and yet makes them available to us. We must first complete our discovery of the properties of things before we can turn to their potential application. Every system of symbols, especially language, manifests this characteristic of relief; time-consuming and difficult experiences are supplanted by ones that simply "suggest" these to us and make them available for more indirect and freer use. Seeing spares us from touching, and the word even spares us from the necessity of seeing but may also replace or represent it.

The objectivity in the world of visible things is thus, as we have seen, the result of many factors, among which, apart from the particular laws governing sight, the processes of active interaction providing relief have a special significance. Our detached awareness of our own movements and sensations is developed parallel to the singling out of "undecided" and symbol-laden things so that our self-awareness ultimately furnishes us with a visual scheme of our own bodies in their changing relationship to the visible locations of things. Along these lines, Scheler writes: "A dog may have lived for years in a garden and may have frequently visited every place in it, yet he will not be able to form an overall picture of the garden, no matter how large or small it may be, or of the arrangements of the trees and bushes independent of his own position. He has only 'environmental spaces' that vary with his movements, and he is not able to coordinate these with the garden space that is independent of the position of his own body. The reason is that he cannot objectify his own body and its movements so as to include them as variable features in his intuition of space and to reckon instinctively, as it were, with the accident of his own position as man is able to do even without science."[29]

We cannot, however, agree with the view subsequently expressed by Scheler that objectivity is ultimately a product of the mind. He writes, "The center, however, from which man performs the acts by means of which he objectifies body, psyche, and world in its spatial and temporal abundance cannot itself be part of this world."[30] In our opinion, consciousness, in which we ourselves and things appear as objects, cannot be considered separately from its substructure—the specific structure of man's sensations and movements, the "two path principle," reciprocal control and relief of the senses, the relief provided by communicative interaction and, finally, man's special morphological position, his erect posture, and so forth. Consciousness cannot, by throwing it into relief in reflection, be set against an as yet merely imagined world as mind. If one is searching for a concept that could serve as a correlate to the concept of object, then perhaps the concept of *will* would prove more productive. For one thing, with the concept of will, the distinction between real and imagined will cannot be blurred to the extent that it can be with consciousness, which can be understood without internal contradiction as imagined consciousness, that is, as self-consciousness; this is what Descartes did. In contrast, there is the great difference of reality, of decision, between real and imagined will. The sentence: *cogito me volentem ergo volo* would be totally absurd. The real objectivity of real things is a correlate of real action or will; the visual objectivity of the same things in our consciousness is a correlate of possible action or possible will and not simply of thinking or seeing. Correspondingly, the subjectivity of utopias and pipedreams is correlated to actions or will that are not possible.

In chapter 14, we saw that the motivating force we call the will finds gratification in the response of real things to the intentions of our actions: the response of things and our actions reinforce each other, regardless of whether a basic drive is involved here or not. The will is in general concerned with how the objects in our world respond to our actions and it finds its gratification therein, even if the responses were not those originally desired. At the same time, the will directs any adjustments in our movements and movement impulses when successful or unsuccessful interactions with things indicate these are necessary.

We have now arrived at a broader concept of the objectivity of things (and of our own behavior in relation to them) which can be summed up as follows: it is not simply that all objective facts are "there" on a visual level and as phenomena and that we are intimately familiar with them: they are also in a state of undecidedness and are potential motivations for actions designed to effect a specific result through them. Furthermore, they may also address other latent needs since, as we explained above, the will can and usually does serve other drives. In this last sense, objective things may prove of value to survival since they represent the potential gratification of an as yet not acute need. For example, anyone who reacts to an object by thinking "I'll take this along, I might be able to use it" is responding to the potential usefulness of the thing.

It is highly significant that an objective thing appears to us in this "intermediate" position—as something that can be changed on its own level, and thus provides the motivation for an action and result involving it (for example, when we decide to repair something). It is also presented as something that may serve to gratify another need, even if this need is not yet pressing. To this extent, all objective things have an immediate or potential value for our survival, and when the appropriate need is awakened, we cease being indifferent to them. On a deeper psychological level, this objectivity can be likened to a *tension stabilisée*. (This expression was used by Przyluski in another context; here, it designates one *category* of the structure of human impulses.)[31] This *tension stabilisée* between mutually exclusive and sometimes latently ambivalent tendencies is of great importance; for example, it explains our "inner equilibrium" toward the property of others. In terms of the world of objective things, it refers to the inner tension between a behavior that manipulates things objectively, for the sake of learning their properties (such as smashing a glass on a table—something one would normally not do) and a behavior that handles things for the sake of other interests (such as drinking from a glass). In everyday life, our behavior vacillates continually between these two poles. Underlying this tension is another between indifference (the state of undecidedness) and thing-actuality (*Dingaktualität*) of action. This system of stabilized tensions is responsible for the visual objectivity of things for, to add a final definition, this objectivity does not exist for me alone. The things in our world are not only seen, as the idealists say, but are also *objectively visible,* and they appear as given in their very phenomenon. The fact that they are seen is not registered in our immediate consciousness for which they are simply "there."

To summarize, any thing we see appears in a specific, constant form and remains undecided and readily available to us. Above and beyond this, it has a type of fruitful passivity, a readiness to respond to any contact we initiate with it. It also has potential value for man's survival, for possibly serving other needs. And it does all this in a concrete form that constitutes the symbolic substance of the indications of its visibility. The intelligence of our perception, which allows us to see, and not think, that this is a cup and that a book, thus is not based solely on the ability to express what we see in language. Its roots actually go much deeper; what we have described in this section is developed from what we perceive.

17. The Imagination of Movement and Sensation

Our examination thus far has refuted all the errors stemming from Kant that are related to the belief that the organization and formation of our perception is the work of our understanding *(Verstand)*. Much in Kant's theory is a product of his times; in particular, there is a lack of deeper awareness of the physiology of the senses, of animal psychology, and of linguistics. Indeed, these disciplines did not even exist in Kant's day. Many of man's unique achievements were consequently mistakenly attributed to his reason, with grave consequences. The senses were wrongly intellectualized and the concept of action was completely overlooked.

In our presentation, we have always been concerned with the role of action in the construction of our perceptual world and with the evidence of how our active determination and development of our own abilities goes hand-in-hand with the process of orienting ourselves in the world. It is appropriate at this point to devote some space to a consideration of Palagyi's important discovery of the imagination of movement *(Bewegungsphantasie)*.

Once sensation and movement have been clearly differentiated from each other, two initially distinct types of imagination become clear. Studies of the imagination are important for us because they allow us to gain a deeper understanding of the development of communicative actions. Because, as visual beings, our imagination is predominantly visual, it is difficult to discuss purely motor images. We will approach this issue from the perspective of abnormal cases.

In 1898, Janet described a female patient as follows: "She said, "I notice that my right arm moves all the time and stops only when I look at it." However, this was in fact not true; her right arm did not move, but she imagined that it did *(elle se figurait qu'il remuait)*."[32]

Goldstein described a patient whose actions seemed to fall into two classes: disturbed voluntary movements and relatively undisturbed habitual movements. The patient could wash and shave himself, turn on the faucet, open and close doors, ring the doorbell, etc. All these activities were successful only with real objects when practical movements were involved. He could knock at the door if he was standing immediately in front of it; however, if he was pulled back a step, his arm remained raised in the air, the movement, already begun, disintegrated. It was impossible for him to carry out the motions of knocking freely. Similarly, although he could hit a nail with a hammer, he was incapable of simply suggesting the motion of hitting the nail. When attempts were made to get him to imitate a voluntary movement by having it first performed in front of him, his movement would dissolve into partial gestures pieced together. While looking alternately at the doctor and at his hand, he would re-start each partial motion under the constant supervision of his eyes.[33]

It is, of course, difficult to say what might have caused these disturbances. However, the situation can be simply and correctly described as follows: this patient lacked the readily available, imagined "free play" of planned actions; his ability to represent and imagine movement was impaired. He could not successfully describe the form of a movement. Another similar case illustrates the same thing: A person who had suffered brain damage was asked to describe a circle on a horizontal plane. Despite various intellectual and tactile aids, he was unable to carry out this movement. He pressed his upper arms firmly to his body and then, haltingly and with great effort, managed to bring his lower arms into a right-angle position; he then made a pendulum type motion with his torso so that his lower arms swung in a horizontal plane. In this manner, he managed to describe a circle bit by bit. Here, it was a combination of intellectual movements and fragmentary gestures guided by touch and sight that sought to make up for the lack of imagination.

Jaensch recounts that a blind geometrist constructed geometric forms by using real motions to begin the lines of the figure and then using his imagination to project where and how these lines would intersect with each other—a process that is possible only through our imagination of movement. When we are considering whether or not to jump over a broad ditch, our decision will depend on the result of an imagined leap. Our imagination allows us to move any limb to any position and to imagine movements and combinations of movements without actually having to carry these out. Athletic ability appears to be based, to a great extent, on a well functioning imagination of movement, which allows the athlete to visualize the new combinations demanded by a sport. Buytendijk speaks of "virtual movements" *(virtuelle Bewegungen)* to which he assigns an important role: "In the social games of children and the sports of adults, virtual movements are essential components of the game. Without them, the so-called empathy and conviviality of the participants among themselves would not be possible. As any billiards or soccer player knows, the movements involving the game object are executed together on a virtual level."[34]

Although the two types of imagination almost always appear as blended together, we should take care to distinguish sensory images from motor ones. The integration of movement and perception—that is, the communicative structure of human behavior—is apparent in this close connection between the two types of mental images. In the area of sensory images, the uniquely human development of a tactile imagination is striking and is related to our mobile limbs. Aristotle was aware of this unique aspect of the human being: He speaks of the "imperfect" animals that possess only a sense of touch: "But how can they have imagination? Shall we say that as their movements are vague and indeterminate, so, though they have these faculties, they have them in a vague and inderminate form?" He argued that in man, the sense of touch is most highly developed. "In the other senses man is inferior to many of the animals, but in delicacy of touch he is far superior to the rest. And to this he owes his superior intelligence."[35]

The unusual range of man's tactile imagination is revealed in the delicate movements that involve minimal spurts of imagination. A skilled surgeon, operating in parts of the body that he cannot directly see, feels with the tip of his probe or scalpel. This brings up the curious phenomenon that when we use inanimate objects to feel for us, we believe we are experiencing the corresponding sensations through the point of the instruments; in addition, we imagine the tactile sensations that should follow the fine movements. If, for example, we close our eyes and aim a pointed object, such as a knife, at our forehead, we will feel quite clearly the imagined sensation which is already occurring in response to the imagined continuation of the movement. The blind have a highly developed imagination for tactile sensations and movements; on the basis of a few tactile attempts, they can reconstruct the shape and surface structure of surrounding things by projecting movements and imagining the resulting sensations. This anticipation of sensation in the course of one's own movements seems to be formed very early in life. For example, Preyer has described that an 18- or 19-week-old child will stare at his own fingers in astonishment if its attempt to grasp something is unsuccessful: "Probably, the child expected the contact and when it did not take place, was surprised by the absence of the tactile sensation."[36]

As we stated earlier, the imagination of movement is usually closely integrated with that of sensation. Palagyi claimed that it is part of our everyday experience that the movement we execute in our imagination can arouse a wide range of sensations. "When I cover the circular opening of a cup with the palm of my hand, I do not perceive the circular form of the opening through the sensation which the glass rim evokes; rather, these sensations must first arouse my imagination and call forth an imagined movement around the rim so that, based on these real sensations I can expand upon the circular form and arrive at a sensation of the entire form. Or, again, if we imagine putting a lemon slice into our mouths, then, as usually happens when someone else does this before our eyes, this imagined movement can call forth such a realistic taste sensation of sourness that the induced sensation seems almost to equal the real one."

These examples should be sufficient for my purposes. For our movements to become perfected, they must become directed and precise; we must be able to use them at will and control them completely. At the same time, they must incorporate expectations of sensation and results along with a range of equally possible variations in the intended use of the movement, a certain amount of "free play." Thus, the product of this process by which movements are perfected is twofold: the efficiently executed movement itself and the free play of equally possible imagined movements. Any movement we perfect, if it does not become automatic, is carried out in an aura of expectations; it is enveloped in images of its execution and the expected result. These images of the course of the movement and the changes it will effect in our surroundings sometimes function as the controlling and initially activated part of the entire process. If we simply approach a highly sensitive scale with our hand, we can "see" its response. At this point, the movement can then be carried out or interrupted.

The *anticipated response behavior* of things is doubtlessly the vital nerve of every purposeful action. Hume's claim, often repeated, that perception can only provide us with the consequence (the *post hoc*) and not the "because" (the *propter hoc*), is not true. Perception can embrace true causality, especially when the unexpected occurs simultaneously in two entities in time and space (for example, a door slams shut and a light goes out simultaneously) or, even more so, if thereby one property smoothly passes through both entities (for example, ink is poured into water which then darkens).

Causality, however, is certainly nothing more than the condition of finality. Hartmann has argued that in a world not causally determined, man's ability to set goals for himself would be an impossibility.[37] Without our *anticipation* of an outcome—the imagined response movements of things to our imagined actions—causal experiences would never prompt us to effect intentional changes in a situation. The relationship of the potential properties of a thing to the *virtual* intentions of our behavior is visibly manifested in these properties as their "suitability" to serve our purposes (such as "something" to use for ladling water or for hammering in a nail).

The concept of this special class of mental motor images, or "virtual" movements, which was first developed by Palagyi, is of great theoretical significance. For one thing, it allows us to define the imagination as a fundamental phenomenon that defies further analysis, as our ability to transfer either ourselves alone—or ourselves and those things with which we form a "communicative system"—into new situations, different from those we occupy in reality. By changing our position in our minds, we can continue our real behavior in the present as the next most likely behavior. Palagyi writes: "It is an unparalleled wonder that life, without moving from the place it occupies, can nonetheless behave in such a way as if it had escaped to another point in space or time."[38] The only explanation for this ability I can see is that it is one of the requirements for man's survival as a world-open being who must change the present to serve his needs.

The tremendous importance of the imagination should now be much clearer. It is the truly communicative power which integrates sensory and motor skills. We will continue to see it at work, especially in the development of language. Above all, it joins together our different senses: in the blind, movements of the limbs are accompanied only by expectations of tactile sensations; in the sighted, these are also accompanied by images of the results of movements. Because our visual perception of things is developed primarily through our movements and our manipulations of things, it also involves expectations of tactile sensations. Investing things we see with symbols of tactile sensations must ultimately be attributed to our imagination. Mead argues this point in his discussion of "imagery," which he understands as the "filling out" of perceptual things with the "contents of past experience."[39] If there is any factual substance to the concept of the "reproductive synthesis of the power of imagination," from the first edition of the *Critique of Pure Reason,* then it must be this.

The discovery of autonomous mental images of movement should be further commended because it conflicts with the view that seeks to break down the experience of movement into "kinesthetic sensations." As long as the idea reigned that "problems of cognition" were the main province of perception (as if its sole purpose was to serve as a sort of preparatory school for science) it was impossible to appreciate the extraordinary processes in the sensorimotor realm. A related error was the attempt to explain all movement as "kinesthetic sensations," which meant that the movements themselves—which were only noted reflexively—were lost in the sensations that at best accompanied them. This error mars Sartre's otherwise excellent work, *L'Imaginaire*. Not only does he lose the insight into the practical significance of perception—into its function of directing action—but he also fails to acknowledge the communicative purpose of action and perception. Yet only through these does a truly *creative* behavior become possible. This creative behavior may consist of developing and utilizing our experiences with things, of forming a practical interpretation of reality, or, in a more intellectual sense, of developing new questions for things and testing our hypotheses. We test hypotheses by placing things in different situations in the course of which we take note of certain aspects and judge their behavior accordingly. Perception alone—without interaction—can only provide us with familiarity, not knowledge. For example, our knowledge about the moon has been gained from experiments with other things, the results of which do not contradict themselves when applied to the moon. The collaboration of sensory data and unconsciously "applied" Kantian categories without action would convey familiarity but not knowledge. Knowledge always involves a change in our approach to a problem; it involves a hypothesis and its *verification*. In other words, knowledge is gained through the test of whether things conform to our expectations.

This insight into the communicative character of human movements—indeed, of human behavior on the whole, including language and thought—is important in relation to the argument that all phenomena of consciousness should be understood from the perspective of or in conjunction with action. Schopenhauer, with his thesis of consciousness as the "medium of motive" (*Medium der Motive*), was the first to recognize the fundamental relationship between consciousness and behavior. Knowledge can be a phase of action: it may precede action and thus function as its motive; it may follow it and thus function as its result; it may even be a substitute for action as an independent, functionalized, and self-sufficient life form. However, it always remains closely connected to action. This is true for the highest syntheses of consciousness, the bearers of which are not so much individuals as entire societies. Religious or philosophical convictions are also motive forces which must be expressed in concrete behavior of real people; if this is not possible, they cannot be upheld.

Schopenhauer was also the first to accord action a central place in philosophy by describing it as the "world-knot" *(Weltknote)*. "Every true act of his will is also at once and without exception a movement of his body ...The act of will and the movement of the body...are one and the same, but they are given in entirely different ways."[40] It is perfectly correct that, in the execution of a real action, the actor is incapable of distinguishing between the spiritual and physical. This is the reason why when we describe direct communicative action here, we are continually compelled to model the internal and external components on each other, and, in doing so, we employ "psychophysically neutral" concepts, to use Scheler's term. In discussing the circular system involving the hands, eyes, and language—the system from which all intellectual development originates and to which it is destined to return—we can avoid the necessity of making the distinction between the physical and psychical if we consider the intelligence, the plasticity, the linguistic nature *(Sprachmässigkeit)* of the movements themselves: the manner in which our movements "converse" with things whereby each newly discovered property is eagerly seized upon and responded to with new achievements and how each interaction is etched in our image and movement memory—a memory that becomes tangible only if an improvement results in the movement's execution and outcome. The subject of these processes is in fact not so much the individual person as the situation itself—the event involving person and thing. Weizsäcker explored the problematic nature of this system affecting both subject and object, organism and environment.[41] One of the great insights Pragmatism (Dewey in particular) was responsible for was that dialogue is part of every human process and that the anticipation of means and goals, which forms the nerve of action, is not a "solitary" process, because an "action directed towards a 'you' " constitutes the basic structure of all human behavior.

18. Movement Symbolism

The most important result of the highly complex cooperation between tactile and visual perception is that visual perception assumes control of experiences formerly obtained through tactile perception. This occurs in the following way: first, our hands are relieved of the task of experiencing objects and thus become free to undertake actual work and to utilize developed experiences; second, visual perception assumes primary control of the world and of our actions and regulates these.

This extremely significant fact is, as we shall soon see, closely connected to language development. One of the specific roots of language—recognition—definitely illustrates this process, in that movements of sound articulation, executed under visual supervision, relieve other movements directed toward things.

When a child is engaged in an activity, its gaze will sometimes stray from the object it is trying to grasp with its hand to the striking sight of its own moving hand; the child may then lose sight of its goal and its hand may come to a stop in mid-air. The child is not yet able to overlook the sight of its own movement in order to stick to its original goal. Until it has mastered this, it cannot exercise fluid movements which find the shortest path to a desired goal and it cannot develop an efficient imagination of movement.

The extraordinary human characteristic of a relieved sense of sight, which is no longer caught up in secondary stimuli but is free instead to incorporate into our visual imagination the substance of our experiences in touch and movement, is thus correlated with the smooth execution of efficient movements. As we said earlier, our eyes can discern the properties of things which we originally could get to know only through touch; we can see whether they are smooth, rough, fuzzy, brittle, heavy, or light. Many experiences must be made before this is possible, of course, but ultimately a mere glance is sufficient. We can also judge with our eyes whether a tool is "useful." (Wernicke described a patient who believed he was a bird and thought that a thin branch could support his weight. These achievements are made possible by our highly developed visual imagination and are correlated with controlled, properly employed actions. Each thing offers to our eyes "specifications for movement" *(Bewegungsvorschriften)*; it suggests which ways of manipulating it are most appropriate, to what actions and for what purposes it is best suited.

Otto Storch discussed these same fundamental phenomena in his studies, independently of my efforts but happily confirming them. He argues that the sensory organs of an animal, limited in function and restricted to use in tasks posed by the specific environment, are attuned only to characteristic features that are part of their particular functional sphere. Man, on the other hand, does not suffer from this limitation; his functional sphere is broken, the sensory organs have become free for other, voluntary activity. In addition, Storch recognized that there is a special set of motor skills corresponding to man's special receptivity; Storch terms these "acquired motor skills" *(Erwerbmotorik)* as opposed to the firmly established "inherited" ones *(Erbmotorik)*. Storch writes: "Man is involved daily, from morning to evening, with objects of his own creation and the manipulations which they require are incredibly varied. None of these skills is 'innate'; all are learned, acquired by man himself."[42] What we have been referring to as "communicative movements," Storch terms "acquired motor skills." He is in complete agreement with the view presented here when he writes: "the acquired motor skills extend far into the anthropic sector, they represent the prerequisite and basis for one of the most distinctive abilities, the ability to speak." The structure our visual world ultimately presents and our "acquired motor skills" are clearly related to our upright stance and basically vertical orientation. In contrast, the perceptual axes of the higher apes shift continually as a consequence of their arboreal existence; hence, they are capable of endowing the things they see with tactile values and of comprehending the statics of individual things. Buytendijk's example of the dummy orange and the mandrils, given above, supports this claim about tactile values; it illustrates the compelling nature and powerful suggestiveness of visual perceptions and the disregard of tactile structures in apes. Köhler's experiments make it clear that apes cannot determine the static values of things. To reach objects placed high, they tried to stick boxes to the middle of the wall; when they piled up boxes, they would pull out one already in use, thereby toppling the whole structure; they were never successful in constructing stable structures with three boxes. Without a moment's reflection, they attempted to stand these boxes on their corners. Tactile symbols, which indicate the weight, static value, and consistency of objects, are conspicuously absent from the visual world of these apes; otherwise, they would not have attempted to use a long cloth as a stick. This absence is due not only to the nature of the particular sensory organs, such as the lack of sufficient tactile sensitivity in the hand, but also to the absence of the corresponding structures for *movement*.

The relief we obtain as a result of this achievement is clear. We move with complete certainty amid *overlooked* opportunities for collision: we are rarely in doubt, from a visual perspective, about the expenditures of energy necessary for a certain task. The things we see offer an extraordinary number of symbols to help guide our behavior. Once a small child can walk upright, its hands are relieved of the problem of body locomotion (the anthropoids did not even reach this phase) and can turn to familiarizing themselves with the world through touch. Once sufficient experience has been gained in coordinating sight and touch, the hands are also free of this task of conquering the perceptual world. The increased visual symbols alone are sufficient and it becomes possible to put acquired manual dexterity to use in work. Given the structure of human perception, and the logic of the functions that cooperate within it, our perception is definitely appropriate for a being who must complete the process of discovering the things in its world in order to move on to making use of them—a process primarily controlled by sight.

It is now apparent that man can develop these complex perceptual symbols only in a space he has first explored through movement. Considering the chaos of conflicting impulses a child experiences in the first months of life, it is clear that the development of perfected and fluid movements is closely tied to the experience of the perceptual world. There is another aspect of this issue, however, which deserves our attention now.

A "perfected" movement is defined by certain features which come about as the result of practice. First of all, it concentrates on executing its *principal phase* while other phases become abbreviated and automatic. A complicated sequence of movements at first demands great effort and concentration because it has many weak points where it could be disturbed. It is not yet secure because the chaos of conflicting impulses for movement has not yet been overcome. A movement becomes perfect and usable only after the working out of certain crucial points on which the whole movement depends and on which the consciousness of the movement concentrates. This "fruitful element" *(fruchtbare Moment)* of the movement carries and represents the entire movement; once it is executed, the entire movement runs its course.

To this extent, we can justifiably speak of a *symbolic structure of movement* which runs parallel to that of perception: just as our wide-ranging vision concentrates on a few productive or fruitful images so does a perfected movement concentrate on the development of productive principal and linking phases of the movement. My meaning becomes clear when we observe the practice of complex movements, in sports, for example: at first, a novice skier or rider has great difficulty in concentrating on holding together the unfamiliar movement combinations which continually threaten to disintegrate. The movements are linked together piece by piece and carefully coordinated under continual control, in the process of which the limbs not directly involved in the movement always revert to their now inexpedient habits. The perfected movement focuses only on the "crucial points" *(Knotenpunkte)* and allows the in-between phases to run their course automatically. The success of a difficult movement combination requires that the proper crucial points be precisely worked through, because it is on these that the aspects of the movements automatically depend; they represent the whole movement. When unnatural movements (such as pole vaulting) involving the coordination of these crucial elements must be learned, this process must take place before it becomes possible to overlook the movement. Another example can be found in handwriting. When writing, our hand focuses only on certain pivotal points in each word. The same holds true in speech: certain sounds which represent the whole word are concentrated on and carefully articulated while others are slurred over.

Perfected movements are therefore symbolic movements in a sense because certain crucial elements that represent the entire sequence of movement* are perfected while the intermediate phases become automatic or are slurred over. This, as I see it, is an extraordinarily important development, which runs parallel to another—the development of the imagination of movement. The imagination of movement is, in a manner of speaking, the product of the process of abbreviation that a movement goes through before it is perfected, before it can consist of the elegant minimal emphases of the mastered movement. The undirected, disjointed, conflicting movements of the infant mask a wealth of possibilities for movement which is realized only once the movements have become experienced and been reduced to focusing on the productive minimum. Our imagination of movement is the aura surrounding relieved and perfected execution of movement; it makes it possible to an-

---

*"Une phase très petite du mouvement (par exemple, une très légère contraction musculaire) peut suffire à réprésenter le mouvement entier" (Sartre, *L'Imaginaire*).

ticipate coming phases and possible variations that can be initiated at the crucial points of the movement.

The range of our imagination for movement thus definitely depends on what has already been achieved, on the store of remembered movements and experiences which fosters the development of the perfected movement. The practiced movement can tolerate a certain limited breadth of variation and, beyond this, further possibilities can be projected as imagined movements. We should, of course, take care to keep in mind that imagined movements go hand in hand with imagined sensations; they produce images of the results of our movements in the world of things, and expectations for change. The symbolic structure of movement and the structure of imagination of movement are of great importance when variations in movement and changes in the point of contact are called for. We will soon examine this issue more closely.

P. Christian experimented in one of his studies with the internal intelligence of movement in the propulsion and maintenance of swinging systems; his findings are often in complete agreement with the views put forth here.[43] He claims we have essentially no idea of the incredible complexity and perfection of higher motor skills and that Nietzsche was right to assert that all perfection is unconscious and not willed. Christian points out that, with a small amount of effort, a pendulum can swing more quickly than it would for itself alone. The critical case is thereby avoided in which the system is released from the hand and a meaningful activity stops. The process must be disturbed in order to observe it and to hold the pendulum in our hands, but the additional expenditure of energy required to do so is only great enough to ensure that we can observe and control it. Similarly, in concrete motor processes, the organism determines the minimal amount of energy necessary to do the task, which also entails a sensitivity for resistance that might be felt. Any excess energy is set against the system in such a way that it is eventually absorbed by the passive energies of the system so that it remains controllable. All conditions are varied to a razor-sharp minimum. As the experimental conditions are changed, the system is stopped in each case at the point of maximal effectiveness. "In this manner, the productive crucial points are ascertained from which the whole of the process (in abbreviated form) is available."[44] The constant process of swinging "is subject to the same law from start to finish and can thus be controlled at any moment in time. It is fixed over other possibilities, it is repeatable and capable of being represented. This factor, which has positive results, creates a standard objectivity, that is, it can be represented in objective invariance.

... On this level, motor skills are themselves intelligent, that is, they need no explanation nor are they capable of providing one, but rather they are themselves the conditions for possible experience and objective explanation."[45] "The great expediency of organic processes, evidenced by the findings in each case, leads one to suspect that, with the mere existence of a perfected movement, a 'problem' has been solved to a degree of perfection that preceeds or even surpasses any conscious knowledge."[46]

The optimal solution, which can be exactly represented mathematically, is found in a precision of movement that has no need of the "planning" consciousness. Only the suspense as to whether the act will be successful and reach its mark gives evidence of the correctness of the act; this is later verified through complex mathematical calculation as an elegant solution. This suspense is the crucial element in the execution of the movement. The basis for what is right and what is wrong does not become visible but remains unobjective.

The views expressed in this chapter could not have found a more faithful confirmation than in this experiment.

19. Two Roots of Language

We can better understand the origins of language if we consider it in the context of the skills we have discussed thus far, those involving the cooperation between hand and eye. Until recently, all philosophy of language, perhaps with the exception of Noiré, has tended to approach language from the perspective of cognition, interpretation, and symbolization. Even when this was not the case, as with Bühler, "representation" was only understood as *one* of the achievements of language, along with information and communication, and although the standpoint has since been correctly broadened to embrace sociological considerations, the *motor* aspect of language is still usually overlooked. On the motor level, language is a movement like any other and can definitely be transformed into other types of movement, as the education of deafmutes has shown us.

Earlier, we discussed the first root of language, the "life of the sound." This is a communicative process whereby we become aware of our own actions. The repeated sound makes us aware of our activity and prompts us to repeat the sound; we then hear it again and it becomes a new stimulus. Humboldt writes: "The articulated sound issues from the breast to awaken in another individual an accord through aural perception."[47] The function of communication, which is later assumed almost exclusively by language, is rooted in this elemental communication. This as yet "unthinking" form of communication is manifested in a second root of language, which I will now treat and designate with the expression "openness" (offenheit). As Geiger put it: "We must assume that such a form of expression, without any purpose other than the pressure to express itself and to voice the joyful interest in what is seen, existed in the primal sound [Urlaut], the seed of all language."[48]

I concur with Geiger. The "joyful interest in what is seen" can be observed in every child as it babbles at striking impressions. This root of language (and the third root as well) originates in the context of man's encounter with the world and his mastery of it through communicative interaction, through the cooperation between hand and eye.

"Openness" is a typically human phenomenon. An animal is "closed." It never becomes free of the pressure of circumstance and it burdens the present with its needs and instincts. It is as little relieved of the world as of itself. Man, on the other hand, is exposed to an excess of stimulation toward which he remains world-open. The barrage of sensation and stimulation that man is exposed to leads one to suspect that there must be some special reason for this. This subject is the focus of the third part of this book, so I will simply state at this point that the *opening-up of oneself (Selbster-schliessung)* toward the external world is the basis for all psychic impulses. Everything that psychology, the study of personality, and so on, terms "utterance" is rooted in this fact and we will later examine it more closely in terms of its principal effects. Man's inner openness is manifested first in his freely accessible realm of ideas and second in the unique, world-open structure of our drives. Together these form the essence of what we call the "soul."

The process of opening up oneself has a clear biological connection to relief from environmental pressure and hence is tied in with the morphological constitution of an unspecialized being which we described earlier. What Geiger calls the "joyful interest in what is seen" is, to a certain extent, an excessive subjectivity, delighting in itself, which is unique to a being that has a free, unspecialized, and open excess of impulses. Such a being lacks the organic specialization which binds one-sided instincts to a few, select stimuli in the environment.

The fundamental phenomenon in all expression is thus openness—man's experience of his inner life—which is possible only when it is *simultaneously* experienced as movement. "Expression *(Ausdruck)* is a uniquely human fact and care should be taken here to distinguish between its two essential aspects: world-open, need-relieved impulses of an excessive and communicative nature and the movements these impulses give rise to—movements that are reexperienced and thereby magnify themselves, movements that are communicative. As we shall see in part 3, human impulses are structured so that they can be invested with experiences, images, and memories of gratification; they are world-open, as Novalis' expression "the inner outer world" implies. We know that animals also have intentions; they can "orient themselves" toward something. Man's intentions are world-open, however, and contain "images" of the world; thus man is aware of these as ideas.

The openness of our inner life toward the external world is "in itself" completely unknown to us. We can realize it only in that the world grows into us so that we find it within ourselves as ideas, as wishes, as interpreted needs; it can also be grasped in that all exhortations to action—wishes and intentions—appear as given to us because they contain images of their goals and substance. Thus, they can be divorced from action, they can communicate within themselves, and a "free" inner life—relieved of the necessity of action—becomes possible. Finally, we can also grasp this openness in the "excess of impulses" *(Antriebsüberschuss)*—in the evidence of a free excess of vitality which can experience itself and which is not bound to instinct or external stimuli.

The basis for this phenomenon is the following: Man's impulses are divorced from action and a "hiatus" is thereby created between the impulse and the action. Our impulses are world-open and can be oriented toward specific things in the external world because they are *not* instinctive and blindly certain of their goal. It is up to man to give vent to them; he behaves toward them in a communicative manner. The mysterious intermediate phase which we can observe in animals, in which stimuli from the environment are translated in the animals into goal-certain actions, is in man, for the most part, still world-open, invested with images, and thereby a given fact for man himself. Certain phases of this transformation process are open to the world and external influence. They are therefore conscious and to a large extent, plastic; they represent the "inner outer world." In making man's inner life world-open and thus conscious and invested with images, Nature ran the great risk that this transformation process may possibly be disturbed. This was an unavoidable risk, for the unique structure of man's inner life is biologically necessary for an acting being whose needs and impulses must arise from the conditions of their own gratification—that is, they must be shaped by the actions necessary to achieve their gratification. Man must be able to orient his impulses. This theory of expression can inevitably grasp only transitory phenomena. The true inner life, which is self-contained, no longer expresses itself. What is expressed is the "inner surface," the world-open phases of a transformation process that is not fixed and not specialized and that does not run a predetermined course. This process may be observed in a child's excessive vitality that delights in itself, before it later disappears to a great extent, beneath established habits and an unshakable structure of attitudes.

We will return later to this important issue. For the moment, though, we will concern ourselves with the child's responses in sound to the impressions streaming in upon him. Anyone who has ever observed children at this age cannot doubt that their babbling is only one of many forms of movement which include squirming, arm waving, and opening the eyes. Nonetheless, it is important and lays the groundwork for audiomotor communication with visual impressions. Because the child hears its own sounds, which automatically involves it in a communicative event, and further, because even its babbling serves to increase the sensory wealth of the world, the child comes to clearly prefer this action over others. I believe that, in face of the external stimuli, the child's self-expression automatically takes a phonetic course. The child experiences itself, enjoys its own vitality, its free and undetermined ability to orient itself and respond to stimuli, and thus prefers to unfold its inner life toward the external world through the medium of sound. I intend to show how the special place of language is determined and becomes "concrete" from several sources, all of which have to do with the function of sound. This system predominates because of the great number of abilities and achievements it makes possible.

As long as language was viewed from the perspective of thought as a *unified* achievement, the perplexing wealth of its power caused it to be considered a wondrous thing, a gift of God, as Haman, indeed, saw it.

20. Recognition: The Third Root of Language

The third root of language arises directly from the second root, from the child's expressive vocalizations, and cannot really be considered separately from it. This is the sound movement that indicates recognition.

Animals are able to recognize, although we can only infer this from their behavior. When an animal finds itself in a situation it has been in before, and its reactions are consequently more "expedient" and "smoother," when it chooses a short-cut, or when its reactions become more defined in the sense that repeated occurrences of the same impression evoke the same specific behavior, we claim the animal has experienced this before and recognizes the situation and its components. We can therefore ascribe recognition to animals only when their motor behavior allows us to conclude that repeated experiences are involved; in animals, recognition is simply a *phase* in the execution of a movement.

This recognition phase of a movement can be clearly observed in young children. Preyer recounts that a child he was observing stared at bottles and infant cereal boxes without making a sound but asked for them by opening its eyes wide and stretching out its arms. In another example, an 18-month-old child had been away from home for six weeks. When, shortly after its return, the mother placed the child on its changing table, it immediately reached for a picture on the wall to play with, just as it had done before the trip. Here, total situations are responded to in old ways such that, as with animals, recognition and action become indistinguishable from each other. Specific response movements are developed for each specific impression. Memory is then awakened at the initiation of the movement and forms expectations. It is a basic characteristic of our imagination that memories are aroused when movements are initiated and then come to anticipate the action as expectations. Recognition has a brief initial mechanical phase: the swift, automatic coordination of an impression with the initiation of movement; this is itself the embodiment and product of earlier experiences and communications. There is also a richer, animated phase: the appropriate memories respond to the impression and action focuses exclusively on what has been recognized, incorporating it in some fashion into our activity and thereby dispensing with it.

It is this entire process that first constitutes recognition and leads to the automatic response to impressions in movement.

In man, as well, recognition basically remains in these motor pathways. It should be readily apparent, however, that the reaction no longer involves the *entire* body but is instead controlled by sound movements. This highly significant, uniquely human experience of *relief* merits closer examination.

We have discussed the relief a child acquires by responding to its sensory impressions in sound. Jespersen disagrees with the view that a child's first utterances are only expressions of its desires and demands. He claims that a child can overtly demonstrate joy at seeing a hat, toy, etc.[49] This is the "joyful interest in what is seen," the openness to the world delighting in itself, which we mentioned above.

Among these movements of response, sounds are clearly preferred because they provide so much more than other movements. On the one hand, they fulfill a clear communicative function, as we saw in our discussion of the "life of the sound." We hear the sounds we make and thereby increase the sensory richness of the world; better than any other means, sounds facilitate the communicative experience of the child's vitality or its detached self-awareness. Furthermore, this action alone can clearly bring results, as when a child calls out or cries and is immediately attended to. Sound movements are thus on the whole the most successful and satisfying of movements; it has been proven that a child masters the imitation of a heard sound more readily than any other skills. Sound movements are the most intelligent, the richest, most gratifying, most successful of movements because, within them, a whole series of skills is consolidated. This system operates in the recognition response, in which the entire body no longer responds to impressions, but rather, to an ever greater degree, sound movements alone.

Although the rule still holds that recognition is also expressed in motor pathways, it comes increasingly to be conveyed through that movement that outweighs all others in terms of its communicative ability, self-awareness, and emotional gratification. At this point, we cannot yet say this is a truly intellectual process. Involved here are phonetic responses to something that is recognized; these become specialized and more defined within distinct, initially very narrow boundaries. For instance, certain sounds are consistently used to respond to certain typical situations or events. Vocalizing in response to pleasurable or painful events is in no sense merely the expression of emotion or the giving of a "name," but rather is a specific response of recognition.

Let us consider the consequences of this. Once a child has begun to respond in this way, then in time all other methods of responding to an impression, of incorporating it into our habits of movement, of developing expectations based on it, become superfluous. There is one very remarkable feature of language: the relief it provides is based on the fact that naming alone becomes a means of coping with sensory impressions. By naming something we can dispense with it; this requires only a minimum of effort on our part. When recognition is no longer necessarily manifested in the adoption of a "better" course for action but is instead expressed in sound movements, language has provided us with relief. All theoretical behavior, which later augments language, is rooted in this relief; it would be impossible without it. *In language, an activity is possible which changes nothing in the factual world.*

This is the basis for all "theory."

I believe this approach, though uncommon, is very important. I have encountered it only once before, in the work of A.A. Grünbaum. Grunbaum identifies a "discharge" *(Erledigung)* or "release" *(Entledigung)* function in language. "In individual development, language soon takes over the role of the primitive explosive 'common movements' of the body, which in a small child clearly serve the function of discharging motor energy. Initially, these motor outbursts play the dominant role in the child's development; later, the irresistible urge to speak in a more or less articulated fashion arises, and the explosive amorphous movements of the body accordingly diminish."[50] Even though Grünbaum is primarily arguing here that energy for experiencing the world is channeled into language development, he recognizes that language relieves motor skills: we can respond to things in sound and so no longer need to engage in action. This has great importance for all higher behavior, in which action is directed toward a specific goal after thought has first assessed the situation and anticipated the outcome. When relief from the pressures of the immediate situation is obtained by mastering it verbally and restraining action, it becomes possible to initiate actions independently of the actual situation, based purely on "imagined" situations represented through language.

This situation will no longer seem so strange if we consider that on the whole the function of language is to facilitate relief and control. Even the development of our imagination involves motor functions. Children enact their imaginary games "with their entire bodies." The same holds true for human expression and communication: initially, a highly active behavior is involved; this is then increasingly relieved by language, which ultimately performs the functions of expression and communication almost alone. Language appears so mysterious to us primarily because of the great number of possible integrations which it contains. We will pursue each of these threads in turn.

I would like to argue that this sort of activity, which is open to experiencing the world and is conveyed through sound movements as well as through other means of expression, also plays a part in the recognition response: recognition becomes specialized in language. To put it briefly, impressions are addressed.

We will now go a step further and consider the origin of names. If the task of responding to perceptual impressions is assumed by the audiomotor system, then this is no longer merely an example of how a verbal response can take the place of response movements involving the entire body; it now points up a fundamental quality of language—its dual nature. The motor and sensory aspects of language are part of the same system. In language, the "long path," which normally leads from the eye to activating the limbs in response to an object, has been abbreviated. A movement with a virtually immediate result responds to the impression. This creates an "association" between visual impressions and sounds.

Although I have little space here to indulge in polemics, I would like to make the point that psychology's rejection of the concept of association after it had been compromised through misuse only shows how little methodologically sound progress is possible in this discipline. Of course associations do not "form themselves." They do exist, however. The creation of associations is facilitated by motor functions. In this sense, the concept of association is fitting; the association between visual impressions and sound is actively achieved through the movement in which recognition occurs. Hence, the word originates through the speech-motor connection between the sensory organs, the eye and ear.

We define intention as the orientation of oneself toward external impressions. When this intention is expressed in language, as is the case here, we have the vital basis for thought. Thought is initially indistinguishable from speech: it is the intention directed toward a thing expressed through sound. Any intention, even in animals, is guided by signs which symbolize something. The unique feature of an intention expressed through language is that here the symbol—the sound—is a self-created one, and, further, the sound movement takes the place of other movements and is thus sufficient alone. Intention and execution coincide here. Once I have named a thing before me, I have usually finished with it.

Intention, as we have described it here, exists only in a community. The sound presupposes communication. When a child recognizes something it sees, addresses it, and thus responds to it, then, although it makes an association, its action is not productive because it is self-contained. Only when the child hears the same sound spoken and then imitates it, is its memory activated to become expectation; in addition, in the medium of the heard and subsequently imitated sound, the same intention can be directed toward a thing without having it directly in front of one. Through this highly significant experience that something is missing, intention—the expectation expressed through language—first becomes aware of itself. Disappointment is in fact the birth of thought.

The intention expressed in freely articulated, precise sounds in response to certain perceptions originates at the same time as the other linguistic achievements that still remain to be discussed; at the earliest, this usually occurs around the age of ten months, although initially only in isolated instances. The frequent naming of individual things that happens somewhere in the second year has the following consequences:

1. Great progress is made toward making the world "intimate," in the sense of becoming familiar with and then dispensing with or neutralizing the things in the world. Individual relief is also thereby obtained in the form of a reduction in the points of direct contact with the world which were not created through the individual's own movements; this reduction is necessary for a planning and acting being. "Check-mating" the world in this manner is the basis for all future intellectual intentions—that is, for thought.
2. A closer look at this process by which we become intimately familiar with the world reveals the following: the self-developing and increasingly more intense processes of detached self-awareness are the first step.

   The sequence of heard sound—imitated sound—reperceived sound is a communicative process that provides delight in one's own actions while also increasing the rich stock of impressions and focusing one's activity. When we involve the things we see in our activity by addressing them, they enter into the realm of our awareness of our own existence, they become part of our delight in being alive, part of our self-awareness and our feelings of satisfaction at our accomplishments. Our communication with them is then purely verbal and our openness toward them experiences itself by "determining" the wealth of phenomena.
3. Communication with others, which up to this point has taken place as the expression of pure vitality without any real content, now becomes *objective*, that is,

when possible, it can be directed toward the *same* thing. Communication with others finds a common point of intersection that lies in the external world and thereby makes all future interest public. That we can enter into a relationship with something external, that we can establish communication with others in reference to this external thing, that we can put ourselves in another's position in anticipation of such a common point of reference—these capabilities provide the basis for the development of all deeper processes of dialogue and communication.

4. How our impulses and interests are then primarily formed through the pathways of language and oriented toward the external world is the subject of a later section in this book. Our interests and impulses become self-aware and intentional; in responding to recognized things, they become diversified and can recognize themselves when they are awakened through familiar impressions. It is highly significant that, with the beginnings of language, human impulses are expressed and become self-aware in that same system which takes over the role of mastering the objective world. This is how, as Herder said, all states of the soul become analogous to language *sprachmässig*.[51]

The processes described in these pages form the vital foundation for thought. We cannot derive the special quality of "thought" from anything else; it is initially one with the intention directed toward a thing, carried in the spoken sound. The act of addressing something real as such, or the intellectual act that focuses on a thing by means of a self-created symbol, is what Herder brilliantly conceived of as the origin of language. He erred only in believing that this was the sole root of language. Herder also linked the birth of the name to recognition, which he described as "singling out one wave, arresting it . . . [collecting oneself] into a moment of wakefulness and dwelling at will on one image, [observing] it clearly and more calmly and [selecting] in it certain distinguishing marks for [oneself] so that [one] will know that this object is this and not another."[52] Herder incorrectly claimed that the first word of language is a repetition of sounds in nature. There is no proof of this. We have already seen that the passage of our sounds to the world of things is facilitated by the *universal* communicative character of all self-perceived movements in several ways. One of these is the response of recognition. To argue that language originates in the context of recognition, indeed, even (as I understand Herder) in the context of human, relieved recognition, was a truly great insight.

There is one significant difficulty in the formulation of my views on language. Man is the most complex being that ever existed. It is impossible to treat all aspects of his being at once, and we have therefore had to gloss over to a great extent such fundamental facts as the historical nature of man and in his ever-present ties to specific historical *communities* in order to bring out other equally important facts. I stressed this biological connection to community very clearly in some places, such as in the prolonged human childhood; but it should generally be assumed as the "background" to all our considerations. Such important categories for our theory as "action" and "communication" should therefore always be seen against this background even if this is not explicitly stressed in each instance.

In my investigation of the roots of language, I have had to speak abstractly as well. In the first place, I do this by speaking of "language" only in an abstract sense, and furthermore by seeking to identify the biological (in a broader sense) "mechanisms" from which language grows. I am, of course, aware that these mechanisms are always activated by external sources, just as a child's surroundings, for example, encourage and guide his language development; nonetheless, they have a function in the development of the total range of skills of human beings and each has a specific place within this system. Thus, the focus of our discussion automatically shifts to the "creative" as opposed to imitative accomplishments. For this reason, we should devote some time here to consider the ways Ammann has supplemented my theory.[53]

It is doubtlessly correct that, in numerous cases, a name is arrived at in an easy, associative manner—that is, when the name is employed by an adult in the context of pointing to the object. If one shows a child a watch and then says "ticktock," the sound, through its imitation and communication, directly receives the intention toward this object. However, all of a child's movements of interaction are communicative, sensorimotor processes, and if the elemental roots of language are viewed in this context they appear as special acts through which man also finds the word on his own with great effort and in a "random" manner, according to each individual case. This "spontaneity" appears quite clearly in the examples Ammann provides, in which the model for the sound does not originate from man at all but is instead a random environmental noise which only *takes on meaning* through its repetition, through the "life of the sound." Ammann cites Schmeiing's story in which he recounts how a small boy heard blasts from a nearby stone quarry and cried "Boom! Boom!" at each explosion. He then turned pleadingly in the direction from which they had come and said, "Please, dear Boom, come back." From then on, Boom became for him an imaginary creature who lived in the closet, ate dinner with him, etc.

This example further illustrates that the word does not always become a constant based on its validity in the community. This validity is only one of the reasons for its constancy; it may, however, be determined by an individual. In this sense, a single word is the same as what will later turn out to be a "truth," a valid statement—an invariant, a guidepost for repeated behavior in the future, a point of support amid the uncertainty and instability of existence, a "certum" to which interests and intellectual acts hold fast and by which they can orient themselves. Of course, this is further reinforced if the word is established within a community.

I would now like to turn to another aspect of these communicative movements—the development of man's inner life through these movements or the repercussions of our interaction with the things in our world on the development of our interests and needs. For the time being, we will leave the topic of language and turn to the simple, self-developing movements of interaction.

21. The Theory of Play: The Fourth Root of Language

It is a curious phenomenon that children become totally absorbed in their play and will devote themselves wholeheartedly to it every day until they are exhausted; for years, this is the basic substance of their lives. For one thing, play is not serious. Thus, only a being who enjoys a secure position in life, whose vital needs are met by external sources, can afford to engage so exclusively in such a pursuit. In addition, we have long been aware that play serves a definite biological purpose. It involves the practice and perfection of movement; thus, there is a hidden seriousness behind it. Spencer's theory of the "excess energy" that is discharged in play definitely contains an element of truth. However, it cannot be that play is mere "childish seriousness." It is far too complex and revealing for this. Since it plays such a central role in a child's life, its importance must be great indeed.

Two skills in particular are developed through play. The first is the practice of motor skills. Through play, a child discovers and develops a versatility of movement. Preyer observed a child of 40 weeks who tried to sit for brief moments without support, attempting to maintain its balance "apparently for its own amusement." Groos rightly pointed out that children obviously delight in experimenting with all types of methods of propelling themselves—limping, twisting their feet, walking on their heels, etc.[54] Of course, manual dexterity is also developed at this age in a similar fashion, always accompanied by great excitement and animation.

To understand this, we need only think of the child's situation which we have discussed earlier—its apparatus for movement—immature but with a tremendous potential—its self-awareness, the relationship between the senses and movement, and its ability to imagine movement. These abilities allow the child to communicate with itself but it must develop them on its own. It is therefore important that the problems in movement contain a certain attraction for the child and, in fact, constitute the basis of the child's enjoyment of play. The child's movements present a problem and a challenge; for it to find pleasure in its ability to overcome these problems, it must be able to perceive obstacles that exist. Each new ability that is gained and perfected consequently enriches the child's imagination for movement, thus creating in turn new prospects for movement.

The second thing a child achieves through play is familiarity with the things in its world. In its communication with the outside world, randomly encountered things become involved in a child's movements and these discoveries are then assimilated. For example: a child of 11 months repeatedly hit a plate with a spoon. The child then, by chance, touched the plate with its free hand; the noise was then muted and this different sound astonished the child. It took the spoon in its other hand, hit the plate with it, muffled the noise, and so on. Here, it is not necessary to go into the entire range of the ways we familiarize ourselves with things through play; this single example should suffice. Other examples would only further substantiate this uniquely human process: the mastery of the world through communication, which is a reciprocal process, and the self-discovery of one's own abilities.

There is a serious aspect of play. I would like to argue, however, that the *true* character of play definitely lies in its imaginative aspect, the *relieved imagined interests (entlastete Phantasieinteressen)*. Of course, imagination forms the true heart of play; if, however, we take a closer look, we will find that play involves the development and delight in "superficial," arbitrarily fluctuating interests which are relieved through play.

The play of adults also shows evidence of this. Such play almost always involves erotic, financial, or aggressive interests. My point, however, is that these interests may only become apparent under the guise of "fantastic" and thoroughly "unpractical" interests. The behavior of jumping balls on the Roulette wheel, the chance distribution of colorful cards, etc., constitute the truly recreational or stimulating aspect of play and encourage active participation in objectively meaningless, random events. The simple redistribution of money is not a satisfying game in itself but must involve ceremony, risk-taking, rules, colorful or stimulating objects, and often even special clothing. All of these make games attractive and also reveal the relieved interests that are actually behind play.

Let us examine more closely these imagined interests which are divorced from needs. Buytendijk believes it is impossible to view games as a means of satisfying particular drives or of practicing for serious tasks in life.[55] The claim that a "drive to play" exists is, of course, merely an expression that does not really explain anything. Indeed, in animals, we can see that specific instincts definitely figure into the so-called play of young animals; when predatory animals play, they use motions of capturing, biting, pouncing, ambushing, etc. Here, instincts announce themselves at an early age in a playful, that is, not real, manner.

In man, however, play is something quite different: the development, diversification, and pleasurable experience of imagined interests—that is, communicative processes that take place in the imagination. But above all, in play, we become conscious of these essentially unstable and changing interests. In general, the movements of the young, whether these be human or animal, are characteristically unstable; fixed or automatic movements are later developments. This fact accounts for the similarity between animal and human play. In humans, however, the instability is of a quite different and more profound nature. The "undetermined being" whose impulses are plastic, world-open, and open to change is able to experience himself through play; play is by its very nature unstable. Its great attraction lies in the imagined, unstable interests that man can pursue only through play. It is therefore incorrect to view the "serious" products of play (perfected movements, and the like) as its sole motivation. A child perceives the loud noise of its rattle on two levels, as movement and as sensation. It develops a drive or need (or whatever one wishes to call it) for this correlation between its movements and the sound. Whenever it sees the rattle, it has the impulse to shake it and the expectation that this action will have a certain result. When it is prompted to act, the child has exact images of the movement and sensation; in this fashion, it becomes aware of its own impulses. As Buytendijk realized, the movement must come back to the player. Of primary importance here is the fact that a definite interest in this type of interactive process is developed and becomes conscious. With this, another important quality of human impulses comes to light: they are world-open, and the pleasure in play is pleasure in the playing out of these impulses which may vary in content but are not dedicated to gratifying basic needs.

Thus, in play, we can observe man's unique world-open impulses which are oriented toward one thing or another, or better yet, are "invested" (*besetzt*) with one content or another. Kant made a brilliant statement that is relevant in this context; I will often have cause to refer to it. He wrote: "The representations of the external senses constitute the material with which the mind is occupied."[56] This process is an active one. Because of the long period of development, a child's world-open impulses do not as yet have specific directions and are therefore perceived as being excessive. Play is the form through which these impulses open themselves toward the world and experience, in their communicative vitality, the way in which many changing needs develop from them. Thus, Spencer's description of the "excessive character" of play was characteristically profound but yet too narrow. The essence of play is not, as he believed, the simple pleasure in the function of movements. Instead, it is ultimately the self-experience of the fundamental qualities of the structure of human impulses which are excessive, plastic, world-open, and communicative. For these very reasons, a certain measure of discipline is called for whenever serious tasks confront man. The best games are therefore "polyphonous" ones which involve several people and make use of a variety of movements—motions of attack, flight, pursuit, ambush, trust, etc.; these are totally inexpedient as "practice sessions" for later real-life situations because they are enjoyable only within the bounds of the arbitrary rules of the game. Pedagogy adopted the transition from play to work ("learning through play") as a method by narrowing the game interest to specific end-goals, by specifying the behavior in the sense of fostering regularity, persistence, and obedience to the rules that ultimately dictate the behavior.

George Herbert Mead convincingly argued that the act of taking the role of the other—that is, incorporating another's response into one's own behavior that is directed toward the other person—is the fundamental means through which the self learns to distinguish and confront itself and thereby develops self-awareness: "It is necessary to rational conduct that the individual should thus take an objective, impersonal attitude toward himself, that he should become an object to himself.... For he enters his own experience as a self or individual, not directly or immediately, not by becoming a subject to himself, but only in so far as he first becomes an object to himself just as other individuals are objects to him or in his experience; and he becomes an object to himself only by taking the attitudes of other individuals toward himself within a social environment or context of experience and behavior in which both he and they are involved."[57]

It is not my purpose here to expound on the great importance of this thesis, which really falls in the province of social anthropology. What interests me is its application to group play (game) and the rules of play. "In the game, then, there is a set of responses of such others so organized that the attitude of one calls out the appropriate attitudes of the other. This organization is put in the form of the rules of the game. Children take a great interest in rules. They make rules on the spot in order to help themselves out of difficulties. Part of the enjoyment of the game is to get these rules. Now, the rules are the set of responses which a particular attitude calls out. You can demand a certain response in others if you take a certain attitude."[58] The actions of the other players, which each player takes into consideration in planning his own behavior, are organized into a system, a unity, and this organization is expressed in the rules of the game, which dictate the individual's response. The organized community or social group that gives the individual such an adjustable unity of his self may be called "the generalized other."[59]

We may therefore interpret the situation as follows: One person takes on the role of another and anticipates the other's behavior in his own behavior; each member of the group has this same relationship to every other member. Thereby, a structure of "roles" is created, in which each one is reflected in the other. This structure becomes the basis for the rules of the game and dictates the behavior of each individual in any situation in such a way that the structure of roles always remains the same. Mead is justified in claiming that in this we have one of the fundamental models for common action.

Thus, rather than explaining play as disguised seriousness or attributing it to a special "drive to play," we should instead focus on the special human structures it manifests: the development of relieved interests, the unfolding of a communicative imagination with an unstable content, the incorporation of the unstable contents into our changeable interests, and finally the gradual process of narrowing down and objectifying which becomes a "rule" in a game and in the course of which the game is transformed, not so much into a serious endeavor as into a system of reciprocal obligations.

We find a similar process, which may also be considered from the same perspective, in the fourth root of language—the call.

Because of its immaturity, a child is not able to interpret its needs and wants and so these are expressed as a state of general unrest, more specifically, in mindless babbling and the like. The child's needs, which it announces in this fashion, are gratified by external sources. In addition, the sounds it produces lead it to develop an awareness of its own actions which in turn fosters the continued use of these actions. In this manner, the sounds that at first simply preceded gratification now take on the meaning of a call even when they are no longer the verbalization of an impulse but rather when the child—with the intention of finding gratification—expects to find it through the sound. The higher animals are also capable of performing a certain activity to get certain results. As we mentioned earlier, when Köhler's chimpanzees would dig up some roots by chance, they would then use their sticks to dig further with the intention of obtaining the same result. A three-month-old child can already use a loud cry to get comfort and gratification.

Here again, the dual nature of the sound is striking: because it echoes back to our ears, it is part of the external world which also provides for the gratification of needs. Through the sound, these needs become part of our awareness of the activity. The strong cry of a three-month-old child allows it to experience its own actions and its ability to control the level and use of the sound. The child thereby alleviates its discomfort; it uses the sound to interact and communicate with the external world. When the child experiences discomfort and expresses its intention of finding relief in sound, we have the call.

The call has the structure of a voluntary action; it is used to achieve a specific result. The crying, which is at first purely affective, soon becomes intentional; even in the first weeks of life a child must be trained not to overindulge this ability. We are most interested in the reciprocal effect this process has on the individual. Because human impulses are world-open, man must give them direction and substance. It is probably safe to assume that a child's physical needs first make themselves felt as a chaos of internal and external unpleasant sensations. With the call, an important step has been made toward specifying these needs: in the sound, a connection is established between certain experiences—for example, between hunger, calling, and eventual satiation. The child becomes aware to some extent of this relationship through its anticipation of gratification; the call is testimony to this and accords the child a measure of control over its experiences.

Later on, we will examine the relationship between human impulses and actions in greater detail. For now, however, I wish simply to suggest that these impulses become specific through those of our actions (including language) that are directed toward the external world. They are thereby given substance and direction. The call can function as a sort of "ground-breaking" action which provides a channel through which we become aware of our needs.

Let us consider another example: A 14-month-old child wanted a clothes hanger that it saw. It called out: "Papa," and paused when the father did not respond. Then, using all manner of gestures to underscore its desire, it cried out "That!" This example illustrates one of the playful, unstable interests we discussed earlier. Here we should take note of the way a desire is expressed through a word; in those cases in which the child already knows the name of the obect it desires, this desire has become an interpreted and conscious interest. In this manner, all our inner states become analogous to language (sprachmässig). If our impulses are not further developed, directed, or interrelated, they remain bound to the images and intentions associated with the situation in which they were first awakened. They cling to the old names under which we first became aware of them. Thus, in the elementary example of the call, we find that a need is identified and, under the guidance of the call, is oriented specfically toward gratification from external sources. In the call, the need is expressed as an action which allows us to become aware of it. We may assume that a child remembers gratification once this has occurred several times; however, these memories can become expectations only after a physical movement first opens up a pathway for them. The call does precisely this: it allows the child to make the association between its needs, the call, and gratification. Thereafter, any discomfort will not simply cause the child to break out in cries; instead, it will expect to find gratification through the sound and is therefore aware of its needs.

With these few examples, we have touched on a highly important topic that will concern us for some time to come. The orientation of desires *(Orientierung des Begehrungslebens)* is a uniquely human problem and springs from our lack of established instincts. It is a biological necessity which can be met only through language. Our impulses must be oriented, invested with images of situations and their outcomes. Our soul, or inner life, consists of the development of an inner world that is accessible. This means that our excessive impulses must be organized and given direction, whereby some must be subordinated to others. We can achieve all this only by experiencing and interpreting situations in which we are aware of our own motivations. The process of mastering the external world is simultaneously one of identifying and giving shape to an inner world. There are two prerequisites to the formation of our inner life: an excess of impulses which are only loosely related to instincts and an uninterpreted, open worldsphere to be mastered. As we come to terms with these two things in one and the same process, our inner life is formed. This is the basis for my theory; I will elaborate upon it later in this book but I must make mention of it now because it is related to the function of the call. When a call is intended to bring gratification, a need has become incorporated into a specific expectation and is then characterized as such.

The call invariably contains an element of coercion, exhortation, or command, even in its later, purely communicative form. The theoretical use of language, such as is embodied in a judgment, is a much later development and should be considered an exception. Intonation, rhythm of speech, tempo, modulation of pitch are all additional expressive elements which are retained even in the highly developed languages, where they often serve a syntactic or designatory function: a certain modulation may signify a question or, as in Chinese, the tone level might have semantic significance.

Finally, in rare cases, the call may act as a bridge to the name. Here, a transition is made from the "ground-breaking" action—from the expectation expressed in the sound—to the intention focused on the thing itself. Because it can be produced at any time, a sound is not bound to the situation in which it was first articulated or to the need it was originally designed to express. The sound then expresses only the intention and is therefore a true word. Here, again, we must assume communication through the sound. For a sound to become a name in this fashion, it must take on a certain life of its own, as occurs in the context of the "life of the sound"; it must have already been detached on occasion from its function as the expression of a need. For example, a child began to use the word *butte* to mean a roll or a cake: this was a true name and arose from the simple call or need-word *bitte* (please).

Later, this possible development becomes important from another angle when names that have been acquired in "theoretical" ways are then employed in the interests of needs. We can then develop interests and needs based on any conceivable thing we may encounter. For example, a child of 27 months frequently began a sentence with "Mama, I want . . ." and then searched about in a long pause for what it might want in order to develop a need for it.

22. Broadening the Range of Experience

In our discussion in this chapter we will see that the relationships between perception, movement, and language enter a new stage.

Even on the physiological level, perception has the tendency to organize its contents into totalities. However, opposing tendencies also exist, which attempt to break down such totalities. For example, the laws of constancy do not harmonize completely with each other on the visual level: the size constancy of an object often takes on an ideal value, which is not necessarily true for the color and form constancy of the same object.[60] Jaensch describes another type of ability to split apart visual fields (optische Aufspaltbarkeit) in his study of spatial displacement (Raumverlagerung)—that is, what occurs when we turn an object we are looking at so that right and left and above and below appear reversed.[61] He states that spatial displacement is significant because it is the first step toward dissecting and analyzing given complexes in our imagination and mind. Similarly, in his work with chimpanzees, Köhler introduced the concepts of "visual resistance" (optische Festigkeit) and "the ability to undo visual units" (Auftrennbarkeit optischer Verbände) to explain why his animals could not recognize familiar objects if these were somehow connected to other objects (such as a table positioned in the corner of a room).[62] In Metzger's recent formulation of Gestalt theory, this concept of the (relative) ability to break up perceptual data does not receive much credence; he does remark, however, that the "singling out of disengaged parts" (Aussonderung von abgesetzten Teilen) should not be confused with disintegration (Zerfall).[63]

In chapter 16, we discussed how perceptual fields are broken down into single, meaningful features (as illustrated in the example of the trained dog). These features can then be transposed to other backgrounds. We also defined the laws governing the constancy of form (which allow us to recognize a form as such despite changes in our perspective) and discussed our ability to understand different variants as being patterned on the same model. Finally, we mentioned the counterfunction of the complex, in which forms become individualized and "filled in" with a "mixture" of data. In general, these abilities explain how an animal learns: its behavior becomes bound to specific signals. In contrast, a symbol is a product of communicative behavior; it can be separated from what it actually represents and thus means something different from what it actually is. We may use the term symbolic to describe what the cooperation between hand and eye effects in perception—how it enriches what we can perceive while concentrating on certain meaningful features. For example, a shadow can indicate a rounded area or a shiny spot might indicate wetness. As we discussed earlier, in this manner we gain an overview *(Übersicht)* of fields of symbols, which not only allows us to orient ourselves quickly but also provides us with a measure of relief. It is then no longer necessary for us to become immersed in the profusion of things. To a great degree, man effects this neutralization or screening off of part of the world on his own.

Only once we have such an overview can we become aware of the inter-relationships between symbols. The symbols are always communicated to us through our movements involving the eyes, the head, the hands, or the entire body. Of course, animals are also capable of comprehending spatial relationships such as "next to," "behind," etc. However, because we do not perceive individual things so much as entire situations in an organized form (whereby symbols provide the elements for this organization), we arrive at an understanding of the relationships between symbols by breaking the situation down into its individual, sensory "accents" *(Akzente)* and their relationships to each other; we do not accomplish this by simply adding in details, one after another, as we perceive them.

Because, in our actions, we tend to group different things together under one common viewpoint, it can be assumed that perception has a symbolic structure. The specific symbol (form, color, etc.) that signifies a specific thing to us is actually "abstract," that is, it has been emphasized while any other, equally possible, related impressions are neglected. When we then encounter something else with the same feature and treat it in the same way, we have again made an abstraction, this time from any differences between the two things which we choose to treat in the same fashion. In this process of abstraction, once the symbolic perspective *(Hinsicht)* has been established, other perspectives are inhibited. When our actions are keyed only to specific perceptual accents or symbols in situations that may differ in other respects, we have broadened our range of experience; the same symbol is emphasized in a completely different context such that perception and action consider otherwise very different things from the same perspective. This perspective is first determined by the sequence of actions involving the thing. Furthermore, adopting the same behavior in two different situations opens up the unexpected possibility of drawing comparisons between them. Köhler's apes show some evidence of this important ability. In the experiments, because of the apes' specific interest in "long and transportable things," they perceived a cloth as a stick and treated it accordingly. Thus, they had acquired the visual accents "long" and "transportable" and used anything with these accents while neutralizing or overlooking other properties.

The animal therefore possesses a type of concept-formation on a practical, sensorimotor level. There is definite evidence of "abstraction" as well as an ability to disregard and generalize. As an indication of the nature of a thing, a symbol is definitely "abstract," that is, it has been emphasized at the cost of other existing, possible impressions which are overlooked. The symbol permits universality in our actions; it allows us to broaden our experience, to make use of the same symbol in the same way in entirely different and similarly neutralized contexts. I would like to propose the following scheme to represent this process: from a group of impressions c d E f g, a dominant, symbolic impression E is singled out. This may occur in a variety of ways: through the simple, compelling nature of a visual, tactile, or other impressions; through precise physiological laws that allow us to "overlook" other factors (e.g., color constancy); through a learned ability to "disregard" the accompanying impressions c d f g; through an instinctive or habitual preference for E, and so on. We can then perceive the context h i E k l, in which the accent appears again, in the same fashion, even *as* the same thing, and we can incorporate it accordingly into our actions. Furthermore, just as we can speak of sensorimotor concept formation, we can also argue that sensorimotor interpretation *(Deutung)* exists. Köhler's chimps interpreted the cloths as sticks—an obvious error. However, when they used pieces of wire for the same purpose, again, by perceiving only the features "long" and "transportable," they met with success: they had broadened their experience in the environment in a very real sense. On an abstract level, we might describe this process as follows: *A is successfully substituted for B; A is taken as B.*

When we organize the perceptual field into symbolic accents within subfields of neutralized impressions, we gain an overview *(Übersicht)* and can understand relationships between symbols on the sensorimotor level. The abstractness of the symbol allows us to broaden our actions, to have true experience, by taking A as B when identical symbolic accents permit this. For example, if I need a cup but cannot find one, then, in an emergency, I could use a vase or bowl; only the properties "round" and "hollow" are important to me in this case. The other properties do not matter. I take A as B by transferring the sensory accent, the specific emphasized property. It should be immediately clear that this process can be described from two points of view. One could say that the things we perceive unite to form certain contexts or relationships. We would then be speaking of the tendency of "stimuli" to be grouped with other stimuli and thereby become involved in actions directed toward these. However, one could also speak of a tendency in our actions to broaden themselves to include other "stimuli" or elements of a situation. These are actually just two different ways of describing the same process. A sensory impression A is "associated" with another impression B when it becomes part of an action directed toward B; or, to put this another way, the action is broadened from B to include A.

For example, if we have "associated"—because of past experiences—a particularly unpleasant impression with the name Peter, our adverse reaction has been broadened from the class of "unpleasant people" to include the class of "men named Peter." We might also say that Köhler's apes had associated "stick" with "cloth," which would mean essentially the same thing.

However, this does not yet fully describe what is happening here. Experience lies not only in considering otherwise different facts from the same perspective, or in broadening our behavior to include different things based on one specific point of view. A very important element is still missing from our discussion—expectation.

Taking B as A means that we expect the same results from B that we did from A. Without doubt, Köhler's chimpanzees expected the same results in their interaction with cloths as they were used to finding with sticks. When they tried to use cloths as sticks, we could say that, to some degree, they expected the following: "With these long, transportable objects we will be able to get those bananas." As I have shown, our mature movements possess to a very high degree images of our actions and their outcomes. When we have practical experiences of the kind in which we take A for B, we expect the same result. This expectation may be fulfilled or disappointed; only in the first case is our experience then broadened. We can now define this process more exactly as follows: on an elementary level, to gain experience means taking A as B based on certain common aspects and to expect the same from A that was true of our interaction with B.

Two things may then occur: A fulfills our expectations. We have then broadened our experience. Or A does not meet our expectations. We have then had a new, initially disappointing experience, which poses a *problem*.

Köhler's apes were not successful with the cloths. These were, of course, unsuitable because they were formless and not rigid. It is very significant, however, that at this point no *problem* arose for the apes; they simply put this experience aside. Why?

The simplest answer would be that they do not inquire as to "why" and "have no category of causality." The question of "why," which arises in us when we are faced with new, problematic experiences or disappointments, is only an intermediate phase: it ushers in a consideration of the problem. This consideration consists of developing a perspective toward the discrepant experience which allows us to account for previous experiences of another type, thus to substitute B for C. Consider the following example: A primitive native is disappointed in his expectation of how another person would behave. Let's say, for example, that this other person becomes sick. This event is a disappointing experience, a problem. The fact of the actual illness is dealt with by grouping it with already familiar experiences—those involving sorcery, evil spirits, and the like. By identifying the illness as a sign of demonic sorcery, the individual then expects that the familiar antidotes to witchcraft will help here; this expectation, however, may be disappointed as well. Then a new problem arises necessitating another change in perspective: the medicine man is powerless and therefore, according to tribal belief, must be eaten.

The basis for causality, for the question of "why," is therefore the following: an expectation is disappointed and this new experience poses a problem. The problem is solved by searching for a new perspective that will account for previous experiences as well. This perspective may demand some degree of abstraction. Perhaps, the perspective required for understanding a troublesome problem A in terms of an already familiar experience B is a very abstract one.

Underlying the concept of causality are two very different experiences. The first (which Hume studied) may be described using the formula "if-then experiences." Distinct from these are the "discrepant" experiences just discussed which suddenly interrupt the smooth course of actions and demand special consideration. Of these, Fichte said, "Only when something is judged as a random event does one inquire after the cause."[64] Thus, we see that the "law of causality" in its abstract form accomplishes two things: coincidence is abolished and all events are formulated as if-then sequences.

Apes ignore these types of experiences because of their inability to change their perspective (Unfähigkeit die Hinsicht zu wechseln). They cannot vary their point of view. In the experiments with the cloths, their instincts determined their perspective and exerted such strong pressure on them that they could not look at the situation from any other angle. Consequently, they could not cope with the resulting problems. This ability is really possible only with the acquisition of language.

To repeat an earlier point, it is clear that, as we broaden our experience in the manner we have described, we achieve a greater freedom from the immediate situation. The extent to which this occurs depends on the number and variety of perceptual symbols available to us. Being able to abstract from the new context h i k l and focus on E means that we have obtained relief from the equally pressing demands and influences of the other elements. An observer who sees the apes take cloths, otherwise used to wrap things up, and use these as tools, shoving them toward the fruit, may think this is a "creative" act: the animals seem to be behaving independently of the situation, if one is not actually aware of the limitations to this achievement. As humans, our perception is not only immeasurably richer in symbols (which are increased still further through language) but, in addition, our actions and movements have a completely different structure because they are self-developed; they contain expectations and are versatile. We have then found complete relief and can use perfected movements, divorced from need gratification, in a variety of ways within a space in which familiar things are indicated to us through symbols and remain always available. Furthermore, our perception and movement are independent from our impulses and motivations (see part 3). By virtue of this ability to change our perspective, our experiences are so removed from those of animals as to be beyond comparison.

At this point, for purposes of clarification, I would like to summarize the "patterns" of experience we have discussed thus far:

1. Conditioned reflex and learning through trial and error: this involves the appropriation of randomly occurring results and the initiation of action to achieve these results.
2. "Taking A as B": perception attends only to certain marked features or symbols and sees A as B. By treating A in the same way as B, our actions are broadened.
3. Any disappointments that may occur are unexpected new experiences and present

problems. A change in perspective is then necessary in order to group these with *other* experiences.

4. Another type of experience involves considering different objects from one *retained* perspective that was earlier selected as appropriate. This was already necessary at that stage in human history when the choice arose between wooden and stone tools (pre-Stone Age). Since abstract perspectives (such as the flammability of objects) are involved here and since it had to be possible to maintain this perspective at any time in the future—that is, independently of an immediate need or situation—this form of experience presupposes *language*.

5. A much higher and more sophisticated type of experience occurs when, in essence, *the experience becomes its own motivation*. Here, the behavior of things, judged from certain perspectives (in particular, any changes in behavior under different conditions) becomes itself the object of ordered experience. This is the *experiment*. In an experiment, certain things are studied from specific, selected viewpoints under changing conditions and any resulting patterns are examined.

The correlation between changes and the experimental conditions which are varied in a systematic manner constitutes the object of "pure" experience. An experiment cannot be performed unless specific expectations have been formed based on previous knowledge. However, beyond having one's expectations (hypotheses) confirmed or disappointed in an experiment, it is also possible that new and unexpected phenomena may surface; these are then studied without the benefit of any theoretical assumptions and in accordance with the laws of the circumstances of their manifestation. Thus we could say that an experiment is "pure theoretical praxis": perspectives and actions are set up in order to study how things behave in situations that have also been selected and artificially created. Modern natural science, with its view to thoroughness, systematically studies in experiments all processes particular to a specific area of research.

The pattern of experience that we have focused on here—taking A as B— is an important model for experience. It figures into every rational deduction (e.g., *A* is *M*, *M* is *B*, and therefore *A* is *B)* but still occurs, as we say, on the sensorimotor level. We will come across it again when we discuss the development of language, for the act of taking a word as a thing is the same type of process of equating as is using one phenomenon to interpret another (metaphor).

Depending on how we choose to describe this process of taking *A* as *B*, it may appear as interpretation, a process of equating, association, or the broadening of action. Ultimately, however, it is a process of the *imagination* in which we "take the role of the other" and form our expectations accordingly. This process is at the heart of our "association" of a word with a thing. The perspective in this case that lets us equate these two things is that of the same intention and is therefore conveyed on the motor level.

This explains why science necessarily simplifies our knowledge, but also increases it immeasurably. If I take A as B, then I have thereby simplified the diversity of experience, but if the consequences of this simplification do *not* meet with my expectations, then this constitutes *new* material for experience. The new material is then simplified in turn and added to what is already known, which then gives rise to new consequences, and so on. In physics, for example, a few laws serve to account for a great number of facts.

Animals have only a very limited ability to broaden experience because of the inferior nature of their perception, and because of the monotony and lack of versatility in their movements. As I documented above, they lack the human ability to develop sensorimotor processes on their own. Furthermore, their movements are not like our communicative movements and interactions with things—which become independent of the immediate situation, removed from the original cause, and therefore productive and open to further development. The perspectives we develop can then be applied elsewhere and carried over to other experiences as I have described. Of course, this is possible only if these actions are not prompted by instinctual urges, that is, only if they have been "relieved"; they must also be relieved of the internal pressure to achieve short-term results. Many animals can learn to remove obstacles that lie directly between them and the objects they desire: McDougall's rats learned to open the complicated latches of their cages. However, these rats disregarded any unexpected experiences beyond the immediate bounds of their instincts.

Let us assume that a child carried out the described transition from A to B and tried to use a piece of wire as a stick; because of the communicative structure of the child's actions, it will be able to benefit from its mistake. It will recognize the specific, visible properties of the wire—its pliability, rigidity, similarity in form to a stick, etc.—and will discover new aspects of the wire through this process; ultimately, it will be able to distinguish the purposes for which both wood and wire are suited from those particular to each material. An animal's experience, in contrast, is restricted because of pressure from immediate attractions or deterrants. It may be greatly refined, but it can be broadened only to a limited degree.

The act of taking *A* as *B,* of using certain stressed symbols to include new objects in old patterns of action, figures into language development.

Our movements of response become abstract when they focus only on particular aspects of things. The motor response in language takes place in precisely the same manner; we observed its origin above in the context of recognition. There, the movements of sound, in response to an impression, triggered and accounted for the entire reaction. Addressing identical symbols with the same sounds was the movement which facilitated recognition and memory and also allowed us to dispense with the original stimulus. If the same visual symbols then appear in other contexts which we can overlook (*übersehen*), the same movement, the same reaction in sound, will be broadened.

In this context, we can examine the all-purpose words children devise. For example, a child characterized all flying things with the expression "pipip"; he grouped flies, bees, and birds under the one simple perspective of things that fly, while disregarding other differences. This is how the random formation of classes or the extension of the scope of a "word" occurs. However, we are definitely not dealing here with true universal words; before this is possible, individual things must be distinguished from "several" or "many" individual things. A child of 22 months of age has as yet no real understanding of plurals. Lindner, for example, showed a child first one ribbon and then another. The (learned) response was invariably "ribbon." Another child, pointing to a door, asked: "That?" The answer was "door." It ran to a second and then a third door, each time repeating its question. It carried out a similar activity with seven chairs in the room. These children were thus involved in the process of working out the difference between singular and plural, between individual and universal words.

The following example illustrates true universal words—that is, responses in sound that have been broadened under one prevailing perspective. Jespersen described a child who divided the animal kingdom into two groups: "he" (horses, turtles, and all walking four-footed beings) and "iz" (fish, birds, flies, and anything that moved without feet). Thus, based on an isolated impression of the form of a thing, he was able to make the transition to recognizing other things.

Obviously, a duck, which can walk, swim, and fly, would contradict this classification. This contradiction would then constitute a problem. The scheme for action might then become more specialized by, for example, limiting the class "he" only to animals that walk; then, a duck-like being would require a special designation, and an *empty place* would be created for a new and specialized response. The unavoidable disappointments and failures thus provide the incentive and the source for new experiences, which must then be worked through and applied in new actions.

The processes we have studied thus far—in essence, those described in the phrase "taking *A* as *B*"—involve a direct practical process of equation, generalization, and deduction. We will now consider the human ability to *change perspective* as it is enhanced by the acquisition of language and thereby gain new insights. Here, communicative behavior simply provides the transition to a behavior with a different orientation.

23. Higher Experiences in Movement

The processes of perception and movement we will now discuss are so essentially human that to treat them without a deeper consideration of language would be of little value, especially as we may safely assume that these processes are developed only in conjunction with language, with which they are so closely integrated that analysis is difficult. I will attempt to divide the task, dealing first with certain higher forms of action alone and then turning to the corresponding process of language which originates at the same time as and influences the development of the former.

If it is true that man develops his movements and perception concurrently, then we can also describe the result of this development as follows: the world is *broadened* beyond what is merely given. The things that surround us contain highly complex visual symbols which indicate to us what is not immediately apparent. We are rarely in doubt as to the total form of a thing beyond the indications that it gives; similarly, we are sure of what we would experience and sense if we interacted with it. The rich store of symbols invites us to engage in specific actions with the things. Our imagined movement toward them is shrouded in expectations and images which would be confirmed if we were to interact with them. Thus, perception has already taught us to rely more on "ideas" than on perception itself. The more deeply and thoroughly we have mastered a field of situations, the more so do perceptions recede in favor of specific sequences of expectations that are embodied in our movements as well as in our symbolic, abbreviated views of things. Our actions respond to our imagined movements and expectations; things have been invested with prescriptions for our interaction with them and suggestions for their use. This development allows us to reduce our direct contact with the world to such an extent that complete automatization of movement can ultimately occur. We might say that our perceptions represent only "momentary views" of things; our movements then follow automatically and unconsciously. We can then vary, transpose, or change the direction of approach of our movements and actions.

Human beings alone can achieve such things because we develop our movements on our own and provide them with a broad base of imagined movements. Animals, with their fixed, innate ways of moving and adjusting movement, cannot perform such feats. A horse who crosses over its hanging reins, for example, cannot perform the simple motion of going backward.

As we saw earlier, a "perfected" movement has certain crucial points from which the movement is directed; we learn through experience that changes in the outcome of the movement as a whole depend on minor changes in the emphasis of these crucial points. For example, if we change the way we grasp something by using our imagination for movement, this may call forth a different result and our experience of movement will be thereby broadened.

It is the human ability to imagine movement and the relief this accords us that make such achievements possible; the relief takes the form of a readiness to initiate action (primarily action involving our hands in coop-eration with our eyes) which is independent of the given situation. This relief sets the stage for the next step in our development, which is the principal focus of this chapter. As the manifestations of this next stage are complex and diverse, I will draw on parallels from the realm of thought to illustrate my points:

1. We are capable of initiating a movement from any of its individual phases, and, under certain circumstances, can even begin with the final phase. By the same token, we are able to interrupt a movement at any phase.

    The parallel to this is as follows: We can begin the act of counting at any point in the numerical sequence without having to go through the entire sequence first; we can also stop at any point.

    Another example: whenever we stumble, the movement of walking must be immediately stopped; we try to avoid falling and the movement changes to the final phase of the movement of getting up. This is quite a difficult feat which all children have trouble mastering.

2. Our imagination allows us to combine an initial phase of one movement with the final phase of another—this is only one of an infinite number of possible combinations. If, for example, we decide to "amble," we must reverse the usual coordination of arm and leg movements so that the right foot and left arm no longer move together but instead the limbs on one side set the pace. This change in the normal coordination of movements has numerous parallels in thought processes.

3. By anticipating what will come, we can stop a movement at any point and undertake a new, different sequence of movements.

This point is very important; it corresponds to the possibility in counting of interrupting the numerical sequence at any point—with the number 7, for example—and then proceeding in another way of counting (for example, the sequence 1 2 3 4 5 6 7 ... 14 21 28 35). Another example: children love to change from walking to skipping, hopping on one foot, and so on. And, as a final example, the movement of reaching out to grasp something can, if the object then happens to fall, immediately become the movement of catching the falling object.

4. Every movement can be stopped at any phase which can then serve as the point of initiation for the same movement.

To draw another parallel with counting: I can count up to 7, then stop and take the 7 as 1, count again to 7, and so on.

Another example is the way we can vary at will the tempo of our stride. No animal is capable of all this.

5. Every movement can first be carried out in our imagination as a planned movement. All that we have said so far applies also to these planned or imagined movements: they may be transposed into each other, etc. Closely related to this ability to imagine movement is our ability merely to suggest movement, that is, to make the "gestures" of hitting, throwing, etc.

6. Finally, the point at which a movement is begun, the zero point in the coordinate system of the movement space in which the movement is executed, may be changed at will. A circular movement with the right hand can be carried on by one of the left foot. A movement of the right hand to the right can be continued by the left hand. There are countless possibilities of moving in counter-directions. Such displacements of the point at which movements are begun become necessary when we operate machines, for example, in driving a car.

These examples should suffice to support my argument. What I have described here is readily apparent and confirms that the structure of our movements is not that of animals' movements. When we try to explain our movements in words, we can only speak of *reflected* movements. This is because our imagination gives us the opportunity to indicate real movements symbolically or to represent them *virtually;* above all, however, it allows us to transpose these symbols or perspectives toward real or virtual (imagined) movements by, for example, retaining one perspective but allowing it to overlap with another. In this fashion, we create a space for symbolic movement in which patterns of movement overlap with each other, lead into one another, or exchange the points of initiations or even any phases of the movements themselves. These capabilities are developed not before or after, but only in conjunction with, the symbolic development of language and consciousness. Thus, it appears they all share the same biological purpose: to respond to the numerous things in our world in actions that our consciousness directs and plans.

When I say our movements are reflected, I do not mean in a metaphorical sense, but rather in a very real sense. It becomes clear how intelligent and clever our structure of movement is when we must resort to parallels from the realm of thought to describe them. It is important to note here not only that a movement is reflected but, in addition, that it has its own field of planned movements by virtue of our ability to imagine movement and interaction. We must take care, however, to distinguish this from the movement's intention, which we have described as follows: in the initial, symbolic phase of a movement, we look ahead and focus on the next phase, which gives us a "perspective" in the same way as does the name we assign to an object. A planned or simply suggested movement "intends" a real, executed one. Because one way of moving may become another, it contains not only a "perspective," but also a "change in perspective." We may alter the point of initiation for a movement in any limb. One limb may take up the movement of another. The possible combinations of movement vary depending on our perspective and we can also quickly change this perspective in the course of the movement. These sophisticated skills would not be possible without language, which shows us that language is closely tied to the human faculty for movement in that this ability can and must be able to respond to an infinite number of possible situations, not only in Nature but also those created by man himself.

Movements do not simply take place in a void; they are directed at things and used in interaction with them and in situations in which any type of activity may be broadened or interrupted. For this reason, any change in our approach or variation in the way we carry out a movement is reflected in the behavior of things. The things themselves take on *different but equally possible values* depending on the different purposes for which or the patterns of movement in which they are used. For example, depending on the situation and the intention, a stick may be used for pointing, for support, or for striking; and it will attract our attention from any of these perspectives which we may adopt toward it. If I need to hammer in a nail but cannot find a hammer, a paperweight will do almost as well. In this example, the purpose and the planned movement are already given; things are incorporated into the movement, depending on the perspective (here, their wieldiness, heaviness, etc.) we adopt toward them as a result of our particular intention. When we are out for a walk, our perspective might cause us to conceive of a fence we encounter as limiting our range of movement; however, with another type of movement, the same fence would have a different value and thus it might occur to us to view it as an obstacle and jump over it. We are well aware that children delight in games of the imagination in which they accord arbitrary roles and functions to different things which may change in the course of their games. The significance of such games lies not only in the power of illusion, which allows a child to assign any conceivable role to a piece of wood, nor only in the communicative ability to take the role of the other and act accordingly; above all, it is significant because a change in the values of objects corresponds to the possible changes in our perspective toward them. On the other hand, the more roles a thing can take on, the more indifferent it appears for any special role and thus the more objective it seems. Ultimately, each thing we experience provides us with indications of its *properties* as well as of its *suitability* for a particular purpose.

One last point: If we add to the abilities we have discussed thus far that of changing our perspective, this entire subject becomes so complex as to defy analysis. Therefore, we will stay with simple examples. When we are handling two things at once and encounter difficulties that require us to switch hands, the process involved is so complex that I believe it lies beyond the capabilities of chimpanzees. For here a change is necessitated in our perspective toward each thing which dictates how each is to be incorporated into the totality of the action. In this context, it is relevant to mention a mistake characteristic of Köhler's chimpanzees: When a stone blocked a door, they combined strengths to try to lift the door over it. I believe a child's attraction to playing with blocks is based on the variety of perspectives from which the same elements can be rearranged in new combinations; as stated earlier, our imagination allows us to change each of these perspectives as well as the point of initiation for the movement.

I do not think further examples or analyses will be useful here. The purpose of a philosophical and psychological study such as the present one can never be to reproduce exactly or exhaust the entire range of existing phenomena. However, it was necessary to go into some detail in representing the *fundamental patterns of movement and communication* in order to show that language is deeply embedded in the system of human perception and movement. In addition, it was appropriate to depict how our sensorimotor, communicative actions let us experience, work through, and become "intimately" familiar with our world at the same time as each movement finds itself in this process, is developed further, and gives rise to new opportunities for movement which are then put to use to effect changes in the meaning and even the appearance of things. Language originates from the cooperation between these abilities. It should be readily apparent that a virtually infinite development is possible when language maintains the perspectives developed through communicative processes or when it goes so far as to experiment with changing from within itself the perspective toward things. The complexity of this topic makes it necessary to rely on only the simplest schemes and the most modest examples in order to be able to discuss it at all. There is, in fact, one aspect of the process that we have only touched upon. This is the realm of human impulses, the development of which is closely integrated with the other aspects we have already discussed. Part 3 is devoted to a consideration of this issue.

24. Sound Gestures: The Fifth Root of Language

Our discussion thus far has emphasized that the aforementioned higher syntheses of movement involving a change in perspective are carried out in a reciprocal process with the acquisition of meaningful sounds and the development of language. There remains, however, one other root of language to be discussed before we can embark on a full examination of language ability. This particular root has to do with the role of a sound as part of the overall execution of movement and communicative experience. To characterize this root of language, I have decided to use the expression "sound gesture," introduced by Stenzel, although I have given it a somewhat different meaning.[65] Stenzel used the phrase to refer to "exclamations" (such as groans or sighs), thus to preverbal interjections which represent the acoustic counterpart to expressive gestures. These sound gestures can be readily observed in small children. A child of 7 months, for example, used "ada" in connection with laughter, "dada" to express defiance and resistance, always accompanied, of course, by other movements indicating agitation and resistance. To the extent that later in life all practiced movements, manipulations of things, etc., are carried out with effort and expressive involvement on our part, they have an accompaniment in sound which is essentially an expressive, motor response that has value as a part of the total situation.

If we establish that specific coordinations of movement have this expressive, motor "accompaniment" *(Begleitmusik),* then the idea suggests itself that there is a purely sensory, physiological law of form dictating that the process by which the outcomes of our actions and perception become more defined and precise proceeds concurrently with another whereby the "accompaniments" in sound also become more specific. If we assume that certain activities promote the process by which initially affective sound accompaniments become more specific, we have found the key to explaining the self-invented "words" children concoct to accompany their actions. Jespersen describes an American child who liked to push a stick back and forth across the carpet while saying "jazing" which was simply the acoustic accompaniment to his action.[66] It is in this sense that I will use the phrase "sound gesture."

Our earlier discussion should make it clear that a *word*—a word with only a situational value—may develop from this sound gesture. We have seen that complex executions of movement of a sensorimotor nature are so versatile that they may be begun from any one of their individual phases. Any phase may act as the point of initiation for the whole movement and may bear the intention of carrying out the movement. Accordingly, the sound "accompaniment" may serve the function of directing the child to a specific sequence of actions which can then be developed further. The child in fact soon comes to prefer this pattern because of the excess of results that are gained. Furthermore, it is better to express the intention to carry out an action in a sound symbol because this particular phase of the entire process is always readily available and requires no real effort. It also facilitates communication with others and creates the possibility of a common focus on the same action. The intention to carry out an action thereby becomes freely available, expressive, and public.

Noiré was really the first to recognize that the "word" could originate in this manner.[67] Next to Herder's work and Wegener's *Untersuchungen über die Grundfragen des Sprachlebens* (1885), this is one of the most important books on the origin of language. In his previously discussed critique of this book, Ammann pointed out that H. J. Chavet's concept of the *imitations d'efforts* corresponds almost exactly to our use of the term "sound gesture."[68] Noiré made the same mistake as Herder in seeking to explain all that language makes possible by one single root. Just as Herder placed great emphasis on the fact of recognition, Noiré stressed the "action sound" *(Aktionslaut)*, with the result that both theories became overburdened and unconvincing.

Noiré's theory does, however, contain a partial truth which has not been sufficiently appreciated. He argued that language originates from expressive sounds that accompanied communal activities and gradually came to signify a specific action. "The sound of language thus originated as an expression of a heightened common emotion accompanying common activity." All communal activity, Noiré theorized, is actually accompanied by song and calling; the word developed from the commonly sounded, commonly produced, and commonly understood sound: "The essential feature of this sound was that it called to mind a certain activity and was understood."[69]

Noiré speculated that primitive humans gathered together for communal tasks that had clear purposes, such as digging and weaving. The sounds that accompanied these activities then came to mean specific actions because the communal understanding was tied to these communal activities; Noiré further believed that the meanings of these "action words" were then shifted secondarily to the products of these activities and thus came to designate not the activities themselves but their results: holes, caves, netting. There are, in fact, cases in language in which the designation of an action has been shifted to the object: plant, wound, erasure, growth, depression, unification, burden, break, speech, gait.[70]

Noiré's theory contains obvious errors as well as deep insights. For example, he knows nothing about the development of movement and perception and the perspectives on the world we develop through movement. He would find it difficult to explain how his primitive people behaved before they grew up and could engage in meaningful communal work. He does, however, have an idea of the practical and communicative motor basis of language and he senses the tremendous importance of the cooperative effort of the hands, perception, and language: "Rational vision or perception is the foundation of all human knowledge. This ability is acquired through the cooperation between the forming hands and language."[71] Because his suspicions are correct, he even touches upon the relief we thereby acquire from the pressures of the immediate situation: "The hand, the grasping hand, the tool of tools, which is itself movement but which can also effect results—this is what creation has opened up for us; our personal activity is transplanted into the world of things and is there reflected as a product of our own imagination, as forms and objects in our own intellectual life, in our inner life. This power of memory, this faculty of our inner vision, simultaneously liberates man from the spell of the immediate present and grants him a standpoint beyond things."[72]

This last sentence is brilliant. Noiré's fundamental position is correct—how correct we will discover later when we discuss the retroactive effects of language on our inner life.

Anyone who has observed children knows that they possess some "words" that were never repeated to them and that designate particular actions, games, needs, and so forth. I understand these "accompaniments" to be phases of pure expression and movement that are part of a total event.

These sounds take on the role of a word when they can serve to initiate the sequence of actions. This development is highly efficient because a sound is easily available, is public, communicative (see the "life of the sound," above) and ensures success, even as a call.

There is no doubt that in this root of language above all lie the beginnings of language learning. I have no trouble explaining why a child, when some-one gives it a toy and then says "ball," will immediately acquire this word. It is not the ball, but rather the sound, interwoven into the movement of play, that is readily available to the child *at any time* so that its intention to "play," to experience all that this entails, is expressed in the sound which also involves the call, help, participation, and community.

Let us now consider the following: this sort of word is not one of those "theoretical" sounds, which a child also develops at this age and which refer to individual things and are the vehicle of recognition. These words instead clearly have a vague meaning: "dada" might mean playing with a rattle, playing in general, movement in general, or even the rattle itself. These words have an undetermined, fluid situational value and are developed or appropriated in the context of movement. One child, for example, was familiar with the particular sequence of actions and perceptions that were the prelude to going for a walk. Now, according to the laws we have described, any one of the elements in this situation could function as the "signal" that initiates the entire sequence of action: an adult points to the street outside or brings over an article of the child's clothing or the child sees the adult put on more clothing. From all this, and also from the word the adults tend to use in this situation, the child will be ready to engage in the appropriate sequence of action and will form the corresponding expec-tations. Of all these possibilities, however, the word alone is always available to the child. It can serve to get the entire sequence underway and can therefore signify situations and actions, although it may also easily be used to indicate some part of the whole and may then become the designation of a thing.

Jespersen provides a good example of this: a small boy used the word "öff" to signify the drawing of a pig. This word was a symbol: (1) of the entire process of drawing a pig, (2) of the pig itself; and (3) of drawing and writing in general. By the same token, when the child heard the sound "öff" he was stimulated to write or draw, or to draw a pig, or to expect a picture of a pig.[73]

This capability is already familiar to us from our examination of human motor skills. Here, too, we find that one individual element facilitates an overview of entire executions of movement and communicative events of a sensorimotor nature. In addition, a sequence of actions can be begun from any one of the individual phases (for example, the sound "öff"). Finally, it also demonstrates the opportunity to act or to "expect" in the same way, based on this or another symbol so that these symbols (for example, the picture of the pig and the sound "öff") consequently appear to be associated.

We have already noted that these associations are always created: they presuppose our ability to change the point of initiation of the action. A 20-month-old child used the expression "bing" to refer to the door, blocks, and building with blocks. It was the similar sound of the door slamming and the blocks toppling to the floor that created this association of meanings. Through the symbol of the crashing noise, through this one retained perspective, the word was transferred from A to B. The same process occurred in the example we mentioned earlier, in which a child used the same word to designate all flying things. In the case just mentioned, the word remains fluid and can designate a thing (the door) as well as an action; further, I expect that it probably referred also to such situations as "going out of doors and slamming them" or could easily have acquired such meanings. One might say that the word still vacillates here between being a verb and a noun. It serves to express the pure intention directed toward a thing as well as the initiation or expectation of an action. It is of great importance that a sound can refer to an entire situation. If this process of coming to terms with situations and actions did not lie at the heart of language, sentences—the joining together of individual words to form a totality which refers to a situation—would never be possible.

I would like to give one further example: a child learns to stand up and to try to walk toward its mother when it hears the words "come to me," because these words are always coupled with the expressive gesture of the mother's open arms.

Of course, for the child, these "words" have only the meaning of a movement or situation as "sound gestures." By trying to reproduce the appealing gesture of the open arms, and thus enter into a pure communication in movement with the mother, the child learns to initiate the movement with the sound that normally accompanies it in order to experience the same situation. In some ways, this resembles a type of training in which acoustic signals also trigger the initiation of a sequence of movement. However, the difference between the type of training we see in the area of animal performance and this process is quite clear: The animal is compelled to develop the habit of behaving in a certain manner at an imperative signal and its interest is always aroused in this action by means (punishment or reward) that lie outside the bounds of the achievement itself. The child, on the other hand, exists in communicative situations and it may adopt the communicative movements on its own from any of their aspects—in this case, from the sound phase. It incorporates this sound accompaniment into its awareness of self; it takes control of it and uses this symbol to intend the whole situation. When we say that a child can understand language better than it can use it, we do not mean that the child can listen better than it can speak, but only that it learns very early on to focus on the sound aspect of certain situations and to use this as the vehicle for its intention.

In our discussion of this root of language, we have above all demonstrated that the word originates in the context of action and practical communication: the relationship between experience and achievement is narrowed down to the word. One path leading to the individual word consists of breaking down the situations to be mastered. Thus, the child mentioned above used "öff" to mean the entire act of drawing a pig, but also to mean pig in general or drawing in general; there is a clear progression here. Once the meaning has been narrowed down and restricted, the other components of the whole contain "empty places" for intentions that must be filled. If "öff" means pig, then drawing must be called something else. The intention, which is expressed in an action word and directed toward a sequence of actions and perceptions, can be narrowed down to motor as well as perceptual elements; this would be puzzling if the word were not itself a sensorimotor fact.

25. Planned Actions

To recapitulate briefly the main points of our discussion, sensitive human movements are developed in the course of our interaction with the things in our world, in a manner relieved of instinct and need gratification. This fosters the development of our imagination of movement, which allows us to abbreviate movement, to change our perspective, to anticipate what will come next and orient ourselves accordingly, to coordinate movements at will, etc.—thus, to develop symbolism in the execution of a movement. Our ability to imagine movement allows us to vary our behavior even though the situation is still the same; to maintain the same behavior in different situations, and to guide or adjust our movements based on visual data or the individual phases of the movement itself. A multiplicity of spaces for movement, in which one movement can be transposed into another, is thereby created, each with its own set of expectations; this multiplicity is saturated with the great diversity of the perceptual realm in which we have invested the things we perceive with symbols indicating which actions are appropriate for these things. The development of language is firmly rooted in these processes.

Language is as much a motor event in the context of movement as it is in the perception of and response to circumstances and situations. A thing we see may serve the function of initiating a communicative interaction, as can a sound we hear; similarly, a sound can be an action just like the manipulation of an object. It can also serve to initiate an action, form the transition from one action to another, or act as the symbol for something we see. The sound can serve equally well as the vehicle for expressing an intention to initiate movements and as the intention directed toward what we perceive.

We now turn to the consideration of a special feature common to all the roots of language—the obscure concept of "consciousness."

We define a "thought" as an intention toward something which is conveyed through sound. The content of the intention itself, of the organism's focus on a "whole" which is suggested symbolically, cannot be further reduced or analyzed. It is definitely one of the vital capabilities of animals.

We learned earlier that the principal feature of a sound is that it is a sensation (it echoes back from the external world) as well as a movement which we execute. The symbol that channels our intention, our focus on a thing, has a dual nature: on the one hand, it is perceived matter, as is the thing itself; on the other, we ourselves have created it and made it available. We may therefore say that because the intention is conveyed through sound, it is conveyed through symbols we have created. This focusing on something through such a readily available symbol is called thinking; speaking and thinking are at first one and the same. It is, of course, impossible and absurd even to attempt to "derive" this special characteristic called thought from anything. However, we may say that consciousness, defined as "focusing on something" through perceptions, expectations, or mental images, may be attributed to all animals; man alone, however, can think, in the sense of focusing on something through a symbol he has created and made available to himself in the course of his interaction with the world.

The implication of this will become clearer if we consider the following: Human movements in general resemble language because they, too, are reperceived (i.e., they can be seen, felt); further, they are communicative; and finally, they are also symbolic and capable of variation. Therefore, because the sound of language originates in the context of these communicative movements, it can also represent them. The role of a sound is by no means limited to "nailing down" *(festnageln)* something we perceive and expressing our intention toward it; it can just as easily take the place of a movement, relieve it, or initiate it. We saw this above when we observed that a sound expresses recognition by taking over the movement of recognition. Thus, we may argue that, because sensation and movement come together in a sound, an intention conveyed through sound can be a valid and adequate activity. When a child is developing its ability to speak, we can observe a good example of this sort of activity in its speech: a typical, relieved self-developed activity of astonishing richness.

In our discussion, we introduced the concept of "perspective" *(Hinsicht)* to mean every symbolic behavior, every focus on or orientation toward something through something else. Every sound associated with each root of language we discussed, has—regardless of the situation it may be used in—the characteristic of being an intention, a perspective. Since every sound can be reproduced at will (because of the self-communication inherent in the sound), it allows us to retain perspectives. The consequences of this ability are great indeed, for the retention of perspectives is the ability to repeat any perspective independently of the situation and the existing circumstances.

Because language is so closely related to movement, it allows us to retain the unstable, fluid intentions of movement. As I pointed out earlier, our more sophisticated movements can be understood only in relation to language, and it was only for the purposes of our analysis that we had to consider the two separately. It has now become quite clear that directed movements—those that necessitate the retention of certain perspectives on coordinating movements—are impossible without language. The more sophisticated human movements are definitely intellectual. That is, they are executed in planned and retained patterns, independently of the pressures of the particular situation, which is necessary if they are to consist of appropriate, anticipatory actions, tailored to the specific properties of the objects they concern.

Here we have touched on the most important fact of human life: controlled and directed action. As we have seen, the prerequisites to controlled and directed action are many and varied and therefore examined here for the first time. We can identify definite types of these as follows:

1. Movement communication. We reperceive our movements and the reciprocal interaction here creates the symbols for action in what we perceive. This involves the cooperation between sight and touch as well as the developing expectations in our movements themselves and the investing of the things in our world with prescriptions for our interaction with them. What we perceive therefore acts as an impulse to motivate actions, just as the sensations and expectations of movements appear as objective facts to us.
2. The ability to vary our movements and change or shift our perspective, which is responsible for the ambiguity in our world and the great diversity of opportunities for initiating and using movement.
3. Verbal characterization of the objective world, of things, of the properties of things: how we identify properties or material values of things previously experienced only through direct interaction; our characterization of the objective results of this in sentences using conjunctions, if-then clauses, etc.

   In addition, there is the ability to retain a perspective through language and to recall it at will.

   Furthermore, it should be noted that a verb primarily designates a perspective toward movement. Such words as turn, twist, bend, stop, leave, stop short, and countless others are not names of objects (such as moon or tree); neither are they designations of the possible abstract perspectives toward things (such as red or hot); instead, they characterize certain perspectives toward movement. They are not established through perception but rather through the act of being reproduced, either in real life or in our imagination (imagination of movement). This difference is crucial for cognitive theory and contradicts any philosophy that proceeds from the simple reflected perception of an object.

4. Finally, as we will examine later, the following is achieved within language and on its own level: (a) the free and readily available combination of the interrelationships between things *(A is B; A is the means toward B; from the perspective of a, A equals B; from the perspective of a, A follows B; A contains the perspectives a b c, etc.)*; (b) the free and readily available change in planned perspectives toward movements *(a is undertaken in consideration of b; c is carried out first and then d; e and f are combined if a appears, etc.)*.

This, then, constitutes a "simple plan." From this purely symbolic anticipation in language, a new combination of motor operations can arise so that this newly created operation becomes readily available when the anticipated situation arises, the result of which has also been anticipated.

These four points are intended to delineate how each of our more sophisticated capabilities arises logically from the one that forms its basis. Our presentation shows, further, that the task of interpreting the world and initiating planned activity within it first gains complete freedom in the medium of language, which relieves us of the here and now and allows us to change our perspective on the world at will.

26. A Recapitulation of the Foundations of Language

We have now laid the groundwork for a comprehensive theory of language which will be elaborated upon in the following sections. I will continue the basic approach I have employed thus far, which treats language as part of a structure of abilities that is specific to human beings. I will now summarize these theoretical points in order to provide the foundation for my ensuing discussion.[74]

A child is extremely open to stimulation because the human perceptual world, unlike that of animals, is not limited to just a few, selected, instinctually important entities. Our nonspecialized nature makes us subject in early life to an unrestrained flood of impressions; we are faced with the task of coping with this barrage, of taking an active stance toward the world that intrudes so forcefully upon our senses. Our response to the world consists of communicative activities that allow us to experience things in our world and then set them aside. However, these activities do not directly serve to satisfy basic drives. Through such activities, we build up a store of experiences. The framework for this process is provided by sensorimotor actions, the development of which we have already discussed. Through our self-perceived, need-free movements, we actively come to terms with the contents of an unbounded, open world—a process that affects all of our senses. In describing our actions as "communicative," I am not primarily referring to their usefulness in sustaining life, but rather to the vitality of our interaction with the world, the fruitfulness of our ever-growing abilities, our facility for making the world accessible to ourselves, and to the "relief" we thereby obtain from internal and external pressures. All these are characteristic of our actions, just as in every communicative act the process of taking the role of the other first opens up to us the world of facts and the profuse abundance of things. Our actions further serve to increase this profuse abundance, by developing it and allowing it to reveal itself to us.

This last aspect of our actions is responsible for the objectivity of our world: things come into their own in the course of our need-free interaction with them.

The immaturity of the child's motor skills poses another set of problems. As we saw, this immaturity of human movements also means that they enjoy a great degree of plasticity; they are highly versatile and can be combined with one another in countless ways. The child explores and develops movements on its own; it is therefore necessary that it become aware of all the phases involved in a movement. Only through interaction with the things in the world does the child develop its movements. There are consequently two sides to this "immaturity": First, it refers to the plasticity of human movement as opposed to the monotonous and fixed patterns of movements of animals; second, it refers also to the self-perceived execution and ultimate command of movements which are achieved through interaction with the world.

Human movements seek to become self-directing and to acquire a wide range of possible coordinations. Because we can reperceive the effects and results of our movements, and because we develop an ability to imagine movements, our movements are capable of being tremendously sensitive and subtle. Ultimately, we build up a great store of experiences and become intimately familiar with all aspects of a situation so that we are able to achieve an overview. Situations are organized into centers, rich in symbols, of what we should expect, what we will perceive—centers that are readily accessible to us through our versatile, anticipatory movements. We simultaneously achieve *relief* and *control:* relief from direct perceptual suggestions and the necessity of immediate responses—relief provided by our movements, which serve to concentrate perception in symbols; at the same time, we gain control by virtue of our ability to subordinate one action to another, to coordinate actions at will, and to control them completely in sensitive, plastic movements that have been invested with images of and expectations of their outcomes.

It is really only in an examination of the higher variations of human movements that we can truly appreciate their complexity. Our discussion was necessarily limited to only the most elementary of these movements; we introduced the concepts of "perspective," "transposition," and "change in the point of initiation." These higher syntheses of movement are made possible by our awareness of our own movements, which we reperceive, by our ability to imagine movement, and, above all, by the communicative character of these movements. The defining feature of all communicative behavior is that it extends beyond itself toward something else that determines it. In such processes of interaction, the values of objects may change, depending on the perspective from which we view them. As our perspective toward objects changes in the course of our interaction with them, for whatever reason, they will continue to reveal new uses and properties to us.

We have now identified the following characteristics of the structure of human actions:

1. Human movements have a communicative, self-aware nature.
2. This nature allows us to change the point of initiation of the movement as well as to transpose perspectives.
3. Our movements have a symbolic structure: one phase of movement can intend the next phase or any other random phase we choose.
4. Our movements facilitate relieved communication, which provides the incentive for its own further development.
5. Our movements are carried out within an "aura" of images of movement and interaction.
6. It is in the course of the movements directed toward things that these things achieve their full validity by virtue of the variety of perspectives we may adopt toward them.

Language originates from these processes and follows the direction of their development; in fact, the more sophisticated patterns of movement can be developed only in conjunction with language. Language has more than one root—that is, the ability to produce sounds initially works in several, distinct directions. Each of these roots is specifically human in its structure, which does not, however, mean intellectual. The roots of language are vital sensorimotor actions involving particular abilities that have an unmistakably human form. It is critical to an anthropological theory of language, however, that neither communication nor the ability to use symbols, neither reflected, self-perceived activity, nor intention, perspective, and change in perspective, belong to language *alone*. To the contrary, all these are characteristic of the entire range of the specifically human abilities related to movement and perception.

The roots of language identified above are as follows:

1. The "life of the sound." Sounds are motor processes as well as self-perceived sensations. Just as is the case with tactile movements, here, too, each movement is echoed in the senses; our awareness of the sounds we make provides the stimulus for us to reproduce these sounds. A child learns to experience itself and becomes aware of itself by shifting its inner activity into the external world, without foregoing subjectivity altogether. Our sounds are played back to us from our

surroundings. A purely sensorimotor communication in sound is possible: we expect a certain result, we expect to hear the sound repeated; this expectation is then gratified or disappointed, and so on.

2. The expression of sounds, prompted by visual impressions. The world-openness and receptivity of the child is documented in the fact that it reacts to visual impressions with unspecific movements of response, including ones of sound. "Expression" is a purely human phenomenon: it is behavior appropriate for a being with a structure of world-open, sensitive, need-free impulses, whose relieved, communicative movements may have no immediate result. Among these movements are those of sound articulation which are directed toward the external world, which are "need-free," and which are characterized by a vitality that is actually excessive in nature: the child "addresses" what it sees out of its sheer joy at perceiving it. A firm association is thereby formed between the seen world and the sound.

3. The call. A child's response to its needs and uninterpreted desires takes the form of a state of overall unrest, into which loud cries also figure. A child's needs and distresses are attended to by external sources; the child ultimately anticipates the gratification that follows its cry in the "call." Thus, it cries with the intention of receiving comfort. This ability to adopt and make use of the result of an action is not uniquely human; the higher animals possess it as well. However, as far as language development is concerned, the child's call for help is significant because it establishes a connection between need, sound, and gratification. The child learns to express its needs and impulses in sound. All of man's needs and impulses become oriented through his experience in the world; they become analogous to language (sprachmässig—Herder); man must become aware of them and interpret them. This occurs for the first time in the call.

4. Sound gestures. Sound as the preferred means of motor expression. At first, a child accompanies its movements and emotional outbursts with sounds. These sounds become more defined once specific patterns of movement have been worked out. Because human movements permit a change in the point of initiation, any sequence of action can be initiated by its accompanying sound phase. The child learns that the specific sounds it makes can intend and usher in a certain sequence of actions. Noiré (1877) first identified this root of language in 1877.

5. The sound of recognition. Herder described this root of language. It can be explained in the following way: repeated impressions are responded to with communicative movements, among which sound movements are given clear preference because they allow us to incorporate even distant stimuli into our awareness of our actions and to answer these in specific actions shaped by our memories. Our sound responses become more precise as impressions are repeated and thereby afford us a greater measure of relief.

27. The Element of Language Itself

The roots of language we have identified are clearly "pre-intellectual." Nonetheless, they are part of the structure of man's unique capabilities, part of a system of relief, which enables man to develop a versatile and yet confident ability to initiate movements and which is also responsible for the character of "acquired neutrality" which the world takes on to an increasing degree. We become intimately familiar with the world and can then overlook it and place it in a state of undecidedness until we need to use it. Only by viewing language in the context of this system can we hope to understand it. We cannot begin to understand language until we acquaint ourselves with its foundations, for language is the vehicle of our abstract consciousness, completely relieved of the immediate situation. It should be clear by now that all the products of human actions in the world—communication within an unrestricted, open world-sphere; orientation in, and familiarity with the world; a free access to the things in our world through the symbols we have created; relief from the influence and pressure of the immediate present—are achieved once again in language, in a more concentrated and perfect form. Language therefore develops in a truly organic manner from the substructure of human senses and movements, and can be described in the same words; ultimately, it consolidates and controls the entire development of human capabilities through our thought and consciousness. It provides complete relief from the present and the necessity of responding to immediate stimuli. It is in language that the processes of our experience in and interaction with the world reach their highest form; it allows us to come to terms with our world-openness in a productive manner so that an infinite number of plans for action becomes possible for us. And, finally, language serves as the best vehicle for communication with other human beings by facilitating a common focus on common activities, a common world, and a common future.

We must now ask ourselves "Where is the trunk toward which all these roots lead?" Or, to phrase our question differently, if these roots all represent vital, pre-intellectual achievements that have an immanent intelligence, where is the seed of thought? Is there not in the entire organism some sort of center of growth for the development of language?

Before we begin to answer this question, we must remind ourselves that a sound has two unusual qualities: it can be repeated at will and it is a movement as well as a part of the world we perceive. We must then recall our definition of intention as that elemental ability of moving beings to direct themselves by means of a symbol or signal toward an entity that appears within the symbol, and further that language directly continues this process of setting up symbols, achieved at first by the cooperation between hand and eye. We will then have all the elements necessary for answering our question. The seed of thought can be found at that point where, in the same relieved, need-free movement, we direct ourselves toward a thing and simultaneously perceive it. In all the movements we have examined, we saw that we behave actively by taking the role of the thing concerned: we experience and become aware of ourselves through our actions directed toward the thing and in response to the thing. When we then direct ourselves toward the thing through a sound, and this focus is played back to our senses so that we experience and become aware of the thing, it is at this point that the lightning bolt of thought strikes. This is indeed the most relieved and effortless way for us to gain intimate knowledge of and access to the world through these self-created symbols. It then becomes possible for us to adopt an active behavior that effects no real changes in the world but is instead a "pure" form of communication, open to all that is perceivable—a form of communication that actually increases the sensory richness of the world and therein finds the incentive for its own continuation.

When the sound functions as a word it simultaneously substitutes for, dispenses with, and represents real perceptions: these become readily available to us through sound, in which medium they can be reproduced at will. The word relieves us completely of the immediate present and yet opens up a free, unbounded "virtual" present, within which the real one figures only as a small segment, and beyond which we can act and plan. This is the final element necessary to the survival of an unadapted, acting being. This "realization" *(Vergegenwärtigung)* is itself an action; in fact, it may go no further than this. At the same time, it is the basis for all (always secondary) theoretical behavior. In addition, language relieves our motor system of the task of direct familiarization with things (through touch, for example), of problems of orientation, of searching movements, etc. The human being can now engage in *work;* he can put his abilities to use in "artificial," self-developed movements to "realize" his plans. By naming the objects in his world, he has already acted; he can now refrain from action and still have ready access to these objects through language.

The word, the central nerve of language, unites the following aspects:

1. An intention that is directed toward a thing by means of a perceptual symbol we have created ourselves.
2. The communicative experience of ourselves through the experience and perception of things.
3. A behavior that is already an action itself; then, no subsequent initiation of action is necessary.

The word is thus a unique act that encompasses the entire structure of human senses and movements; the form of consciousness we achieve therein is called thought, and, at first, as is generally acknowledged, it is indistinguishable from the word: it is even the word itself. Obviously, all animals possess some awareness of what they see, hear, etc.; however, they lack true action (in the sense of directing themselves toward a thing and then acting), which culminates in something that is perceived through the senses. This aspect of language as an action that changes nothing on the factual level is extraordinarily important. Humboldt alone has touched on it: "The sound, however, does not displace any of the other impressions which the objects are capable of producing upon the external or internal senses, but instead becomes their bearer. Moreover, it adds, in its individual association with the object, a new designative impression."[75]

In his excellent essay entitled "Sprache und Wirklichkeit" (Language and Reality)[76] H. Ammann drew a distinction between representation *(Darstellung)* and determination *(Feststellung)*. Before treating this issue in depth, I shall briefly recapitulate his discussion of the subject of representation: In a spoken sentence, temporal reality is represented as follows: "A Being *[Seiendes]* is represented in the sentence; it 'gets a hearing' in the sentence, in the mouth of the speaker himself. . . . In a series of sentences such as 'the sun is shining,' 'the birds are singing,' 'the flowers are blooming,' it is in reality the sun, birds, and flowers that have the word. . . . by letting them express themselves, we are agreeing with the manner in which they announce their existence and we exhort the hearer to do the same."

Ammann explains this as follows: "What is essential to the act of representation is the subjectivization of the objective, the unification *(Ineinssetzung)* of the thinking and speaking human being with the bearer of the process." We would recognize our own concept of communication in this "unification" even if Ammann himself did not go on to speak of "changing roles" *(Rollenwechsel)*—the act of taking the role of the other and experiencing oneself from another's perspective, as occurs in communication.

Stenzel[77] has investigated this subject further and acknowledges its dual nature: Linguistic representation simultaneously involves making the world come alive in sounds and making consciousness part of this world, or objectifying it. Let us compare this to Humboldt: "In its intellectual striving [language] makes its way past the lips, its product wends its way back to the speaker's own ear. The concept is thus shifted over into a state of objectivity, without losing its subjectivity. Only language is capable of this. Without this feature, that is, without this continuous regression of objectivity to the subject, in which language collaborates, the formulation of concepts (and consequently all true thinking) is impossible."[78]

The communicative nature of language has thus always been acknowledged. However, this remains an isolated insight if it is not accompanied by the recognition of the sensorimotor substructure of language, which provides a true picture of what language achieves.

These theories all center around one main point: they describe intention, which experiences and confronts itself by taking the role of the thing it is directed toward and experiencing itself from this other point of view. It is the self-created symbol that gives us access to a thing; we behave actively toward a thing and at the same time can dispense with it. By drawing the things in our world into our self-awareness, we become intimately familiar with them.

Thus, the other theories I have briefly detailed here all treat essentially the same thing, although from different points of view. I would like now to reintroduce my approach from another angle.

For the moment, let us turn away from language specifically and think about a random action concerned in a communicative way with an object. It is not enough just to say that each phase of such an action will become aware of itself through the changes it brings about in the object. We must go a step further and argue that our imagination of the movement takes the role of the object so that we can experience our own movements from the point of view of the object as well. Consequently, we can initiate movements toward phases of a thing which are as yet only anticipated and not actually perceived. But, in addition, in the course of moving, the various adumbrations *(Abschattierungen)* of the thing take on a reference to each other and come together to form specific effects. These are the effects of its properties, which can always be repeated and which provide guidelines for our movements. Thus, through this communication process, through this act of taking the role of the other, *objectivity*—that is, the particular effect of the data contained in a thing—is established.

This last sentence has a vital importance for cognitive theory. If we apply it to language, we will see that the sound is itself a communicative movement, in which we take the role of a thing and reexperience this act of role-taking from the thing's point of view, whereby we then perceive the thing. To follow this line of reasoning one step further, if we then express the effect of the thing or the impression it gives (such as "light") in another word (such as "the sun"), then we will experience, from the perspective of the thing, an objective result in the course of our communication, precisely as we described above. The sentence "the sun shines" is then simultaneously a statement (action), an objective experience, and the behavior of the thing itself. Here again, we find objectivity in the context of communication. Ammann made the same point: "Linking a naming subject with a verb form allows us to represent temporal events in the sense that it lets the subject of the action express itself, it allows it to give the sound that symbolizes action. We could say that agent *[agens]* and action *[actio]* designate the actor and the script in the drama of the sentence. In this sense, the predicate of the sentence ultimately becomes the 'statement' or speech of the subject. The verbal sentence is based on transformation into action through speech; it therefore signifies the subjectivization of the objective."[79]

The verb is a word that can be realized only in images drawn from the world of human action; it is "subjective" and yet for this reason has the great power of objectivity. As Humboldt says: "The idea...abandons through the verb its internal dwelling place and steps forth into the realm of reality."[80] This is not simply a purely linguistic phenomenon but is closely tied to the human ability to execute communicative movements. When man enters into a mutually enriching relationship with things through these communicative movements, the movements become objectified (detached self-awareness), and at the same time the effects contained within these things become objective, reexperienced processes. This remarkable feat, of vital importance in understanding human behavior, is reenacted in the realm of language by the verb or predicative sentence.

The "drama" of the word, of the simple act of naming, as yet remains subjective and "locked" within our inner life. In its interaction with the thing, in its focus on the thing, the word seems to originate from the thing itself to allow the thing to express itself. This is the fundamental experience of language; however, it remains locked within the speaker, it is the inner birth of the concept. For this reason, this action is bound to the visible existence of the thing itself and does not rise above the immediate present. Hence the isolated word a child uses is only a sign that it has noticed an object, or a call, or the expression of a desire; however, it remains effective only on the subjective level.

In contrast, even in the simplest verb sentence, such as "lightning strikes," thought has expanded itself and has fulfilled the potential contained in the word: it makes the world come alive. The drama becomes concrete, the word takes the role of the other and begins to come to terms with this other. We could also say that the thing takes on a very specific, communicative, unified perspective toward another thing. For example, the individual words for "lightning" and for describing the process of "striking" may have been mastered for a long time, but once these have been "synthesized" (Humboldt), thought can refer back to itself so that the change in perspectives is facilitated by the thing and is experienced as the drama and vitality of the thing which is expressed from a second perspective.

As Humboldt writes, "In language, there is an original *prosopopoeia* which broadens itself out from this base in that an ideal being, the word, is conceived of as the subject and represented as active or passive while an action which takes place in the depths of the soul, a statement made in judgment of an object, is imposed externally upon this object as a property. This as it were imaginative aspect of languages is a necessary and unalterable factor in all speaking."

Elsewhere, Humboldt comments further on this topic: "By one and the same synthetic act, the verb joins the predicate with the subject through its being. But this is done in such a way that the being, which is transformed with an energetic predicate into an action, is in turn attributed to the subject itself. Thus that which was conceived as combinable actually becomes so in reality. One does not merely conceive of lightning striking; it is the lightning itself which descends."[81]

Thus, in the verbalized word, it is the exchange of roles between the state and the object, between subject and object, that permits, by means of a change in perspective, the things to express their own relationships; or, to put it differently, as formulated above, this exchange is facilitated by the thing and is reflected as its own drama and vitality. Fichte expressed this thought with his characteristic clarity: "The need for having different words to designate subject and predicate arose after the objects took on so many different relationships toward each other that the predicate was not immediately obvious when the subject was identified. The means for distinguishing the two was quickly found, for it existed in Nature herself. One simply put two tones together: the first designated the subject, and the concept that the subject had an inherent relationship to man was dropped because a special relationship was added."[82] This last sentence is of extraordinary significance. The subjective use of the word in existing immediate situations and experiences, this purely demonstrative or expressive use of words, is completely overcome in the sentence. The sentence is self-sufficient, self-contained, just as the thing designated in the sentence is liberated from every reference to actual situations which is not expressed in the sentence.

Finally, the difficult question of what exactly a sentence is cannot be separated from the issue of grammar, since isolated words can often be used as sentences themselves, as verbless statements. We can come up with the following definition, based on the quotation from Fichte, above: "The sentence is a complete unity of meaning which is sufficient for purposes of communication and in which a subject matter is established as real solely through the medium of language." This definition allows us to weed out those single words that may function as sentences but that are always dependent on the immediate situation to get their full meaning across (e.g., "Rain!") as well as the statements of mathematical logic in which there is fundamentally no relationship to reality.[83]

28. The Further Development of Language, I

When a thing is intended in a word, then it has meaning in itself; it is set off from the world and "nailed down" *(festgenagelt)*, so to speak. Thereby, it first becomes for our consciousness a concrete "itself." It is "held fast" *(gebannt)* in the original sense of the word (to designate, to give a sign).[84] Whenever philosophy attempted to determine the "essence" of things by abstracting from the things themselves, it could only propose the concept, the meaning of the word, as this "essence" of a thing; the original and naïve abstract philosophy is therefore always platonic. However, when the word isolates a thing for our consciousness and embodies it within itself, therein the characteristic mute strangeness of the thing also appears, the embodiment of unintended fullness. Once a thing has taken on a specific perspective in our eyes, it gives up all the unintended perspectives; similarly, our practical interaction with a thing, guided by a specific perspective we have adopted toward it, gives up anything that is not part of this process. Reality extends far beyond what it is taken to be in our thoughts and actions. The reason for this lies in the "resistance of things" *(Sachwiderstand)*, a category that is also theoretical; this resistance makes it necessary for us to change our perspective. From the point of view of the thing itself, one spoken word demands the next, so that it becomes a never-ending challenge to contain a thing within a word.

Our discussion has brought out one of the reasons why, as has often been remarked, the potential for all language lies in one word, why the word strives beyond itself. A second reason has to do with the transitory nature of the word: as it dies away, it cannot hold fast to the intention, which must then be recaptured by immediately repeating the word or else it will evaporate along with the word, and, following the course of the river of life, will be produced again at another point.

It is impossible to analyze further this gradually developing intellectual vitality. However, one factor in its development is related to the nature of sound. As Humboldt writes, "what one has heard does more than merely report information to oneself. It also prepares the mind to understand more easily what has not yet been heard and clarifies that which has been long since heard, though only half or not at all understood at the time. This is because the similarity between what has been heard long ago and what has just been perceived suddenly becomes obvious to the perceptive power which has become more acute in the interim. This sharpens the urge and the capacity to channel material heard into the memory more rapidly and it permits increasingly less thereof to pass by as mere sound."[85]

The "life of the sound," the reexperienced, dynamic self-perpetuating activity which circles back upon itself, has a certain excess vigor: it causes the individual sound to represent itself as a part of a larger whole and thus splendidly stays in step with our awakening consciousness.

We have now identified the resistance of things, the transitory nature of words, and the sensory vitality of our imagination of sound as factors that are responsible for the great energy of language and that encourage its further development which is the same as the development of consciousness. Nonetheless, we have not yet exhausted this subject. In addition, we must consider something that happens once communication is actually attempted: this is the productive effect of any misunderstandings whereby any perceived failure of the two intentions to coincide prompts a renewed effort to communicate. Furthermore, most words are at first somewhat fluid and imprecise; thus, once they have been limited to a specific meaning, empty places are opened up which then must be filled by new expressions.

Further factors regulating the development of language have to do with the "pressure of meaning" (Sinndruck). This phrase was originally introduced by Stenzel, but I use it here in a very different sense to express the difficulty that arises when the entire complex of intended statements comes up against the merely one dimensional series of words. Because what I wish to say is necessarily conveyed piece-by-piece because of the inevitable passage of time, the resulting feeling of discrepancy leads me to search for new words and expressions. In addition, in every language, only a small number of models of form must suffice for expressing an infinite number of possible connections and interrelationships between thoughts; another type of "pressure of meaning" arises which requires that any ambiguity be overcome by creatively using language and its forms.

Let us for the moment return to the relationship between the word and the thing and the "resistance" of things. A word intends and successfully designates a thing, but it then dies away while the thing remains. Although the thing was first set off and called to our attention by the word, and its objective fullness demanded changes in our perspective, it nonetheless remains unattainable. The word becomes aware of itself as mere word. Language is a sort of "twilight world" *(Zwischenwelt)* between consciousness and the real world, linking but also separating the two. To the extent that a word intends to embody a thing, it is thrown back, reflected, upon itself. The intention contained in the word is disappointed; it searches beyond the word, differentiating itself from the word and yet not really different from it until it finds a new word. Stenzel writes: "As a linguistic sign, the word cannot hold fast to the thought but instead releases it as it dies away to new connections. In this ongoing process, the mind gains control of one "portion" of reality after another for our classifying articulation is carried over in a progressive reciprocal process to the similarly classifying concrete world."[86]

The meaning of a word, the concept, exists only on the level of language, not above or behind the world. Thought is an intention directed toward a thing which is conveyed in a word; however, because the word-thought *(Wortgedanke)* encounters resistance from the thing, it is reflected back upon itself and realizes that the word that is dying away has not completely exhausted it. It then strikes back in order to be re-created in another word. The point must be made here, however, that in direct usage, in the flow of dialogue, or in the direct function of designating, word and concept are indistinguishable from each other. Only in the course of being reflected does unspent thought set itself off from the word and become "pressure of meaning" until it is once again contained in a word. We may therefore give a brief answer to the question of the difference between word and concept by saying that this difference lies not in intention but rather in reflection. Aside from this one reservation, I agree with Weisgerber's statement "Meaning exists only in words, as a function of the phonetic part.... The word is the indissoluble bond between the phonetic and semantic portion based upon the function of a symbol."[87]

As Weisgerber sees it, then, the "indissoluble" word has a phonetic aspect (its "name") and a semantic one (the "concept") (see next page).

Weisgerber calls the relationship of the word to the thing "naming" *(Benennung)* when looked at from the point of view of the thing itself, the thing-content *(Sachgehalt)* of the word. "Meaning" is based on the name

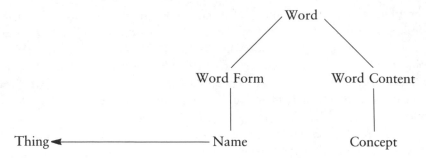

and refers to the concept to the extent that this is part of the phonetic aspect; from the opposite point of view, this relationship is called the "designation" of a concept with a name.

At first it may seem paradoxical that Weisgerber makes this distinction within the word when he has warned against making such distinctions in his theory of the indivisability *(Unteilbarkeit)* of the word. However, we will understand his point if we consider that this difference is manifested only in the process of reflection in which the two aspects (whose unity in direct usage Weisgerber correctly emphasizes) separate from each other.

This relationship between concept and word is significant because we can identify therein one of the forces that fosters the development of language. The word strives to go beyond itself; we must keep in mind that as far as thought is concerned, the role of language is not to create a material "sign" to convey an already existing concept but instead that thought and the articulated word work together in a reciprocal process to clarify each other. This is the only possible way of describing this relationship in the process of reflection. Saussure argued with great insight that language *[langue]* "acts as the intermediary between thought and sound *[son]* in such a way that the coming together of these two inevitably leads to a reciprocal process of defining units.... Thought, chaotic in origin, is compelled to become more precise as it dissects itself. Thus, there is neither a materialization of thoughts nor an intellectualization of sounds; instead, involved here is the somewhat mysterious fact that the thought-sound *[pensée-son]* contains possible divisions and that language works out these units as it is developed between two amorphous masses."[88]

On the one hand, claims Saussure, we have the amorphous mass of imprecise kernels of thought, and on the other the mass of already versatile images of sound; language develops as these masses are analyzed through each other. Humboldt argues along similar lines: "The emotion expressing itself in sound contains everything in germinal form. However, in the sound itself, everything is not immediately apparent. The hidden portions of the sentence gradually become clearer and emerge in individual sounds only after the emotion has become more sharply defined, after the articulation has gained freedom and precision, and after the success of an attempted mutual understanding has elevated man's spirits."[89]

When a single step in intellectual reasoning conceives of itself as articulation, the word cannot hold onto the thought but instead, just as it separates from the word in reflection, so does the word, dying away, release the thought. Thus, the fleeting nature of the word cooperates with thought; in addition, the rhythm of the sounds functions as the "fly-wheel of thought" (Schwungrad des Gedankens).

I see no point in arguing for "extra-" or "supra-linguistic" meaning, or "pure meaning" and the like. Weisgerber claims that the meaning of a word is clearly valid independently of whether I have ever encountered it; but this being (Sein), this validity, is not yet universal, does not exist "for me and everyone else" but just for a specific linguistic community.[90]

Thus, above all, the word is a real action and its motor aspect should never be overlooked. The fact that this action is reexperienced on a sensory level (in this case by our ears) is also true of other relieved, communicative actions, such as tactile movements. We have often made the analogy between language and the use of our hands; just as the tactile sensations produced by the movements of our hands provide incentive for their own continuation, so, too, do the sound masses function as the "flywheels" for repeated articulations. It is therefore possible that in the ancient forms of language, a relationship existed between sounds and communicative movements, whether these were demonstrative gestures or imitative movements. As we know, there is an affinity between verbs referring to speaking with verbs referring to showing (dicere; δείκνυμι) or making something appear (ψαίνωιψῶς ψημί).

Language always retains its character as action in the course of its development even at the point where it is distinguished from gestures. Language could even be described as an ersatz-action (Ersatz-Handlung). This expression is meant to convey the self-sufficiency (Selbstgenügsamkeit) of language. An intention directed toward a thing can be fulfilled and gratified in a word; indeed, this type of perfect intention which appears in a word as a completed action is called "intellectual" (geistig). When an animal perceives a stimulus and focuses on it and what is manifested therein, we can watch this intention become transformed into movements of pouncing, fleeing, etc. Since this "transformation" is absent in language, and intention and action are directly "telescoped" into each other in its place, we can say that this is another example of the fundamental human fact of "relief." In language, relief takes two forms: relief from the pressure of what is perceived, and also, from an internal perspective, relief from a pressing, instinctive interest in what is perceived.

Man thus exists in a world that is detached and neutralized; consequently, vital desires and instinctual interests do not figure into language. For this reason, man's intelligent behavior may often appear to be cut off from his biological needs, particularly if one adopts only a superficial view and does not take into account the special biological circumstances of the human being. The intentions that appear in language and that are conveyed through these unique communicative movements are need-free and removed. All communicative behavior is a relieved, human process of coming alive in a world which is first experienced and then "used" in some manner. The inner development of language runs a course designed to continue this relief: it forfeits a concrete content referring to things beyond language and instead increasingly broadens itself within itself in symbolic relationships.

We remarked in our discussion of the structure of the human perceptual world that there is a tendency toward obtaining relief from the world's confusing and overwhelming profusion of impressions. The communicative interaction with things in our world promotes a familiarity with the world through symbols. The result of these experiences is a complex, symbolic world within which we conduct ourselves in perfected, controlled, confident movements and actions; we live in an implied world of perceivable, self-developed symbols. Language simply carries this process further. Communication alone, the act of taking the role of the other, manages to make it seem that the sound we hear comes from the thing itself and expresses the thing; it becomes the principal symbol for the thing. However, because the sound is essentially an action, it is then possible and important that man use these readily available sounds to create a world of the symbolic presence of things, even if the things are not actually present, in complete independence and detachment from the "objective" presence of things. In language, the continuing process of relief from the pressure of the immediate present leads to the complete "exploding" of the present. The human being becomes a thinking, imagining being in a world he has "realized" (*vergegenwärtigt*) at will, and time and space, the future and the distant, open up around him.

29. The Repercussions of the Development of Language: The Idea

The complete freedom that the human being achieves through language from the given situation takes several forms, one of which we will examine in this section. This is the specific repercussion an acquired word has on the human imagination—ideas *(Vorstellungen)* which are readily available and plastic in nature.

Ideas are actually products of language, which uses the raw material of our immediate, remembered images to create the freely mobile and readily available idea—an image that intends itself *(ein selbst intentionales Phantasma)*. As we have already indicated our memories, formed passively within us, become mobile and undergo a process of selection as a result of our movements; they then function as expectations for our actions.

Every vital process, whether of a sensory or a motor nature, or even of a vegetative nature, is determined in part by its past states and thus has a "historical basis of reaction." Thus, a present state is impressed unconsciously upon the organism in a way I term passive. We can most clearly witness the power of our imagination on the level of motor functions, where our executed actions are later reflected as a readiness to carry out the same actions again if necessary. An animal also incorporates its perceptions into itself, particularly those frequently repeated. It is impossible to tell how deeply our perceptions penetrate within us; we experience the process of their becoming historical *(Historischwerden)* as after-images or echoes of our actions. Dreams provide astonishing evidence of the strength of this passive power of imagination.

These images are stored in our memory where they lie dormant until activated by our actions directed toward the future. When we are about to initiate a movement and are evaluating the existing situation, all the memories appropriate to the situation are aroused and appear as active images and expectations of what will happen. Memories are awakened that conform to the general direction of our actions. As our activity consequently becomes more focused and specific, these appropriate images come together to form a new present, appearing in the future. This sort of active imagination is first and foremost a total imagination—that is, it projects all the necessary transpositions of the entire organism, including motor images and expected sensations.

The biological function of the passive imagination will become clear if we consider the following: it seems that the organism preserves whatever situations it has already experienced in order to be prepared for similar situations in the future. In view of this, we would logically expect that the ability to remember the past will be more greatly developed, the greater the chance is of encountering unexpected and surprising situations, as is true for a world-open and vulnerable being. This is indeed the case with human beings. However, our active expectations can only make use of the essence of previous experience; we therefore possess insufficient means for guiding our existence in the future because this future is not simply a repetition of the past but rather is more likely to contain unexpected events and new situations. The future is "dark" to us; all the more so, the more world-open a being is. We might describe this vital human process in which memories, new experiences, and expectations are synthesized with each other as "experience sensu eminenti". Every step forward we take is at the same time an action against ourselves because the events do not always comply with our expectations. Thus we must continually rid ourselves of established memories and habits which not only tie us to the past but also render us defenseless against the incalculable future.

Given this situation, it should be clear that man has a great survival advantage, because he can actualize his memories at will and combine them freely with one another in anticipation of the future. This ability to "mobilize" and summon up images from our memory may also be attributed to language because language does have a motor aspect. The material for ideas is definitely memories, but memories that the word has made mobile and available. From this material, language creates relieved, mobile images which, like words, can be repeated at will, independently of the particular situation, which can even take part in the intentionality of the word. Because these ideas, like words, can be produced at any arbitrary time, they both appear not to be tied to any specific time. The "timelessness" of a concept is actually only the ability to repeat its placement arbitrarily, independent of the existing situation; in other words, timelessness is the indifference of an intention expressed through language toward the time and "background" of its execution. For example, an image of a tree that we conjure up in our minds is "timeless."

Through language, memories become ideas. This is particularly true of sensory images, as opposed to motor ones, which remain non verbal and for this very reason were not really studied until Palagyi rediscovered them. Language gives us ready access to the images in our memory which can thereby become part of the intention of our thought. Ideas are relieved, "deactualized" (entaktualisiert) images of memory that have become intentional. I described above how a thought is disclosed through the word, and further that the articulation of a thought is the intention directed toward a specific thing expressed in a specific sound. I also described how our ability to repeat a sound facilitates our ability to repeat an intention. In this manner, the real thing is divested of its power and is distanced from us. Once the thought becomes free, the word then forms a "twilight world;" it is closer to us than the actual thing and it shatters the power of visual impressions. Insofar as language is action, it has the ability to release and call forth memories, as do our movements; these memories then follow our words, take part in their intentions, and become ideas. When I say the word "tree," a remembered image is evoked which then, like the word, "intends" the real tree.

In sum, our intentions become completely available to us through language; they become independent of what is actually given. The images activated through language now take part in the intentionality of language. In our idea of a person, we focus on the person himself. In the process of reflection (Reflexion), as discussed above, one can easily distinguish between the thought and the image because the latter appears as an image that corresponds to an intellectual act: the word-thought (Wortgedanke) "oak" can apparently materialize as easily in an idea of an oak as in an oak we actually see.

In 1916, Segal[91] studied the imagination of objects and situations and argued that imagining situations involves a total displacement in which images of actions and movements also play a role, with motor displacements tending to preceed visual ones. Eventually, a realm of ideas (Vorstellungsraum) is created in which the imagining person moves about in virtual movements while the things he imagines change in the ways perception would indicate they should in response to changes in his own virtual movements. Breaking down these total displacements causes isolated images to appear which seem to have "no present" (gegenwartslos). An essential part of this process is that language takes over the role of total movements.

An idea can be an act as well as an object: as we speak, our words are swathed in idea-images; this is true even when language is not metaphorical, plastic, and sensuous. In reflection, the idea can appear as the object of the concept. In any philosophy that retains this concept of reflection (Descartes, Fichte), concepts or ideas consequently appear as the object of thought whereas, in fact, thought is essentially an instrument; it is the intention directed toward things and the means for symbolic interaction with them, independent of the immediate present. There are basically only three real solutions of a philosophical nature to the problem of thought:

1. The Platonic solution: the reflected concept, detached from the word, is elevated to the status of a special, higher reality because of its apparent timelessness.
2. The Idealist solution: Thought is simultaneously act and object, it is its own world and reality disappears within it.
3. The Instrumental solution: Thought is the means toward a relieved, symbolic interaction and is closely related to action. It is the method of "taking something as" *(Nehmen-als)*, of changing our perspective, of planning and instituting new combinations independently of real situations. Thought can become its own subject; it achieves a second level of symbolization, and can develop itself systematically, according to certain laws, in specific steps. This is what occurs in mathematics. Only in recent times has mathematics become something more than pseudo-ontology *(Scheinontologie)*, that is, since it has learned to renounce any content, to retain the intellectual act alone, and to contain only symbols of intellectual steps that have already been taken and that are defined according to certain laws in order to be able to establish new symbols of the same nature.

To my knowledge, Noiré alone remarked upon the important fact that our actions, our directed movements, actualize our memories, that, in general, an ability to remember makes sense only for moving beings who continually encounter new situations. "The reproduction of an idea is only possible for beings with a will." "No memory of the external world is possible unless it is linked to an awareness of one's own voluntary activity."[92] These are excellent insights, especially in view of the primitive state of psychology at that time. In Noiré, I also came across the fitting remark about the "uninterrupted reciprocal action of external objects upon us which awakens a word in us and of the words which awaken in us the idea of external objects."[93] Even Herder's theory of the origin of language seems to me to be rooted in this problem of "word-ideas" *(Wortvorstellungen)*. In his well-known passage on addressing a sheep, Herder writes: "[The] soul in reflective exercise seeks a distinguishing mark—the sheep bleats!... This bleating makes upon man's soul the strongest impression, which broke away from all the other qualities of vision and of touch, which sprang out and penetrated most deeply, the soul retains it. . . . It has recognized it humanly when it recognized and named it clearly, that is, with a distinguishing mark. . . . [without such distinguishing marks] no sensuous being can perceive outside itself, for there are forever other feelings which it must repress, annihilate as it were, in order to recognize. . . . And what was that other than a distinguishing word within?"[94]

According to Herder, this distinguishing mark can only be a word, which contains or reproduces an idea of a heard sound—an intention directed toward an object expressed through a word which can be repeated. In this word, memory is activated and what was once heard resonates again. Furthermore, the final words of this quote make reference to relief, to overlooking or "repressing" all else that could be perceived apart from the chosen symbol.

In conclusion, I understand ideas to be remembered images that become readily available, repeatable, and intentional through language. They thus enjoy the independence from what is actually given that language has achieved. This is the most important point in our discussion of man's complete liberation from the immediate present for an "anticipatory" existence. In this section we have also broached the issue of the orientation of our inner life toward the world, of the inner and outer worlds, which come to approximate each other through language. This important topic has two aspects: the problem of the world-open structure of human impulses (treated in part 3) and the problem of finding the "same level" for idea and reality (treated in the following chapter).

30. Repercussions, Continued: The Mutual Approximation of the Internal and External Worlds

Language brings the internal and external together on its own level. In the previous section, we traced the mobilization of our ideas through language and saw that language makes it possible for the intentions of our thoughts to be fulfilled in ideas. Language docs not differentiate between *imagined* and *real* things. For this very reason, language obscures the difference between reality and imagination for our consciousness. It is not necessary here to go into the countless examples from the history of philosophy that show that the standpoint of reflection immediately cancels this considerable difference; we may say, however, that those philosophical systems were possible and even necessary only as long as philosophers remained unaware of their bond to language. Because the idea originates through language, the internal and external (here, above all, idea and perception) are inevitably transformed into each other.

If we then consider ideas in terms of what they effect for us, we will find that they serve a vital function: we can visualize any reality even if it is not actually given; this, in turn, allows us to anticipate its continuation into the future and to figure into our conception of the immediate present this imagined extension of the visible present into the invisible future. In addition, the ready availability of ideas and our ability to combine them with other ideas enables us to plan for possible new events. This ability to project perceptions and ideas on the same level has great anthropological significance and is one of the factors that has enabled man to survive. A being who acts in preparation for the future must be able on occasion to suspend the difference between imagined and real situations. Our experience is so structured that to an increasing degree ideas and verified images are superimposed on reality. From another perspective, this is the same situation that we described in our discussion of relief as the reduction of direct contact with the immediate world.

My argument here will become clearer if we acknowledge that the ability to retain a perspective is a fundamental achievement made possible by language. For instance, when we use the word "red" to express that perspective toward a thing that has to do with its red coloring, then this perspective has been singled out from others and can enjoy all the advantages language grants. If I hand this thing to someone else and say "red," I have already dictated how that person should relate to this thing. Precisely because it is neutral toward reality, language can retain the perspective embodied in a word and can preserve it in spite of any changes that may occur in the situation or in one's inner self. Something is established and firmly fixed that is independent of the inner state of the person, of the mirror of experience and emotions, but also independent of the nature of the immediate present. Indeed, it even becomes possible to change and transpose these perspectives. By basing our actions on a plan for the future in which we anticipate our future selves and our future positions, we make this plan a reality. The existing state of our psyche, our inner state of being, is pushed into the realm of the "unreal" along with the existing external situation.

Let us again contrast this situation with that of animals. Köhler's chimpanzees were unable to recognize a stick that lay behind them even though they were searching for one. We can explain this in three ways: (1) because they lack language, they did not possess the isolated perspective of "stick"; (2) they could not free themselves of the pressure of their needs, of their desire for the fruit, which lay beyond their reach and which they were able to get with a stick if it happened to lie directly before them; (3) the fruit was such an intense stimulus that it constrained the animals so that they were unable to search freely.

Apparently, these animals were unable to retain an idea of what they were looking for; they had no concrete idea of what was not present because they did not have language, and vice versa. By opening up our inner life toward the outside world—a process that is effected through language—we also invest our inner life with impressions of the outside world (memory). We encountered this same situation in an earlier discussion in which we found that our silently collected memories have to be superimposed again upon the world in the form of ideas directed toward the external world. The term "inner life" *(Inneres Innenleben)* is a purely anthropological term. Basically, it has to do with the fact of man's world-open nature; it is in fact this nature as experienced by a world-open being. The "soul" *(Seele)* and the "inner world" *(innere Welt)* are equivalent concepts. Furthermore, the narrower term "inner outer-world" is intended to convey the idea that certain processes in man take place under the direct influence of the external world, that they are "invested" with impressions of the outside world and thus should be considered as phases in the process of coming to terms with the world which an acting, world-open being must carry out.

"Consciousness," however, is not a purely anthropological concept; it has a broader validity. It signifies a process of transformation *(Umsetzungs-vorgang)*, the mechanism of which we do not yet understand, which takes place at the points of contact between an organism and the world; in the lower animals, it takes place primarily in the perceptual act. However, because the human being is world-open, these contact zones extend much deeper within him; hence, even our impulses and motivations have been invested with images of the external world. Any consideration of the physical aspect of the human being focuses on only a few phases in the circular process of interaction, which actually encompasses the entire person and the external world with which the person is coming to terms. The expression "inner outer-world" *(innere Aussenwelt)* characterizes a specific part—better yet, aspect—of this as the scheme of "subjective psychical processes" *(subjektive psychische Prozesse)*. Novalis, probably influenced by Fichte, wrote: "There is also an outer world within us which has a relationship to our inner life that is analogous to the one the outer world outside of us has to our exterior."[95]

Language is primarily responsible for incorporating the outer world into us. When we discussed the "call" above, we noticed that through the sound, an association was created between a need and an expectation of definite gratification, with the result that this need was interpreted and became conscious. The call provides us with an isolated example, as if in an experiment, of the relationship between expression—the process of opening up our inner life toward the outside world—and the act of investing that same inner life with images from the external world. Orienting our impulses in this fashion is one of the most significant events in an instinct-relieved being's mastery of the world. Herder first described how the world grows into the human soul through language and, conversely, how language directs the soul toward the outside world: "If the first state of reason in man could not become real without language, it follows that all states of reason in him become utterable. . . . Because the thread of his thoughts is spun by reason, because there is in him no state which, taken as a whole, is not reason, and because man is not ruled by emotion but instead his nature is centered on the finer senses of sight and hearing, it follows that *there is no state in the human soul which cannot be expressed in words* or which becomes real through the words of the soul. As we know from dreams and from observing the insane, in the human soul, no condition is possible without thinking in words."[96] These sentences contain only a few of the timeless insights which appear throughout Herder's *Essay on the Origin of Language*.

If the inner life can be expressed in language, it is also by the same token the "inner outer-world," which means that it can be described only indirectly in images drawn from the external world: words such as open-minded, brooding, reserved, tense, high-spirited, depressed, shaken, are just a few examples from a long list Klages has put forth containing phrases that describe one's state of mind in images from the external world.[97] It is necessary to use these images because our inner state is crystallized in such images from the outside world and thereby becomes wish, yearning, interest, and drive.

The process whereby the internal and external world approximate each other proceeds as we use the external world to interpret the internal one and vice versa, because we really only experience these as interpolated in each other. Language forms the center, the heart, of the relationship between expression and impression. The inner outer-world merges into the outer inner-world. It is completely natural for us to conceive, as children do, of the external animate and even the inanimate as being "expressive," as alter ego, for in a world of experiences that have not been subjected to rational processes, all are equal targets for us to perceive and address.

This point is so central to anthropology that I would like to document it further by drawing on other thinkers who have discussed it in greater depth.

Plessner, in 1928, undertook a philosophical examination of the nature of plants, animals, and man.[98] Here I would like to show how our present topic evolved from the anthropological premise he presents. An animal lives from its "center" *(Mitte)* but it does not live as this center; it constructs a self-reflexive system *(selbst rückbezüglich)* but does not experience itself. Its body as a whole has not yet become completely reflexive. In man, the center of positionality *(Positionalität)*, the distance of which to man's own body forms the basis for the possibility of all factual reality, acquires distance from itself. The human being is consequently aware of himself and can perceive himself and is therefore "ego" *(Ich)*, the "vanishing point" "behind" man of his own inwardness *(Innerlichkeit)*; removed from all possible life processes that proceed from this center, it functions as an onlooker toward the scenario of the inner field. The division into external field, internal field, and consciousness is thereby completed. Man can create a gulf between himself and his experiences; he exists on both sides of the gulf, tied to the body and tied to the soul, but at the same time he exists nowhere; he is beyond space and time and is therefore human. Although the human being cannot break through this centering (Zentrierung), his life is nonetheless "eccentric" (exzentrisch).

An animal's relationship to its surroundings is mediated by the animal itself but appears to it to be direct and unmediated because the animal is hidden from itself. It stands in the center of this mediation and forms it. For the animal to become aware of this mediation, it would have to stand "next to" it but not lose its mediating centrality. This "eccentric" position has been realized in man, who stands at the center of his standing (Stehen). The ego stands behind itself, beyond space, in nothingness; it experiences its own timelessness and spacelessness as standing outside of itself. The ego observes the desires, thoughts, drives, and feelings, and yet at the same time lives directly within them. Thus, it has a dual nature: the ego lives on this side of the gulf as body and soul and on the other side as the psychophysically neutral unity of these spheres. This unity, however, should not be viewed as a third element but is instead the gulf itself, the hiatus, the empty passage through which the mediation is channeled.

The physical features of human nature have only an empirical value. Being human is not bound to a specific form; it could take many forms as Dacqué has speculated. Man exists in a world, which—in accordance with the three-fold nature of his position as body, soul, and ego—is made up of the external world, internal world, and social milieu (Mitwelt). Just as an eccentric organism is not bound to time or space and is dependent on nothing, the things in the external world exist in a "void" of relative space and time. This is also true of one's own body (Körper). The abdomen (Leib) on the other hand, is the center for absolute directions (above, below, in front of, behind, and so on) and for the organism in its surroundings. These two aspects exist side by side and are mediated only at the point of eccentricity, the unobjectifiable ego. However, even in the act of thinking, feeling, and willing, the human being stands outside of himself and can be divided from himself and may come to doubt the character of his experiences as experiences. The internal world is what man is, what he feels, suffers, endures, and perceives. The true inner world is being at odds with oneself (Zerfallenheit) from which there is no escape and for which there is no compensation. This is the radical double aspect that exists between the soul and the act of experience. In order for one's own being *(Sein)* to encounter itself as a reality *sui generis,* it must be an intrinsic part of its nature to stand outside of itself.

This exposition of Plessner's anthropological model provides new categories for understanding what we have described as a reversal of the internal and external world. The ego, the center and possessor of body and soul, can lay claim to the spacelessness and timelessness of its own position for itself as for any other being. It therefore can say to itself and to others "you," "he," "we." The social milieu *(Mitwelt)* is that form of one's own position which we understand as the sphere of other human beings. Conversely, the very existence of this social milieu is the basis that enables a living being to comprehend its own position as a member of this social milieu. The intellectual character of a person is based on the "we" form of his own ego; between "me" and "me," between "me" and "him," lies the sphere of this world of the mind *(Geist)*. The sphere we designate as "we" is the mind in the strictest sense. Man does not possess mind in the same way that he does a body and soul; mind is the sphere that allows us to live as persons, the sphere in which we stand precisely because the form of our positions preserves it. We could say that because of the structure of the social milieu, different positions of the human being in time and space are devalued. As a part of this milieu, we stand where another stands; the concepts of subject and object are not applicable to the mind as a sphere because this sphere is neutral, indifferent toward the distinction between subject and object.

In this section, we have treated one of the most important subjects in anthropology. We conceive of the human being as having a soul, as the inner outer-world, because we open ourselves toward the external as we express ourselves; thereby, we devalue ourselves within the inner relationship and become socialized. In this sphere, the mind is realized. G.H. Mead used the behaviorist approach to describe this same process.[99] To begin with, he describes social acts (gestures) or ways of behavior (attitudes) which act as a stimulus for another person and call forth his attitudes in response, similar to the exchange of blows, for example, in a boxing or fencing match. On the level of language, this corresponds almost exactly to what we described earlier as the "life of the sound" of communication in sound.

The critical transition from the merely communicative sound to the significant symbol is invariably conditioned by social factors and occurs when an individual incorporates into his own gestures the response that these gestures evoked in others. At this point, the gesture takes on a meaning on the virtual level: "Gestures thus internalized are significant symbols because they have the same meanings for all individual members of the given society or social group, i.e., they respectively arouse the same attitudes in the individuals responding to them."[100]

This means that in making a particular sound gesture, a person can anticipate the initial attitudes that this gesture will call forth in others: "Gestures become significant symbols when they implicitly arouse in an individual making them the same responses which they explicitly arouse, or are supposed to arouse, in other individuals, the individuals to whom they are addressed; and in all conversations of gestures within the social process . . . the individual's consciousness of the content and flow of meaning involved depends on his thus taking the attitude of the other toward his own gestures."[101]

If in our gestures, we anticipate the reaction of another, we have created a common basis which can serve as a new point of departure. We can then respond to the relationship of another's reaction to our own initial gesture. The *meaning* of the first gesture is then the same for both. An individual's awareness develops of the meaning of a gesture which he makes when he has taken the role of the other. To put it differently, the first form of our inner life is that act of taking the role of the other which creates this common basis of meaning. Only at this point does a gesture become symbolic or meaningful. For example, when a child reacts to its own sounds as if to another's (life of the sound), it is taking the role of the other and has become aware of the meaning of its sound gestures. Thus, imitation, often overestimated, is actually only one part of a complex process. Guillaume astutely claims: "Imitation cannot have such a simple structure, otherwise its biological validity would be much greater, whereas in fact it is manifested almost exclusively in man alone."[102]

Mead calls this process "taking the role of the other." It is on the one hand the basis for the significant symbol, for a gesture becomes symbolic when it has incorporated in a reciprocal process the behavior of another into itself. On the other hand, this same structure is also the basis for self-awareness. "It is evident that out of just such conduct as this, out of addressing one's self and responding with the appropriate response of another, 'self-consciousness' arises. The child during this period of infancy creates a forum within which he assumes various roles."[103]

"One participates in the same process the other person is carrying out and controls his action with reference to that participation."[104]

Taking the role of the other means objectifying oneself, becoming distanced from oneself, possessing oneself. A child's role playing and imitation games are the vehicle for the development of its self-awareness through its awareness of others.

It is necessary to rational conduct that the individual should thus take an objective, impersonal attitude toward himself, that he should become an object to himself.... For he enters his own experience as a self or individual, not directly or immediately, not by becoming a subject to himself, but only in so far as he first becomes an object to himself just as other individuals are objects to him or in his experience; and he becomes an object to himself only by taking the attitudes of other individuals toward himself within a social environment or context of experience and behavior in which both he and they are involved.[105]

Because the awareness of oneself is distilled, in a manner of speaking, from the various processes involved in taking the role of the other and the alienation from oneself that is part of this process, the child acquires the specifically human relationship toward its own body: "Through self-consciousness the individual organism enters in some sense into its own environmental field; its own body becomes a part of the set of environmental stimuli to which it responds or reacts."[106]

Mead differentiates in terminology between the I and the Me: "The 'I' is the response of the organism to the attitude of the others; the "me" is the organized set of attitudes of the others which one himself assumes. The attitudes of the others constitute the organized "me" and then one reacts toward that as an 'I.' "[107]

The I responds to the social situation which determines in part its own behavior; it is the incalculable, individual I as opposed to the socialized I, or to put it another way, the I is the response of the individual to the behavior of society as this is manifested in his own experience and as it figures into his own behavior.

In this chapter, we have approached the same fundamental phenomenon from several converging directions. Its great significance, particularly for understanding primitive cultures, should be readily apparent.

31. Silent Thinking

Until now, we have purposely equated language with thought and have used both with the same range of meaning. In our discussion thus far, this should not have caused any misunderstanding because we have defined thought first and foremost as the intention directed toward something which is expressed in sound. There can be no doubt that in a narrower sense, thinking is a form of "inner speech" *(inneres Sprechen)*, a "subvocal Talking" (Watson), because it remains so closely bound up with language (for example, one thinks in one's native language).

However, as we are well aware, we do not have to express or announce what we are thinking; this fact seems to indicate that speaking and thinking are separate. We can now identify two different problems: inner speech as opposed to voiced speech (the problem of "silent thinking" *[lautloses Denken]*) and secondly, the question of whether, as Watson asserts, thinking is really one and the same as this inner speech (in other words, the problem of nonverbal thinking *[sprachloses Denken]*).

The first problem of inner, unexpressed speech is quite puzzling. In the first place, quite generally, it signifies an increase in our indirect behavior toward the world; in other words, a direct motor response or sound-motor interaction with things does not take place. Because the expression of sensorimotor processes is also checked, it appears that this inhibition extends beyond consciousness down into the vital depths of the individual. A person sitting quietly, who seems not to be seeing or hearing anything, is most likely thinking. It seems that some sort of process of turning back or blocking our human impulses and drives must be the prerequisite to this internalization. I would like to argue that this process of turning back might be one sign of the excessive nature of impulses, of the fact that we are overburdened with impulses that cannot be completely gratified in direct actions. To this extent, the process of turning inward our intentions that can no longer be directly fulfilled in reality is an essential human characteristic. On a purely descriptive level, thought is first and foremost a means of reducing the urgency of sensations. It behaves toward language as language does toward the perceivable abundance in the world. In thought, our intentions follow a course that is detached to a great extent from the concrete material of ideas and memories as well as from the phonetic material of word-ideas. Our intentions follow a course that skirts the "kernels" of word-ideas without these actually becoming concrete, and in this way, intentions apparently become free to link up with each other and thereby form trains of thought. We can thus describe thinking as the highest degree of relief—a form of behavior that reduces our contact with the sensory world, that is abbreviated, and that is purely suggested.

For anthropology, the great significance of this higher indirectness lies in the fact that if fewer intentions are actually expressed, then more can come to terms with each other in our mind. Our real trial and error behavior, guided by perception, our controlled manipulation of things and versatility of movement, are completely transformed through thought and are shifted internally while all real action, including verbal action, is suspended. Dewey writes: "We will begin with the claim that deliberation is a dramatic test in the imagination for the different competing directions of action."[108]

The same drama that our language and our actions develop through interaction with the outside world is now drawn inward—with the difference, however, that the lability, and instability of these inner situations in the "inner outer-world" is, especially when an experimental action is involved, infinitely superior to the stubborn unequivocality of situations one encounters in real life.

The expression "inner outer-world" and the concept of an inner realm of experimental action in which we enjoy a greater range of freedom do not yet completely explain this phenomenon. In thought processes, a person always comes to terms with himself, his own interests, desires, and so forth. Hence, these processes involve a certain amount of self-interpretation. All thinking is a form of communication with oneself, a monitoring of oneself down to the level of basic drives and impulses and is thus, in a manner of speaking, an internal process of socialization.

In an excellent study by Selz,[109] the internal drama of thought is brought out very clearly with simple problems which illustrate how thought makes use of mobilized ideas and images as points of support for anticipated actions. He also discusses how we transfer motor response from one situation to another on the virtual level, that is, the processes whereby we construct an "inner stage." As Selz rightly states, "The changing material of the objective world bears the same relationship to the coordination of movements—by means of which it achieves realization—as the changing material of the processes of consciousness and the bases for their reproduction have to the coordination of intellectual operations, in which they actively participate." As we know, thinking about concrete problems takes the same form as actual actions do, in which one action leads to another, certain actions stand out and are maintained, in which direction can be reversed or the approach changed, etc. On the other hand, a thought process is a product as well as an operation; this aspect of thought is also related to the nature of language in which intention and movement coincide in such a way that the heard sound is already the result of a movement and this activity does not actually change anything in the world. This movement, with its special motor type of intention, lets the world resound and makes it part of our self-awareness of the interaction. This movement cannot be separated from human intelligence and permits it to become self-contained. Nonverbal thinking (sprachloses Denken) can therefore promote self-sufficiency.

The second problem we posed above addresses the question of whether there is such a thing as "pure" thought, unsupported by language. This question is related to the one we have just discussed of silent thinking as opposed to expressed thinking; it is actually the same question on two levels. As James has said, every word, or every word-idea (Wortvorstellung) is a "halting place" for thought; the "transitional parts" are not conscious as a rule, not on a linguistic or any other level. From these unconscious genetic processes, a "feeling of meaning" sometimes penetrates into consciousness, most often when discoveries are made or new insights gained; however, real meaning is present only if a word or at least an imagined scheme exists to which the feeling of meaning can be attached. An idea or a mental scheme may on occasion take the place of a word in order to serve as a vehicle for thought, to relieve it of internal "pressure of meaning" (Sinndruck) as a "dehors fugitif de la pensée" (Sartre)[110] which only indicates thought's direction to it. However, it appears that there is no "pure thought" as the result of something that is carried out. We can thus agree with Kainz when he says that there is a form of nonverbal thinking which is nonetheless fortified by perception as well as a form of thought unrelated to perception that is facilitated by language.[111]

In The Interpretation of Dreams (1900), Freud came to the conclusion that thought processes are essentially without qualities and unconscious and that they only gain the ability to become conscious by being tied to the residue of verbal perception. This means that the system of action is actually more closely related to intelligence than is that of perception; furthermore, language, as an organ of action that is perceivable in itself, has a reinforcing effect on the intellectual acts, unconscious in themselves. Freud suggested as much at one point: "The representations of words arise in turn from sensory perception in the same way as the representations of things, so that one might well ask why the representations of objects could not remain conscious by virtue of their own perceptual residue. Most likely, however, thought takes place in systems which are so far removed from the original perceptual residues that they no longer possess any of their qualities and need to be reinforced with qualities in order to become conscious. Furthermore, by being bound to words, such systems might take on qualities although they could not carry over any qualities from perception themselves because they simply correspond to relationships between representations of objects."[112]

The belief that the psychical knows no spatiality needs to be amended because the question can be posed as to whether the experiences we call psychical do not in fact have a specific range. If this is true then the concepts of "expanded" (ausgedehnt) and "material" would not necessarily be synonymous. In one of his later aphorisms, Freud came close to the standpoint adopted by Kant: "Spatiality might be the projection of the expansion of the psychical apparatus.... The psyche is expanded, but knows nothing about it."[113]

Metzger did us the great service of studying the problems of space in psychology.[114] In his view, there are degrees of psychical spatiality; in their emphasis of the spatial, the type of thought constructions and structural models that modern science employs today are still closely tied to the perceptual realm. When psychology speaks of the "depths" of feelings and of spiritual "levels," it is not clear that it is only using "images" of something that is essentially nonspatial; instead, the results of experience itself dictate this spatial representation. Moreover, all experiences take place "within us," and even within the ego, one can differentiate a "further ego" from a punctiform, central ego: the latter can be defined only by its position in space and in this sense cannot be distinguished from any concrete point of emphasis. Even "spatiality" is psychophysically neutral.

32. The Origin of Language

At this point in our examination of language, we will consider the initial stages of language and delineate the general tendency in development which is found in virtually every language. Humboldt was the first to discover that there is a general law governing the development of language which dictates that language becomes increasingly abstract. From our discussion thus far, this should come as no surprise. It refers to the way in which the relief from the immediacy of the present, which constitutes the basis of language, is carried still further in language itself. Through language, we gain increasing freedom to undertake versatile, abbreviated, and increasingly indirect actions. To an ever greater degree, language loses its reference to things beyond itself, its concrete content, through a process of "fading" *(abblassen)*; at the same time, it becomes possible for the words to refer to each other, to fulfill each other, and to express this function themselves. In other words, it becomes possible for thought to remain by itself *(bei sich bleiben)*. This possibility is realized in every complete sentence but to an even greater extent in the degree of inflection of a language. As this process of "fading" continues, the inflection is ultimately worn down again so that the late stages of highly intellectual languages (English, Chinese) are not as inflected as they once were. My presentation of this law is necessarily brief; I mention it only to provide further verification for the views set forth to this point.

In inquiring after the origin of language, we should not ask ourselves such questions as how primitive man could have invented language. If we assume that language is one of the uniquely human capabilities, then it must be as old as mankind, so that the problem of its origin is tied in with that of the origin of mankind. Consequently, as long as practically nothing about man's evolution from some primate species in the Tertiary period is known, we can similarly make no claims about the relationships between the subsequent functional changes in the human being as a whole. When we pose the question in this way, we are really only linking it to an even greater mystery.

We have, however, made one positive statement about language: it is one of the essential features of the human being. We are thus asserting the fundamental nature *(Ursprünglichkeit)* of language; in concrete terms, this means that children raised without language, without the benefit of adult teachers, should nonetheless develop language on their own. The Pharaoh Psammetich is said to have carried an experiment along these lines and Friedrich II as well.[115] More recently, such linguists and psychologists as McDougall, Paul, Wundt, and Kainz have adopted a common point of view on this subject. Kainz, for example, assumes that a group of small children raised without any external influence on their speech would reach "a form that although rudimentary in structure, would nonetheless approximate perfected language."[116] The distinguished Danish linguist Jespersen came to the same conclusion: "Children left to themselves... in an uninhabited region where they were still not liable to die from hunger or cold, would be able to develop a language for their mutual understanding that might become so different from that of their parents as really to constitute a new stock of language."[117]

Jespersen expressed this opinion when he was asked to explain the astonishing variety of Native American languages. In California, there are a great number, which can be grouped into no fewer than 19 separate families. The situation is similar in Oregon (30 language families). In Brazil, it seems that a language is often limited to a group of related individuals so that it constitutes a true family institution; for example, of twenty random people in a boat's crew, only three or four would be able to converse in a common tongue while the others would silently look on.[118] As early as 1886, Hale proposed that the mild climate and natural abundance of these American regions enabled children whose parents had died for whatever reason to get by even without the help of adults, whereby it was necessary for them to develop a language among themselves. Jespersen discusses a very interesting Kaspar Hauser type of case from this century: a pair of severely neglected Danish twins were raised by an almost totally deaf old woman. They developed their own language which was incomprehensible to others. When Jespersen saw them, these twins were 5½ years old and had picked up some Danish from a children's home. When left alone, however, they immediately reverted to their thoroughly incomprehensible gibberish. They used sounds unknown in Danish as well as totally different word placements and multiple negatives in their sentences, such as occurs in the Bantu language. *Lhalh* meant *water* but also *to wet* and *wet;* this is reminiscent of similar manifestations in English. Most of the words that Jerpersen managed to understand he was able to explain as garbled Danish *(lop—sort* [black]); however, a considerable amount of what they said was unintelligible to anyone else.

That something like this could occur in a civilized country in the twentieth century lends credence to Hale's assumption that children in an uninhabited but hospitable environment would develop their own language. Adults do not teach children to intend something through symbols—this is taught by Nature herself. From this great teacher a child would probably also learn to use sound to express its intention. Of course, it is far quicker and easier for an adult to point to a clock and say "tick-tock." Because a child readily imitates what it hears (life of the sound) and because the adult points to it, the intention is directed toward the clock and a direct association is created between visual and acoustic impressions; the repeated sound is thus inevitably directed toward the thing. A child of one to two years of age learns this easily because it is a preferred short cut between processes the child would otherwise develop on its own without any guidance but with numerous detours and great effort. For a child to be able to adopt a word that adults repeat aloud, certain prerequisites are necessary which are in themselves uniquely human.

1. The already existing, highly symbolic structure of the perceptual world, as well as a cultivated ability to use these symbols in articulated movements requiring a minimum of effort and to carry out communicative interactions.
2. A comprehensive overview of situations, facilitated by this symbolic perception.
3. Intentions; that is, the ability to focus on something by means of symbols.
4. The ability to "shut down" the entire organism, which is contingent upon the delayed development of human impulses and is further fostered by man's single-handed mastery of the initially overwhelming barrage of perceptions.
5. Rendering the world "intimate," familiar, and "undecided" (dahingestellt) down to the last detail.
6. Openness, that is, the unstable, world-open, excessive human impulses and movements which are expressed in communicative interaction—"expression" (Ausdruck).
7. The ability to adopt and make use of the results of communicative movements of every sort; furthermore, the ability to anticipate the results of our actions and use these as the motivation for initiating these movements in the future.
8. The life of the sound. The wealth of possibilities for articulation, the sensitivity to acoustic form, and communication through sound.
9. The ability to express recognition in sound motor pathways in "minimal movements."
10. Sound gestures, the increasingly precise nature of the sound accompaniment to an action and our ability to intend the initiation of a sequence of actions through these sounds.
11. The sound as call and "ground-breaking" action.

These points represent the essential things that must be mastered before language development can be further guided by adults. As we look these over and reflect on them, our suspicion is confirmed that children would in fact develop language even without parental guidance, although of course only through communication with one another. Thus it appears that language is indeed original and part of the basic nature of the human being.

There is, however, one further aspect of this problem of the origin of language. Ancient languages actually surpass living ones in their extraordinary wealth of words and forms; of course, since we estimate the age of *Sinanthropus* to be at least 400,000 years, these ancient languages were developed gradually over very long periods of time from very primitive beginnings. Thus, the development of language and of the mind must have taken place parallel to anthropogenesis. As we indicated in the introduction to this book, it is hardly possible to form an idea of the biological mechanism involved here, let alone to understand the "origin" of the categorical novum which language and thought represent. In this mysterious process, however, the roots of language we have identified most likely played an important role. The question arises whether there are not in fact "key situations" *(Schlüsselsituationen)*, from an anthropological perspective, in which a few or all of these must have worked together. This type of situation would necessarily have been a uniquely human one and must have involved some sort of collective action. In fact, four very different, distinguished linguists (Noiré, Ammann, Jespersen, and Vossler) concur on this point and their views encompass our prerequisites to language development. Noiré's hypothesis has already been discussed. He writes: "The first sound of language must thus have originated as the expression of a heightened common emotion which accompanied common activity." He argues that all common activity is accompanied by song or calls and that from such a commonly produced and universally understood sound, the word developed: "The essential feature of this sound was that it reminded one of a specific activity and was understood."[19] Thus, because these actions involved collective participation, the sounds that accompanied such actions took on the meaning of specific actions; they "reminded" one of these actions or this commonly understood sound allowed one to focus on a specific action.

Vossler argues along the same lines: "Let us assume that in primitive times, some sound, for example *mar*, accompanied the movements of grinding or polishing stones. This sound had no special meaning, but was simply a natural reflex, a habitual sound. This does not yet constitute language. If then, however, one of the "*mar*-criers" who wanted to grind stones but had not yet actually begun to do so, said *mar* in order to convey that he wished to do it or that the others should do it, this was language. He had now used this natural, habitual sound to represent the wish to grind stones or the need to grind stones which was not yet the actual act of grinding itself. He made an association and created what is called a metaphor or permutation or symbol, and this is the essence of all linguistic thought. At the same time, this first speaker might have used a gesture or an accent to accompany and underscore his *mar* which might have implied a challenge, invitation, or command, and it would then be clear that he had an awareness, a logical consciousness, that saying *mar* was not the same as doing *mar*."[120]

Ammann uses Vossler's example as a basis for a more extensive examination of this topic which I will not go into here in detail because it draws greatly on linguistic theory. However, his main point is as follows: "The sound gesture, which was originally closely tied to action, serves, on the one hand, to call the action itself to life and on the other, to call to mind the past action in a representative fashion."[121] Thus, we could say that the sound functioned as an imperative (the call) as well as the first-person past indicative. Ammann goes on to say that one could speculate that the other people in Vossler's example would have declared their willingness to participate by "joining in the call." And, finally, Jespersen writes:

If a certain number of people have together witnessed some incident and have accompanied it with some sort of impromptu song or refrain, the two ideas are associated, and later on the same song will tend to call forth in the memory of those who were present the idea of the whole situation. If one of our forebears on some occasion accidentally produced a sequence of sounds, and the people around him were seen (or heard) to respond appreciatively, he would tend to settle on the same string of sounds and repeat it on similar occasions, and in this way it would gradually become "conventionalized" as a symbol of what was then foremost in his and in their minds.[122]

These four scholars concur in their reconstruction of this prototypical case. I do not believe, however, that this says something definitive about the *first* historical use of language, although these authors no doubt intended this in their discussions of these primitive humans. Nonetheless, I feel this example does have a kernel of truth, for it pinpoints an important, if not the most important, point: It describes a basic human situation that occurs repeatedly, in which several roots of language operate jointly with the result that we can recognize this as one of the fundamental directions of the development of language, probably the most essential one. Let us use these four similar examples to construct one of our own.

There is a group or community of human beings concerned with some sort of actions. These actions are "accompanied" by affective sounds which become more specific over time as the form of action itself does, and which thus come to refer to a specific situation. These are sound gestures, in the sense we described above; because they are rooted in an ability to change the point of initiation of a movement, they can express the intention to carry out the action as a whole. Similarly, we must also assume that communication on the level of sound, the "life of the sound," existed. Then, indeed, through this common sound, an action can be initiated, if at first on the sensorimotor level; at the same time, as Vossler correctly realizes, this sound phase would be perceived as distinct from the action itself, as the purely intellectual intention toward something or toward an action which is expressed in sound. The sound comes to mean the action, and frequent repetition reinforces this association because it offers the acoustical and visual means for recognition.

Another aspect of this process is that a sound produced on a similar occasion will evoke the memory of this entire process. Ultimately, only the sound phase will need to be stressed and carried out in order to create, based on the effect of the call on all participants, an expectation of the result and subsequent phases of the action. We have here a case in which all the roots of language are concentrated, a definitely significant point where they all come together in *one* achievement: communication and mutual understanding of common activity. These sound gestures or situation-words must have been relatively indifferent toward the distinction between action and object; or better yet, they must have both caused these early humans to focus on an action and provided the impetus for participating in it. Hence, such sounds must have been used before noun and verb had been differentiated; they would therefore have not had much independence, because they were so determined by their specific context which served to make their meaning clear. Linguistic theory confirms this.

In addition, we must view this example in the light of the open human world which we master through communication and interaction. Other experiences also contribute to the development of language such as, above all, when we discover that a sound can serve as a means for dealing with recognized things so that only a minimum of effort is required while still involving them in the vitality of the interaction experience—and further, when we discover that this intention expressed in words can now be broadened to recognize the "same thing" anywhere else. With the entire range of human relieved experiences of interaction as the basis, individual centers where language and action are concentrated will be formed and will promote the further development of language; one of these centers, the most important one in fact, was illustrated in our example.

33. The Further Development of Language

There can be no doubt that over long periods of time, the use of language would not have progressed much beyond direct communication within concrete situations, if the word and the sentence had not originated at the same time. In a sentence, a process is represented or something is established. Every language is capable of expressing this. In children, we can observe a stage in which they begin to use uninflected sentences of several words. To give one of countless possible examples, Lindner's child said "fall chair leg Anna Hans" *(fallen tul bein anna ans)* which was intended to convey that Hans had tripped over the leg of a chair on which Anna was sitting. Here, too, as with naïve story telling, language remains within the confines of representing experienced situations, and one may safely assume that the actual primitive beginnings of language must have had this same structure.

On the intellectual level, the sentence grants us an overview of the situation and permits us to focus on a few essential elements in it; in addition, it fosters our ability (which Humboldt termed "synthetic") to join together on their own level a sequence of words, each of which signifies one element in an entire process, to form a total meaning which corresponds to the situation as a whole. One intention is directed through the words toward the things they signify; another is directed through the words toward the other words in the sentence. This would be impossible if a distinction had not been made through reflection between word and thing in their relationship to each other. A 15-month-old child who saw a group of soldiers playing music could represent this event in a two-word sentence as "solda la la la." Just as the synthesis of perceptions, processes, and situations provides us with an overview so too does the synthesis of words describe these processes, represent them on their own level, and communicate them. With the sentence, an important and necessary step has been taken which makes it possible now for language to remain by itself *(bei sich selbst bleiben)*.

While it is generally accepted in linguistics that word and sentence originated simultaneously, this should not lead to a failure to appreciate the difference between the two. The development of language in children reveals that there are words that are wishes or affect-words (such as the call) and other words (such as *öff*, mentioned above) that have a fluid meaning. These words, like sound gestures, may refer to situations and are the "seeds" of sentences. This does not preclude the possibility that at the same time very specific individual names may appear by chance, particularly in the context of recognition, which may persist unchanged. A child must use a sentence of several words whenever he must communicate information or give a simple narrative—that is, whenever the actual situation itself cannot make clear what the child wishes to say. In the last case, the child may not progress for a long time beyond simple "signals"; to narrate an event, however, it needs to have at least a few individual words to designate the focal points of the situation. The sentence *Lightning strikes* signifies a qualitatively new step beyond affective language interaction or the use of situational aids. In this sentence, thought remains by itself.

The significance of this theory is great. In speech, words are relieved in a certain sense of their "image-content" *(Bildnisgehalt)*. If we had to refer directly from the individual words to the things they represent (which might be appropriate in another situation), if each individual word had to be fulfilled in our mind and realized, then their ability to refer to each other and to enter into a relationship with each other would be negated. It is this last ability that liberates thought and allows it to remain by itself. Heinrich von Kleist was aware of this when he likened a word to the "flywheel on the axis of thoughts" *(Schwungrad an der Achse der Gedanken)*. Language sidesteps the need for its signs to be realized concretely by letting them refer to one another, so that it is not the things themselves but rather the sounds that represent the things that keep this linguistic process going. To put this another way, the word's meaning is temporary, which is precisely why it is able to expand through other words and direct the intention toward these. Only in this manner can the amorphous mass of thoughts, which exercises a "pressure to mean" *(Sinndruck)* on man, be quickly developed into a sequence of abbreviated symbols; each articulation is allowed to divide up the mass of thoughts and to continue through these articulations.

This topic can be approached from another angle. The purely demonstrative type of communication definitely represents one of the earliest levels of language. Even today it is sometimes vitally necessary to use appropriate signs to underscore what one is saying. Some categories of words still retain this particular demonstrative function which refers words directly to the particular situation. In such cases, thought is sent directly from the word to the thing and thus is pushed beyond language toward perception.

A similar process occurs in simple narration, which makes up the bulk of daily linguistic interaction. In this case, an immediate situation is not described, but instead one that has occurred before and is now called to mind again through the narration. Such an account always demands an effort on the part of the imagination because the listener removes himself from the real present into an imagined one. Language still preserves ties to immediate situations; the difference here is that the sentence could not carry out its representative function without thought also being directed to the level of the words themselves.

In contrast, let us now consider an observation or statement involving true knowledge in a general sense, such as the sentence "the rain cools things down." This sentence does *not* intend to say that I or we have once or frequently noticed that things are much cooler after a rainfall. However, it also does not mean that up until now it has also become cooler whenever it has rained; this would be narration. Instead—although this sentence originally resulted from perception—it has broken off its relationship to perception. It is a "synthesis of concepts" *(Synthese aus Begriffen)*. It establishes a fact but it does so *for thought*. Its purpose is not to refer to actual situations or to be amplified in ideas and visualized, and it is in essence not the communication of information—although all these may also be present within it. Through language, it is possible to represent a perceivable fact, to relate it, to refer to it, that is, to direct our attention toward it concretely or through our imagination. It is also possible to abandon this direct route to the thing and to remain instead on the level of thought, leaving other intentions which could have been developed in a suspended state.

This ability of thought to remain by itself is the basis of knowledge. Knowledge is essentially based on thought processes, even though it may follow from perception. Language not only allows us to focus directly on a thing through a symbol but can also suspend this particular focus and bring out another one to which it is similarly predisposed: it can provide relief from the immediacy of the meanings of words by allowing the words to be fulfilled through each other, thereby—to use Leibniz's phrase—"helping out thoughts." Language can prefer this particular route and make it possible for thought to remain by itself. Knowledge is the act of establishing each specific instance in which thought remains by itself. Although this invariably occurs in reference to a thing, it is in itself an action of our thought which no longer directs the intention toward a thing but instead retains it within itself.

I referred earlier to Fichte's example. He wrote: "The need to have different words for subject and object arose after objects became involved in so many different relationships with each other that the predicate was no longer immediately obvious when the object was given."[123] In other words, in language usage that is demonstrative, concrete, and refers to specific situations in nature, it is sufficient simply to identify one element in order to be able to infer the meaning of this embryo of a sentence from its concrete context. However, with situations that are constantly changing or that are ambiguous, this purely demonstrative function is no longer enough: "The means for differentiation was quickly found for it existed in Nature herself. Two tones were put together; the first referred to the subject and the idea was dropped that the subject had a unique relationship to man [I would say: a relationship to particular circumstances and interests] because a special relationship had been added to it."[124]

We now have an explanation for this process. Because thoughts can be linked together, their reference to the immediate external world, as well as their contact with immediate emotions and interests directed toward the external world, acquire a position of secondary importance. They are "suspended" (aufgehoben), as Hegel says. With thought, a significant degree of relief from immediacy is obtained. When a fact expressed in a sentence such as "the rain cools things down" takes on an apparently timeless validity, this can be due only to the fact that thought remains by itself and suspends its always possible demonstrative function, and thereby also suspends its relationship to immediate interests.

To take this argument one step further, it is clear that language recasts the relationships among the word-concepts and expresses and formulates these on their own level, with a marked preference for "faded" (abgeblasst) words, which have lost their concrete or demonstrative character. According to Humboldt,[125] the particular method of inflection "takes every element of speech in its twofold value, that is, in its objective meaning and in its subjective reference to the concept and the language." In an inflected sentence, then, the interrelationships between words are expressed on their own level in addition to the factual meaning of the words which is retained. The sentence *"Caesar urben expugnatam destruxit"* can stand alone because it also expresses and represents the fact that thought remains by itself in the relationships between the words, as opposed to a child's uninflected sentence of several words that has a direct reference to the immediate situation.

Consciousness experiences relief by learning to dwell on its own fleeting, linguistic signs while disregarding the concrete and emotional aspect of the words. This enables consciousness to develop in time all the individual elements in a complex subject and to express this in the relationships of the words to each other. We have already seen in many forms how an overview arises from being able to overlook *(Übersehen im Absehen)*. We are able to overlook fields of symbols in perception because these symbols indicate the potential utility of objects to us and we can then disregard them. Similarly, language is also a field of symbols which we become able to overlook once the individual weight of the words "fades" along with their situational relevance and their reference to immediate interests. The word that disregards the immediate situation is unfulfilled; the intention forces its way beyond the word, and this tension is relieved only by constructing syntactic entities.

That language develops further in syntax and inflection is clear proof that thought originally worked directly in language. Every turn that thought takes is carried out in the material of the word and the words articulate their relationship to each other so that each word takes on an *expressed* relevance to the other words within the context of the meaning of the whole. One consequence is that the power of language is also increased to incorporate the perspectives of the things into itself. The more real thought is, then the more relevant and appropriate it will be. In a language with a highly developed syntax and inflection, thought has perfected itself within itself by not leaving one single perspective unarticulated. It is able to do this only because it can remain by itself and not strive directly from the word to the thing. The prerequisite to this "theoretical" achievement is thus a certain reduction in the emotion (which is already given with our unrestricted ability to repeat any word as an imagined sound) in addition to allowing the demonstrative function to recede. At this point, a high degree of relief from the immediate situation has already been achieved through the sensorimotor functions; this process is then completed and perfected in language.

It is reasonable to expect that with the loss of their immediate relevance to things, the words would assume, in their "faded" form, the function of reference within language itself. The material elements of language, once they have lost their concrete or demonstrative meaning, become for the most part independent, "formal" word-elements and thus are responsible for expressing abstract relationships within language. I will provide a few examples of this.

The Scandinavian passive was formed by combining the active verb with the pronoun *sik: finna sik* (Old Norse: they find themselves), then *finnask, finast, de finnas* (Swedish: they are found). A similar process occurred in the formation of the Latin future tense: *finirai* from *finire habeo* (I will complete). In the same manner, the demonstrative pronoun, which was directly tied to the situation, is reduced to an article: *mann, land* plus the demonstrative pronoun *en* or *et* (neuter) becomes *mannen* (the man), *landet* (the land—Old Norse). Humboldt was aware that it is difficult for certain languages to conceive of the third person as a pure concept and to distinguish it from the demonstrative pronoun. This is a crucial distinction, because while the first and second person pronouns (I, you) are always tied to the particular situation, the third person makes possible a purely intellectual objectivity. Personal pronouns often become the endings to verbs: Greek *esmi* from *es* plus *me;* and *esti* from *es* plus *to;* the Indo-Germanic demonstrative in which this transition, noted by Humboldt, was complete.

Another example is words that were originally independent but then become mere abstract appendages, reduced to the level of secondary elements which simply modify the main concept. As Paul[126] has explained, the word *lîka* ("body," German *Leib)* developed on the one hand into *Leiche* (German, corpse), but was also reduced to the abstract suffix *-lich: wibo-lîkes* ("female body") became the perspective embodied in the adjective *weiblich* (feminine). The suffixes *-keit* and *-heit* come from the Gothic *haidus* (rank, worth). *Heute* (today) and *heuer* (this year) once contained the complete words *Tag* (day) and *Jahr* (year) *(hiu-taju, hiu-jaru).*

Greek verbs with the stem *lyein* are formed by combining two verb stems, *ly* plus *ein:* the latter is a remnant of the complete verb *einai* (to be). Similarly, the French adverbial suffix *-ment* came from the Latin *mens* (feramente = fièrement).

Finally, a late development—subordinate clauses—proved to be of great significance in the development of a form of thought that was independent of the given situation. In subordinate clauses, parts of the sentence are dependent on other parts, rather than simply juxtaposed with each other. Here, as Humboldt recognized, relative pronouns play the principal role. The Melanesian and Ural-Altaic languages originally tolerated no subordinate clauses and dependent sentence structures. In contrast to this, the Finno-Ugric subfamily of languages, as well as many Indo-Germanic languages, developed the relative pronoun from the interrogative. In other words, an interrogative pronoun closely tied to the given situation "faded" to express the relationship between elements within the sentence (qui from quis?). Conjunctions such as because, in that, although, were late acquisitions even in Indo-Germanic. The effect of this reduction or "fading" process on the affective aspect is very clear in those cases in which combinations of affect and statements have resulted in new syntactic constructions. Wegener provides examples of this phenomenon: "Timeo! Ne moriatur!" to Timeo ne moriatur"; εἴ μοί τι πίθοιο! Τό κεν πολὺ κέρδιον εἴη! (Oh, would that you would obey! That would be much better: εἴ here has the meaning of "if," as in "If you would obey, it would be much better.")

As far as allowing thought to remain by itself and expressing relationships within thought are concerned, the loss of the tension of interests (Interessenspannung) is just as important as the process of "fading" or "sinking down" (Herabsinken, Brugmann) which happens to the material contents. The emotional utterance Censeo! followed by Carthaginem esse delendam! is an ancient, original combination of narrative and direct speech: "I meant: Let the battles be fought! I did not believe: I will live after them!" (Old Egyptian). With this loss of the affect, the logical construction of the accusative plus infinitive becomes possible, i.e., censeo Carthaginem esse delendam. To give one final example, the purely logical copula "is" in the sentence Copper is a metal was originally a true verb with the concrete meaning to exist, before it became the mere form word for an intellectual synthesis.

I believe these few examples are sufficient, because this fact has long been recognized. As Grimm put it: "At the beginning, the impression of the words was pure and spontaneous, but yet too full and overburdened, so that light and shadow could not be properly distinguished. Gradually, however, an unconsciously governing Spirit in language allowed weaker light to fall on the secondary concepts and appended them as diluted and abbreviated elements to the principal idea. Inflection arises when certain determining words (Bestimmwörter) become incorporated and function as wheels for the main word that they encourage; they have turned from their originally sensual meaning to take on a more distilled one through which their original meaning only shimmers now and then."[127]

Humboldt believed highly inflected languages, such as the Indo-Germanic languages, were perfect because they were able to express every nuance of thought, and every relationship or aspect. I think he was justified in this. For example, many American Indian languages, which "incorporate" or condense the meaning of a statement into one sentence-word by adopting entire words and articles into the heart of the sentence to define its meaning more exactly, are essentially still bound to the immediate situation. They can represent a concrete situation down to the last detail, but cannot rise above this to the level of real intellectual universality.

All highly developed languages show a tendency to carry this process of "wearing down" still further and become more simple, more abstract, and less inflected. This illustrates the development in the human mind toward a certain mechanical abstractness. Humboldt had the following to say on this subject: "The human intellect, in keeping with its great strides forward and influenced by an increasing confidence in the integrity of its own internal view, finds it appropriate to regard as superfluous a too careful modification of the phonemes of a language.... The more mature the intellect regards itself, the more boldly it operates within its own confines, and the more confidently it abandons the bridges which language has built for the understanding."[128]

Apparently, this tendency toward an increasingly abstract disregard of a former richness of form is common to all languages, and it doubtlessly signifies a waning in the creative power from which indeed certain new possibilities may arise. For example, Jespersen writes

Colloquial Irish and Gaelic have in many ways a simpler grammatical structure than the Oldest Irish. Russian has got rid of some of the complications of Old Slavonic. ... Bulgarian has greatly simplified its nominal and Serbian its verbal flexions. The grammar of spoken Modern Greek is much less complicated than that of the language of Homer or of Demosthenes. The structure of Modern Persian is nearly as simple as English, though that of Old Persian was highly complicated.... Of [one of the Bantu languages] we have a grammar two hundred years old, by Brusciotto a Vetralla.... A comparison of his description with the language now spoken in the same region (Mpongwe) shows that the class signs have dwindled down considerably and the number of classes has been reduced from 16 to 10.[129]

Another of Jespersen's examples will give us an idea of this "progress." In place of the Gothic forms *habaida habaides hadaidedu habaidedium ha-baidedum habaideduth habaidedun habeidedjan habeidedies habeidedi ha-beidedeiwa habaidedeits habaidedeima habaidedeith habaidedeina*, present-day English has only *had* linked with a personal pronoun. Where Old English used *god godne gode godum godes godre godra goda godan godena*, today *good* alone suffices. In modern English, the word *water* is the same in all cases and can serve as a verb as well as a quasi-adjective (watermelon). This means that the word has one general meaning (water, watery) but its concrete meaning can be inferred only from the context of the sentence as a whole; in contrast, an inflected word, such as *cantavissent* contains six aspects of meaning: to sing, the past perfect, the restriction implied by the subjunctive mood, the active voice, third person, and plural.

At this level, word position becomes very important and the listener must correctly interpret what is being said from the context of meaning. Humboldt wrote of Chinese, which is uninflected, that the ear takes in only the materially significant sounds, the formal relationship between words is expressed in the sounds only in their relationship to each other, in the word position, and subordination. Thus, the Chinese must have a keen ear for recognizing the formal context of speech.

The loss of inflection thus permits languages to become "abstract." The meanings, formulated earlier, which are contained in the relationships between words now become nonverbal relationships between intellectual acts! In the sentence *puer amat puellam*, it is the accusative ending that indicates the object in the described process; in the sentence *the boy loves the girl*, the position of the words prevents any misunderstanding. Thus the meaning of the object lies unformulated in the direction of thought that is clearly prescribed. This example leads to the interesting insight that by becoming less inflected, a language becomes more mathematical. Sentences which have lost inflection become topographical schemata in which position is significant. One could say that a word first gains its full meaning by virtue of its place value *(Stellenwert)* and that all nonmaterial meanings are based on regular movements of reference of thought itself.

Thought becomes mathematical when it consists of a simple intellectual act without any real content and preserves this in remnants of linguistic signs. This unity is established by the intellectual act as such. The mathematical movement consists of arbitrary, willed, but nonetheless regular and maintained relationships between such intellectual acts. Signs are chosen to symbolize these relationships. Each symbol indicates the relationships between these intellectual acts or between other similarly symbolic ones, and the operations made possible by these symbols are carried out for the express purpose of establishing other equally symbolic ones.

For example, the "meaning" of a mathematical symbol, such as the number 3, lies only in the intellectual movement, without any real content, which is prescribed in it: act, act, act all condensed in this one symbol. This same intellectual movement, which has been freed of language, is necessary in uninflected, highly abstract languages, when the place value of a word constitutes the nonmaterial part of its meaning (such as the role of object) so that this meaning can be reached only by a specific, regular direction of relationship without explicitly stating this. This fact explains, as in mathematics, the ability of these languages to become mechanical and simple and yet avoid misunderstandings. Certain aspects of English clearly bring to mind mechanical mathematics: for example, the collective genetive: all good old men's works = (all good old men)'s works.

The basic human phenomenon of relief always involves an act of drawing back from points of direct contact with the world. From the simplest motor skills to language, thought, and above all to our basic drives and impulses, all human functions are developed in conjunction with each other; indispensable to this development is mechanization, the formation of habit; in other words the creation of a basis for the further refinement of skills. To realize this, we need only consider a skilled artisan who has developed, through thousands of hours of practice, an unconscious certainty of movement even when the most refined movements are called for, so that anything beyond these movements, which might simply require more effort and concentration on his part, would be almost impossible for anyone else to execute. In this chapter on language, I have attempted to show how remarkable this law of relief is here in the very core of the human being. Originally, the domain of language was certainly confined to the here and now, the existing situation. However, by finding relief from the present, language learns to move within itself; the mechanism of associations, of forming analogies, of understanding formulas, is integrated into language to the same degree that it loses its demonstrative function and purely affective value, and is reduced in image and emotional content. This process sets the stage for a richer and more greatly refined form of thinking; it is the basis for our ability to think in the nuances of subordinate clauses and for the entire range of intellectual richness that is expressed in syntax and inflection. This process continues until the path to perfection leads downward once again, as stereotypy becomes stifling, an impoverished schematism sets in, and the pervasive absence of problems associated with "terrifying simplification" results.

34. Images Peculiar to Language

Etymology is a truly fascinating area of study. The original images and thoughts that once lived in a language can be reawakened from its now functionalized forms; we can trace our way back to those early times in which a graphic imagination produced thoughts in world-images.

In his *Philebos* (ch. 23), Plato writes that there is a picture-maker and a logos-writer at work within us whenever we perceive anything real. Aristotle writes: "As far as concepts are concerned, the power of thought constructs these on the basis of images in our mind."[130] I agree wholeheartedly with these views. When we study a language, we experience and revitalize the original direction of a people's interpretative imagination.

Thought's movement through sound is a manner of communication that is active and directed toward opening up the world; it is also creative because it increases and concentrates the richness of the world. Through the images in language, this world of concrete, condensed symbols becomes accessible to us once more on a symbolic level. To do so, of course, language draws extensively on the human imagination, for language represents the system that ultimately directs and integrates human experience and comes to monopolize expression and communication. Man's ability to transfer himself to other situations in his imagination allows him to indulge in a relieved, removed form of activity; because the intentions of language are fulfilled in each other, this ability eventually allows us to transpose these intended contents into each other. It is this last skill that we will now discuss, a skill which is distinct from that other ability also made possible by language to shift oneself into other situations in the mind.

There appear to be two directions imagination takes in language: The first is in the image content of the word itself; the second in the "inner form" of language—the choice of perspectives possible in the imagination which guides its interpretation. I would like to discuss both these aspects briefly.

The symbolic nature of language, language's ability to portray objects metaphorically in words, shows us that the imagination is already at work on a fundamental level in every word as such. In this sense, assigning one specific sound to one thing, taking one thing as another, is already an imaginative act. Its intellectual aspect lies in the intention of this act, in directing oneself toward a thing through a word. This act is the same in many languages. In contrast, when the imaginative act of assigning a sound to a thing, of taking A as B, becomes aware of itself and then functions independently (as in a game), we have the interesting imaginary languages that children concoct. I believe it is quite possible that a portion of the vocabulary was developed in this manner. As we saw in our discussion of the origin of language, the sound gestures (action-sounds) and the responses in sound to something that is recognized must indeed have led to the word, but beyond doubt the imagined word also played a part in this. Once the value of a sound-image for representing a thing becomes clear as a creative event, as a result of a successful communication, then this ability becomes conscious and unleashes the "game of naming." There is a fundamental arbitrariness to this game: a child conceives of the words that he learns as nominal relationships. A child stood in the center of a room, pointed toward the individual objects, and said, "lamp," "closet," "wastebasket." This arbitrariness of the rules is part of every game of the imagination and is a necessary aspect of imagination. Thus, along with the other sources of words, naming can be a type of "betting game" *(Setzungsspiel)* of the imagination.

I am indebted to Jespersen for a very nice illustration of this point which he found in a work by Martius, an explorer of South America. He recounts that among the Botokude tribe, words were often spontaneously invented: "One of them called out the word in a loud voice, as if a thought had suddenly occurred to him, the others repeated it with laughter and amidst excited shouts and it was then universally accepted by all of them, even for very familiar objects." Thus, the horse was called "head-teeth" and the ox "cloven foot." In general, the languages of primitive peoples allow a certain degree of spontaneous word invention. Kainz reports that a member of the Ful tribe, when asked about the word for lungs, immediately invented one. From *fofa* (to blow), he took the intensive form *fofta* and then added the suffix of the instrumental class, *ki,* to form the word *foftoki*—"forceful blowing instrument."[131]

In our discussion thus far, it seems that the word, considered as a sound-image and picture of a thing, already possesses a metaphorical content. Language is in fact fundamentally metaphor, simply because it does not contain the objects themselves, but instead "expresses [them] in reflection" (Goethe). The narrower form of metaphor, which involves a truly imaginative use of language, is based on the possibility of taking A as B.

Within the meanings of individual words and the words, there is an image of fundamental meaning (Grundbedeutung), which in the majority of cases is an image of concrete movement with an unequivocal form and which tends to allow the meaning and validity of a word to extend to similar objects. This should appear as no mystery to us, considering what we have been saying all along. Different objects which are similar in some way from the perspective of this fundamental image of meaning become associated with each other. One might also say that our act of naming extends throughout the world. It is these processes that make the area of etymology so exciting.

In Ancient Egyptian, kod meant many things: to make pots, to be a potter, to create, to build, to work, to draw, as well as picture, circle, ring, etc. Behind all of these images lies a fundamental one of "turning around, turning in a circle." The action of turning a pot on a potter's wheel and representing a potter's work led to the development of these other meanings of "forming, working, creating, building."[132]

In the Ural-Altaic languages, tob is an element associated with flying, feathers, wings, butterflies, etc. This developed on the one hand into tev ten den siw sub lob leb röp, rb, jep, etc.; and on the other hand into tagv, tog, däk, len, lij. Thus, in Finnish, for to fly, to flap, to soar, we have lobal, lobog, lebeg, leg, röpül, repül, etc.; and for leaf: lipet, luopta, lopa, level. Butterfly: lependek, libindi, lapoch, lablok. Fly: legy. Feather: togol, taul, toll, tolke. In Tungusic, doguatten means he flies, däge = birds; däktilä, feather; lopara, wing; jepura, wing.[133]

Stenzel contributes another example.[134] In Greek, χεο means "to pour," but it is also tied to another specific image of movement and can refer to the action of falling (as in "the snow falls"), of pulling out the base of support by overturning a vessel, of sliding fish off a spit, and of sliding arrows out of the quiver. Thus, the meaning of being fluid, which cannot be avoided in German, is not essential here. What is, however, is the form of movement of dropping, sliding out, or running down. In Latin, on the other hand, fundo, which means "to pour," implies the form of movement that involves active flinging or throwing; in addition to pour, it can also mean to shoot or to throw someone to the ground. χεο corresponds to a twisting movement of the hand turning over a container, whereas fundo is associated more with a powerful thrust.

As a final example (Jespersen), in Swedish, the word hoppas (hope) has an older meaning of refuge *(to-hopa)* and to find refuge *(hopan to)*. Within this is hidden an even more ancient meaning of *hop* as to hop or jump (Old Nordic, *hopa),* to move back. Thus, the original image of movement here was that of bending over, of jumping away, or jumping toward something good.

These examples are intended to convey a sense of the original meaning of words. The precise images embodied in words refer to mental pictures as well as to movements; as Stenzel recognized, they existed before noun and verb were differentiated. They represent truly creative achievements, for the act of giving a name to a process or a thing is at the same time the act of selecting one perspective from which to view the thing. This perspective is then retained by our imagination as an essential element in the word. The abstract nature of these images makes it possible to apply them to other processes, based on one dominant perspective. Strictly speaking, this constitutes the truly metaphorical process.

Children frequently make use of this sort of metaphorical interpretation of the world. When a child calls a soup with dumplings "ball soup," or refers to the rubbing motions of a butterfly's legs by saying that it is "knitting socks," the child is carrying out a metaphorical transferral of images of form. Words often come about in this manner. A child may say "I pailed him out" when he uses a pail to get a turtle. A long list of such childish metaphors is available in Bühler's book, *Die Geistige Entwicklung des Kindes* (1924).

There is also, of course, a broad area of metaphorical interpretation of aspects of reality that do not directly involve the senses—the dimensions of time, for example. Time can be described only with metaphors of space: before, after, a long time, short time, an extended time, etc. The same is true of abstract spatial directions: *Süden* (south), Old High German *sund,* is related to the word for sun *(Sonne;* Gothic, *sunno;* Old Slavic, *slunice).* Above everything else, all inner spiritual states, all emotions, drives, or moods, can be described only in metaphors drawing on sensory images: to be struck by a thought, to break one's heart, to be consumed by jealousy, to stir up emotion, to toss around an idea, are only a few of a great list of such examples in every language.[135] Another aspect of this rich metaphorical use of language is apparent when we use verbs to describe processes involving inanimate things: the fall "obeys" the law of gravity, the sky "threatens" to rain, the woods "are silent." In the use of the verb in the Indo-Germanic languages, there is a "personification" of all things which are described with verbs; these processes are thought of as actions.

We have now touched upon the second major area in which the imagination acts in language—the fundamental perspectives that constitute the inner form of every language. Here, too, I will provide only a few examples because much attention has been devoted to this subject in linguistic research, even though it has rarely been considered from the solely correct viewpoint of the imagination.

In Indo-Germanic languages, for example, the verbs are based on actual images of activity; in addition, although this may not be readily apparent, external processes are also conceived of in images of activities, insofar as these are described verbally. Other languages, in contrast, show a different trend and think not in images of action but rather in terms of the "manifested process." Such languages, instead of saying "I killed him," might have something along the lines of "He died to me"; not: "I threw it away," but "It fell away from me" (in the Ural-Altaic languages, for example). This represents such a totally different way of understanding the world that one must assume the basic categories of the imagination are different. To translate such a sentence as "he died to me" into another language involves translating it into another spirit of language, which captures the same fact but not the spontaneous manner in which it was understood. The language of Greenland does not have the fundamental image "I hear," but instead has a completely different one that might be rendered as "sounding to me." This conception cannot actually be translated or faithfully reproduced; we can only transpose the basic fact it expresses into a completely different feeling for language or image. Only the substance of what is being discussed can be translated from one language to another, not the original way in which the imagination of a language mastered these facts.

Let us consider the following: in the Indo-Germanic languages, there is a distinction between noun and verb. This means that assigning a characteristic to an object and describing a process are fundamental and distinct categories of thought and perception, of interpretative imagination. In the Ural-Altaic language, there was initially no distinction between noun and verb. The expressions Man-I," "big-I," "There-I," "go-I," were part of the same basic point of view. In Turkish, *min padishamyn* means "I Lord I" or "I am Lord"; *mänäkkälgän min* is literally "I have brought I" or "I have brought." This undifferentiated "verb-noun" can certainly be rendered in our language by using substantivized infinitives, participles, and so forth, but we cannot fully adopt the basic outlook that lies behind it. The image that assigns a property to a thing is here the same as the one that portrays a process or one's own actions.

Simple indications of tense can be added to a noun-adjective relationship:

sawa-dam (good I), *sawa* + *dam* + *s* (good I was: Jurassic). This "predicative conjugation" primarily involves intransitive verbs ("go-I") although
of course these languages also have transitive verbs. Here we must marvel
at the imagination that allows the languages to incorporate both the relationship to an object and the specification of the person who is doing the
action (we took them) into the image of a thing. The possessive pronoun
serves this purpose. In Vogul, *kuäl-on, Kuäl-än, Kuäl-änel* means: "house-
our," "house-your," "house-their"; similarly, *us-l-on, us-l-än, us-l-änel*
means "took-him-our," "took-him-your," "took-him-their," or "our having
taken him," "your having taken him," etc. The stem *-us* acts as a verbal
noun to which an object and a possessive pronoun have been added. Thus,
it is possible for a verb to be declined. In Turkish, for example, the syllable
-lar/ler functions as the plural suffix. *Severler* means: they love. In Japanese,
in which this characteristic feature appears most strongly, these substantive
formations even affect particles and adverbs of place *(ko-no koma,* "this
horse," literally means "the hereness horse," whereby *no* is expressively
genetive).

These examples show us original ways of understanding the world that
are radically different from our own. The various language families differ
so greatly in their elemental language imagination that one can go crazy
trying to render them in one's own language. Finck rightly points out that
in Turkish the personal ending *-im,* which is also a possessive suffix, has
combined "I, mine, me" into one "inconceivable unity." To render a verbal
noun as "the going" is basically illogical because our substantivized verbal
forms can only bridge the gap between noun and verb in very special cases,
since after all they define this gap. The verbal noun, however, lies before,
or better yet beyond, this differentiation. I doubt whether it is really possible
to express the image "going" or "going-I" as a genetive: "going's not being."
For this reason, there are clearly things that are beyond translation. In the
language of the Hamites, there is a grammatical phenomenon known as
"polarity," which also exists in Somali.[136] In Somali, a masculine singular
noun becomes feminine in the plural, and vice versa. To explain this, Meinhof points out that among the Hamites, the sons often belong to the family
of the mother, the daughters to that of the father, and that (among the
Nandi) young boys don girls' clothing and the girls boys' before the passage
into manhood. This might indicate a very curious and deep-lying polarity
image that is expressed in language. In Fula, the class of singular persons
begins the same as the class of plural things. Why in Fula, which has 21
class-defining suffixes, the fifth one *(-al, -gal)* should designate "birds, tools,

infinitives" is beyond my power of understanding. This language is in no sense primitive; indeed, the possible combinations of suffixes and verbs are in fact extraordinarily ingenious.

We can close our rather elementary discussion of the images inherent in language without treating the higher processes that involve creative use of the imagination in language. It seems that linguistics generally shies away from the topic of the "imagination," probably because the lack of understanding about it causes any discussion to dissolve into vagueness. For this reason, the concept of the inner form of language remains quite obscure and can be defined only in terms of the imagination. Once the critical role that imagination plays in the development of our senses and movements has been acknowledged and once language is studied in its vital relationship to the imagination, we can begin to comprehend, in the deepest levels of language, the imagination as it takes the role of the other, equates one thing with another, and interprets the world accordingly. This is metaphor. Even the inner form of language, which equates "processes" with "actions" or "actions" with "manifestations," etc., is ultimately metaphor.

35. Knowledge and Truth

Thought's ability to "remain by itself" is already prefigured in language, which is its foundation. This ability makes it possible for us to isolate and examine a context of meanings and thereby establish a fact as such. We must then repeat Pilate's question: "What is truth?" I wish to explore this question in this chapter.

As we know from our previous discussion, perception provides us not with knowledge, but with familiarity: for example, a child might be familiar with *(kennen)* the moon but really know *(wissen)* nothing about it. A statement about the moon must be made before the issue of truth can surface. Xenophon, for example, made the following statement: "The moon is a condensed mass of clouds." It is immaterial for our purposes that this sentence is actually false. What we should be aware of here is that this statement (like all other statements) exists in the social medium: it is formed from words that everyone knows, it contains a message, it is addressed to anyone who might not know this fact. In addition to its implicit, mysterious claim to be true, it makes the claim that it is valid for any number of people who should understand it and accept it as true. As Schiller wrote, "Truth is one of the few things which no one wants to be the sole possessor of."[137]

This particular statement was interesting because it said something new; every true sentence was interesting at one time before it became self-evident. It is the acquisition of truth that is attractive, not the possession of it. The sentence is interesting in another sense because it establishes a connection between an unknown quantity and a known, between the moon and the clouds. A person hearing this thinks of the clouds, then imagines them coming together and balling up like cotton. The end product is the moon. This person might then perhaps ask, "But what exactly are clouds?" Xenophon can answer this question: "When moisture is drawn up from the sea by the sun, the sweet particles are separated out because they are so fine; these particles then become dense like fog and form clouds, eventually producing rain."

This statement represents a whole system of knowledge. As one can easily observe, the sun draws the fog up from the sea. The salty, heavy parts are cast off, the fog condenses into clouds which then, like a squeezed sponge, give off fresh water. The moon is one such concentrated mass of clouds.

We can now identify how knowledge is obtained: by letting an unknown follow from a known, re-creating it in our minds or by using some sort of intellectual operation to change a known in such a way that an unknown results. This involves a process of reconstruction *(Umkonstruktion)*. Xenophon begins with the observation that fog rises and adds in the concept of condensation which he has also obtained somehow; finally, in his reconstructing imagination, the clouds, rain, and moon appear in turn.

We could consider this from another angle and say that the unknown becomes incorporated into a greater, already established system, a context of familiar facts: that the fog rises toward the sun, that the sea is salty, and rain is not, that condensation occurs, and that a sponge "rains" when it is pressed—all these are known facts to which the unknown fact is then grouped and by means of which it is understood.

Finally, there is yet another aspect of this issue: the sentence itself ("the moon is a condensed mass of clouds"). This sentence is the result of a reconstruction process, an isolated, self-contained structure. This sentence then enters circulation like a newly minted coin and thus comes to another person who might question it and ask "Is this true?" What does this other person then do?

He "verifies" the statement, he *makes* it true or false. He also uses a process of construction to accomplish this: he predicts the observable consequences that should exist if the sentence is true. If the moon is a condensed mass of clouds, why does it not produce rain like all other clouds and why does it not change its position in the skies with the wind direction, as clouds do? If the sentence were actually true, these expectations would have to be confirmed by experience; since this is not the case, this second ancient physicist would reject the sentence as untrue.

Thus, we see that there are several important factors that affect knowledge. First of all, the process of acquiring knowledge is just as constructive as that of verifying it, for in both cases something new emerges from what is already given. We define and verify in a fundamentally constructive manner. We can say that knowledge is productive because it involves this process of letting something new emerge; it is also productive on a psychological level because of the intellectual freedom it provides, which allows us to

isolate a fact from its usual, familiar surroundings and relate it to an unexpected other that explains it.

Second, once a fact is known, it becomes part of a system of already
known facts and bears a certain relationship to these. It might appear to
be connected to facts that direct experience would indicate have nothing to
do with the unknown. The true sentence is assigned a place value in a system
of other true sentences. It is significant that this connection exists in knowledge, and probably in reality itself, but *not* in the concrete world of perceptual situations. A falling stone and the movement of the planets are part
of one system in Newton's mind and in the real world of natural laws, but
not in direct experience of perception. At this point, the truly gnosological
problems of cognitive theory arise.

The third important point is that of *verification*. The sentence's claim to
be true and the proof of its truth are two different things. A good truth
grants us certainty, not in its conviction that it is true but rather in its ability
to predict certain consequences which in hindsight confirm its truth. A truth
is fruitful, something can be gained from it. An expectation known to be
justified is as deeply satisfying as its result.

Finally, there is the sentence itself: this isolated and self-contained structure, in which the truth becomes transportable, is released from the lonely
mind of its inventor, and enters into circulation. Thus, because of the sentence, one can determine one's actions not only on the basis of one's own
insights but on the insights of others as well. When we know something, a
specific content of thought, related to an objective fact, is established and
a specific set of meanings can remain by itself. In this way, an invariant is
created in the ocean of experiences, an island, a handhold for guiding behavior in the future, a point of support for further actions.

This final point about the "closed" sentence can also contribute much to
anthropology. Because of the freedom of thought the sentence grants, freedom to develop further in itself and to use one idea to intend and refer back
to another, the sentence is removed temporarily from the world, has its own
momentum, and at some point encounters the facts again. Thought's ability
to remain by itself allows more indirect and circuitous behavior, which in
turn permits us to retreat in a series of conclusions and hypotheses from
reality only then to move back toward it once more. The highest degree of
relief comes about because relieved behavior can perpetuate itself for a while
within itself and is self-contained. Dewey touched on this in his *The Quest
for Certainty* in his discussion of symbols or words: "Even more important

was the fact that instead of being adapted to local and directly presented situations, they were framed in detachment from direct overt use [relief!] and *with respect to one another.*"[138]

A formulated truth is an inner invariant which allows us to deal with a fact "in absentia" since in the majority of cases we did not even determine the fact ourselves. Acute impressions are then no longer the motivation for our behavior. We act in a world that has been completely restructured and in which the things that interest us most and that we are constantly seeking to explain are not actually present. It is language that enables us to form attitudes freely about reality, to draw back from it temporarily, only then to remerge ourselves in it. Language lets us remove ourselves from the immediate world; it aids the articulation of our movements, opens up our imagination, extends the present in space and time, expresses our mind's intentions, and allows us to base our behavior on the knowledge of others. Finally, it functions as the "flywheel on the axis of thought," so that thought can perpetuate itself and become self-contained within the form of a sentence. Thus, because a sentence can stand on its own, the relationship of thought to being *(Sein)* becomes merely *possible.* This virtual verifiability is the "pretension to truth" that one attributes to a sentence instead of to the person who spoke it. As far as factual statements are concerned (as opposed to purely formal constructions, such as mathematical theorems), the supposed timelessness of a truth, a true statement, does not mean that it is rooted in a higher sphere of "pure values." Thought alone does not guarantee this other world. The timeless quality is caused by a suspension of the reference to unique situations in time—situations we would have to examine closely if we wished to verify the statement. Thought can of course choose to make this reference. A *possible* relationship of what has been established to reality must also exist; it figures into all knowledge as its pretension to the truth, as the tendency of suspended thought to lead back once again to the real world.

The model of knowledge we have presented here can be verified wherever any factual problems in reality are concerned, whether these are of a scientific nature or not, from the technical expertise of a craftsman who must assess his material carefully to the science that deals most heavily in ideas—the study of history. The historian draws on incomplete documents and remnants to reconstruct historical events in his imagination; his work manifests perhaps the greatest distance between reality and theory.

The concept of knowledge we have presented here is by no means new. As I have argued elsewhere,[139] very different philosophers (such as Aristotle,

Hobbes, and Vico) have referred to the view that knowledge constructs its object or allows it to emerge in a generative fashion. Kant made the following thesis a principle of his theory: "Reason only perceives that which it produces after its own design."[140] He puts this even more strongly at another point: "However, we cannot really understand anything properly if it is not something that we could immediately make ourselves if we were provided with the appropriate materials."[141] F. H. Jacobi writes: "If we discover the mechanism of things, what makes them work, if we have the appropriate means at our disposal, we can produce these things ourselves. Whatever we can construct in this fashion, or at least in our minds, we can understand and what we cannot construct we do not understand."[142] Novalis wrote: "What I comprehend, I must be able to make, what I wish to comprehend, I must be able to learn to make," for "we only understand something to the extent that we can express it, that is, make it."[143] Similarly, Nietzsche claimed: "If there is indeed any understanding at all, then we can only understand what we can do."[144] Fichte also expressed this pragmatic concept of knowledge: "I have compared my different experiences with each other and only once I realized exactly what their relationship to each other is, only once I could explain one through the other, derive one from the other, anticipate the outcomes beforehand, and have the perception of this outcome agree with my calculations, was I then reassured."[145]

These initial forays in this direction of understanding knowledge were not carried further in idealistic philosophy, however, even in the works of these writers. It was Pragmatism, under the guidance of Peirce, James, and Dewey, that fully developed this concept of knowledge. James argued that the essence of the agreement between knowledge and its subject lies in the process of "being lead"; a theory must above all lead toward something, away from eccentricity and isolation, from unfruitful thoughts, and toward something important and fruitful.[146] In *The Will to Believe*,[147] James very convincingly contrasted the uncertainty of the future with the secure expectations that rational knowledge affords. In many of his works concerned with cognitive theory, and above all in *The Quest for Certainty* (1930), Dewey examined this subject. He put forth the thesis that the goal of thought in its rational cognition of things is not to approximate an existing reality; instead, thought is interested in the features that are characteristic not of things at rest, but rather of their dynamic interrelationships. Thought considers these features as indications of what these things could possibly *become* if specific operations were performed on them. Knowledge invariably involves experimentation through which a problematic situation is transformed into a manageable or "resolved" one: "Sensory qualities experienced through vision have their cognitive status and office, not (as sensual empiricism holds) in and of themselves in isolation, or as merely forced upon attention, but because they are the consequences of definite and intentionally performed operations. Only in connection with the intent, or idea of these operations do they amount to anything, either as disclosing any fact or giving test and proof of any theory."[148]

I am devoting attention to Pragmatism here because it has been the only branch of philosophy to view man as an acting being. I am pleased that W. Burkamp, in his learned and thorough work *Wirklichkeit und Sinn (Reality and Meaning,* 1938) shares this view: "I am in complete agreement with the fundamental principle of Pragmatism."[149] It is only fair to mention here that, independently of the American movement which began in 1878 with Peirce, Pragmatism had already been proposed on several occasions, for example, by Sorel in 1899 *(De l'utilité du pragmatisme),* by E. Mach, and by Bergson as well. It should be noted further that Pragmatism does not so much solve the problem of knowledge as give it a new form. It does this by modeling its theory of knowledge on the experimental natural sciences. Any branch of philosophy that does this takes on a certain pragmatic tone, as Georges Sorel rightly identified in Kant: "Like Kant, the pragmatists take society's highest scientific achievement as the first datum of intelligence." Indeed, Kant, in the *Critique of Judgment,* wrote that natural science must confine its study of nature to what "we are able so to subject to our observation or experiment that we could ourselves produce it like nature, or at least produce it according to similar laws. For we have complete insight only into what we can make and accomplish according to our conceptions."[150] This sentence contains the central thought of Kant's theory and is in essence pragmatic. It was most likely the compelling influence of Newtonian astronomy that led Kant to claim that Reason *(Vernunft)* has a purely intellectual power to act in experience and to overlook the role of the real actions of the body in this development. Indeed, no experimentation was involved here; a supposedly *a priori* law was discovered through perception and calculation.

From our discussion, we can come up with a specific understanding of the truth of all knowledge that is expressed in the form of a sentence. If, as is generally recognized, the truth of a sentence cannot be determined from the sentence itself ("the average life span of a European is 52 years"), then it must lie in a relationship that can be created. This relationship may, as is immediately apparent, take three forms: (1) it can be the relationship of the sentence to the facts it asserts;(2) it can be the relationship of the sentence to other sentences; (3) since sentences are "inner invariants," and as such provide guidelines for our actions, it can be the effectiveness of the sentence for this purpose—that is, its productivity in terms of practical and theoretical consequences in the future.

Thus, truth is never inherent to a sentence but is rather the mark of a function or service the sentence performs. As far as consciousness is concerned, the sentence as such is always hypothetical and "undecided" *(da-hingestellt)*. It may remain this way if I rely on its possible confirmation without testing it out first or if I do not doubt its validity. This happens frequently. It is possible, however, to prove the truth of a sentence and this always involves setting it in motion: we trace it back to its origin in experience, we ascertain its effectiveness by determining its future usefulness, or we compare it to other sentences in order to see what pattern emerges. Thus, the established sentence must always be set in motion again to determine its truth; this truth is a function of the result of such an attempt. An isolated sentence, as the mere object of reflection, cannot even be questioned as to whether it is "true or false."

The first meaning of this function we call truth, which we conceive of as contained within a sentence, is the relationship of the sentence to the facts it asserts. This is essentially a relationship that extends backwards, a test of origin. I assume that it is true that the Brocken [The highest peak in the Harz Mountain range.—trans.] is 1142 meters high but if I want to be sure of this, I would have to measure it myself. Any valid scientific concept must be able to be proved in this same manner; it must be open to verification. Determining the sources of experience from which the statement originated is a sometimes necessary but in essence unproductive way of reassuring oneself that a certain bit of knowledge is correct. In fact, this way of proceeding is only productive if one item of knowledge contradicts another and then becomes open to doubt itself. In such a case, the attempt to verify it could lead to far-reaching changes in the system of knowledge. However, because some branches of philosophy (above all, Sensualism) were preoccupied with determining the origins of concepts and judgments in experience, they always described the cognitive process as one of combining and comparing beliefs that ultimately must be traced back to experience. In this view, knowledge becomes a sterile function that simply leads us back via circuitous routes to what we already know.

Now we come to the second meaning of truth which is closely related to the first and third meanings. This is the relationship of the sentence to other sentences.

A certain degree of indefiniteness in the meanings of words is part of the nature of language. This is cleared up by the context of the sentence. Words can be brought together to form a sentence because the meaning of each individual word is first tentative and somewhat loose, which allows it to refer to the words that follow; thus, in the sentence, it gains back its own meaning from the meaning of the sentence as a whole. Because in language this direct reference toward what is present can be suspended, it becomes possible for thought to continue within itself. Thereby, a certain provisional variable becomes part of every word which is resolved by the word that follows and by the overall context of meaning in which the words appear.

Saussure first argued this point: "La langue est un système dont tous les termes sont solidaires et où la valeur de l'un ne résulte que de la présence simultanée des autres". ("Language is a system in which all the terms are interdependent and the value of one is determined only by the simultaneous presence of the others.")[151]

This indefiniteness is avoided through definition, that is, by willfully determining the content appropriate to a meaning. A definition is a contract, a process in which thought comes to terms with itself, and agrees to think in specific, individually formulated perspectives in one concept and to stick to this interpretation. The definition thus arose from the truly constructive areas of thought—logic, mathematics, and jurisprudence. However, apart from the definition, an indefiniteness in meaning of words does exist and allows the words to enter into the unity of a sentence and to gain definiteness from it, even if no situational aids are available to facilitate this.

We encounter this same situation on a higher level in the relationship of sentences to each other. Idealism was completely correct in stating that all our knowledge strives beyond itself toward a system, a whole. Fichte and Hegel were not successful in describing this whole; it is basically impossible to do so because all experience operates in an as yet indefinite future. Schelling, however, does make a valid point: "In true science, every sentence has only one specific and so to speak localized meaning, and . . . because it is removed from this specific place and becomes absolute, that is dogmatic, it either loses its sense and meaning or becomes enmeshed in contradictions."[152]

As Schelling correctly argued, the meaning of a sentence, on the basis of which its truth can first be debated, is closely related to the context of sentences in which it exists. Its truth is thus a function in a second respect: The sentence has a place value which is important as far as its truth is concerned. The place value of a sentence, of an item of knowledge, can differ greatly; in our only loosely coherent everyday knowledge it is quite slight, but in the highly organized sciences it is very great. Similarly, the consequences of the change that results whenever we withdraw a sentence believed to be true and replace it with another can also vary. The importance and range of validity of a sentence are doubtless part of its meaning and thereby become a function of the theoretical context in which the sentence exists. In the descriptive or classifying sciences, a new discovery or an error may remain quite isolated; however, in physics, for example, in which a high level of systematic representation exists, an individual statement has a great deal of weight. The fundamental tenets of quantum mechanics contradicted the earlier conceptions of atomic events and furthermore necessitated a new understanding of classical physics and its models. It appears, however, that this movement extends even beyond the boundaries of physics. The problems of concreteness and of causality crop up; and further problems for cognitive theory appear: the "objectifiability" of concepts and the element of "choice" that figures into the formation of concepts. The basic assumptions of logic become questionable if one has to use a "polyvalent" logic to describe something. There also appear to be cases in which the statement no longer holds for an excluded third element.[153] This is only one particularly interesting example of the fact that wherever our experience provides a context, the things we know are so closely related to each other that a change at any one point inevitably causes changes elsewhere as well.

The third element of meaning of truth is its productivity or effectiveness as far as the future is concerned. Of the four great branches of philosophy to date, the rationalists (Platonic philosophers and logicians) could not come up with an understanding of truth because they believed in the existence of the contents of concepts and sentences in themselves and they consequently ascribed truth to the sentence itself, rather than seeing it in a movement of the sentence. The Sensualists argued that our first concept of truth is the only correct one; the Idealists chose the second, and the Pragmatists the third. One should not judge the Pragmatists solely by the mundane formulas they resorted to on occasion, as when James said that the truth of a sentence lies in its "cash value" (meaning apparently *pour épater le bourgeois*). What James meant here is its effectiveness for the future; this may be a purely theoretical effectiveness but can just as easily be a practical or moral one as well. On a theoretical level, it could then be asked: What new and productive points of view could be gained from new knowledge? What does it illuminate that was previously obscure and what new light does it shed upon what is already known? On a practical level, this productivity could refer to the ways in which knowledge can be applied, the new orientations for action that might result or the possibility that things once unrelated might now be brought together.

It is also possible, as Kant realized, that a conviction, the truth of which cannot be directly verified, might take on the status of an "inner truth," that it might bring about a greater degree of harmony between moral impulses and ourselves which will then be manifested in how we lead our lives. Thus, Kant believed the idea of God was "empty" in an empirical sense but he felt that it had a great range of effectiveness in moral life. When James translated this Kantianism into the conceptual world of Pragmatism, he carried it beyond the bound of a theory of science. All these efforts are fruitful. Fruitfulness has to do with the potential for knowledge to become an inner invariant, a guideline for leading one's life. An insight is not productive, it is *made* productive; for this reason; it becomes the starting point for a new action. Dewey writes, "The test of ideas ... is found in the consequences of the act to which the ideas lead, that is, in new arrangements of things which are brought into existence."[54] The Pragmatists, and Dewey in particular, chose to emphasize this particular meaning of truth. Dewey writes: "The business of thought is not to conform to or reproduce the characters already possessed by objects but to judge them as potentialities of what they become through an indicated operation."[55] To this end, perceived data and data that serve as possible perspectives to guide our actions continually work together and regulate each other. Every step in one direction carries a corresponding improvement in the other. The effect is that the original material of experience is reorganized to construct a new one, which then has those qualities that allow it to be understood or known.

It is quite apparent that this third direction of truth encompasses the first two because what we already know invariably figures into any productive problem-solving. What is already known then no longer needs to be directly verified but rather becomes valid retroactively and receives a higher place value through its relationship to what has just been learned. Now we must turn to the question of why there are these three meanings of truth. This has to do with the nature of knowledge once it is expressed in a sentence. Then and only then is it able to refer to something, to be joined to other sentences while essentially remaining by itself, and finally to act as a guideline for future actions. Let us now develop these thoughts and apply them to man's situation in particular.

We represent the world in our consciousness. It is not restricted to the narrow realm of the here and now, to the perceivable; instead, in our consciousness, we exist in a spatiotemporal world which knows no boundaries and in which what we know is just as valuable as what we have experienced. This is the basic phenomenon from which Kant proceded. What is past and distant, the factualness of anytime and anyplace, can be realized in our minds at any time to the extent that it has been established as knowledge; it can be called into play at any point in the present. In knowledge, "anywhere" is available to us symbolically in the here and now. This is where we encounter our first concept of truth. It takes note of the distance between knowledge and its origins, of the fact that it was once the concrete present. This understanding demands that the unreal process of visualization, of imagining, remain aware of its own unreality so that we will not blindly rely upon the truth of an item of knowledge, that it must be able to become part of the present, an apparent fact.

However, even by identifying our ability to focus in our freely available intentions on some fact in space and time and then to use this in the immediate present, we have still not exhausted this issue. Our thoughts must remain in their own domain and be able to follow their impulses, to adopt circuitous routes within themselves, to move over toward other perspectives, and to establish connections on their own level between distant facts. We must be able to take action in sequences of events that do not fit into direct experience, such as the beginning and end of a lengthy process. Our thought is able to duplicate the spatiotemporal world almost exactly and to create connections between random points in this system because it is itself energy; it develops and broadens itself and it is infinitely diverse. Thus, it is essentially the world all over again, and as it moves from knowledge to knowledge, it tests the truth of one item of knowledge against another, just as the second meaning of truth confirms.

36. The Certainty of Irrational Experience

It can hardly be doubted that Pragmatism went beyond the old dispute between the Rationalists and Empiricists. Let us take an isolated piece of knowledge such as the statement "The rain cools things down." If we look at it not as referring to a special event of this type but reflect instead on the universality of the statement, which embodies a set of interrelated concepts, then it would appear that there are eternal truths, a realm of pure values, such as Plato described. The Empiricists, in contrast, preferred to concentrate on the factual, as exemplified in the Greek philosopher who responded to the Eleatic philosophers' claim that there is no movement by silently walking back and forth. However, just as there was too much truth with Plato, there is too little truth here. The meaning of knowledge does not necessarily have to send us on abstract detours toward concrete perceptions, although it sometimes has this very effect. The Rationalists disregarded reference to the world of facts, although such reference is definitely contained in knowledge, even though it may choose to leave it "undecided" and not focus directly on it. This sort of thing occurs in narration or informative statements. By choosing to disregard its reference to the factual world, knowledge can attempt to establish one specific thing in order to build on it and advance toward a system. The Empiricists, however, overlooked this; they tried to lump together thoughts and facts and denied that thought could refer to itself.

In view of this state of affairs, Pragmatism represented a great step forward, although it did tend to rely too strongly on an instrumental understanding of knowledge. Dewey was overly optimistic when he posed the problem of a "directed reconstruction" of economic, political, and religious institutions, the "construction of values through experimental behavior." "Operational thinking needs to be applied to the judgment of values just as it has now finally been applied in conceptions of physical objects."[156]

This is pragmatic rationalism. Rationalism itself suffers from an interesting paradox. When we consider the whole range of functions language performs, the variety of interests and impulses that it serves, in addition to the by no means negligible ones that already exist within language itself, we will find the following: because language, and thought as well, can serve such a great range of interests, they therefore appear to be independent of any particular, specific interest. Thus, they may appear to be self-sufficient, autarchic, and ultimately the organ of "pure truth," which transcends internal and external reality. Pragmatism should not attempt to counter this form of Rationalism merely by substituting pragmatic rationalism in its place, which argues for pure action and the autarchy of "operational thinking."

If we consider modern man living within the modern industrial state, and attempt to assess its overwhelming meaning, then, indeed, we can hardly overestimate the importance of knowledge and rationally directed action. Man exists in a "second Nature," a world he has transformed to serve his own needs, *"une nature artificielle,"* as Georges Sorel called it.[157] This nature is not simply "artificial," but actually a "cultivated" Nature, because we discover possibilities in it which, if left to itself, Nature would not pursue. In the original Nature, there are neither beasts of burden nor explosives.

Pragmatism, however, does overlook the broad area of growth in human life, the silent processes that unfold unconsciously in the social setting. Pragmatism fails to see—not on a fundamental level, but in the interpretation of its standpoint—that experience is far richer and broader than what can be readily translated into "controlled behavior." Furthermore, not all problems in life can be turned into experiments. Kant contributed an insight that appears paradoxical from the point of view of the Rationalists. We might express this paradox as follows: *Our need to act extends further than our ability to know.* The fundamentally irrational, "broad" experience, which is not conducive to scientific study and which cannot be directly controlled, has its own certainty. It also has its own form of action—a nonexperimental type founded on tradition, instinct, habit, or conviction. Even the particular orientations we acquire in time, under the influence of the group but shaped by our own individual natures, would need to be conscious before they could command action. Here, however, the image becomes the flywheel of actions, and truth becomes a state of nonrational certainty seasoned through experience. *"Phantasia certissima facultas,"* wrote Vico. Just as rational metaphysics claims that *"homo intelligendo fit omnia,"* so does the metaphysics of the imagination teach that *"homo non intelligendo fit omnia."* As Vico writes, "Perhaps there is more truth in the latter statement than the former, for through his understanding man enlightens his mind, but through his nonunderstanding he creates the things from himself, transforms himself into them and becomes a thing himself."[158]

Only experimental knowledge resembles an operational hypothesis. We live, however, amid many certainties that are manifested as truths in our minds and that do not have the function of "leading us toward something," but serve instead to orient our behavior based on images of a particular state of being *(Sosein)* or particular obligations rather than on techniques of becoming different *(Anderswerden)*. By their very nature, these certainties are unshakable, and to a great extent remain unaffected by any failures that might occur. Any changes in them occur beyond the horizon of individual existence. They appear illogical from an experimental point of view. Nietzsche wrote: "One of those things that may drive a thinker into despair is the recognition that the illogical is necessary for man."[159] We find evidence of the illogical in a practical group of these certainties—ethical norms. These have no logical foundation; they appear simply as rules that must be obeyed. The reluctance to provide an empirical, and thereby immediately debatable, foundation (such as a utilitarian one) for ethical norms—indeed, the reluctance in general to bring them into consciousness and thereby open them up to possible changes and recombinations—this reluctance justifies itself. As Nietzsche wrote: "High culture demands that some things be left unexplained."[160] In fact, propriety, or even our spiritual well-being (or whatever one wishes to call that organ that refuses to challenge its own certainties) already demands this. James's brilliant effort to use the typically modern condition of the "will to believe" as the point of departure for a pragmatic theory of religion and his assumption that belief has the meaning of a working hypothesis have ultimately proved themselves only on a literary level.[161]

Basing our behavior on assumptions about being and on rules we should unquestioningly obey is apparently one of the conditions necessary for forming a will and for cultivating the ability to find closure, that is, to bring to a halt the chain reaction of recurring problems. There is an experimental way of thinking, according to which, in contrast to Goethe's remark, the observer, not the actor, has no conscience. Our impulses become invested with images of their goals; they establish themselves in relation to each other, they are open to experiences, and must remain versatile and capable of being deferred when necessary. In short, they must be able to adapt to conditions that change independently of them, to hold fast to these or withdraw when necessary. A person who cannot reject or turn away from certain avenues of action when this is called for will "lose his spark" *(ver-glimmt in sich)*, as Hegel says, for only by rejecting other possibilities can he maintain his course. The decision to finish something, to defer gratification, is often a conscious one, but in important cases it may result from an instinctive, darkly certain "feeling." What we hear when we "listen to ourselves" cannot be expressed as a hypothesis but can take the form of convictions that guide our lives and that could not be measured by the objective control of the experimental way of thought. We are acting beings and our impulses are structured accordingly: we possess an excess of plastic, world-open impulses, which are shaped by our actions and which must be developed into long-term drives to carry us into the uncertain future. Hence, we must continually dispense with and reject some in order to maintain others.

We exercise only a slight amount of conscious control over this process; most of it is guided by a nonexperimental certainty of experience. Each individual enjoys a certain range of variation here within an overall order of what should be rejected and what pursued; this order is necessary for survival. Consider how little one actually knows about the history of one's character. Consider how the process of character formation began at an age before memory was formed and how it transforms us in ways we cannot fathom. To use Hobbes's terms, it is easier to see than to express in words that there are processes of nonrational, broad experience that regulate, select, and determine what will become conscious. Vilfredo Pareto has compiled evidence from six languages and sources spanning centuries to present the convincing argument that human beings primarily behave in "illogical actions" *(actions non-logiques)*, that there is a "logic of feeling" *(logique du sentiment)*, which means that we often believe something *because* we have acted accordingly *(on croit cela parce qu'on agit ainsi)* and then formulate certainties to cover any discrepancies; Pareto calls these certainties "derivations."[162]

The rational bent of western European culture is not really standard for the human being. In every century and on every continent, human history has been characterized by experiences of the sort that "your cattle would not die, if your neighbor were not evil" (Hesiod, as cited by Pareto).[163] Judgments of this nature (which appear just as frequently in the "enlightened" ages of pseudo-rational cultures) exemplify what we may call an ascertainment without a preceding problem phase *(Vergewisserung ohne Problemstadium)*. Usually we do not respond to problems or disturbances by investigating their sources; instead, we react with shock. Avoiding fire because one has been burned can be just as expedient as experimenting, on other occasions, with how one can use fire without getting burned. Countless shocks of this type occur and they are often "rationalized," that is, tied in with a certainty that explains them. Even Hesiod's "truth" is one such simple rationalization that works because a guilty party is found or, more exactly, because one already knows someone who is responsible and lets this thought surface on this particular occasion. The sacrificial victim is also a classic form of dealing with shocks by means of imagined certainties. There is much ethnological evidence to the effect that sacrifice can take place on an abstract level, purely as a ritual or suggestion, and still calm or help deal with such shocks.

One could argue that these illogical actions have disappeared for the most part because they were replaced by more successful rational methods. This is undoubtedly correct, but in essence means only that the boundary between extralogical and controlled experiences is fluid and is at present quite deep, although it appears to be rising once more. These illogical experiences will never disappear completely for the following universal reason: the process of human experience is inevitably at the same time a process of character formation. External circumstances change independently of our history but nonetheless always demand our active involvement in them. We must be able to interpret and respond to these changing circumstances; we do this by drawing on the enduring system formed by our certainties and needs. To a third observer, this would appear as an irrational, nonobjective, biased approach, although we would "believe" we were encountering familiar situations. In this sense, as Novalis expressed it, belief is "the effect of the will on the intellect."[164] At the heart of this phenomenon is one law that dictates that our experiences guide the development of our impulses and a second that specifies that one of the most important things language and knowledge achieve is to make our past experiences available to us in the future, so that we do not have to reexamine and resubstantiate them every time. Thus, we always respond to an event from a "historical basis of reaction," which is fundamentally nonobjective in nature and which does not involve a "problem stage." If reality changes drastically but we still maintain our old values, certainties, and habits (which then represent earlier experiences in another world), it will appear that there is a necessary and chronic discrepancy between the internal and the external; this is the basis of departure for idealistic philosophy. Or, what is even worse, this discrepancy may take the form of two classes: a traditionalistic, romantic, or conservative class loses touch with the class that labors in the world of the new facts and must draw its convictions from this world alone, having been intellectually betrayed.

It can therefore be argued that the process of experience is also one of character formation because, as Aristotle noted, "it is [a person's] persistent activities in certain directions that make [him] what [he is]."[65] By the same token, our inner certainties are also to a great extent reflections of our individual natures. A discussion of an individual's convictions can easily become a discussion of that person's nature. Our character figures into many of the truths that guide our lives; as the French existentialist Lequier put it, each individual represents an *accident absolu*. Psychology must realize that there is an irrational constant in the problems that concern man, in his way of thinking as well as in his certainties. Even convictions of a theoretical nature are often the reflection of the effect of the will upon the intellect. It is therefore generally impossible to validate the viewpoint of experimental truth on this level of irrational certainties. Whenever convictions come into conflict with each other on a grand scale, history will ultimately decide where the truth actually lay and will leave it up to the historian to announce the decision.

A further, equally significant form of irrationality exists on the social level. Generally, it is the attitudes and experiences of others, that determine our actions. Only in truly scientific, experimental thinking can we abstract to a meaningful degree from the social milieu. This is not possible in the sphere of broad experience and public opinion in which our experiences are primarily those of others. Karl Vossler was quite correct in stating that it is more the psychical constellation under which a concept or principle appears that is identified and passed on and not so much the actual concept itself.[166] In addition to the meaning that a particular speech (such as the Sermon on the Mount) has in the mouth of its speaker, there is another, sometimes very different, meaning which is the one that is accepted and passed on. The historical meaning is often the dynamic effectiveness of the speech rather than the originally intended meaning. Because such a speech is made in the social sphere, its implications, unspoken associations, and emotions, the inherent attitudes in it, not to mention the actions it may prompt, all belong to the *meaning* of a message. A message is a type of action that is almost always intended to make an impression on others, convince them, appeal to them, command them, exhort them, etc. In response to asking where a certain street is, we do not learn where it is, but how to get there. Because we initiate new actions on the bases of certain motivations or insights—habitual actions require no forethought—the only way to change another's behavior is through communication, which has an effect on his behavior through his consciousness. Even the communication of facts hardly ever takes place without an underlying purpose.

For this reason, we must distinguish the certainties based on the current understanding of a statement from the truth of theoretical knowledge, which can be verified in three ways. The process by which we ascertain the validity of something is based on countless earlier experiences, which often remain unconscious but which orient and shape our impulses and lead to new ascertainments. This process does not involve a problem stage. It is essentially irrational. Any attempt to explain it would inevitably become mired in contradictions. I would like, however, to give an interesting example of how deeply this irrationality of broad experience penetrates. Let us consider the statement "All men are mortal." Exactly why is this true?

If we consider the sentence from a theoretical point of view, it demands some sort of proof. It is a statement based on experience and, as such, has only a statistical validity; it is simply highly probable. Biological science can of course provide many reasons for this statement; however, it had been universally accepted as true even before science existed. It cannot be verified directly for "all men." We cannot even prove that it is true for all men whom we assume have lived because they can no longer be found since they are all dead. Indeed, precisely if this statement is true, it can never be proven. Furthermore, the class of "all men" also includes oneself, which presents a new difficulty. I can only believe this sentence to be true on an abstract level but I cannot imagine that "I" could cease to exist. It is impossible for me to comprehend that I will cease to exist. I cannot think myself away, cannot actually carry out this insight on a concrete level. There is a blind spot in consciousness because the ego cannot temporarily be suspended for purposes of experimentation.

Thus, the absolute value of the sentence, which one must indeed acknowledge, is only its certainty. This certainty is not simply a generalization based on the fact that for as long as we know, all men that we knew, that they in turn knew, and so forth, have all died. Instead, this certainty is "irrational," unverifiable. It is part of the context of human experience as a whole. No number of further claims could make the sentence as certain as it already is; it is the universal presence of death that places it beyond doubt. This presence penetrates our daily existence, sits with us at table when we eat, lives in our children who will outlive us, lies in the uncertainty of every plan and thought we make for the coming year, accompanies us on our travels as the everpresent danger, and is the transience of every passing second. If the sentence were false, then the context of our total experience would be meaningless; this sentence partakes of the certainty of life itself. It is thus a *certum,* although it is essentially beyond our comprehension.

Thus, a certainty may be impossible to verify but yet not conflict with reality. When, in other cases, such a certainty becomes practical—that is, when it takes the form of a belief in a particular result that is not necessarily inevitable—this belief is often the only thing that allows this result to occur. The spirit of belief is opposed to the spirit of science insofar as it desires that events take a course different from the one they actually do. One cannot really wish for such a thing unless one possesses certainties that appear to be static, to be existential statements to the effect that reality is essentially different from how it appears to be. Convictions of this nature are in fact vitally necessary for human survival. The human being must act in consideration of the future. However, because we cannot know the future, how else can we act except on the basis of belief in a possible situation which is only truly possible if it is basically already real? *Phantasia certissima facultas.*

The modes of behavior of everyday "broad" experience, which are for the most part illogical (to use Pareto's term), and in which quasi-instinctual certainties, habits, and unfiltered convictions play such a great role, exclude by virtue of their very nature a practical, experimental approach toward the same object. To put this another way, the theoretical technique of observation, experimentation, and the drawing of conclusions, which could be described as a method of "inventing artificial experiences in order to draw out the properties of things" (Hamann), brings about a change in man in the long run. Not only the economic sphere of life, as Schumpeter believes, but also the military and political spheres have long been the "culture-medium of logic" *(Nährboden der Logik);* and it is from these that rational expertise or science has always developed. Modern European thought, only three hundred years old, has transformed the living conditions of mankind. This was achieved only at the cost of a grand, laborious, highly disciplined process of *renunciation.*

The first step in this process was the renunciation of the direct gratification of religious interests in scientific knowledge. Newton's description of space as *sensorium Dei* represents an almost self-evident way of thinking for his time. Bentley, with the express approval of Newton, believed gravity to be "direct and positive proof that an immaterial, living spirit guides and influences the inanimate material and preserves the world-edifice." Even as late as 1763, Kant, in his essay entitled "Der einzige mögliche Beweisgrund zu einer Demonstration des Daseins Gottes" (The Only Possible Argument for Demonstrating God's Existence) used certain laws of the natural order, such as Maupertius's law of the "economy of Nature's effect," to support his contention that there exists "agreement in the possibility of things" and hence that God must exist. It is already "ascetic" that Kant, in contrast to the prevailing view of his times, no longer saw God's hand in individual natural events. Lambert, a contemporary of Kant, claimed that the increase in the atmospheres of comets as they approach the sun was designed to protect the "comet men" from the great heat. Kant still believed it was necessary to contest the idea that the mountains had been created to punish our sins or that the northern lights were created to aid the Greenlanders and Lapps. It was his *Critique of the Power of Judgment* (1787) that first overcame this naïve way of thinking. By naïve I mean the direct, natural way in which human interests gain control of and interpret knowledge, thereby reaffirming themselves. As long as these interests were not pushed off course by knowledge as a result of a process of renunciation, purely objective insight was not possible.

A further renunciation becomes necessary where our direct desires toward facts are concerned, including the desire to exert a magical influence on them. In this area, indeed, time seems not to have effected any changes. Herodotus recounts that the Athenians believed Boreas, the god of the wind, had come to their aid when they fought the Persians;[167] on August 5, 1923, the Bishop of Montpellier asked that prayers be said for rain. From these examples, one could conclude that the optimistic belief that we can somehow influence events so that they will conform to our wishes and needs is natural, but that the interest in the purely objective "capricious" behavior of things is a relatively late and difficult acquisition. Here, I am not so much referring to grand interests such as the desire to make gold, which had to disappear before alchemy could give rise to chemistry. What was actually much more difficult to renounce were the "instinctive" mental and emotional associations, the probabilities, and the suggestions of appearances: "A thing that is warm, moist, and soft to the touch is cold, dry, and hard on the inside; this is because the exterior of a thing is invariably the opposite of its invisible interior [body vs. soul!]. Thus, there is a power in every thing, even if we cannot perceive it. . . . Lead is cold and dry on the outside but possesses the opposite properties on the inside" (the doctor and chemist Rases, cited by Bousquet).[168]

In this passage, I noted the sort of association of ideas that are present in such a "science" and that prevent true knowledge of the nature of lead. Are there not countless such examples from antiquity and the Middle Ages? Does not mercury represent the "middle ground" between liquids and solids and is not "10" a "perfect" number? Comte himself was an admirer of the number 7.

As long as many people believed that a sick person was possessed by a demon and could not be given nourishment or help for fear of drawing the demon towards themselves, there was no foundation for medical science, but a very favorable one for sorcery. As long as trials were conducted against animals in which witnesses, defendants, and prosecutors all appeared (as late as 1741 in Poitou a cow was brought to trial), there was no chance for zoology to develop as a science.

One of the most difficult ascetic acts or necessary renunciations is the renunciation of appearances and our instinctive reliance upon the ways of thinking that are dictated by appearances. This achievement immortalized the names of Columbus and Copernicus. An entire book could be devoted to the wild goose chases undertaken by science before the renunciation of appearances had established itself (non-Euclidean geometry). In the present day, physics also encourages us to renounce our familiar ways of thinking: it describes obscure, subatomic, objectively undetermined (not undeterminable) processes, and substitutes for the law of causality estimates based on probability. Since calculations can be made based on these processes and since predictions are possible, we are asked to surrender for these formulas our most tenacious instinctive ways of looking at the world; resistance to this is naturally great.

These few examples should suffice to show that it was necessary to break down certain natural human emotional needs, habits of thought, beliefs about the world, expectations, and the like which had prevailed for centuries before the wondrous and unique tool of truly rational thought employed in European society could develop. The objectivity of thought, including the difficult act of disregarding those factual properties that are not productive on a rational level (an art which is manifested in the way problems are posed), is the result of its enduring struggle to be completely liberated for the thing it is directed toward. This way of thinking is responsible for the "self-less" results of whole generations of dedicated research. It calls for patient dedication and a refined disciplined awareness at every step of the way of what is being disregarded and what is actually intended. This type of thought relies on a highly mathematical imagination and is always able to discard its basic assumptions when these no longer fit the facts. The results of such thinking support modern culture. This way of thinking has learned to adapt itself completely to reality and the capriciousness of Nature and to hold their astonishing powers in its hands, but it has paid a dear price for these achievements. It has paid through renunciations that extend deep into man's very nature and that are "inhuman" and dangerous. For, in broad experience, human nature continues to be guided by irrational impulses and convictions, although it is actually moving away from these; it is corresponding to an ever lesser extent to the "filtered," highly artificial experience of the sciences.

Because science seeks knowledge for its own sake and because the findings of experimental science are always controlled because they are understood, the inevitable outcome is that science is incapable of justifying, or even simply specifying, any obligations it may have. It knows no goals beyond its own progress. Its ethos is ascetic, negative. Nobel's dilemma is a representative case: as the inventor of dynamite, he can only hope that *others* will prevent its use, and so he creates a peace prize. The other side of this negative ethos is the pathos of science for its own sake which science develops because of its very nature. However, those certainties that are the foundation of our moral, social, or religious life do not require acts of renunciation; they exist in the immediacy of broad experience.

The alliance that the natural sciences formed with technology and industry unhappily involves partners of which the same is true: technology, by its very nature, has no conception of limits to its permitted means. In addition, as Max Weber realized, commercial business develops its own special logic and set of rational laws which cannot be measured on an ethical level. This trend is even more pronounced as business becomes increasingly technological. The three areas of science, its technical application, and industrial utilization have long formed a superstructure, which has become automatic and objectified to such a degree that ethical considerations appear only to be inappropriate objections. The hopelessness of placing ethical controls on modern civilization hovers over the earth like the Fates of antiquity (as Marx said) and is one of the reasons for the widespread despair and resignation. Earlier, pretechnological cultures, despite their great internal frictions, nonetheless created certain contexts of obligation at those points where their nonrational experiences showed gaps or discrepancies and they systematized these experiences on a moral if not theoretical level.

From what we have said here, it follows that science, which by its very nature is "enlightenment," cannot function as a substitute for an absent guiding system, for the *idées directrices* of a society. It cannot propose sufficient reasons for a total orientation toward the world, for an acting belief,* it can offer no genuine motivating power for fundamental decisions as well as no compelling, universally valid certainties. The repercussions of the widespread disappointment over the failure of the popularized sciences to bring about a stabilization in world view could very well become serious precisely because of the artifical nature of the scientific approach. The level of science's "ability to know," which has created and supported modern culture, must be continually increased. It also follows from our discussion that because of the onesidedness of its ethos, the scientific world has only a limited power to create institutions. It appears that the vision of scientific corporations which could supervise the application of research findings (such as atomic energy) will never be realized.

The first steps in an emotional counterattack against the spirit of science were taken 200 years ago. In 1755, Rousseau wrote in his *Discours sur l'origine:* "If Nature has designed us to be healthy, I could argue that the state of reflection is unnatural *[un état contre nature]* and that a man who meditates is a corrupt animal *[un animal déparavé]*." Diderot, in his *Le Rêve de d'Alembert,* carried further this extreme line of reasoning: "Nothing stands in greater contradiction to Nature than the habitual practice of meditation or the state of mind of the learned scholar. The natural man is made to think only a little and act a lot. Science, on the other hand, thinks a lot and acts little." Diderot claimed that the scholar was a "système agissant à rebours" (a system running in reverse).

This dangerous prelude to a large-scale emotional retaliation has remained an isolated case. Scientific, and especially philosophical and literary culture quickly reach a degree of independence that invites questions about their purpose. A fundamental human phenomenon is at stake here which has to do with the "risky" organization of the human being. I would like to devote some time here to discussing one of many possible examples of the *dangers* of relief although this subject falls more properly in the province of cultural anthropology.

Even in the very nature of his physical constitution, man has been relieved of the necessity of responding in a blind, instinctive manner to the immediate present. His sensorimotor functions, his impulses, his language, and so forth

---

*"To think that unrealistic blueprinting, propaganda, or artificial morale techniques can construct new myths and functions to support a social order of extraneous imposition in an individuated age similar to the organic folk buttressing of a simple people is something like mistaking a house of cards for a granite monolith." James W. Woodward in Gurvitch, *Twentieth Century Sociology* (New York, 1945), p.234.

are all characterized by the availability *(Verfügbarkeit)*. They are not subject to the pressures of the immediate present but have been released from these. To put it differently, they possess their own vitality as self-perceived, communicative functions and they are capable of animating one another. This brings about a significant reduction in the direct contact with the immediate situation. These functions become separated to an ever greater degree from their original cause because they are both self-perceived and self-alienated— that is, they are at the same time experience and object. They become increasingly indirect. They do of course achieve their goal in circumspect, efficient, planned actions and hence are directed toward the world again, but they use the present situation as a starting point to effect changes extending beyond the present in time and space. They also lose to a great extent their direct reference to the actual present. This makes them extremely valuable to a being like man, who must anticipate new combinations of experiences.

There is a grave danger here. Human impulses are plastic and excessive, and their gratification can be deferred. Indirect actions become needs for even more indirect and refined actions. Our motivations and impulses are developed in conjunction with our actions; they become specialized and more defined along with these actions and come to embrace their increasingly conditioned objects. The more refined appetites, the functionalized, highly conditioned interests, such as the lust for power, greed, and the various manias, show us how complexes of impulses can achieve an independent power. There is a danger inherent in man's constitution that actions and impulses will not find their way back to the world but instead will become ever more refined and will perpetuate themselves; this danger can be avoided only through rigorous discipline. This danger also exists for the relieved, higher intellectual functions which can easily cross the fine inner boundary beyond which they are seen as intellectualism or artistry. In all these cases, the risky organization of the human being can function as an advantage or disadvantage, for if man were completely unable to gratify his impulses in direct forms of behavior, he could not undertake activities with a more distant purpose. All human impulses, even the highly conditioned ones, easily become functionalized; they move beyond their original context, become increasingly independent, and enter into the state of repetitive automatism and herein find their own value for gratification.

The only means of avoiding this danger we have described is through open social contact, which the social system should promote and even enforce. Discipline in the form of education and self-discipline, subordination and control, activity and work directed beyond oneself, is the basic skeleton that gives form to our impulses; the forms of discipline are vital to the impulses of a being whose biological structure contains some inherent dangers. The broad level of open and ordered actions in a community is thus the medium in which the sciences should continually lead into actions and so find their way back to the world.

The so-called "naturalists" of the Age of Enlightenment probably had this danger in mind when they described a form of scholarship that could easily lead to a "fine, intellectual egoism" (Gervinus), which they perceived as "perverse." Gervinus himself expressed a similar view when he discussed the spirit of romanticism, its flight from the present, the real, the active— a spirit which "grew up in language and natural science, in art and antiquity, in all those subjects that have nothing to do with real life." In his *History of German Poetry,* he wrote: "At the time Goethe was learning Chinese, or even earlier when he was concerned with studying Nature and the plastic arts, in order to have nothing to do with public life, Jean Paul also turned his back on these public relationships to devote himself to writing, Fouqué became absorbed with chivalry, Hoffman with the supernatural, Tieck's tender soul fled from history and time to solitude and Nature, Seume and Chamisso empathized with the natural life of the savages. Historical research turned its back upon recent history to dig down into early history where it also channeled the mythological research of the philologists."[169]

37. Toward a Theory of the Imagination

Now that we are approaching the end of this Part of the book, I would like to present the foundation for a theory that will link together the numerous references made so far to the human imagination. We know so little about no other human faculty. Palagyi formulated a theory of the imagination (1925);[170] Segal's excellent study *Über das Vorstellen von Objekten und Situationen* (1916)[171] is still indispensable today as is that of Lacroze (1938)[172] which was published in the same year as Sartre's "Structure intentionelle de l'image."[173] In 1936, Sartre's *L'Imagination* appeared, followed in 1940 by his great work *L'Imaginaire*[174]—a careful and comprehensive phenomenological description. Klages and Scheler made a significant contribution in this area with their theory of "images" (Bilder); Bergson delineated a sweeping biological and sociological theory of the "myth-making function" in his *Two Sources*[175] and finally, Hans Kunz[176] presented in 1946 a comprehensive presentation and critique of the psychological research in this area and other related areas and put forward his own existentially oriented theory.

Despite these efforts, however, one could still claim that the research has only just begun. Herder's statement still applies: "The imagination is still by far the least researched and perhaps the least researchable of all the spiritual faculties of the human being."[177] An anthropology that considers man from the point of view of action might be able to shed light on the function and significance of the imagination. Such an approach might allow us to avoid the mistake of beginning our investigation of this topic at too high a level. For the word "imagination" usually makes one think of poetic or artistic "transfiguration," of the type of imagination that is expressed in language, or the highly cultivated visual or musical imagination, or perhaps even of dreams; but we rarely consider that above all, the imagination is a very real and vital phenomenon.

By imagination, we generally mean an organism's ability to assimilate the states it has experienced in order to base future actions on past experiences of situations. The first of these skills, if considered alone, could be called memory in a general sense. This direct memory that passively assimilates and retains is a vital ability possessed perhaps by all living things, certainly by all animals; it cannot be explained further. In 1870, Ewald Hering held a notable lecture entitled "On Memory as a Universal Function of Organized Material." Nietzsche contended that an organism's ability to "collect" experiences was the essential feature that distinguished it from the inorganic: "There is no forgetting in the realm of the organic; instead, experiences are digested in some fashion." An organism's memory burdens it with its earlier reactions and impressions, binds it to the past, thereby making past experiences available to it for use in coming to terms with the present and preparing for the future. When we consider the imagination from the point of view of the future, we call it expectation, planning, or active imagination in a narrower sense.

Palagyi brilliantly identified the power of the imagination as the vital ability which enables a living being to transfer itself beyond its location in space and time without actually moving from its actual place. It is an incomparable wonder, he wrote, that life, without moving from its place, can nonetheless behave in such a way as if it had moved to another point in space and time. "This process in which life removes itself from the spatiotemporal position that it occupies in reality is called the imagination."[178] For a being whose survival depends on its ability to liberate itself from the brackets of the immediate spatiotemporal present, the imagination naturally has tremendous significance. In fact, we would be equally justified in describing man as a being of imagination (Phantasiewesen) as well as a being of reason (Vernunftswesen). True actions are possible only for a being who has found relief from the immediate influence and pressure of its surroundings to such an extent that it draws its highly versatile ability to transfer itself from this relief. Even before very young children have developed sophisticated symbolic images and fine motor skills, they are able to make their very limited range of experiences available and to accustom themselves to other situations by means of their imagination. The example Guernsey provided of the child who hit his forehead by chance and then went on to repeat the action attests to the child's ability to use the total form of a movement as a blueprint for its freely repeated execution. A child of eleven months of age played at being asleep by squirming around in his bed and saying "baba." I myself observed a one-and-a-half-year-old child who could barely walk begin to dance spontaneously at the sound of the church bells, that is, he made a transition to another type of rhythmical movement. These examples give sufficient testimony that the ability to transfer from one movement to another is formed quite early and this ability is often exercised independently of the nature of the immediate situation.

Studies of child psychology have reported such things as a child of approximately a year who "dusted off" a chair with a piece of paper, and a fifteen-month-old child who pretended to smoke. Such studies illustrate the fundamental process identified in my earlier discussion of G. H. Mead— taking the role of the other. Imitation is not an adequate description of this process, since what is actually involved here is that an individual realizes a relationship to himself in the course of taking the role of the other. By taking the role of others, a child objectifies and experiences himself. From this, it follows that there can be no *direct* behavior toward oneself; instead, identification with another is the prerequisite for experiencing oneself.

Even Mead did not exhaust all the ramifications of this brilliant insight, which for one thing means that, like an individual, a group also has no direct relationship to itself. Group consciousness comes to be in an indirect manner—in such a way that all the individuals identify with the *same* other, an "X," and behave accordingly, so that their self-awareness has a common point of intersection and is further supported by a sameness of behavior.

This point is crucial to understanding all primitive societies and totemism. All the members of the Bear Clan formed a group symbiotically. They became "we, this group" on an intellectual level only to the extent that each person took on the role of the other, indeed, of the same other—the bear. Originally, the awareness of belonging to a group was not on an abstract level, but on a concrete one. The experience of "we" was re-created in such rituals as the bear dance. The experience of being in the group is gained only by representing it through a process of taking the role of a common other and acting accordingly. Thus, the clan members experience themselves as the bear clan in their representation of the bear.

It is very significant that totemism is so widespread throughout the world. Even in the foundations of Greek religion, "animal gods," the ancient group symbols, can be unearthed if one digs deep enough. In Homer, Hera is still referred to as the "cow-faced one," just as in Rome Isis was represented with the cow horns of Hathor. Erinys was originally a single goddess from Thelpusa in Arcadia who took the form of a horse. Artemis Brauronia was originally a bear, worshipped in ritual bear dances. It is quite certain that the difficult and yet highly important problem of identification has its roots here. Our modern boundless quasi-communities do not allow any such stable identification; our civilization offers no real gratification for our psycho-vital needs. The abstract context of a people is too great; the family too small. Sociology has just discovered the "secret of proportion."[179]

The explorer Steinen was astonished to hear the Brazilian Bakairi Indians seriously claim that they were parrots. When a group, tribe, or clan has a mythical ancestor, worships it in a cult, and calls itself after this ancestor, the process is in essence the same: self-awareness is gained indirectly by identifying with the other.

We cannot help but conclude that imagination is actually the fundamental social organ. Here we are not referring to the late phenomenon of single, imagined ideas conceived of as being unreal; these are in fact quite rare if we thereby understand concrete images. Instead, we are referring to a chronic condition of semi-alienation (*chronische Zuständigkeit der Halbentfremdung*), which develops from the role-playing and imitation games of early childhood and which constitutes the unconscious background for our social existence, including our awareness of this social existence. Perhaps the best way to approach this phenomenon is in a step-by-step fashion. Sartre, for example, described what he calls the "emotional abstract."[180] For instance, some people when told about an accident, cry out "Oh, how horrible!"; they use this gesture to rid themselves of their fear and shock. By means of a simple affective scheme, they assign the character "horrible" to the represented images. I believe this process briefly actualizes one of the possibilities in the chronic, affective background that is part of our self-concept and that is the unbroken resonance of the average affect of the group. This self-concept is itself already an *état imaginaire*. Blondel has shown us that even those emotions which we believe to be the property of our own hearts are actually modeled on the social customs of our lives and times.[181] The satisfaction gained from being able to use a catchword to represent a sudden emotion is essentially no different from the satisfaction gained from experiencing its individuality. The vocabulary and syntax of emotions are just as binding as those of language. This means not only that we have passions à la Werther or Kierkegaard but further, that what can be called our basic state of mind is itself an *état imaginaire*. What we are is a relationship to ourselves and in this sense has been thoroughly socialized and is to a great extent a state of chronic semialienation.

Modern collective psychology has determined that our feelings and emotions have a sort of socially conditioned quality of obligation. We regulate not only the expression of our feelings but also the feelings themselves. This subject is actually much more complex and we should avoid drawing the same conclusions as Gide did: "Psychological analysis ceased to interest me on the day I realized that man feels what he imagines he feels." One could also argue, however, that only at this point does this issue really become interesting on a psychological level, for here the imaginary begins to lose its arbitrariness and becomes compelling and begins to be stored up in the very constitution of our social existence.

Gruhle claimed that patriotism, familial feelings, and notions of social position are all simply social structures.[182] The feeling of justice did not create justice, but rather justice created the feeling of justice (Jhering). These concepts are all highly abstract: if applied to reality, they merge into universal concepts which designate attitudes such as those embodied in the terms *pietas, maestas, auctoritas, dignitas, gravitas, constantia, mos maiourum, potestas, disciplina,* etc. These "ideas," as Rothacker realized, are not ways of acting but are instead "pole stars" which guide our development.[183] They are the embodiment of social experiences in our own development. They can therefore refer to personal attitudes as well as to the normal ways of dealing with social situations. In certain ages, they were even revered as gods. Their medium is definitely the imagination; we can only "have" these ideas by representing them, incorporating them into ourselves, and identifying with these ideal situations in order to come to an awareness of ourselves thereby. We might say that only by reproducing a social model can such concretely moral ideas be given life and substance until the other has become part of ourselves and the attitude becomes an enduring, habitualized relationship to oneself in the representation of this relationship. The imagination as the ability to take the role of the other is the basic underlying structure of societies.

I would like to discuss the final, and perhaps deepest, level of the imagination, which I have chosen to call the primal imagination (Urphantasie). This is a difficult topic because it stands at the boundaries of the conceivable. Only by identifying the common direction and goal of several very different lines of reasoning can we begin to approach it.

In part 1, we presented the argument that man is characterized by a certain delayed development or juvenilization process. This would indicate that something unspent, some untapped power, must lie on the level of vegetative functions. The apparent existence of certain inhibitive factors, perhaps in the endocrine system, which influence man's development, suggest the idea that suppressed powers exist. Furthermore, the relationship of the retarding forces in development to those already retarded is not necessarily stable. It is completely possible that the eventually achieved state of balance is in fact postponed. This explains Naef's contention that in the future the curvature of the human forehead will become even stronger and more pronounced. In any case, from Bolk's theory we may assume that a "disharmony" exists deep within man's constitution, in direct contrast to the equilibrium in animals. This disharmony does have a positive side, however—the "pressure for development" *(Entwicklungsdruck)* which it gives rise to. Even if we choose to bracket Bolk's theory and adopt Darwin's line of reasoning, we will still come to the same conclusion. If, over the course of hundreds of thousands of years, there is a development from lower to higher forms which takes the form of a creative, enriching process, then we should still expect to find this tendency in man, who constitutes the end point of this series. This fact must be registered in some way in our impulses and drives. The phylogenetic law, the particulars of which are still obscure, must indeed have affected all animals not only in terms of a metamorphosis of form but also in the organization of instincts, for it is these instincts that guarantee the preservation of the species and provide the framework for progressive development.

Let us then assume that life develops "upwards": How then is this tendency manifested in man, in whom the essential growth processes form part of his attitude toward himself, in whom there are practically no true instincts at all, and in whom the preservation and reproduction of life (the framework for further organic development) pass through the medium of consciousness and are thereby exposed to potential disturbances.

We also expressed, in very different concepts from those Bolk used, the suspicion that man is prey to a pressure to become formed, which places a great burden on him because of the nature of his constitution. This "pressure for development" most likely shifted toward the area of self-realization, because those impulses that motivate our actions have been, to an unspecifiable depth, "laid bare"—invested with images—and have become directly or indirectly objects toward which we form attitudes. Thus, in man, this tendency toward "more life" must affect the area of self-realization because it cannot work in the direction of instincts.

We should keep in mind, however, that consciousness is primarily a "surface" *(Oberfläche);* it lacks knowledge of the nature of the external world in itself as well as of the "how" of vital, internal processes in which we live without knowing how. The internal and external worlds are wholly appearance. The concept does not achieve what our desire to understand intends it to achieve. As Nietzsche wrote: "That which we call our 'consciousness' is innocent of any of the essential processes of our preservation and growth."[184] In another very important aphorism Nietzsche wrote: "The distinguishing feature of our consciousness which we usually think of as standing alone, of our intellect, is that it remains protected and closed off from the great diversity of the experiences of the living being which constitute our body, and as a consciousness of a higher status, as a reigning aristocracy, it is presented only with a selection of experiences, experiences that have been simplified, made comprehensible, and thereby falsified, so that it in turn will continue with this process of simplification and falsification and lay the groundwork for what is commonly called the will.... And the same type of operations that take place here must continually take place at all deeper stages, in the behavior of all the higher and lower beings towards each other—this same selection and presentation of experiences, this process of abstraction and thinking together, this wanting and retranslating of indefinite wanting into definite activity. There are strengths within us which are stronger than anything that can be formulated about the human being. The body teaches us that our life is possible because of the cooperation of many unequal intelligences and hence only because of a constant, infinitely diverse process of obeying and commanding, of the practice of many virtues—physical virtues."[185]

If we then assume, as we said above, that there is a tendency operating in man toward "more life," it would seem logical that this must penetrate to the level of basic impulses, and consequently, by virtue of their relationship to action, to the edge of human consciousness. However, we cannot really know what happens at this level because consciousness is essentially directed toward the external world and is in this sense simply a surface. This situation suggests that man would feel that he had an ultimate, very serious responsibility but had no possible way of knowing the exact nature of this "task" precisely because he himself is such an intrinsic part of it. We do not know how our actions and vital processes take place and how some metabiological problem is developed and resolved through these processes, perhaps over a span of thousands of years. We can "speculate," however, that we are deeply involved in some unknown way in the essence of the life process and it is here that the primal imagination appears.

This view is not simply a construct. It is possible to show that we cannot understand primitive societies without the aid of the category of "unspecified obligation." This unspecified obligation is anchored in a confusing diversity of highly concrete, plastic, and thoroughly fantastic interpretations that form a system which in turn constitutes the basic skeleton that supports a particular culture. A belief in magic can arise only because of this fundamental idea of a nonrational, concrete, fantastic channelling of this unspecified obligation toward "more life" (more power, greater fertility, greater longevity, and so forth). Rothacker[186] suggested that the imagination aids vegetative growth processes and Kunz[187] conceded that it is possible that the imagination represents the internalized organic formative power *(Bildungskraft)* perhaps in the sense that these share a common origin. I have expanded these hypotheses in two ways: by adding the phylogenetic dimension and by proposing that in man this process begins to enter into a relationship with itself. At its point of contact with consciousness, our imagination would produce inadequate, but concrete, compelling images of a "more from life."

Nietzsche's symbols of the "superman" and the "will to power" are abstract concepts illustrating this point of contact. The symbol of the superman implies that man is still his own greatest challenge: "It is our nature to create a being higher than ourselves. To create beyond ourselves! This is the procreative drive, the drive of the deed and of achievement." However, this symbol does express another purpose of life, as the rest of the above quote indicates: "Just as all desire presupposes a purpose, so does man presuppose a being which is not itself but which provides the purpose of his existence."[188] I would like to argue that Nietzsche was well aware of the problems inherent in such a catchword and that the "will to power" was intended to be a better formulation of the concept of the superman. The will to power is formulated as follows: If consciousness is a means and is "directed outwards," then we might ask "whether or not all conscious desiring, all conscious purposes, all judgments, are perhaps only the means by which something is to be achieved which is essentially different from how it appears to our consciousness. I believe our likes and dislikes are involved here—but these likes and dislikes could be the means by which we must achieve something that lies beyond our consciousness."[189] Nietzsche sought other ways to characterize this difficult concept, the purpose of which is unknown to us, this "X," which is carried out "underneath the table." He described it on a purely formal level as the increase and expansion of power, as processes whereby strengths are determined, as a process of incorporation, overcoming, as a creative effort, and ultimately as an abstract, biological "more." He refrained from giving any indication of its purpose or meaning as he did do in his scheme of the superman. Nonetheless, the two symbols are analogous: in man and in all living things, there is a meaning (superman) or a meaning of meaninglessness (will to power) to which consciousness is not privy but which is expressed in the actions of our lives, indeed, in our very existence. It constitutes the guiding force in our lives. We participate in it. It makes up the substance of the unspecified obligation that Nietzsche attempted to define. These symbols do not work, however, because they are abstract exaggerations of Darwinism or Schopenhauerian metaphysics: they lack the indescribable, compelling power of the plastic images of a "more of life," they lack the awe-inspiring beauty. Nietzsche's symbol of the eternal return has even less substance and one may well question whether a refined logical mind was still at work here.[190]

If we now step back and see where these various lines of examination intersect, we will find the concept of the "primal imagination": this is manifested in the detritus of our dreams, or in the periods of concentrated vegetative processes, in childhood, or in the contact between the sexes; in other words, wherever forces of developing life announce themselves. There are, amid ever-changing images, certain primal visions or images of the overall purpose of life, which senses within itself a tendency toward a higher form, a greater intensity of current, so to speak. An immediate vital *ideality* exists, a tendency in the *substantia vegetans* toward a higher quality or quantity (whereby it should be noted that the right to make this distinction remains questionable). In idealizing the world, the creative imagination traces out the goals for the development of its inner striving. A "biology of poetry" is by no means an impossible thought and has in fact been proposed by such profound thinkers as Schelling, Novalis, and Nietzsche.

We now come to one of the fundamental sources of art. For identifying the impulses that live within art, I have always found the ancient naïve conceptions, such as those in the Pygmalion saga, to be the most enlightening. Cicero wrote that when Phidias was working on a sculpture of Jupiter or Minerva, he did not use a human form for a model but instead envisioned in his mind the sublime idea of beauty which he then attempted to reproduce in his art and work.[191] This, in its incomparable simplicity, is really all that needs to be said about this particular root of art. This is the primal imagination and art is the means by which one establishes an active relationship toward it. Only the visual arts, and sculpture above all, can convey a real idea of the degree of vital perfection that our primal imagination still perceives within itself as possible. There is no doubt that the fine arts can exert a great influence as far as form is concerned on the easily influenced primal imagination of man. Lessing said that the state of the ancients was indebted for its beautiful people to its beautiful statues. True art wields an irreplaceable authority. In architecture, this authority really takes form; as Vitruv said of the edifices constructed by Augustus: *"Verum etiam majestas imperii publicorum aedificiorum egregias habet auctoritates."*

This view of art as a model of the vital ideality is in agreement with the basic tenets of idealistic aestheticism since Kant. The artistically creative powers of the human being are portrayed as identical to the organic, form-fashioning ones. As Schelling wrote in his essay *"Über das Verhältnis der bildenden Künste zur Natur"* (On the Relationship of the Fine Arts to Nature): "This entire essay argues that the basis of art and thus also of beauty lies in the vitality of Nature."[92]

In my opinion, a work of art has a dual effect on the viewer: first, it addresses the imagination, that is, it initiates a process in which the viewer transfers himself into the unknown depths of the primal imagination, which become clear and comprehensible in a painting; secondly, because the painting awakens and fulfills the imagination, continually draws it toward itself and concentrates it, communication is established between the otherwise silent, unexpressed levels in man and the reality standing before his eyes. However, the viewer's awareness of the "painting," of its unreality, allows it to *remain* in this movement without perceiving this as insufficient, as would be the case with a movement of the imagination toward *reality.*

Religion also finds one of its roots here, one that it shares with art. "The world of the gods," wrote Schelling, "is not an object of mere understanding or of reason, but can only be comprehended with the imagination."[93] I must, unfortunately, allow this thought to remain in its unsatisfying universality because it must remain abstract, as it is detached from any historical and ethnological material. We can say, however, that whenever religion represents living beings who are more perfect than man, it is tapping the primal imagination. And, although it may seem paradoxical, this also holds true for the animal cults, which appear almost everywhere in various forms. Ipsen provided me with a persuasive explanation of this universal phenomenon. Man admires the animal's mode of existence, which is not possible for him—a way of life that cannot be disturbed or influenced. In other words, he admires the animal's "power"—a nonhuman perfection which his imagination interprets as superhuman. The disharmony in the human constitution, the unique burdens man bears—his excessive impulses and drives, his need to control himself, the necessity of work, the need to anticipate the future, and the constant awareness of mortality—all these risks and complications are not part of the secure, effortless vitality of the animal.

This is what distinguishes man from the animal, which appears "godlike" as a result of its mysterious, calm mastery of its existence. In this form, religion remains "vegetative"; it is a statement a living being makes about himself by taking on the role of another living thing.

PART III

The Laws Governing Human Impulses; Character; the Problem of the Mind

38. Refutation of the Theory of Drives

The final problem to be treated in this book is that of character development. Because we will approach this problem from our all-encompassing perspective of man as an acting being, we will discover that here, too, there is an underlying order to the facts. Part 3 will conclude with an exposition of the problem of the "mind" *(Geist)* which I have chosen to undertake in the wake of numerous misunderstandings, for which I accept partial blame although these were in part tendentious. The focal point of my discussion of this subject will once again be action. I will address the general question of the structure of the impulses of a world-open being—a being who can be said to possess only a few true instincts, a being characterized by a deficient organic specialization, and the absence of an environment to which he is naturally adapted, and finally, a being who must not become trapped within the confines of the given situation, the fluctuating present, but who instead must anticipate future needs and work toward meeting them. It thus seems logical that the basic impulses of such a being, whom even "future hunger makes hungry," must also be oriented in some manner toward the future.

It should be clear that our formulation of this problem makes it necessary to adopt an approach that is far removed from those prevalent in psychology today, for modern psychology is bound to the following method of abstraction: A specific human being is described in terms of what he does and in terms of the nature of his inclinations. By pursuing this abstract way of thinking, one inevitably ends up with a series of universal "qualities," such as steadfastness, cunning, cleverness, lasciviousness, etc., from which action as well as the concrete nature of the individual's inclinations have disappeared. In other words, on the basis of real behavior, one has deduced the "predispositions manifested therein." The inevitable second step in this line of reasoning is to make complete this abstract, qualitative inner life by introducing the "environment," the "milieu," etc. We are now faced with that all-powerful pair of concepts, "inherited predisposition—environment"

(Anlage—Umwelt); because of our basic premise, we have completely lost sight of the reality of actions. We are now dealing with an inner life that has been invested with certain qualities and that is set counter to the external world. This method of procedure is not inappropriate for descriptive purposes; however, if we believe that human impulses can be understood only in relation to action, then it is clear that this way of proceeding would obscure certain underlying laws governing the structure of human impulses.

There is another possible way of proceeding from the premise described above: this involves carrying even further the process of "tracing back." Might it not be possible to reduce the great number of these qualities by, for example, understanding vanity, ambition, and initiative as variants of the "desire for power"? This would then lead to the formulation of a theory of "fundamental drives" *(Grundtriebe)* and bring us to that branch of psychology concerned with the theory of drives *(Trieblehre)*. This branch originated with Schopenhauer and was later developed extensively by Freud and Klages. However, such attempts will fail without exception, for the same reasons that theories of types *(Typenlehren)* also fail—because of the arbitrary nature of the decision as to which drives are most important. Power, egoism, sexuality, the drive to imitate, the drive to assert oneself, the need for prestige and recognition, the destructive drive, the drive to succeed, and many others have all been declared, in various combinations, to be the essential factor in human motivation. McDougall has identified eighteen fundamental drives (including curiosity, the need for comfort, the migratory drive, and the need for companionship) while Watson has discovered approximately fifty. Shaffer claims that in 1924 Bernard found 14,046 human activities identified by several hundred different thinkers as "instinctive."[1]

If we consider this problem more closely, it should be clear that even if we believe the human being is a unity of certain inherited predispositions, qualities, fundamental drives, etc., this "unity" is never manifested in all its aspects at the same time. Furthermore, if we truly wish to remain within this conceptual scheme and yet still approximate reality, we would have to argue that this structure of qualities and drives is fluid. In different situations, the human being manifests very different qualities which may, moreover, disappear entirely in the course of history, with the passage of time. Hoffmann,[2] for example, has described how Friedrich Wilhelm I, the "Soldier King," manifested a different behavior depending on the specific situation he was in: As a ruler, he was serious and conscientious, but at the same time brutal and ruthless; as a family man, he was the same way. Among friends, however, he was jovial, sociable, and good-humored. In his positions on foreign policy, he was timid, weak, and indecisive. Other monarchs felt he was unreliable. Similarly, the young Bismarck was docile, polite, and well mannered: "A delicate youth with a tender and malleable nature." By age twenty-five, however, he had become a wild, violent, and domineering Junker. These examples are important because they point up the necessity of reintroducing the world previously "bracketed" into attempts to understand human nature; we are thus ultimately left with biography, the description of one individual's life. We may conclude, therefore, that all efforts to determine specific characteristics, predispositions, or basic drives ultimately evidence basic logical flaws. One can either argue that man constitutes a set of concepts which have lost all real content or, if one wishes to be concrete, one must necessarily lapse back into descriptive biography. Typology, of course, attempts to find a middle ground here, to remain in the sphere of the average and the general; it would, however, congeal there into a pseudo-science. We must not forget Dilthey's original and logically correct understanding of the type *(Typus)* as an approximation *(Annäherung)* of the description of an individual.

Our purposes require that we now undertake a refutation of the "psychology of drives" *(Triebpsychologie)*; this should prove particularly instructive because it is the ambiguity of the concepts of drive and instinct that is responsible for a considerable amount of confusion.

We could say that the human being behaves instinctively whenever his organs function "appropriately" and automatically—for example, when an infant nurses, or closes its fist, or perhaps even when it makes the motions of embracing. Sexuality, clearly, has an instinctive root.

From these and a few other examples which may be open to interpretation, we can determine that we really know human beings only as cultural beings, as beings who are active in infinitely varied, socially mediated actions—actions which have been learned and cannot be understood out of the context of the actions of other human beings. It makes no sense here to speak of inherited patterns of movement, that is, truly instinctive actions, which are activated in key situations. On a subjective level, however, all these forms of behavior can run their course in an *instinctive* manner, no matter how highly conditioned they may be. They may achieve a degree of stability, single-mindedness, and automatization which could make them appear to be the emanations of underlying drives or instincts. All forms of learned human activity, from philosophy to head-hunting, which might just as easily spawn variations as disappear altogether, have the potential to be invested with impulses *(Antriebsbesetzung);* this fact is of tremendous significance and can be attributed to the reduction of instincts *(Instinktreduktion)* in the human being. The reduction of truly instinctive actions apparently goes hand-in-hand with the morphological fetalization of man and his advanced cerebral development. This reduction signifies a process of "dedifferentiation" *(Entdifferenzierung)* of the structure of human impulses, which means that any form of behavior, whether it belongs in the realm of work or play, can appear as compulsive and can serve to gratify some basic impulses. Because of this inner plasticity in the structure of human impulses, it becomes necessary for every culture to formulate its own specific hierarchy and law of apportionment of required, tolerated, and prohibited actions, and thus also of needs, and to inculcate these into its young members. We do not act in a certain way because we have specific needs, but rather we have these needs because we and those around us act in certain ways.

Dedifferentiation apparently affects to some extent even that system of impulses which is hormonally regulated—the sexual. There is hardly any activity, even the most intellectual of pursuits, which could not draw part of its dynamic impetus from this system; by the same token, the sexual system can always yield to other determinants—social, esthetic, ritual, etc. A similar situation can be found wherever we are inclined to assume that an instinctive root or a residue of instincts *(Instinktresiduum)* exists. For example, the mere fact of togetherness, of the group situation, appears to function as a releaser toward the need to assert oneself or dominate others, which has the character of an instinct residue. However, here, too—if we consider the diversity among cultures—we will see that almost any activity may take on a prestige value, from the Polynesian art of boat-building to the shaman's art of inducing trances, to the quality of "sexual charisma," which can convey power in certain situations. Because every human behavior is in fact *overdetermined,* it is hopeless to attempt to set up a catalogue of instincts. Every concrete behavior "X" is socially conditioned; it is a part of a system in the context of a culture. It is learned, it may take different forms, it may become compulsive, or it may be able to be gratified in itself to the point of satiation (and not, for example, simply be stopped because of fatigue), and very often has a distinct instinct-residual quality. The concepts of the reduction of instincts, residue of instincts, and the dedifferentiation of instincts are genuine and indispensable anthropological categories.

We may also justify our approach from another angle. In popular speech, those actions are characterized as "instinctive" *(triebhaft)* which run their course in a strikingly uninhibited fashion. It makes sense to describe the desperate thievery of a starving person or the sexual excesses of a prisoner as instinctive, for these are actions occurring at the lowest limits of existence—actions designed to relieve basic distress which surface when higher controls are absent. On the other hand, such actions as those involved in the participation in a hunt or in agricultural cultivation are not instinctive actions, although one might argue that, in the final analysis, hunger is their driving force. The expression "instinctive" in the above examples refers to the sudden gratification of basic physical needs which have been denied to the very limits of tolerance. In normal circumstances, however, the human being is "driven" beyond these lower limits of existence precisely because he *cannot* gratify his overdetermined needs, his hunger, his sexual needs, in an "instinctive" fashion, but must do so instead in an orderly and "limited" fashion. We could even argue that man has a need for needs that extend beyond the basics of existence: for example, the "drive" to drive a car, to dance, or to collect works of art. Thus, we have again come upon the fact, mentioned above, that highly conditioned and derived forms of behavior can be invested with drives.

The word "instinctive" is also employed in another sense to refer to those actions or emotions which are not carefully and intelligently considered and which are not kept under tight control. For example, we could say that someone has an instinctive inclination toward exaggeration, although he is aware that those around him see through this, or that he is inclined to be extravagant although he is aware of his limited means. By the same token, we would not call a sudden outbreak of anger "instinctive" if it occurred in an appropriate situation. In such cases, it appears that an emotion, or basic urge, has not been successfully integrated into a structure of attitudes (Haltungsgefüge); thus we could say that the individual has somehow been deficient in forming an inner attitude toward himself.

Finally, we might also call actions "instinctive" that represent attempts to master the here and now, in contrast to those actions that focus on long-term interests. Thus, we could say that a child's urge to destroy objects, or the fear response, is instinctive—as is, in general, all short-term emotional behavior focusing on whatever happens to be present and directly available. This includes, for example, the behavior of a pasha who had the bearer of bad tidings decapitated.

In sum, our language characterizes those actions, inclinations, etc., as instinctive which are fundamentally opposed to nonminimal actions, to conscious, willed, controlled, directed actions, to actions oriented toward long-term needs. It is important to note here that the latter set of concepts, those opposed to "instinctive" actions, are interrelated. A structure of interests, needs, inclinations, and habits—in sum, impulses that are discriminatory and controlled, that have been appropriated and singled out in a selective, reciprocal process, and that are long-term in nature—is called *character*.

I therefore feel that proposing a catalogue of instincts or a list of fundamental drives holds little promise. We can discover a common point of reference for understanding this problem if we take the reduction of instincts as our premise and use it to understand how *all* intelligent behavior is invested with impulses; we will then see that the formation of character becomes a necessity.

39. The Two Laws Governing Impulses: The Hiatus

The fundamentally different premise that we have adopted in this book grants us a few insights which are not possible if one chooses the other paths of abstracting qualities or reducing everything to drives. Our approach is necessary because anthropology, as man's understanding of himself achieved through science, must not become mired in the methodological uncertainty of the theories of character, typologies, and so forth. Our premise is the philosophical one I have described above: it is based on a total understanding of the human being with action as the focal point. Before proceeding further, however, we must briefly consider a few facts relating to the mechanism of action.

The human being has voluntary control over his organs of movement and perception—those organs that facilitate the sensorimotor circular processes involved in perception and movement. In part 2, we examined in great detail how our perceptions cooperate with and inform our versatile movements and how language, and ultimately thought itself, arise from this cooperation and feed back into it. Whenever we see an object, we have not only an interpreted and understood perception of it, but also a seasoned ability to manipulate the object and, beyond this, to respond intelligently to any experiences or surprises we may have with this object. We exercise our judgments, assess the situation, and make use of the object in question. Thus, we discovered that the "circle of action" (involving our hands, eyes, and language) may become to a great extent self-contained and may draw the impetus for its own initiation, continuation, or change from within itself. These organs of perception and movement are distinguished from those involved in digestion, circulation, respiration, etc., in two ways: (1) they are not directly and necessarily dependent on each other—the latter set of organs function beyond our control; (2) they are capable of becoming fatigued. Thus, these organs require periods of rest; they can function independently of each other, whereas the heart, lungs, and circulatory system, for example, are directly dependent on each other and hence are not subject to voluntary control. We can walk without speaking, see without exerting effort, hear without seeing, work without thinking, move without perceiving, and so on. At the same time, however, we may choose to connect all these activities to each other and find the impetus for employing one function in another function.

Because these functions can operate independently of each other while they can also be related to each other, it is possible for us to change the order of dominance: any one function can be subordinated to any other. To give simple examples, our eyes will guide our grasping movements when we must orient ourselves by sight in order to act. However, the reverse can also occur: we can handle or even destroy a thing in order to see what is on it or inside it. We can also walk in order to hear (to a concert, for example) and hear in order to walk (if we have lost our way and are listening for some clue to guide our movements). On the whole, our faculty for action is to a great extent self-contained. It can find its impetus in the things we encounter, in its own habits, in practical "ideas," or images of goals—in any case, it finds its motivation largely within the confines of the circle of action itself. Thus, at least at times, this circle may become independent; but independent of what?

It may become independent of our impulses and drives. In the discussion to follow, I will use the terms impulses, needs, and interests synonymously and always in the plural form. Because man is an unspecialized being dependent on his own initiative and because he possesses no environment to which he is naturally adapted, he is denied the direct gratification of his life needs that an animal enjoys. He cannot pursue the "short cut" taken by the animal, whose instincts operate through its senses to find its goals, which Nature, in her great wisdom, has made readily available. Man must confront the world and its constant surprises and render it available, knowable, intimately familiar, and usable, so that he can engage in planned and appropriate work to create what he needs, what is not readily available to him. For precisely this reason, the range of human action is not limited to the given situation, to the boundaries of the here and now. By anticipating the future, the human being creates the conditions that enable him to survive in it. These facts provide the basis for the structure of human impulses and explain their orientation. After considering the unspecialization and lack of organic means of man, his world-openness and intelligence, we can examine his use of action to maintain his existence and ask ourselves: what is the nature of the impulses of such a being?

There is a whole series of answers to this question which illuminate each other; we can launch our examination of this subject from any point in it. First and foremost, human impulses must be understood in relation to action and the problems of action. It is vitally necessary that man, as an acting being, be able to *defer* the gratification of his needs, because the preliminary activities he must engage in—the activities in which he discovers and manufactures from existing circumstances what he needs to survive—have their own set of laws peculiar to the given situation. It is of the utmost importance here that experience and the assimilation of experience run their course in an objective, logical fashion and not be swayed by emotional or other disturbances because the gratification of human needs depends on the outcomes of practical interaction with the things in our world. Nature provides two means of dealing with this problem: First, she makes the circle of action fluid so that it can be initiated at any point and directed at will; second, she makes the ability to inhibit impulses a *need* to inhibit them while also providing the means for accomplishing this. The means to accomplish this have to do with a fact, the great importance of which I have already stressed: human beings are subject to an excess of impulses (*Antriebsüberschuss*), which makes it imperative that these impulses be managed and controlled in some manner, specifically, by using some impulses to inhibit and restrain others. That all human impulses, even organic ones, can be inhibited is of tremendous importance and can be understood only in the context of human actions which must be "detached" from human needs, in order that man be able to experience the world fully and thereby develop an unrestricted and vitally necessary faculty for action. The deferral of gratification thus creates a void, a *hiatus*, between the needs and their gratification; action lies in this "void," as does thought. Like action, thought cannot fall prey to disturbance by impulses if it is to be proper and fruitful. We might describe this hiatus as the reality of completed experience (*vollzogene Erlebniswirklichkeit*); physiologically, it is an objective fact in the diversity and relative independence of the organic and animal realm.

It is not within our power to avoid feeling an impulse or need; it is within our power to decide whether or not to gratify it, as Fichte has pointed out.[3] In order for a need to be gratified, it cannot determine the particular circumstances of its gratification. We must be able to "unhinge" our actions from our impulses; we must create this hiatus, because in order for our actions to become appropriate, well thought-out, and open to repetition and improvement, they need time and experience. This process of finding the means to gratify our needs—a process in which our actions naturally intermesh with one another—has no limits; it may go on indefinitely and take many forms. For example, which actions of a mechanic or accountant actually serve directly to procure those things necessary for gratifying their vital needs? The indirect nature of human occupation has grown into a monstrous apparatus in modern culture. Within this apparatus, however, each individual pursues his livelihood, and even the smallest component represents an act of disciplined work such that any attempt to undermine the foundations of this system must be prevented, even if this attempt involves only lowering through romantic babble the standard of dedicated research and knowledge that supports this system.

Culture is therefore more than simply reasonable for man; it is in fact vitally necessary to his survival. Its basis is the hiatus, the ability to separate actions from impulses, which is the condition for man's survival. Our mind, our eyes, and our hands are all directed toward the external world; we employ them actively in reality, in cooperation with or in opposition to each other. They can always be employed independently (not in an absolute sense, of course, but under certain conditions which are learned through experience) of our rhythmical needs, which are the foundation for our impulses.

In our discussion thus far, we have touched on only one aspect of this many-sided problem; we shall now consider another, which runs counter to the one already mentioned.

Because man is an active, planning being who must first create from the world the means for his survival and who in the process becomes caught up in unforeseeable ways in the laws of the factual world, it is of course inconceivable that a clear boundary could exist in him between those actions that serve immediate biological purposes and those that serve indirect, removed purposes. To make such a distinction would in fact be life-threatening for man. Thus, we must again ask ourselves: What is the nature of human impulses? Human impulses can be developed and formed; they can arise from actions themselves which then become needs. This astonishing fact is as vital to human survival as is the other point we have stressed—that human impulses can be detached from actions. We may argue further that there is no objective boundary between impulses and habits, between primary and secondary needs; instead, whenever such a distinction does appear, it is made by *man himself*. To put this another way, man allows certain needs to be transformed within himself and to spread themselves out in the world through him until they become interests in very specific actions directed toward specific, individual facts. For an acting being, a being who is exposed to the unrestricted randomness of reality, it is crucial that even the most refined abilities be able to become needs and to be executed with great interest. To accomplish this, man must possess a type of peripheral or external will which will spur him to take up, maintain, and pursue certain activities oriented toward solving any disturbances and problems he will encounter in the course of his actions; more important, man must possess the ability to find gratification in even the most removed, special problems and activities so that these can become needs. It is therefore important that "as far as it is possible, the means are also in a sense ends, that is, they are desirable not only on account of what they do, but on account of what they are."[4]

Human impulses demand a certain amount of cultivation. They must be *developed* in order to conform to the facts of the world. They can also follow from actions, since they themselves can be inhibited when necessary and detached from actions. We develop an interest in aspects of our world and in interacting with the things in our world; in addition, our actions may become habits—needs—which we cannot even call secondarily instinctive. This situation only makes sense in light of our understanding of the total human being: this being must not act "instinctively" because his survival requires him to delve into the facts and come to terms with them. Thus, it must be possible for even the most unusual methods of responding to and coming to terms with these facts to become needs. This explains why habits and interests, even of a superficial nature, can tell us something about the human being, that is, about his orientation toward the world which has given form to his impulses. If we consider man on a simple level—that is, without any "scientific" prejudices—we will find that we can best discover his personality, his "self," in his longing for specific activities, in the hierarchy of the interests he pursues, but clearly not in the "traits" he possesses. To date, psychology has usually chosen to consider the character of the human being separately from his actions, thereby relegating him to an "inner life," whereas in fact one can easily read a human being by his actions, his successes and failures, his habits and interests. All these have been shaped by attitudes which the individual continually adopts toward himself and which his surroundings have also validated for him since his childhood, educating and influencing him.

The character of a human being thus inevitably encompasses what he *himself* has become; the self, however, does not figure into the pair of concepts of inherited predisposition and environment. Regretably, this pair of concepts still holds sway in modern psychology, although it is completely useless for two reasons: first, these predispositions are simply deduced from an individual's behavior, while ignoring the factor of action, for every inclination that is expressed actively has already passed through a stage in which an attitude was formed toward it; at least, it is the potential object of such an attitude. Second, the term "environment" *(Umwelt)* is completely vague: it certainly does not mean environment in the biological sense, for this, as we have shown, is a concept restricted to the field of animal psychology. In the realm of the human being, this term can only mean a "cultural environment" and what is this other than a highly complex, definitely historical field of genuine facts—the results of the actions of longstanding communities? We can know a character by where and by what means it enters into the action field of culture, how it behaves in active encounters, and how it effects *changes* in these facts and encounters, to create the desired environment. To put it simply, the "environment" contains nothing more than human beings and things: the former actively influence each other and the latter are "preformed" actions, preexecuted deeds: the simplest tool attests to this. Thus, the main element is missing in the scheme of predisposition and environment—the self and the insight that *action* contains the self and creates the environment. This scheme is one of those misleading biological intellectual aids which have actually obstructed the development of a true biological understanding of the human being. It is an essential feature of man that he forms and orients his impulses and needs in the course of experiencing the world because he must simultaneously come to terms with himself and the world so that his character, the product of this disciplined process, is established through his actions and their results (including the actions of others).

40. The World-Openness of Impulses

In our investigation of the problems of man's inner life, we have been guided by our view of the total human being; we have concentrated on the question of the nature of the impulses of such a being whose survival depends on action. This approach has revealed that human impulses characteristically operate in two opposite directions. On the one hand, the prerequisite to the gratification of all human needs is that we explore and come to know thoroughly all the things and situations in our world; in the human being, knowledge and mastery of the world are achieved in the *same* activities. For this reason, all human needs are "higher" needs—that is, interests in the conditions necessary for their gratification, in the obstacles and aids to their gratification, in the activities and their effects which serve to transform the world to suit man's purposes. The impulses are necessarily plastic in nature: they conform to the given circumstances; they can adjust to changes in the situation and in actions; they are not determined by the situation itself *(situationsbedingt)* but instead correspond to it *(situationsentspre-chend)*. This is their essential feature. On the other hand, these impulses must also be able to be restrained to the greatest degree possible. They must at the same time be independent of, or more precisely "detachable" *(ab-hängbar)* from, the processes of action and experience. The infinite diversity of potential situations makes it necessary for us to experience the world on a concrete level, that is, to become intimately familiar with it, to experiment with and experience it. We must be able to check our needs and interests because their future gratification depends on our being able to allow the circumstances to "express themselves" as they are. The "hiatus" between needs and impulses on the one hand and their gratification and the actions necessary to achieve this on the other is what first opens up the possibility of an "inner life" for the human being.

At this point in our discussion, I have formulated several significant insights I wish to develop in detail. The two basic features of my understanding of human impulses indicate deeper, underlying peculiarities in them—the conscious nature *(Bewusstheit)* and the worldliness *(Welthaftigkeit)* of man's inner life. Those features are usually described with the term "soul."

Let us for the moment rid ourselves of all the notions that commonly cling to this concept, particularly the idea that a dualism of body and soul exists. Let us focus only on what we already know of the human being. A world-open, that is, unspecialized, being who must depend on his own initiative and intelligence in order to survive, a being who is vulnerable to the external world in every respect but yet must maintain an existence within it by assimilating it, working through it, becoming familiar with, and gaining control over it—such a being would be doomed if it had only a few rigid instincts such as an animal has, even if these instincts could be tempered somewhat by experience. Even then, this being would be doomed because there are no guarantees that those situations would come about which would awaken the appropriate instincts if man himself did not create these situations. In order to create such situations, however, this being needs impulses and drives that are fundamentally different in structure from those belonging to a creature of instinct—in a word, its impulses must be world-open. We can therefore understand only those characteristics of human impulses we have identified thus far—their worldliness, world-openness, and conscious nature—if we consider them in the light of our fundamental anthropological interpretation. For the purposes of clarity, I have chosen a simple term to embody all the aspects of this complex subject—the human ability to orient impulses *(Orientierbarkeit der Antriebe);* my choice of words is intended to indicate that the human being must accomplish this on his own.

In order to gain an understanding of the "inner life" of the human being, we must above all relegate *thought* to its proper place. It is not part of this inner life from the start but rather is derived from language; it is a system that belongs completely in the sensorimotor realm—a system of interpretations and characterizations that is focused outwards, an organ that facilitates planning and achieving an overview, an organ that directs action. As a system of relief, it is also designed to reduce further the direct relationship to the sensory world, and above all to allow its intentions to continue their course within themselves and to find gratification within themselves. In this manner, it becomes nonverbal inner thinking *(sprachloses inneres Denken),* touching only on the "seeds" of the complex of ideas; nonetheless, it never loses sight of the problem with which it is ultimately concerned—the direction of behavior. Ultimately, it discovers within itself the motivations for directed development; it discovers within itself problems which allow it to exercise its potential fully. It becomes purely intellectual and technical (mathematics) although, of course, this development could take place only after writing had been invented, because writing allowed thought to confront itself and to set down the individual steps in its reasoning process as instructions for subsequent execution. However, all this does not alter the fact that this system is primarily directed "outward." It has evolved to aid the human being in mastering his world, to provide total freedom for action as it moves within itself from one concept to another, taking A as B, and forming new expectations accordingly, as it weaves the absent into the present, as it broadens the range of perspectives available to man. When action comes to a standstill between two possibilities, it will follow the impulses it has formed which see good prospects in one of these possibilities. Schopenhauer's statement is apt: Thought is the "idea if ideas" [*Vorstellen des Vorstellens*]; it is the extension of what is present into the future, into what is not-present; it is closely tied to action. As Schopenhauer says, it is the "medium of motivation" *(Medium der Motive)*, the agent of our motivating impulses.

Now that we have come to understand thought as a sensorimotor process, we can broach the topic of how and why our impulses become conscious. If we consider the reality of our own inner life, leaving aside all abstract notions, we will discover first of all that this inner life generally makes itself felt in the state of complete rest, where action is absent. In other words, it is detached from actions; it is a hiatus. At times of very intense activity, such as in moments of extreme danger, there is no inner life; in such moments, we engage in lightning-quick actions, our mind is focused on the external world, and we experience a keen perception of the changing images, but no emotions aside from a feeling of great energy. However, when we do not act but instead remain still, or when we are only superficially performing actions that have become mechanical habits which run their course smoothly, we will experience internal pressure from our excessive impulses. Above all, at such times, we will discover within ourselves desires or interests, compelling images of problems we face, or plans or hopes we may have, as well as strong urges to undertake certain activities with very specific goals of which we are well aware. Our impulses then dominate our thoughts; the particular obstacles and situations we face, the fears and plans we have, awaken certain memories and expectations within us. A world we have come to know through movement is developed within us; it is not subjective, but rather contains possible situations in which we feel an urge to act. In this world, the ever changing and yet clearly defined situations play just as important a role as do the specific persons we imagine in our mind.

We can now pose a further question: For what reasons would Nature allow a being to be aware of its own impulses, thereby exposing it to grave dangers? The answer, of course, is that this being cannot automatically gratify its needs in its immediate surroundings to the extent that these can be perceived by its sense. To put this paradoxically, this being must find gratification for its needs *within itself* because it cannot find it *outside* of itself. Man's inner life is world-open: this means above all that it can be shaped by a wide diversity of experiences and impressions, any of which can give rise to a striving or aspiration. This signifies further that human needs and impulses contain images from the past, longings for what is absent, yearnings for future situations. As should be immediately apparent, this structure is necessary for an acting being who must exist within the open abundance of the world, responding to whatever situation it may encounter by forming expectations dictated by experience.

Thus, the fundamental phenomena we have discussed here explain each other. Man provides direction and substance for his impulses and needs. By experiencing the world—indeed, simply by speaking and interpreting the world—he facilitates the process whereby his impulses are given concrete substance. These impulses arise in the course of his actions and are shaped by the objects they concern; they remain attached to the images of experience. The human being experiences himself and inevitably becomes a *problem* for himself, an object toward which he must adopt some sort of stance, form some opinion. Nietzsche called this process *Einverseelung* (incorporation into the soul). Kant has made the profound statement that our minds are occupied with representations, the external sense(s); he further emphasized that inner experience is really possible only through external experience.[5]

As we have seen, then, the system of action can be set in motion independently of one's particular needs. This inhibition or deferment of gratification of impulses, this hiatus, first exposes an inner life which nonetheless does have a specific orientation: it has been "invested with ideas of the external senses," steeped in images of desires, of situations, hopes, and habits. This is the only form that human impulses, needs, and interests can take, because this structure of impulses befits a being who cannot travel the direct path from instinct through innate patterns of movement toward the selected stimulus. The external world must therefore grow into this being so that, as Herder put it, all inner states become or are made analogous to language *("sprachmässig")*.

We can now go one step further, while we keep in mind what we have established thus far so that we may integrate it with the new discoveries we will make. The question now arises of how a need is oriented, how it becomes *sprachmässig*—how it becomes conscious, how it comes to possess a specific content. Our earlier discussion will prove useful in finding an answer to this question.

Let us recall our discussion of the roots of language, specifically, the call. A small child expresses its intense, uninterpreted feelings of discomfort in restless movements, including sounds and cries. The distress is alleviated, the child's need (which it does not as yet fully understand) is met, the gratification of this need is perceived, tasted, felt, seen: this association is frequently repeated so that the child actively assimilates it. It comes to expect the gratification that *follows* the cry—that is, it cries with the intention of alleviating its discomfort. The more advanced animals are also able to assimilate and then use such random sequences of actions. If the call is then employed to obtain a specific result, if it is invested with expectations, then a relationship has been firmly established between need, sound, and gratification, which is under the direction of the sound. The sound expresses impulses and needs and facilitates their gratification. Whenever the need begins to make itself felt, it is anticipated in the sound and in specific images; it thereby becomes conscious as a specific need with a particular content.

Thus, some form of action always serves as the vehicle for the development of our needs. Action is the medium through which they become comprehensible, able to be oriented, and conscious of their goals. In the example provided above, this action took the form of a call in which, along with the accompanying images of the call's effect, of gratification, a goal-conscious need becomes aware of itself as such. When we say that an infant "associates" the feeling of hunger, the call, and the image of nursing, we have actually missed the most important point: for such expressions as the "feeling of hunger," "drive to eat," etc., already incorporate the image of gratification, the ultimate goal, and do not refer to action. Yet, the nature of our impulses first becomes comprehensible and clear to us in the context of specific situations involving action. A small child's impulses are as yet unappropriated and uninterpreted; they are first characterized by the fact that they can imagine goals. Some form of activity is necessary to facilitate this process. The human being experiences himself through action; to put it another way, man's impulses belong in the realm of those achievements that involve appropriation and interpretation, the realm of human problems. This is an essential, fundamental human reality. Our interests and needs surface in active situations which furnish images of their goals; they then become conscious impulses. The two-year-old child who says "Mama, I want..." and then looks around for what he might possibly want, has certainly already experienced and assimilated this fact—the crystallization of the initially formless impulses into definite images, into real, oriented needs.

We stated above that man's inner life is wordly *(welthaft)*. This expression now takes on a second meaning because man actively experiences, appropriates, and interprets this inner life, as he does the external world, and these two can really be experienced and mastered only through each other. Novalis called it "a most promising sign" when idealism described the inner world in images drawn from the external world and vice versa; this method of procedure proved most fruitful because it is appropriate and correct. Clearly, language plays the principal role in this process. It accompanies all actions and movements, as, for example, in a game in which we experience our impulses, with the result that language can detach these from factual activities and allow them to continue movement on its own plane. We can experience interests in and needs for goals and situations that are purely imagined. Above all, however, language remains indifferent toward the distinction between the real and the imagined; in other words, language itself is "the most promising sign" because it allows the external world to grow into us. Thus, we invest our mind with the ideas drawn from our external senses, and we orient our world-open, conscious impulses—impulses that befit an acting being who must establish himself in relation to the world from the inside outwards.

When, in this fashion, a specific, living impulse is established, it becomes an inner source of energy and can power other processes. Our versatile, controlled actions can now carry out or not carry out this impulse. Let us express this another way: An interest becomes an object toward which we must form an attitude; we can permit it and gratify it or we can choose to reject it by allowing other interests to inhibit action. It is of great importance that man is capable of forming an attitude toward himself, and there are several aspects to this. For the moment, we are concerned with the hiatus between impulses and actions and our awareness of ability to comprehend every established impulse. Only when an impulse can be detached from action, so that it becomes conscious and comprehensible, can another be opposed to it. Indisputably, one of the simplest experiences is that we can form an attitude toward any need; on the other hand, every impulse we have allowed to come to expression has the tendency to broaden itself, to draw into itself the energy of other impulses, until finally it becomes an established habit, part of the organic rhythm, and no longer easily disturbed. The borderline between impulse *(Antrieb)*, drive *(Trieb)*, and habit *(Gewohnheit)* is therefore not an objective one: it is determined by each individual who personally regulates the transition from one to the other. Aristotle expressed this same idea:

It is by no means true that [a person] can stop being unjust or dissolute merely by wishing it. You might as well expect a sick man to get better by wishing it. Yet the illness may be voluntary in the sense that it has been caused by loose living and neglecting the doctor's orders. There was a time when he need not have been ill; but once he let himself go, the opportunity was lost.... Similarly, it was open to the dishonest and dissolute fellow to avoid becoming such a character; so that his original action was voluntary.[6]

We can form attitudes and judgments toward our own needs and interests—once these have become crystallized, comprehensible, and conscious—as soon as they have been laid bare through the hiatus. They will surface as inner urges if the action is inhibited or just occupied with other matters. It is necessary for us to make decisions of this nature because of the excess of impulses we are subject to and because the vitally important diversity in human actions and interests does not afford a great amount of room for the development of individual needs. Only in relieved, favorable circumstances and at the cost of other impulses can such excesses be expressed. There are, however, other reasons why we must make these sorts of decisions: only through them can we form an *attitude (Haltung)*, that is, a system of exclusive directions our striving takes, directions that define each other and are part of a hierarchy we work out. As I intend to show, this system is actually vitally and organically necessary for the human being. This fact should come as no surprise to us, given our biologically based understanding of man as an acting being; we would expect that even the purely vegetative processes are related to this as well. As impulses are crystallized in specific situations and actively invested with images of their goals, they become conscious and eventually develop into true inner strengths. At the same time, however, we are able to form opinions and attitudes toward them; they become the object of our efforts at discipline, education, self-control. The fundamental fact that man is a challenge and problem to himself is responsible for the nature of his physical constitution.

The more general philosophical question we must address here is not one of cognitive theory; it is not the question of how our "ideas" relate to the external world. The question is instead how the external world grows into us. We have now provided an answer to this question. The "inner outer-world" (Novalis) is formed when we feel our needs and urges erupt in certain situations we actively experience; in the course of our actions, and in accompaniment to our activities, these interests and urges become specific impulses that are defined and invested with a specific content. This explains why our needs and interests continue to be tied to the situation in which they were first perceived and why they retain their old names rather than being automatically "rebaptized," so to speak, or newly adapted. These concrete experiences that every human being has cannot be replaced by any process of consciousness or thought, except in cases of self-delusion. Moreover, these experiences usually begin at an age before examination of their "elements" is possible—in the first days of life. For this reason, our inner world consists of a system of significant, goal-conscious interests, needs, and aversions which represent true human aspiration, impetus for actions, habitual ways of acting, as well as images of the world and situations. They are the embodiments of earlier actions and experiences which can be expressed in language and which propel our actions into the future. This is why we really can describe an individual's character only in terms of what he wants or does not want in the realm of politics, professional life, culture, and everyday existence, and in terms of what he has done and what now constitutes the basis for his future attitudes. Above all else, we really can describe a person only in terms of what he would *never* do.

The imagination becomes thoroughly permeated by language and thought; all impulses are imbued with thoughts and images. A child who says "I want the ball" is not experiencing the "expression of the drive to possess" but rather the clear, interpreted desire for this familiar thing along with all the experiences, movements, and images that are part of his play with this thing. I argued earlier that language sets ideas free and makes them versatile. Because language and the imagination work together, our imagination allows us to incorporate into ourselves a great many images of possible encounters, events, and acts which we can then use to test our inclinations, aversions, impulses, and emotions. Our hopes and expectations unfold in these freely imagined settings; true dramatization of our thoughts and ideas takes hold. By imagining ourselves in another's shoes in different situations, we can tap into our own interests and inclinations and can then construct our plans for the future in relation to our impulses. This dramatic process of testing ourselves, accepting certain aspects and rejecting others, always takes place in an imagined "inner world," which contains images of actions, situations, and problems we may encounter. If the human being were simply bound to a few "basic drives," such a process would not only be superfluous but would in fact be impossible—just as impossible as acquiring different senses from those we already possess.

There are only a few philosophers who have treated this particular issue, among them Nietzsche: "Character" he wrote, "appears to be an idea that is poured over our drives. Under it, all expressions of our drives come to light." In the same context, he also remarked that "here we see how the idea is capable of differentiating the different expressions of our will from one another."[7]

I argue that in the course of concrete, active experience, certain interests, inclinations, and impulses announce themselves in man; furthermore, as a result of a specific behavior we adopt in these situations (even if this be no more than naming), an impulse is established and defined and becomes conscious. This is a highly abstract description which makes use of images: We say that an impulse becomes "crystallized" (the image is taken from Stendhal), that it is given "eyes," or that it makes the transition to another aggregate state (Aggregatzustand) through the action that has unlocked it; we resort to such images because our language has no word to describe this singular relationship. The situation was different for the Greek philosophers, who could easily describe such relationships with their concepts of *dynamis* and *energeia*. They also used the term *entelechy* to refer to an ability that is transformed into actuality and can only be understood in terms of the result of this actuality. I have therefore had to describe this process in detail to make it completely clear. Our discussion has also had a polemical purpose: it was directed against the belief that there are specific, innate, fundamental drives in man which are concentrated on specific things in our world. Even hunger and sexuality, which are embodied in specific organs and which seem to lend the greatest support to this notion of fundamental drives, constitute a special case. These also enjoy (one might even say *malgre eux*) the plasticity and dedifferentiation all drives possess; they too should be viewed "from above," and considered in light of the fact that human impulses are predisposed toward intelligent actions and practical needs. It is in this system that they are defined, adopted, and incorporated. Furthermore, the way an individual appropriates these drives (which have a clearly instinctive root but which function as "drives" in the sense that they form the chronic background of latent urges) will reveal much about that individual. This aspect of human impulses represents one side of the coin; the other is that they are "overdetermined" through experience. These two aspects together are responsible for the highly selective sensitivity of our impulses, which is completely different in nature from the high threshold of sensation of corresponding instincts in animals or the exclusivity of the coordinated releasers. Even Buytendijk has contested the idea that hunger and thirst are drives directed toward something; I agree completely with his statement: "It is incorrect to believe that drives are inherited as ready-made powers."[8]

Our scheme demands further clarification from another angle. When we say that, in the course of our actions, our impulses become crystallized or first become conscious and defined, we primarily mean that human impulses are essentially predisposed toward *communication*. They first manifest themselves in early childhood and are developed over the years through play. In play, we can observe the development of world-open, unstable needs for contact which are closely intertwined with the vitality of our senses and the sensitivity of our movements. At first these are so excessive and fluid in nature that it is impossible to name them. Gradually, they become more concentrated and stable although as yet no distinction can be made between intellectual, imagined gratification and the gratification of impulses. Once we realize that the primary achievement of these years is the establishment and growth of lasting impulses, we have taken a big step. We have come to the realization that all impulses, even those of the adult human being, are communicative. Ultimately, even physical needs appear in the costumes of the particular time and society. We see them only as if refracted through a prism, which habit, society, and the *accident absolu* of one's own character have fashioned. Just as man penetrates the world, so does the world penetrate man; we might also say that all things man has experienced, mastered, and strived for, as well as those he did not achieve, urge him on. Our earlier image of the "eruption" of impulses in man must now be amended because it suggests the mistaken view that powers already present and latent in man suddenly find their object. We may at times speak of such an eruption, but we are then referring to syntheses of needs which suddenly come about after long preparation and which are brought together in *one* object based on earlier experience. When we do so we are referring to breaks in the inner dam.

In view of the insights we have gained thus far, it makes sense to reject the idea of a "catalogue of instincts" as well as the scheme of predisposition and environment, because even a consideration of environmental influences fails to take into account the essential aspect of this subject. All these views (even the typological) do not understand the human being and his impulses in terms of action. However, if one adopts action as the focal point, the unique feature of all these human phenomena becomes clear—it is that of the second nature. The world of the human being is a second nature he has created himself; in so doing, however, he necessarily becomes his own problem. His nature is such that he continues to find problems within himself, the solutions to which represent progress in this world. We have described this singular development in our discussion of perception, language, and of movement. Every behavior directed outward is simultaneously a behavior directed inward, and vice versa—this is the fundamental reality of man as the "undetermined" being. Human impulses are no exception. They are themselves ultimately an organ of experiences of the world and other men and are therefore reflexive. Here, too, there is only a second nature. We cannot banish the hiatus from what we term the soul. This hiatus is the level of oriented, image-invested impulses which is first laid bare when it becomes possible to detach these from actions. The context of these impulses are formed from earlier experiences and actions and their focus on specific situations is experienced as internal pressure only until we take action. In this relationship there is at the same time the possibility of immorality, which occurs when there is a contradiction between impulses and actions that has become habit. In essence, this immorality is cowardice—the only vice that cannot be hidden, just as courage is the only virtue that cannot be feigned.

41. Additional Laws Pertaining to Human Impulses

We can carry our discussion of human impulses further by casting another look at the animal, which always lives in the present. Concerned with the here and now, it is secure but not creative. It remains bound to its instincts which indicate in every situation those stimuli to which the animal can respond given its particular organs and physical structure. In contrast to this, man's accomplishments, even the most lowly, involve developing his needs through his activities and developing interests in the specific problems he faces. The primary means that Nature employs to achieve this masterpiece is the "hiatus"—the investment of human impulses with the images of their goals, the incorporation of the external world into man, and the concommitant opening up of his inner life. This is not yet enough, however, to solve the problem man faces. The solution is found only after the practical necessities of action become needs themselves, so that, even when our actions become more deeply caught up in the laws of facts, they will not bridge the hiatus but will instead maintain contact, no matter how indirect, with all our needs, including the organic ones. The boundary here is incidentally quite fine; a strongly introverted individual who has drawn too far away from action, will become an artist at prolonging longevity and will refuse to allow himself to be consumed by everyday life, although indeed this is the way things should be. In general, our inner impulses must grow from the world of action and the infinitely varied human interests which intersect there. This process involves the development of qualified interests—or "higher" interests, as I have termed them. The prerequisites to this development are our ability to check impulses, our awareness of these impulses, and their ability to be affected by the attitudes we form about them, etc.

The first step is to inhibit actions concerned exclusively with the here and now. We could say that all the spontaneous actions of a small child are instinctive, or impulsive, from reaching for shiny objects to throwing away something that is placed in its hands; all these are examples of actions concerned with the immediate present. Such actions must be inhibited so that higher interests may be cultivated. These higher interests are inevitably long-term in nature. For example, as long as a child cannot restrain his urge to destroy the objects he handles, he cannot develop an interest in discovering the relationship between the properties of a thing. Clearly, no other area in psychology has been less explored and remains as uncharted as that of these productive restraints. However, we can see that, at times, the social impulses will inhibit the egocentric ones and draw them toward themselves, resulting in a higher synthesis. For example, children love to handle colorful, bright objects and will only be parted from these reluctantly, because they provide the impetus for continuing the enjoyable play with the objects. However, by its very nature, any objective thing is also readily available to many other people as well, and this is a source of conflict. Upon this quick reacting mechanism, another is superimposed—the fundamental social configuration of "taking the role of the other." This mechanism allows the original desire to retain the object to adopt a completely different constellation: one individual takes over the other's interest in the same object and in return relinquishes his interest in other things. In this manner, the concept of property evolves. Property is not based on one person monopolizing his interest in a thing, but rather involves a reciprocal process of adopting and relinquishing virtual interests—a process that is apparently built on complex systems of productive inhibitions.

Immediate concerns are not sufficient to command all human energies. In other words, the need of our impulses for a higher form is itself an organic need; it is the result of the excess of impulses. Because the human being focuses on action, he must try to expend this excess energy in action; any response to immediate situations is ultimately unsatisfying because it precludes the development of long-term impulses. Immediate instinctive responses tend to leave a feeling of deep dissatisfaction. We do not know much about the philosophy of Aristippus, but judging from the accounts of Aelian and Diogenes, we know that he believed that we could find happiness in immediate pleasures, renouncing any concern for the past or future. This relegates him to a position beneath Epicurus, for whom pleasure still possessed an element of obligation, and his despairing point of view is impressive only because of the naïveté of the ancients and the absence of nihilistic instincts, the good conscience of the ancients. *Non erubuit,* ("He did not blush") wrote Cicero of him.[9]

The human ability to inhibit impulses affords us a different view of man's inner life. All human strivings are influenced by earlier activities and their repercussions; they remain ready to be transformed into actions when the appropriate situation arises and if no other interests inhibit their expression. However, even in this state, they will have a "subterranean" effect: it seems that the very inhibition itself allows them to move up in the structure of subordinated impulses and to disperse themselves among differentiated interests. Long-term interests are not simply interests that have been established and adopted into the structure of attitudes, where they congeal into habits—this process is in fact one of the general prerequisites to the cultivation of impulses. These impulses presuppose that some sort of choice or decision was made at one time, but then does not need to be made again in each new situation. In fact, long-term interests have conformed to and incorporated the fundamental law of man's existence—namely, that activities are decided upon, intelligently directed, and oriented toward the future. Every educator is aware of how many resistant impulses must be overcome before a practical work interest can develop, or of how much constant discipline involving renunciation is necessary to form an enduring set of attitudes. One very common misdirection of a true long-term interest is what we call greed, which is fundamentally different from the form of avarice that is accompanied by a *consomption forte* of worldly pleasures. Greed is related to anxiety about the passage of time; it is based upon the desire to preserve a measure of security while expending as little energy and effort as possible. It is a very powerful "drive" with a complicated history.

The plasticity of human impulses is a biological necessity related to man's organic development, or more precisely, to his organic deficiencies, his lack of specialization, and his ability to act. The term "plasticity" has many meanings. First, it indicates the absence of established, distinct instincts. Second, it refers to man's ability to develop his impulses—that is, to establish or break off connections between them, to provide new orientations for them, to shift toward similar or related interests, or even to form new ones. New needs may arise at any time in one's life, even in the later years. Third, this term refers to the world-openness of impulses. Fourth, it indicates man's ability to make decisions about these impulses, to inhibit them, control them, subordinate and superordinate them to each other. Fifth, this term suggests that all impulses are capable of undergoing a higher development and sublimation so that if certain inhibitions are enforced, qualified, cultivated needs may arise. Finally, plasticity also means that impulses can be exhausted; they may degenerate and become denatured or superfluous.

If an individual's structure of attitudes *(Haltungsgefüge)* is shattered and if his problems disappear or undergo significant, irreversible changes, a "workless" *(arbeitslos)* or "alienated" *(entfremdet)* existence may result because the individual's impulses can no longer find an anchor in objective situations. In such a case, there is not only an opportunity for a subjective morality, as Dewey as shown;[10] in addition, the further development of impulses can be prompted only by stimulation: extravagance, comfort, decay take hold and spread and must be combatted—the Platonic situation.

By now it should be quite clear that it is completely futile to attempt to attribute an individual's character and actions to distinct, innate drives, instincts, or the like. Thorndike, for example, has identified six or seven separate aggressive instincts. There is the instinct to resist an obstructing force, to overcome obstacles, to launch a counterattack, to react unreasonably to pain, to fight rivals, and to be aggressive in competition for a mate. It is clear here that a series of specific situations has been imbued with drives. I fail to understand why there could not then be an instinct to hit the tennis ball over the net. Thorndike has fallen prey to the compulsion to name. Stage fright is quite distinct from other fears, such as fear of retribution, fear of loneliness, agoraphobia, etc. Furthermore, as Ernst Jünger has pointed out, there is also the fear of fear.

Abstract theorists would thus assume that a fear instinct exists and would attribute social drives (as Hobbes did) or religion or what have you to this instinct. They do not realize that such drives are formed by complex internal and external conditions and that they are in fact always overdetermined in a way we cannot figure out retrospectively. These impulses are designed to be experienced "forward" *(nach vorne)*, not "backward." This also accounts for the peculiar sterility of such theories: they allegedly lay bare the underlying causes of our behavior but never actually give us motives or reasons so that, next to our true inner life, an unrelated, intellectual double appears. It is quite easy to make the common mistake of localizing human intelligence in the brain, thereby overlooking the great reason of the body, which is left to the physiologists and other specialists; the theory of drives reduces to a primitive level the foundations of man's inner life and neglects to take into consideration the deep experience and intelligence of human impulses.

We can now identify the following characteristics in all the higher attitudes and long-term interests:

1. Actions confined to the immediate present must first be inhibited so that higher interests can be cultivated. The actions focusing on the immediate present are in any case inherently unsatisfying; human impulses have an organic need for a higher form.

2. These higher interests are long-term and enduring in nature. They are focused on the future, become firm habits, and are unaffected by any changes in the immediate situation; this structure alone is fitting for an acting, anticipatory being.
3. These interests are based on an intimate familiarity with objects in the world. Because they are capable of qualitative development, they become familiar with objects and develop a refined sensitivity.
4. They become "instinctive" in a secondary sense. Every orientation and direction of human activity which is specific in content can become habitual and ultimately function as a source of direct gratification in itself.
5. Finally, these interests can be combined with one another and their gratification deferred to an unusually great degree. They are so closely integrated with human senses, with man's facility for action, with experiences, that they conform to the particular requirements of concrete things and actions as well as to intellectual acts and the imagination. This allows their gratification to be deferred, but at the same time they can be recombined in new ways with each other and developed further. Let us consider a simple example: one's fondness for a person may extend to his relatives and his possessions, and may even lead one to adopt his interests and attitudes. An interest in any thing or phenomenon will extend to its causes, to the causes of these causes, and so forth—regardless of whether these can be actually experienced or only imagined.

We must take care here to avoid a certain intellectual pitfall. If one loses sight of action as the focal point, it may appear that man's impulses are modified or redirected by his consciousness. This would lead once again to a dualistic way of thinking, especially if consciousness is understood as the fundamentally irresponsible realm of fluid "ideas." However, if we choose instead to conceive of consciousness as being directed toward the external world, if we understand it correctly as the dominant organ that allows man to process the interrelationships between things and the circumstances of his actions, then man's ability to change his attitudes means that these can be affected by the system of action—a vital necessity because as oriented, long-term impulses, they are responsible for man's survival. The structure of human impulses—their plasticity, their ability to be cultivated, the pressure to be formed that they experience—is related to action. Our challenge as human beings is to discover and bring out within ourselves the specific existing, appropriated details and problems—the "themes" of the world—and further, to incite our infinitely diverse impulses, needs, etc., to select some, to combine some with others, to inhibit some—in short, to organize these impulses so that a directed activity that has been agreed upon by other human beings can be carried out regardless of any changes in the situation, indeed, perhaps even profiting from such changes. As Novalis wrote, "The ideas of the inner and outer world are formed parallel to each other, in a continuous process—like our right and left foot."[11]

We can only begin to understand the structure of human impulses once we have developed an all-encompassing theory of man and of the elemental challenges he faces. Only then can we understand how the particular human traits are related. If Nature desired "the production in a rational being of an aptitude for any ends whatever of his own choosing" (Kant),[12] (which indeed she must have wished so that this "deficient being" could maintain an existence) then the impulses of such a being would have to be world-open in accordance with this determination—that is, they would have to be oriented by experience, by the "world of purposes," and would have to be able to incorporate these experiences into man's soul.

Because man's impulses can be inhibited and detached from action, they appear as part of the inner world and constitute a special, colorful inner life. These features of human impulses are as necessary to action as is their counterability to become specialized in accordance with the diverse circumstances and particular intentions of man, such as an artisan's concern for a certain quality of material or the sensitivity of technical instincts. When random, short-term impulses are inhibited, long-term interests, attitudes, and needs for more enduring activities arise in accordance with the long-term problems that man faces given his orientation toward the future. At the same time, however, corresponding to this necessary fact of human life, is another fact: it is vital that, within certain limits, man's impulses be able to adapt. When necessary, a given need A must be able to switch its focus from goal a to goal b if b is the means to a or a necessary "detour" toward it or if it is easier to achieve than a, if it is related to or similar to a.

Every thought process offers examples of such adaptation and adjustment. When we are debating which of two needs or two impulses should be satisfied or pursued, we do not draw on an empty "will" which we arbitrarily direct in one direction or another. Instead, we weigh the situation, searching for additional reasons that will make one of the needs more attractive, richer in content, more urgent, so that ultimately no real choice will exist. One impulse will automatically come into effect while the other pales or pours its energy into the first. In this example, however, the interest has become different from what it originally was: it is no longer an interest in a, but rather an interest in a plus b; it has shifted, or adapted to a new situation. This type of adaptation occurs fairly frequently although, in many other cases, such a problem might also be resolved by letting one alternative be related to a long-term interest so that it then becomes unquestionable.

We can also view the important combinations of impulses as very successful adaptations. In a dance, for example, a variety of distinct, higher needs are fulfilled, such as the need for music, for rhythmic movement, for attracting the opposite sex, for ceremony, and so forth. Another example is the passion for hunting: here, in addition to the very real goal of catching the prey, there is also the impulse to move in the outdoors, to carry out an activity with others, the need for excitement, perhaps the desire to kill—who knows how many other possible needs might be thereby fulfilled? It is immediately clear that only a being capable of developing language could adjust and combine his impulses; language makes available to us specific ideas directed toward things. It makes imagination possible, which in turn conveys relief because it allows us to focus on any situation, real or imagined.

Because our impulses are conscious, they can follow the great versatility of reality and the ideas conveyed by language and imagination; above all, they can incorporate the attitudes of other human beings into our communication and interaction with others. In man's interaction with others, a vast, silent game unfolds involving attempts to coerce or persuade others, to adjust to them, agree with them, etc. The complex nature of the conditions for human existence are aptly illustrated in man's ability to retain long-term impulses despite the inevitable changes, detours, and adaptations as well as his ability to respond to these changes. Anyone who ponders these facts will become convinced that the so-called qualities are fundamentally ambiguous. Hoffmann lists very fitting examples of this. Industriousness can be related to ambition, greed, a passion for accuracy, or it may even contain all of these.[13] Furthermore, even unfulfilled or imperceptible needs can function as constitutive elements of an individual's character and of an activity; disappointments, renunciations, and losses can essentially not be surmounted.

By abstracting these features from different modes of behavior, one might conclude that a "fundamental drive," such as an unfulfilled ambition, exists. However, the question of the history of this basic drive would remain unanswered—a question that can no longer be posed in those by no means rare cases in which certain clear, unambiguous, enduring impulses are manifested in early childhood and remain in force throughout an individual's entire life. For example, Klaatsch, the well-known anthropologist, was added to the list of founders of the Berlin Aquarium when he was only six years old—does this mean that an innate drive to study animals exists? Two enduring impulses shaped the life of Pierre Loti: as a child he wanted to be a minister as well as a sailor and hoped to combine these in a career as a missionary. He finally became first and foremost a poet, but in addition commanded a submarine, and so was able to indulge both of his principal interests. How can it possibly help in understanding such a rich and active life to argue that the human being has eight or eighteen or even fifty instincts?

42. The Excess of Impulses: The Law of Discipline

In chapter 7, we introduced the concept of the excess of impulses. Now, we will take up this topic again and put forth a few new ideas.

To say that the human being suffers unceasing pressure from his drives which command even his dreams at night is a purely descriptive statement. It is no simple task to transfer this energy or gain control over these impulses. Their quantity of energy far exceeds what is expended in the gratification of basic physical needs. If we consider that human activities have been responsible for reshaping the face of the earth, for conquering the seas and skies, razing mountains, and delving deep inside the earth—if we simply think for a moment of the nature of our daily work—it will be clear that what human culture has achieved cannot be wholly explained by the concept of the preservation of the species. On the contrary, as far as the preservation of the species is concerned, the excess of impulses appears irrational and at times consumes itself. The "biological hardiness" evidenced in the creative minorities that propel the culture forward, the precarious artificiality of all social institutions when first formed, and the fate similar to Icarus's of countless, nameless pioneers and inventors, are all sufficient testimony that the *élan vital* is unstable in a dynamic way and that the "preservation of the species" is only a secondary product.

We do know a few things about this important and obscure subject of the excess of impulses. Several factors are clearly responsible for it. It is initially indistinguishable from the reduction of instincts, which finds external expression in the morphological unspecialization of the human being. Let us imagine that quantities of impulses are disengaged from organs, detached from the environment. In this case, the reduction in instincts would not signify a quantitative weakening but rather an inner dedifferentiation of instincts such that the numerous instincts and specialized behaviors we observe in animals are either lost completely or never even arise in the first place. Even the sex drive takes part in this inner restructuring process. On the concrete level, this process of dedifferentiation means that great amounts of energy from these impulses, which still bear the taint of instincts, can be applied to any other arbitrary habitual actions and development of interests. The consequence, as Portmann realized, is, for example, the constant, enduring sexualization of all systems of human impulses on the one hand and the investment of all sexual activity with other motivations on the other. The residue of social instincts—an area not yet adequately studied—might also be affected by this same pattern: for example, residues which according to the law of instinct reduction are not coordinated with specific forms of behavior could above all be the drive for power and the communicative processes of "taking the role of the other," as Mead described. Thus, it is conceivable that a human being who experiments with a thing in a given situation might not only be satisfying a rational interest in the object but also be experiencing a drive for power, a form of pseudosocialization of interaction, or even a libidinous urge.

The reduction of instincts and the absence of firmly fixed, species-specific releasers create a chronic pressure. There is a direct correlation between a human being's requirements for survival and his chronic state of need. Man must survive all the changes in the external world, including seasonal changes; in every situation, even the more favorable ones, he must constantly devote his energies to initiating actions. His impulses cannot be attuned to specific things in his surroundings and cannot cease in accordance with the rhythm of Nature. Such an instinctual rhythm would prove to be a serious disharmony in a being whose survival depends on constant action.

The human being must master an essentially hostile world. He must develop and maintain long-term impulses, because they will serve to sustain his actions into the future. In addition he must approach and respond to the present in terms of the future and what it holds for him. Furthermore, building his second nature poses one problem after the other for him and demands his constant attention. These factors make it impossible to gratify directly the immediate vital needs, the basic necessities of existence; these can be gratified only if an excess of impulses exists.

The sex drive is also basically chronic in nature, although it still manifests remnants of periodicity; it is always in effect. Incidentally, this is the reason why, from an anthropological perspective, the choice between the terms "drive" *(Trieb)* and instinct *(Instinkt)* is quite arbitrary. We cannot clearly distinguish one from the other in the human being as Lorenz was able to do in his work with animals, where he distinguished between the animal form of impulsive appetitive behavior and the truly instinctive patterns of movements triggered by releasers. Animal psychology can identify specific patterns of movement as instinctive. The human being, on the other hand, experiences all his impulses with all their conceivable qualitative and substantive variations as fundamentally *distinct* from his behavior, as urges that can be gratified in a variety of behaviors. The concepts of "instinct" and "instinctive" can therefore only be defined exactly in the study of animal behavior; when applied to man, they become imprecise, arbitrary, and are difficult to distinguish from the concept of drives, which, in turn, blends in with that of needs and even of interests. Our feeling of being alive, our awareness of reality are so completely dependent upon this chronic pressure that even the most primitive tribes will resort to artificial stimulants when involution or exhaustion or impotence sets in, simply in order to create again the experience of the drive. Here, the drive is not striving for the consummatory action, but instead the consummatory action is striving for the drive! One could also argue that the overdetermined nature of impulses— it is not clear whether this is a cause or result of the excess of impulses— suggests that some drives are never completely gratified. Some portion of our needs inevitably remains unfulfilled. As the pessimists claim, longing, once disappointed by fulfillment, simply surfaces again in a new form.

Furthermore, the excess of impulses is most likely related to retardation, the delayed development of the human body. Buytendijk and Plessner related the excess of impulses to the long period of immature motor skills (human childhood) and the late awakening of sexuality.[14] To use a mechanical image here, a type of dam forms. The human being never expends certain energies that are present in his constitution; thus in a manner of speaking, he ages in a chemical sense but not in an organic one. A series of fetal characteristics persists into adulthood, except in certain pathological cases in which endocrine action is disturbed, resulting in excessive growth of body hair, for example. We could then argue that the "macrobiotic" instinct of human beings, which I believe is an important source of social phenomena (certain forms of ascetism) is the reflection of a fundamental human fact—namely, the juvenilization and retardation that has penetrated into our very consciousness so that a normal life span appears too short.

These three perspectives on the excess of impulses—which, I freely concede, I might not have related to each other in the best way possible—show us that this excess is by no means an anomalous fact, but is instead completely appropriate in view of the unique biological position of the human being. We can argue that man lacks the organic means, that he suffers a reduction in instincts, and is relieved of an environment and must therefore draw on an excess of impulses. We characterized this relief in great detail earlier in this book. By taking upon himself the dangers inherent in his nature, by liberating himself from the pressures of overstimulation in his senses, his movements, and his language, man reduces to a minimum on a sensory as well as a motor level the points of contact with the immediate situation. He thereby gains control over his world, acquires an overview of it, and can transform the field of surprises into a second, artificial nature.

This last point brings up a fourth aspect of the excess of impulses—relief. Gaining freedom from the pressures of the immediate situation is apparently only another aspect of lack of specialized organs to absorb this excess of impulses and expend it in the environment. Indeed, we can find further support for this belief if it is true that the ability to find relief—to neutralize stimuli in the world, leaving them undecided but yet easily available, and to relay human behavior "upwards"—serves retroactively to increase the excess of impulses. This type of sublimation actually continues the process of detaching instincts from the immediate present and encourages impulses to be managed internally, in the intellectual realm. It is thus inappropriate to describe this sublimation as an "ersatz development." It is in fact in complete harmony with the general direction of human development. There is, however, an element of dissatisfaction in it. More accurately, the *tristitia ingenii* might be explained by the fact that the continuation of this sublimation process diminishes the opportunities for expending the energy contained in these impulses and thus actually increases the excess secondarily. However, such assumptions are really only metapsychological hypotheses.

The hiatus, the inner distance between our impulses and our actions is, however, a constitutive fact of the human being. It creates an image-conscious inner life. Conscious impulses are those which have been inhibited, most likely by other drives. It is clear, furthermore, that only an excess of impulses could be responsible for the ability to inhibit impulses which is presupposed in every oriented need. Even in the physiology of the senses, inhibitory forces act to prevent response to common stimuli; these can be suspended in experiments with animals by using electric shocks. Furthermore, beyond the general fact that conscious impulses are inhibited impulses, certain selective impulses with a specific goal are sustained in part by inhibitions; the removal of these inhibitions through toxic agents or sudden outbreaks of emotion results in a lowering of the threshold (indiscriminate response) as well as the unconscious transition of the impulses into action.

It is vitally necessary, however, that the human being be conscious of his impulses and able to check them, because this makes it possible to orient the impulses, to combine them with each other, to defer their gratification, etc.

Impulses of a plastic nature are necessarily excessive as well. The absence of specialized organs and the excess of impulses, allow man to follow his impulses or check them, to redirect them from one goal toward another, and so forth. It is striking how few animals are capable of behaving "negatively"; the anthropoid apes are incapable of confidently removing obstacles to their desired goals. De Jong conditioned a dog to get out of a cage by training the animal to step on a horizontal board, which opened the door; however, the animal was at a loss when the board was placed upright instead of horizontally.[15] These represent the limitations not only of the animal's intelligence but of its impulses; it is unable to shut off or redirect an immediate or learned impulse.

We stated above that every oriented human drive is also an object toward which man can form an attitude or opinion. In other words, man can choose to accept or reject it. However, this is only *one* statement about the structure of human drives. Only an array of excessive drives, fluid in structure, can provide the energy for reactions and counterreactions and only to the extent that impulses can be inhibited, do they become conscious. The underlying expediency of this structure is now apparent: man's ability to develop habits, to keep sight of goals despite the changes in the nature of the present, is based on inhibitions; from another perspective, this fact appears as the *pressure to form*, which man feels because of the excessive nature of his impulses. This relationship has always been recognized in the area of moral problems, although it is usually misinterpreted. "Moral laws" have always been considered shaky. While there is a demand to maintain certain moral attitudes, these obviously must be asserted against, and are often overwhelmed by, other impulses—a fact related to the very nature of human impulses and indeed to the very nature of the human being in general. It is also related to man's status as an "undetermined being" who does not possess unshakeable instincts but instead must come to terms with his impulses on his own, making them enduring, organizing them into strengths and counterstrengths, fitting them into a structure of attitudes. Man's consciousness of his impulses, his ability to inhibit them, to orient them, and to defer their gratification are all part of this same context. This inner view of man also makes sense of his external situation: he must engage in selected, learned actions, which then become needs themselves and which are directed beyond the immediate present. Indeed, such activities involve other humans and their impulses are mutually corrected.

Thus human impulses compel their own formation. The excess of impulses must be managed and accomodated somehow because it cannot be expended in actions which gratify immediate urges. Once man's impulses have been successfully formed, this excess produces an almost inexhaustible directed energy which is channeled into activity and into work. This energy is primarily responsible for maintaining the existence of this threatened being; it does so creatively by finding motivations for new feats in the ever changing factual world. Thus, the products man creates may, unlike those of animals, serve as the material for higher products.

My earlier statement that the human being is a creature of discipline (*Zuchtwesen*) has now been confirmed. The problem man faces of giving form to his impulses is an ever-present fact of human existence and it is formulated anew in each generation. In man's upbringing, and later in his efforts at self-discipline, this task is continually reinterpreted. This formation process is in essence morality (*Sittlichkeit*); as we have seen, it is a uniquely human biological necessity. The statement that man is a creature of discipline has another meaning as well: the process of giving form to and ordering man's impulses has a deeply injurious or disciplinary effect on the vital levels of the human being (affecting even the sexual imagination) so that man's body, his physical constitution, becomes a problem he must solve.

Before proceeding further, I would like to take time to bring up an important question. The reader might perhaps have noticed that I have avoided until now any reference to the "will"; I wish to substantiate my reasons for doing so. The prevailing belief that, in addition to human "drives" and "reason," a will exists is of no real value. I would suggest, although it may sound paradoxical at first, that, as the Greek philosophers contended, there is no special faculty of the will.

The question of what is the will has usually been answered by attributing this unknown X to an already familiar quantity Y. Philosophy has vacillated between understanding the will as a special form of thinking or a special form of a drive. These two possibilities eliminate the question altogether. However, there is a third possibility: to assume that a special faculty of the will exists.

In order to approach this problem correctly, we should focus first on the realm of the involuntary. Our heartbeat, respiration, dreams, reflexive movements, sudden passions, etc., are certainly not executed by a will. Instead, as we look more closely at this issue, we will see that the problem of the will encompasses the entire human being so that we cannot logically propose that the will exists as a single, psychical faculty. We can speak of voluntary, willed movements of our arms, of "willed" thoughts, of maintained and conscious desires, etc.; the realm of the will thus extends to embrace every facet of the human being. On the physical and motor level, on the level of impulses and emotions, and in the realm of thought—everywhere there are willed acts and experiences.

Therefore, no reason exists to argue for the presence of a special faculty of will; in fact, Greek philosophy managed quite nicely without it. It had the concepts of *noos* (mind), *epithymetikon,* and *orektikon* to refer to desire and longing; it also had the concepts of *hairesis* and *prohairesis* (choice and deliberate choice or preference). Aristotle described *boulesis* (translated as "will") as a wish or desire in the specific sense of a wish for what is impossible (for example, the wish not to die) or in the sense of a wish for something over which one has no control (such as the wish that a particular contestant win).[16] *Boulema* is that which is willed, a plan, and in all the words derived from it, there is the sense of giving advice or counsel, of deliberation, of careful consideration. The Greeks did not conceive of a substance like the "will" and thereby proved their great wisdom.

Thus, when the Greeks use the idea of deliberate desire where we would speak of "will," they wisely retained the idea of a relationship—a profound insight.[17] For Aristotle and Plato always accord the dominant function *(hegemonikon)* to reason in reference to desires. We can view this relationship from another side, as Kant did when he argued that it is the "culture by way of discipline" *(Kultur der Zucht)* which first allows reason to "tighten or slacken, lengthen or shorten" its reins on man's drives—this is the "will."[18]

Let us now consider more closely the idea that the will is the ability to take control of all movements initiated by the body. The human being is capable of objectifying movements he carries out involuntarily or randomly; he is capable of distancing himself from these and then adopting them and initiating them intentionally, based on a certain plan he formulates. This was illustrated earlier in this book in the example of the child who fell and struck his forehead and then purposefully repeated this sequence of movements as a controlled movement. Any sort of randomly occurring sensorimotor process can be adopted and controlled. I described this phenomenon above when I argued that the result or effect of the action becomes its motivation. In other words, the human being can repeat actions and movements by using the projected result of the movement as the motivation and goal of the controlled efforts to repeat the movement, the contours of which are plotted in advance by our imagination. I also stated in the same chapter that the adoption of a movement in this fashion and the ability to reproduce it, based on the effect it will have, constitute a willed action. We must keep in mind in our discussion that man has a unique ability to realize his sensorimotor experiences in emotion-free activities. In addition, his capacity for movement is versatile, and he is able to gain relief from the immediate situation. He is not bound by his instincts, to specific types of situations; he develops his movement variations independently of his surroundings. This cultivated ability to move freely and independently of the dictates of drives and the immediate situation cannot be observed in animals. Children, however, happily indulge in all sorts of curious methods of walking, gesturing, and moving their bodies.

The objectification, utilization, and control of movement in the sensorimotor realm represent a transition from involuntary to voluntary actions. Volition *(Wollen)* is thus the exercise of control over movements in the broadest sense which are projected beforehand by the imagination. In other words, it is the fundamental phenomenon of the human being himself. Volition is the structure of actions of an unspecialized, undetermined, relieved being, a structure unique in the sensorimotor realm. Man leads his life, and this should be in evidence throughout the entire breadth of his being; the special faculty known as the "will" is then simply another word for what is human in the human being. It is now clear that we must reject this idea of a special faculty of the will not because we question the importance of the will, but because it constitutes the universal essential quality of the human being. To use a phrase we have employed often before: the human being is a creature of discipline; he is undetermined by nature; he is a challenge to himself; he does not *live* but rather *leads* a life—all these formulas express the idea that the human being is essentially volitional.

Two particular conditions are necessary for purely automatic processes to become conscious or detached to the extent that they can be initiated at will: these processes become conscious either as a result of the inhibition and the resistance they encounter or as a result of the effect they have, if this effect is striking and consequently reexperienced by the individual. In both cases, the person's attention is drawn to the action itself which he then appropriates and executes at will. A child who reaches for an object but is distracted in the course of doing so by his own movements is experiencing an inhibition of two impulses and must decide to assert one of these. A child who becomes aware of the favorable effect his crying has will then adopt this action because of its effect and will cry out "intentionally" in the future.

We can apply this same approach to our impulses and desires. As we discussed above, these are essentially conscious: When they are followed through, we become aware of them because of their effects; if they are inhibited, we become aware of them as conscious, internal urges. Even without the present and the effect of other people's attitudes, which lend support to or contradict our impulses, the simple changes in situations would make it necessary for man to gain lasting control over his impulses. Furthermore, the excess of impulses has the effect of overburdening some drives while allowing others to be expressed; with the result that it is necessary for man to choose and make decisions about these impulses just as he does with the execution of movements: these impulses must be expressed or rejected, fostered or suppressed.

The same is true, of course, of the imagination, of language, and of thought. Because these are conscious processes, man can control them. The distinction between automatic processes, which simply run their course, and the directed processes of thought, which are initiated to obtain a specific result or in response to a specific motivating factor, is the same as the distinction between an infant's accidentally successful cry of discomfort and his "purposeful" cry of alarm. We can agree with Bostroem, who argues that in the type of associative, undirected thought that perpetuates itself there is a phenomenon similar to what is manifested in the "ideomotor" activities of walking, riding a bicycle, and so forth.[19] Both of these are semi-automatic processes of a self-perpetuating nature. In contrast to these, thoughts directed toward a specific goal constitute what we can call contemplation or reflection (Nachdenken). Thus, the otherwise simply automatic acts take on the character of willed activities; indeed, even expressed rejection, such as the rejection of a thought, involves an act of will. For these reasons, to describe the thoughts of the human being we can use the same expressions that we employ for his character: a person's way of thinking is genuine, convincing, fantastic, sound, irresponsible, rigid, and so forth.

All human functions that can be initiated in the world, that are directed toward objects, that can be controlled, and that respond to themselves and to each other, should be characterized as willed acts. However, this expression really refers to the specifically *human* functions of movements, impulses, of language and thought. Because man is an acting and world-open being, he is just a much as part of the world as it is a part of him. His behavior toward the world is at the same time a behavior toward himself and vice versa; this very fact is the universal meaning of the expression "the will."

Once the human being has practiced and developed his movements, once he has acquired a lasting ability to act in specific directions, once he has appropriated an array of impulses and interests while rejecting others, once he has made his actions into needs, formed his convictions, and established a system of experiences and interpretations—then, all subsequent expressions of life take place within this framework and are the results of what has been previously established and determined. Our habits are the embodiment of our earlier actions and also provide the foundation for the further development of action. Similarly, our long-term interests and convictions define all our subsequent desires and thoughts. In other words, the subsequent development of life, particularly of the excess of impulses, unfolds "involuntarily" and essentially automatically along the lines of what has already been established. This is a narrower definition of the will; it is the ready access to the energy of impulses through prescribed and established pathways. It is true "will power" (Willenskraft).

Beyond any doubt, this will power is a product of discipline, and follows from a hierarchy of man's abilities and impulses. It presupposes that specific long-term interests have been cultivated and have become needs, that consciousness has become able to concentrate completely on the tasks at hand, and that a constant disciplined use of action has been achieved. Once these things have been achieved, the excess of impulses can be expended in these pathways. As we are well aware, human will power is responsible for extraordinary feats. At this point, the human being is truly able to disregard the immediate nature of a situation and can employ his energies and his imagination toward future goals. Man's challenge is not simply to experiment with the world, to glide by the present, but to transform this world with a view toward the future.

When we speak in broad terms of an individual's will power, we are referring to the energy he possesses for dealing with this challenge; at the same time we are also stating that he has a disciplined character and that the way he leads his life conforms to this challenge. The human being makes basic decisions which serve as the foundation for future actions. It is not necessary for the human being to call these fundamental decisions into question again and again; instead, he relies on what he has already established within himself and on the increase in his directed energies. Even in this narrower sense, the will is still a phenomenon involving the entire human being and is not one "faculty" among others.

On the topic of the will, Nietzsche wrote: "The multitude and disgregation of impulses and the lack of any systematic order among them result in a 'weak will'; their coordination under a single predominant impulse results in a 'strong will': in the first case it is the oscillation and the lack of gravity; in the latter, the precision and clarity of the direction."[20] This is the order provided by what has already been "established," as we discussed above. Once this has taken place, we can speak of will. The excess of impulses is expended in well-defined pathways. Every action can be studied in terms of the guiding consciousness (the plan) behind it, the convictions manifested therein, and the problem it is addressing. Psychology has always been uncertain as to whether to understand the will in terms of consciousness or impulses or as a special faculty. It would have been more correct to view it in relation to the pressure of the problems man faces. Rodin, for example, found himself constantly beset by the demands of unfinished sculptures and finally expressed this in the words "il faut toujours travailler" (one must always work), just as Fichte said: "Ich arbeite immer" (I am always working).

Nietzsche's statements about the will contained in his book *The Will to Power* express a great deal of truth. He argues that psychology's understanding of the "will" is basically an unjustified generalization and that this sort of abstract will does not even exist: "One has eliminated the character of the will by subtracting from it its content, its 'whither.' "[21] "The will is only a simplifying conception of understanding, as is "matter.' "[22] In contrast, the correct view is to understand man as a system of functions, from which certain dominant, commanding, shaping forces stand out which continually simplify; thus, the will presupposes a system of obedient and well-disciplined forces which posits fixed magnitudes in place of indefinite entities.[23] In another of Nietzsche's aphorisms, the will is described as the master of desires which prescribes their direction and degree.[24] In our brief recapitulation of Nietzsche's thoughts on this subject, we get a glimpse of his important insights into the "substructure" of the will and the fact that the will in its narrower meaning is cultivated from what has already been established and that it represents the liberated energy of the excess of impulses. Aristotle expressed essentially the same thought: Once habit, once attitudes, once the *ethos* has been formed, then actions will follow in the *direction* of these developments. Through abstention, we become moderate; however, if we are moderate, we will then best be able to abstain in the future with an increasing firmness of resolve.

Only serious vital disharmonies can impede the development of such attitudes or willed attitudes. Otherwise, these are achieved even under the most unfavorable of conditions and are then reinforced by inhibitions. For example, an individual detects within himself an inherited indolence or an inability to concentrate—errors in his basic functions. However, if he trains himself properly, he will not have to fight against these tendencies each day. Instead, he may be able to develop through experience certain limiting, cohesive habits or he may find within himself another predisposition to tenacity or punctiliousness which he can then choose to encourage. His trick then involves not allowing the will "to wait" but instead developing it in the direction of these predispositions. Reserving a regular time for work and strictly avoiding possible disruptions will bring out the same degree of success with the problem as would an inherited tendency to industriousness. A type of "subterranean" will power, which draws on weaknesses and is perhaps for this very reason unshakable, will result when the force of habit (which is itself indolence in a certain sense) is employed against indolence and when anything related to the instinct of self-preservation is pushed forward in the direction of the persevering mastery of things. Another individual may be lively but easily influenced and will therefore have to develop his will power in a completely different manner. He will have to learn to curb his ability to be easily swayed by relying on purposeful planning to determine his actions. In both cases, the physiognomy of achievement will be very different although both presuppose a similar process of discipline: to avoid those situations in which aspects of one's needs surface that one wishes to suppress because they have shown themselves to be detrimental to the formation of higher interests.

Passionate, focused impulses are part of all creative achievements; in these, the imagination unites all the human being's energies and employs them to these ends. This is the imagination for action; it is in a manner of speaking a type of practical sensuousness; it is the imagination of the things themselves and on the deepest level; it represents the vital ideality of life in man and his aspiration toward "more life." Acting in concert with the imagination is a superior, efficient, controlling intellect endowed with memories and intimate familiarity with the laws of the world of things and their mysteries.

The final element is human ability, the gradually developed art of mastering the material. Truly creative *intellectual* achievements are actually rare because in such a case all these conditions—idea, planning, ability, and execution—have to coincide in *one* organ, in the mind. In all creative activity, the hidden possibilities within the material itself are added to the powers of the individual human being; it is truly astonishing how ingenious, as well as how useful, a good concept or an isolated natural process can be (the wheel, the trap). Truly inspired creations do not work against their material; they are sparing, elegant accomplishments, they are *telos*, perfection. As Freyer wrote, "If the different layers of personality from which action originates and which provide its fuel, were not capable of independent movement," if man were not a being capable of developing specific interests, combinations of interests, and attitudes to fit the variety of problems and plans he faces and constructs in the world—indeed, if man were not capable of developing different aspects of his intelligence, then it would not be possible to develop that concentrated diversity in *one* direction which constitutes true creativity.[25]

Aristotle wrote: Τά θηρία... πράξεως μὴ κοινωεῖν (animals do not act).[26] An animal's activities are not planned; they are not creative. They are dynamic only in their process; in terms of their outcomes, they are static and always the same. This is not because the animal possesses an inferior intelligence but has to do instead with the absence of those uniquely human factors we have grouped together under the broader heading of "relief" and the "excess of impulses."

In contrast, the human being is as a rule not bound to the pressures of the immediate situation; but whenever he is bound to such pressures, his behavior becomes truly inventive, creative, and unpredictable. He has obtained relief to the highest degree through his language and the movements which he has developed on his own, through a minimum of motor exertion, through a primarily symbolic type of behavior. This relief must of course always be viewed in relation to man's intelligence and to action; we must realize its appropriateness for a being who must gratify his needs in anticipatory, variable actions. And, as I have shown here, also correlated with this is a very specific structure of impulses: human needs are actively appropriated; they are conscious and able to be inhibited; they are also world-open—that is, they can adjust to the particular problems man faces. This excessive energy results in the formation of the will which, directed outward, plans and acts and, directed inward, disciplines, appropriates, or inhibits, engages or rejects. The human being is compelled to manage this excess of impulses in some way; thus, man is created to be creative, he is compelled to be so. The self-control in face of the distracting impulses, the careful consideration that characterizes the human being and allows him to maintain goals different from these impulses, to change the nature of these impulses by thinking of or creating something else, to unite these impulses with others, and then to initiate the appropriate actions and use the mind to project their outcomes—all these are active, self-created steering mechanisms which produce creative results. And all these conditions illustrate the basic difference between man and animal, who remains bound to any changes in its environment but who does not oversee the development and shaping of its own impulses through experience—in the broadest sense—and thus has no responsibility.

43. Character

If, as we have argued, man lacks the organic mechanisms present in animals to dictate actions—and furthermore, if this lack necessitates that he cope with the overwhelming pressure from his impulses by directing his energies toward the bare necessities of life—then we could argue that man needs to be able to restrain his impulses, to select some over others, and to cultivate and discipline these. We say that a person has healthy drives when these have been converted into strict orders of controlled and selected abilities, contained in habitual actions, and categorized in terms of the objective world. Thus, when there are no true "drives" *(Triebe)* anymore, this is because they have become part of the *natural* order.

This is a highly complex subject. Every level of the human being, even those in which lie his vital possibilities of overwhelming energy or exhaustion; in the very tempo of our lives, the waves of tiredness or spurts of energy, the tense alertness or fatigue, the healing sensation of strength or the silent vulnerability—even at these levels, a measure of indirect control and economy is necessary. Form is provided by the skeleton of an ordered utilization of our abilities and habits; our responsibility extends even as far as the vegetative level. Drives that are not controlled in this fashion tend to expand their realm to a point where we can no longer control them. In such cases, man's vital energies are sapped; a process of unchecked growth in some areas and devastation in others sets in which will affect and overburden the nervous system. On the other hand, anyone who acts without knowledge and experience of his underlying abilities and limitations will inevitably find himself in situations that either demand too much from him or leave him unsatisfied; such an individual will then most likely seek gratification in other, self-destructive stimulating acts.

Because man is a creature of discipline, and because discipline is a vital need of the body itself, even the deepest, vegetative levels of the human being figure into his range of self-experience, self-understanding, and consequently also of responsibility. Although these levels cannot be changed directly, they can be indirectly affected by what the human being does or does not do, by what he sustains in his actions and what he neglects, and by the types of needs he develops or allows to develop. For example, in these depths lies the imagination of the race *(Geschlechtsphantasie)* and whether this will remain intact and discriminating depends on the quality of the image of the species, thus directly that of the next generation. This movement is very important from a biological perspective and, significantly it takes a path through our consciousness—in other words, it is possible for it to be misdirected. Just as man first develops—indeed, first characterizes—his abilities and strengths in the course of his interaction with the world, we must imagine that this process is continued within him: in the inner world of his decisions and their consequences, opportunities arise for a rise or decline in the direction of ascent of his life state. Because man is the "undetermined animal," his very body presents a problem and challenge to him; therefore, in seeking to understand human nature, we cannot ignore the important factors of discipline, control, responsibility, and value. It is necessary to consider the following when attempting to understand the human being: the concrete world with its problems and tasks, the world in which every individual lives; the work the human being engages in to master these problems; the habits, opinions, and attitudes of the individual which are developed on the basis of the results of man's activity; the order of impulses which have now taken on a specific form; the concentrated will; and, finally, the vegetative processes of the body that are healthy only if the above conditions have been met. There should be no break in this order; if at any one link in this chain the problems are removed, man will become sick at another point and deteriorate.

For the human being to develop to his greatest potential, all organ systems must expend energy. The American physiologist Alexis Carrel wrote a very important book entitled *Man The Unknown;* in the chapter entitled "Adaptive Functions," he puts forth the theory that the human being has "degenerated" as a result of modern civilization (comfort).[27] Man, he argues, achieves the highest level of development only if he is exposed to the hardships of the passage of the seasons, if he must sometimes make do without sleep and sometimes sleep for many hours, if his food ranges from overabundant feasts to meager meals, and if he is only able to find food and shelter by exerting himself untiringly. The human being must exercise his muscles; must tire himself out and then rest; must struggle, suffer, and also be happy; must love and hate. He needs the constant fluctuation from exertion to relaxation. He must struggle against his fellow men or against himself. This is the sort of life he is designed for, argues Carrel, just as the stomach is designed to digest food. When these processes of adaptation are operating most intensively within him, he becomes most fully a human being. Carrel argues that with the advent of civilization, the diversity in physical conditions has been lost, the necessary exertion and moral responsibility have been eliminated, and all the forms of expression of our organic systems (the muscular, nervous, circulatory, and glandular) have been altered. This "law of effort" states that it is the expenditure of these reserve energies of the body and its organs that is responsible for physical well-being. Carrel defines adaptation as the mobilization of an organism's potential for achievement when internal or external changes occur. Thus, every illness is a process of adaptation: scurvy, for example, to a vitamin deficiency, Bright's disease to the secretion of toxic substances through the thyroid gland, etc.

Carrel's theory is as follows: the organism, even in a healthy state, has a need to exercise its ability to adapt; only an existence involving exertion and work can fill this need. All the comforts of civilization have a neutralizing effect; they supply stimulation without requiring any work on man's part. By eliminating muscular exertion from daily life, we have inadvertently removed the constant exercise that our organ systems require in order to maintain their equilibrium. As is well known, when the muscles are exercised, they use up sugar and oxygen, produce heat, and release lactic acid to the circulating blood. To adjust to such changes, a whole series of organs are set in motion: the heart, lungs, liver, pancreas, kidneys, and sweat glands, in addition to the cerebrospinal system and the sympathetic nervous system. A sudden burst of anger, for example, produces a deep change in all organs: the muscles contract, the sympathetic nerves and the suprarenal glands become active, which causes the blood pressure to rise, the heart to beat faster, and the liver to give off glucose which the muscles use as fuel. A similar process occurs when the body responds to extreme cold: the circulatory, respiratory, and digestive systems, as well as the muscles and nerves play a role in this response. In short, "The adaptation of the individual to a psychological, intellectual, and moral discipline determines definite changes in the nervous system, the endocrine glands, and the mind. The organism acquires, in this way, a better integration, greater vigor, and more ability to overcome the difficulties and dangers of existence."

"Certain forms of modern life lead directly to degeneration."

"We utilize our adaptive functions much less than our ancestors did.... we have accommodated ourselves to our environment through mechanisms created by our intelligence, and no longer through physiological mechanisms. . . . We have mentioned how the physical conditions of our daily life are prevented from varying. How muscular exercise, food, and sleep are standardized. How modern civilization has done away with effort and moral responsibility, and transformed the modes of activity of our muscular, nervous, circulatory, and glandular systems."[28]

Carrel provides many insightful examples of this: for example, he argues that "the inhabitants of the modern city no longer suffer from changes of atmospheric temperature. That they are protected by modern houses, clothes, and automobiles. That during the winter they are not subjected, as their ancestors were, to alternatives of prolonged cold and of brutal heat from stoves and open fireplaces. The organism does not have to fight cold by setting in motion the chain of the associated physiological processes, which increase the chemical exchanges and modify the circulation of all the tissues. When an individual, insufficiently clothed, has to maintain his inner temperature by violent exercise, all his organic systems remain in a condition of repose if cold weather is fought by furs and warm clothing, by the heating apparatus of a closed car, or by the walls of a steam-heated room."[29]

Carrel's theory provides confirmation from a physiological point of view of our belief that the human being, as an acting being, is oriented toward work and action right down to the vegetative processes of his body. What Carrel terms adaptation is the utilization of energy reserves which are tapped only in the course of strenuous activity; this utilization contributes to well-being. Man will by nature find himself in difficult, demanding situations (if his powers of reason do not provide him with a ready way out) and these conditions will then elicit from him highly disciplined achievements and abilities, toward which he is already predisposed.

When Carrel writes that "we know how strong physically and morally are those who, since childhood, have been submitted to intelligent discipline, who have endured some privations and adapted themselves to adverse conditions," it may sound like a banality but it is in fact an age-old truth.[30] If impulses are not controlled, not formed into attitudes, man will deteriorate. This perspective will allow us to develop an understanding of the concept of "character."

When we say that "character" is the system of impulses, long-term interests, and needs that have a specific content and correspond to the external world, then we are really saying that it is at the same time action and the substance of action, that it is ultimately a system of attitudes constructed upon impulses which man has followed or rejected but in any case always evaluated in some way. These impulses have been oriented actively in the world or they may have emerged as secondary results of our actions. However, the building of character—which, according to Kant, results from "weariness of the fluctuating nature of instincts" and which is rarely completed before the fortieth year (anthropology)—is not achieved until the reality of man's action and his conscious orientation in the world have emerged so that even man's sensory expressions and reactions approximate convictions and so that his thoughts have the clear unequivocality of actions. In order to have a clear view of the disciplined world of character, we must above all liberate ourselves from the modern, unjustified habit of overestimating the "river of consciousness" *(Bewusstseinsstrom)*.

One of the natural results of our actions and our active life is that consciousness will come to adapt to a certain degree to the natural vital processes. Those fundamental resolves and decisions that allow us to consciously lead our lives must not be subject to influence by stimuli on the surface of consciousness but must instead be relegated to the safety of the realm of selected, controlled, and so to speak "charged" *(geladen)* abilities. These abilities should manifest themselves only when resistance is encountered, for example, when we encounter a ditch on the road and have to jump over it. At the bottom of the river of consciousness, beneath the level at which internal and external stimuli are processed, there must be another consciousness—or better yet, an awareness of a totally different type: an awareness of self-evident fundamental decisions, of the horizons of our abilities, of cultivated instincts to choose one option and avoid another, a readiness to undertake whatever will conform to the direction of our prevailing interests, and a sense of what is not appropriate. It is this deeper awareness that regulates what things can be admitted into consciousness and there dealt with further. In addition, we demand of character that everyday habits remain symbolic to a certain extent, that they express in some way our fundamental resolves; we have an intuitive sense which lets us distinguish very precisely between those habits that are "valid," that mirror our fundamental decisions in indifferent everyday existence and those other "simple habits" that represent the shallow, superficial autonomy into which a vital soul, released from control, sinks.

We can describe character from two perspectives: seen from "above," it appears as an order of attitudes and rules of control which man has incorporated—a set of "instincts," which in order to function smoothly have become almost unconscious and which are crystallized from impulses and then exposed to the world in actions and selected accordingly. Seen from "below," however, character appears as the continuation in the range of the self-executed, of those directed, rhythmical, and closed processes with which the biological life process is in harmony overall. Any individual habit can appear to consciousness as somehow arbitrary; however, the habit of cultivating and incorporating habits—that is, of forming attitudes—is physical and is necessary: if it does not occur, the nervous system will become disordered. A healthy body exudes a certain tenseness, a charged readiness to engage in actions and movements.

The same is true of the readiness of an individual's character to accept certain things and discard others. This will come across more strongly if there is little or no need to provide justification, and if other possibilities are not acknowledged. In all experience and education, the tendency can be found toward making a choice, coordinating possibilities, eliminating some and preferring others; this tendency will result in dominant habits of actions and the "acquired instincts" that grow within us. Even the involuntary, purely physiological life processes are oriented toward this process of formation—these ordered and disciplined demands—for when these deeper energies are expended, the organism is in a state of good health. In the inner life of the human being there is a level of semi-conscious interests, convictions, and developed aversions which constitutes the invisible skeleton of our intellectual life, that gives form to our reactions, and that is in turn kept in form by these such that even our physical constitution is required to make adjustments and changes. Without them it would degenerate because of its reservoir of underutilized energies. Therefore, if we say that our experience extends as deep as this level, our responsibility does so as well.

From our discussion thus far, we can see again the logical necessity of the method proposed: we must choose those descriptive concepts that are indifferent to the distinction between the physical and psychical, concepts such as our categories of relief, the excess of impulses, availability, control, intention, variation, adoption, utilization, etc.

In our understanding of the concept of character, we are conforming more to the usage in English psychology than in German in the sense of acquired character. We must then deal with another issue as well: the question of "innate" traits—those traits that are viewed as inherited. This is by no means an exclusively modern issue. In the Odyssey, for example, Pallas Athena speaks to Telemachos in the guise of Mentor as he is undertaking to travel to Pylos and Sparta:

Telemachos, you are no thoughtless man, no coward if truly the strong force of your father is instilled in you; such a man he was for accomplishing word and action. Your journey then will be no vain thing nor go unaccomplished. But if you are not the seed begotten of him and Penelope, I have no hope that you will accomplish all that you strive for.[31]

Clearly, this speech already presupposes that certain traits are inherited and even concludes that "if you do not have the great soul of Odysseus, you cannot be his son."

To appreciate the problems involved in this issue of inherited traits, we need only consider the following: strictly speaking, only a longitudinal study spanning many generations could give us information on what is inherited. This is not possible. Second, beyond any doubt, deep, pervasive changes can result from external factors affecting the inner life; for example, urbanization, as the condition for a universal "infantilism," has an indirect effect on the constitution and the effect on his psyche cannot be measured. Third, the processes of the inner life form a unified whole which is difficult to analyze. Analysis, however, is the method of procedure of all empirical investigation, which becomes helpless when faced with complex interrelationships. In all areas of biology, it is the defective states, pathological manifestations, and obvious malformations that are most amenable to analysis. This makes Panse's remark all the more significant: "Compared with what genetic research has produced in the way of clear results in the area of simple somatic traits or even in that of experimental genetics, the state of research in this borderline area between normal and pathological, psychical events is quite disheartening."[32]

Nowadays it seems highly questionable that certain clearly defined core traits or "radicals" *(Radikale)* of an inherited nature could ever be identified, as Enke, Pfahler, and others have attempted to do.[33] Stumpfl made this point quite forcefully; he argued that "an approach based on the model of exact genetics is not appropriate for the genealogy of character because structural relationships of a highly elastic and changeable nature are inherited."[34] Along the same lines, Kroh maintained "that it is in the structure of functions which is the basis for our cognitive, experiencing, and forming activities, that we should seek the true dispositional element which could be directly identified as inherited. It is virtually impossible to describe the wealth of factors that come together in this unity of functions."[35]

Despite these points, however, diligent research has not remained entirely fruitless. To gain an idea of the research on this subject, we will examine those areas in which it has the best chance of achieving results. I am convinced that "character," in the narrower sense in which we have defined it here of a system of specific interests, attitudes, and lasting impulses, is *not* one of these areas. If we call the range of definitely or probably inherited "predispositions" *(Anlagen)* of a human being his nature *(Wesensart),* then at best all we could assume is that this nature shields or blocks access to specific areas of things or values; however, we could not assume, for example, that such things as a good head for business or a passion for collecting things are inherited. The concrete orientation of interests, lasting impulses, convictions, and the like—which culminates in a structure of attitudes—is quite obviously dependent on what the given social organization demands, suggests, or prevents. Wherever firm norms of discipline prevail, we will find that they correspond to the prejudices and preferences of the human beings in a particular society; comparative historical social and political psychology can teach us more about this than the psychology of the individual. We should modify our standpoint by adding that some talents, such as musical ability, are inherited to a striking degree and that in such cases the development of a specific interest is already prefigured.

Research has thus determined that specific "basic functions," "essential tendencies"—or better yet, the structures for these—are inherited along with certain "abilities" or talents. To understand what this really means, we will try to gain an orienting overview although we cannot of course encompass all aspects of this issue.

It is clear that "temperament" and the related habitual fundamental disposition in life are hereditarily conditioned, since these are so closely related to the physical constitution. The sanguine and phlegmatic temperaments, above all, with their differences in emotional excitability, in will, as well as in mood, are inherited, as studies by Stumpfl (60 families), Frischeisen and Köhler (over 1000 individuals) and Davenport (600 individuals) have shown.[36] Similar findings in this area of the hereditary nature of temperament were obtained by Hoffmann as early as 1922.[37] Stumpfl studied approximately 260 families and determined that the temperament of the hyperthymic (jovial, sanguine, hardworking) is inherited.[38] The same is true of one's overall "tempo"; human beings are born with an innately fast or slow tempo of all expressions of life: from the ability to grasp things quickly, to excitability, developmental ability, motor skills, and so forth. Stumpfl writes: "If, under otherwise similar conditions, each specific process generally runs its course quickly, regularly, and energetically in one individual whereas in a second, it runs slowly, weakly, and erratically, and in yet a third individual, may run its course quickly but irregularly, in spurts—if, in one individual, the processes of the inner life peak sharply and then fall off slowly while in a second individual they begin slowly and fall off precipitously, and in yet a third individual, they follow a gentle, uniform curve, then these differences are due to a close relationship between physical structure and character which is genetically anchored. For this reason, we can recognize all of the individuals described by their gait, the manner in which they knock at a door or raise their hand in greeting and by many other similar gestures."[39]

Similarly, in the area of emotions, a general increase in superficiality, and effusiveness, emotional excitability, and passionateness also appears to be inherited just as, on the other hand, an emotional coldness or lack of feeling appears to be (Stumpfl). Here, too, we are dealing with entire complexes; hence, emotional shallowness is often related to an anxious self-consciousness and tendency to be easily upset or related even to a heavy-handed, dry, egocentric stiffness. As far as the will is concerned, Stumpfl found that the ability to stick to decisions once made as well as an abnormally weak will clearly ran in families. Among the relatives of weak-willed, abnormal individuals, he found a frequent incidence of similar psychopaths as well as, in otherwise normal individuals, an easily influenced will and unusually malleable nature. The combination of a lack of emotion, an abnormally easily influenced will with a sanguine temperament and increased activity constitutes a special group here. Enke put forth a good argument that an additional inherited complex exists which he called "perseverations" (Perseverationen), which are related to the schizothymic constitution in intellectual, psychological, affective, and psychomotor areas.[40]

These findings indicate those traits of a species that the psychology of genetics can study with hope of success. Genealogical comparisons and the study of twins are the primary approaches available and for the most part they have produced the findings thus far.

The fundamental qualities of the vital psyche are most likely, and have in part been proven, to be constant and inherited. These have nothing to do with the question we examined in the last few chapters of the orientation of the contents of human impulses. They tell us nothing directly about the question of whether the human being has clearly defined instincts, and reveal nothing directly about how impulses and interests are invested with specific things and values, etc. It appears likely that a hereditary constitutional habitus draws with it or suggests additional, qualified, and similarly formal "secondary traits" such as lack of independence, superficiality, imperturbability, calmness, pedantry, shyness, formality. It is also possible that from encountering unavoidable, universal experiences, certain ways of "processing" these will necessarily take place if the appropriate predisposition exists. In this regard we might consider, for example, insecurity, adventurousness, carefulness, deceitfulness, propriety, cautiousness, and so forth. However, so far, no careful studies have been undertaken to substantiate or disprove these ideas. To my mind, the frequent, stereotypical reactions of ambition and the need for approval seem only superficially to be directed toward specific objects, but in reality represent the individual's failure to work through himself completely.

There are several reasons why I have taken care in this book to differentiate between character and "nature" (Wesensart) or, if one prefers, between the content and form of the "soul." On the one hand, character, as the embodiment of oriented, worked-through impulses, of enduring interests and convictions, cannot be considered apart from an individual's actions, life circumstances, history, or particular social community. The comparative historical approach adopted by political psychologists has shown us more than any other that an exact correspondence exists between social systems and concrete inclinations and interests. For example, in ancient Egypt, because the bureaucracy broke down the genealogical order, the entire system of interests of the ethos of kinship was absent, including ancestor worship, despite a highly developed worship of the dead. In contrast, the strict kinship ties of the Chinese, along with the legal insecurity of the individual in the patriarchal state, doubtlessly encouraged the development of business acumen. The sense of honor of the feudal ruling classes could tolerate a warlike, fatalistic religion or even the personal world regiment of a god, but not the idea of real "sin" or a system of morals oriented toward the concepts of duty and reward and punishment. Very often, firmly established orders will make certain "talents" taboo, as in Rome, where a proconsul who painted suffered a damaged reputation.

Because we define character as the embodiment of *stable* habits and convictions, which influences an individual to choose certain behaviors over others while remaining indifferent toward other possible options for action—in other words, because we understand character as an individual's permanent formula for behavior consisting of invariable inclinations—then we can say that character is a product of discipline of the society in which the individual lives and of its particular distribution of interests. Every formative educational process, to which children in a stable social order are exposed, strives for types, not individuals. A "disintegrated" society such as ours—that is, a society that is highly complex and rapidly changing—breaks down the traditional forms of discipline that lend a primarily social content to the relationship of the individual to himself. Individuals now fall back into a directness, they experience the whole breadth of their natural strengths and weaknesses. They must solve conflicts, which are magnified by their lack of distance, by drawing on the slight reserves of whatever traits they happen to possess. This explains the astonishing general psychological knowledge of our times. If we consider this phenomenon more closely, however, it also explains the unprecedented unfolding, the pronounced nature, indeed, the nonchalance, of the psychologically aberrant. Amid the complex forms of modern life, the wide diversity of special conditions, random natures develop. In this close world, they reflect one another, and sensitize their souls no longer protected against stimulation by the bastions of respected habits. This world provides the substance for the art form that truly represents the Western world—the psychological novel. The subtlety of an inner life that has become reflective and caught up in itself can be refined to an extreme degree; in many people, a thought or emotion automatically functions as a stimulus to which they in turn respond. The complex disintegration of society, of ideals and values—which has its correlate in the enormous changes in the inner life of the individual in our times—has been productive in the sense that it has fostered an astonishing degree of psychological differentiation. This "indiscrete character" of the inner life is manifested in man's compulsive need for information, in the nonchalant uninhibitedness of its particular nature, as well as in the methods psychology has adopted and tailored to this very phenomenon. This indiscrete nature coupled with the awareness of the average person makes it impossible to distinguish the soul from the imagined soul. From this point of view, the author of the psychological novel is representative of an entire culture. "Tous les voiles du coeur ont été déchirés. Les anciens n'auraient jamais fait ainsi de leur âme un sujet de fiction" (All the veils of the heart have been stripped away. The ancients would never have made their own soul into a subject of fiction in this manner).[41]

The expression subject of fiction should be related to the soul itself. The chronic awareness of the inner life is not purely passive but in fact serves a formative function. It is the form of productivity that is left over when deep perplexity and uncertainty in regard to ultimate spiritual values prevail. I have pursued this topic in greater depth in my book *Man in the Age of Technology* (1962).

If the views presented here are correct, then it is logical to conclude that there must be a specific order for the psychological disciplines. Anthropology could identify the universal structural laws of the psychical as they relate to the human constitution. Then, social or collective psychology could be seen as part of sociology. The descriptions provided by these sciences of concrete social conditions could then provide the framework for a psychology of the individual. The psychology of inheritance *(Erbpsychologie)*, on the other hand, has a methodology adopted from the natural sciences; it takes individuals as its starting point and attempts to form statistical groups, which are intended to refer to specific sociological groups, such as criminals, the "classe dirigente" (leading figures), etc. In addition to the area of formal character traits mentioned above, another promising area of research is that of talents. The various types of talent, such as intelligence, musicality, mathematical inclination, artistic ability, etc., have long been the objects of fruitful study.

44. A Few Problems Relating to the Mind

In describing the approach put forward in this book as "biological," I have given this word a broader meaning than it usually has. On the one hand, it is clearly a biological question to ask how a being such as man manages to survive—a being who is, in physical terms, ill-equipped for survival and who clearly does not fit into the framework we use for understanding animals' methods of maintaining their existence. On the other hand, because this question necessarily concerns the acting human being, it will inevitably lead us to areas, such as language, cognition, and the imagination, that have until now been studied by the cultural sciences *(Geisteswissenschaften)*. As we have shown, our particular approach does give us access to these areas. The tendentious claim that we are thereby reducing these to the biological level only fosters an unfortunate misunderstanding. We can furnish convincing proof that to a very great degree, factors that until now were considered purely physical (such as the interaction between the senses of sight and touch, the great breadth of variations in motor skills, the reduction of instincts, indeed, even the immaturity of man at birth [Portmann's "physiologically premature birth"] appear to be the foundations or prerequisites for the higher intellectual abilities. Thus, to adopt the language of the new ontology, we have developed a few of the general categories of being human *(Menschsein)*, in particular those that cut across all levels—that is, such categories as relief, action, availability, communication, and so forth.

With this approach, however, we cannot hope to treat all the extraordinarily complex problems associated with the subject of the mind *(Geist)*. For one thing, our entire theory necessarily deals in abstractions, specifically, an abstract concept of the individual acting human being. This model does not permit discussion of certain higher problems in the cultural sciences because religion, art, law, technology, etc., are, from a scientific perspective, *social* facts. These great collective phenomena of the historical social world have long been studied by their own highly developed sciences which have recently made increasing use of sociological methods. The relationship thereby created between the social institutions and the historical formations of the objective mind can under certain circumstances be carried very far and may produce illuminating insights. For instance, the absence of any mythologically or dogmatically founded theory of gods among the Romans[42] can be clearly correlated with the fact that Roman nobility never allowed the rise of an independent priesthood. For this reason as well, education was in general not fostered by the priesthood, as it was in India and in Europe in the Middle Ages, but was instead adopted from a foreign country—Greece. As is well known, it was Max Weber who developed this approach, the sociology of religion, to an unprecedented extent. In principle, however, it should also be possible to formulate a sociology of law or of art, making use of the same methods; forays in this direction have in fact already been made.

Any serious scientific study of the "worlds" of the objective mind in their historical concreteness must nowadays introduce a sociological dimension whereby it is possible to avoid the error of "sociologism." At this point, I face the task of correcting the mistake of an exceedingly narrow premise which I adopted in the final chapters entitled "Oberste Führungssyteme" (The Highest Directing Systems) in earlier editions of this book. I still adhere to this designation; it has subsequently been employed by other authors. However, Carl Schmitt has cited a study by Maurice Hauriou[43] which emphasizes the important fact that a directing system *(Führungssystem)* or *idée directrice* is always that of an institution; in other words, a directing system, such as Puritanism or Confucianism, can be understood scientifically and objectively only in relation to the social institutions in which it exists. Sociology confirms this theory time and time again.

It then appears impossible to propose a *direct* relationship between this directing system and the biological constitution of the human being (even in the broader sense of the word). I undertook to do so, however, by describing the *imagination* as the "god-creating" power *(götterschaffende Kraft)* and by arguing that the great achievement of this theogonic, imagination lay in its power to carry man beyond his awareness of his own instability, vulnerability, and powerlessness: *"Deos fecit timor* is not expressed correctly; it is not the fear or the threat of a superior power that creates gods but rather the conquering of fear. It is *natural* not to want to believe in death and thus to formulate ideas about the Beyond and life after death. It is natural to want to fill the void, the space between what we have direct possession of and the results which are beyond our control, with benevolent figures drawn from our imagination.... For this reason, the interests of powerlessness, the expression of this inexhaustible excess of driving force, actually serve life; man's imagination is a power that promotes life, that carries us into the future and that counters our feelings of resignation."[44] From a purely historical point of view, I should mention that the definition of the imagination as the organ for "the world of the Gods" stems from Schelling.[45]

I wanted to emphasize here that religious ideas have a reciprocal effect on the sphere of individual motivation. In the course of doing so, however, the entire world of social institutions was bracketed, although the directing systems are indeed essentially bound to this world. This type of "short-circuit" suggests itself readily; a number of other authors have argued along these lines. For example, the theologian Karl Beth argued: "Religion is the response when the human being acknowledges the truth and authenticity of his feeling of ultimate powerlessness but at the same time affirms his own vital drive by acknowledging an extra or superempirical power which he conceives of as having a will and as wanting his life, as it is, so that he surrenders to it humbly and trustingly."[46] Let us compare this statement with Scheler's argument: "Man could ... yield to the irresistible urge for safety or protection, not only for himself, but primarily for the group as a whole. By means of the enormous surplus of fantasy which was his heritage in contrast to the animal, he could then populate this sphere of being with imaginary figures in order to seek refuge in their power through cult and ritual. The purpose was to get some protection and help to "back him up,' since the basic act of his estrangement from, and his objectification of, nature—together with his self-consciousness—threatened to throw him into pure nothingness. The overcoming of this nihilism by means of such protective measures is what we call religion."[47]

These views are in total agreement with Bergson's theory which he formulated in his last work *The Two Sources of Morality and Religion*. Here he conceived of religion as a compensatory measure orginating from vital depths which served to reduce the hazards posed by our intelligence. As he often remarked, he saw religion as Nature's means of self-defense against the potential biological damage intelligence could inflict. "We postulate a certain instinctive activity; then, calling into play intelligence, we try to discover whether it leads to a dangerous disturbance; if it does, the balance will probably be restored through representations evoked by instinct within the disturbing intelligence; if such representations exist, they are primary religious ideas."[48]

If we consider these various views all together, we will discover a common scheme which appears to be intellectually necessary. This is why I hit upon it myself. Once religion, law, customs, are considered in a neutral light, as objective life phenomena, a teleological form of thinking inevitably suggests itself and the question ultimately arises of what these actually effect. Kraft, for instance, has argued: "Among primitive peoples, religion is essentially centered around the ability which the tribe believes to possess as a result of its conviction that it can meet any danger, which gives it a feeling of security and superiority." Kraft goes on to cite Marett, for whom "The basic criterium for religion to have an effect on the human being's consciousness is whether it serves to heighten the individual by making him believe that he can be equal to any situation in life and thus serves to make man happy and to preserve the species."[49] Thus, if we consider these cultural worlds objectively and concretely (empirically), we will come to see them as living facts among other facts and we will necessarily come to propose the fundamental category of expediency as Jhering did quite a while ago when he grouped law under the general concept of "ensuring the conditions for society's existence." The same interpretation is applied to customs and ethics: "Let us then give to the word biology the very wide meaning it should have, and will perhaps have one day, and let us say in conclusion that all morality, be it pressure or aspiration, is in essence biological."[50]

If we examine law, religion, etc., from an analytical point of view, if we consider these objectively and scientifically, it will at first appear that, apart from the esthetic point of view, only the following approach is possible: these phenomena are part of the purposeful natural organization of the human being and serve to equip this human being for survival. They are antidotes to the feeling of powerlessness, to resignation, and in some sense, they function as encouraging images. Only once we have acknowledged this fact can we realize fully the great weight of the philosophical problems we are treating here.

In sum, the situation is as follows: on the one hand, there are the historical, cultural sciences *(Geisteswissenschaften)*, buttressed by sociology; these disciplines consider it a legitimate area of study of examine the position of a specific religion, a specific legal system, or a particular art form in relation to the social structure of an equally clearly defined society. The directing system is an integral part of the system of institutions of these societies. On the other hand, we have the attempts cited above to find the universal meaning of religion, law, etc.; these attempts always end up focusing on the psychological or psychobiological effect of these ideas on man's inner life. They necessarily, not voluntarily, make use of teleological forms of thought. These approaches appear unrelated to each other. Thus, if we wish to delve deeper into this problem, we should seek a common ground between the two.

This common ground is historical consciousness. Language, law, religion, morals, art are social facts for this consciousness: they arise in the course of history through the interaction between human beings and then take on an independence of their own as individual worlds, which over the course of long or short periods of time undergo transformations in a recognizable fashion. We can detect this historical consciousness in Scheler's and Bergson's theories; it provided them with the material on the primitive, simple forms of religion which enabled them to develop their theological theories. This historical consciousness, which now cannot be lost, is definitely a product of the Enlightenment. In Montesquieu's *Esprit des lois,* we can clearly identify the field of study that historical consciousness has opened up and within which sociological and psychological concepts explain each other. By applying its objective way of thinking to the sphere of religion, by on the one hand developing rational psychology and on the other exposing in the area of history the numerous religious, legal, and sociological formations, the Enlightenment took a spiritual reality laden with emotion and conscience and created a cosmos of "ideas"—that is, of representations that exist on the same level as all other concepts thought up by the human brain and that can hence be examined with interest by a neutral third party. The belief that religious "ideas" have some psychological effect cannot be considered separately from the idea that they vary with the times and from people to people and social system to social system.

Once this step had been taken, the religions and world views of exotic or primitive peoples became possible *objects,* whereas, previously—to the pre-Enlightenment mind which did not "believe in religious ideas" but lived instead in the medium of the word of God and thus understood all events as *preordained*—these appeared as false doctrines, pagan superstitions, or at best as curious nonsense, and as such had to be avoided at all cost before they could reach the bounds of theoretical interest. For a consciousness for which religious, legal, moral concerns qualify as *realities*—that is, function as motivations for behavior (for one does not react to simple conscious representations or ideas in one's own head)—other concerns impinging on the consciousness from the outside world may also function as motivations; from their own inner dynamic, they find rejection or acceptance, but not objective, concrete interest.

Because the Enlightenment developed its rationalized form of thought to the extent that it could no longer refrain from turning back its own beliefs, which were experienced as reality, these beliefs themselves became *historicized*. In other words, the evidence of their validity was no longer tied to the immediate reality of social and natural experience, but instead found support in the uncertain and mutable material of history. Hegel illustrated this phase. In the course of this process, these beliefs were also stripped of their power, their potential as motivating forces was diminished, and they became "ideas." Kant clearly took this step. Hellpach correctly argued: "Where conscience does not appear as the voice of God within man, but where instead the assumption (!) that God exists appears as the voice of the human conscience, at this point religion is essentially over and done with and the pure theory of morality, the exclusive ethics, has appeared in its place, the power of the beyond has become a mere epiphenomenon of the obligation of the here and now."[51]

We must distinguish here between two different types of consciousness. For one, consciousness, or religious, moral, or legal concerns appear in a peculiar intermediate position between Being *(Sein)* and Ought *(Sollen)*, which they contain, as long as these concerns at the same time represent categories for understanding the world and structural principles of institutions. This consciousness is distinct from the other consciousness, for which the same concerns have become ideas and are thereby simultaneously experienced as being subjective and renounceable. The difference between the two is of great importance, particularly when the concern is the same in both cases: *haeretica voce recta clamant*. As long as both standpoints interfere with one another within the same consciousness (and also correspond to a specific historical period), the troubling questions will necessarily arise (as Kant says they will) when reason *(Vernunft)* enters into conflict with itself. For it is this second enlightened and reflexive type of consciousness for which one's own spiritual world, as part of a tradition, appears at the same level of visibility at which the great abundance and mass of the historical social ideas become visible.

As we saw above, the natural, traditional belief in truth rejected these ideas as false doctrines or the like and did not allow them to enter into the realm of "possible truths." In that zone in which both forms of consciousness interact with one another, the urgent question presents itself of whether all these obviously heterogeneous directing systems could be true, of whether truth can exist in the plural, and of whether these things are in fact only illusions, albeit highly expedient ones with a certain amount of utility in terms of the "fabulatory function." The question arises of whether we ourselves, with our ultimate convictions—if we still have any at all at this point—are not the deceived ones. If nothing is true, then is not everything permitted? This is the problem of relativism; following its thorough going treatment by Marx, Nietzsche, and Freud, it has become the "acid test" that has proved to be the downfall of philosophy. Like Kant's antinomies, it originates from the interaction between the two different structures of consciousness which we have developed here in their historical collision as the Enlightenment and traditional religion, and which we will now investigate more closely.

The first logical possibility is to attempt Hegel's route again, unhampered by his Christian beliefs, hence, to attempt to distill definitive convictions from an investigation of the historical, social forms of the mind (Geist) itself. Dilthey chose this route. One of the things that motivated this complex scholar was the hope of finding "inner security," "firm purposes," and the power to "give form to life" by pursuing an interpretative understanding (Verstehen) of the historical world. With Dilthey, we can clearly retrace the process whereby the reflexive consciousness within him (the psychologist) gained control of the as yet traditional and immediate intellectual impulses and, before these could become translated into action, pushed them into reflection where they were arrayed among the "understood" foreign ideas that streamed at him (the historian) from all sides. The reverse process was then inevitably the need to come to belief and action from understanding. In his correspondence with Count Yorck, he writes the following: "The catastrophes come upon us at a frightening speed: the lack of faith of an age, that is, its inability to hold onto its convictions which make the human being free in comparison to the poor . . . social masses. The question is what powers can be utilized to overcome this influence. My book proceeds from the conviction that the independence of the cultural sciences and the knowledge of historical reality these convey can contribute to this."[52]

This passage contains one of the important themes in Dilthey's philosophy. He argued that the "relative nature of every sort of historical understanding of the connection between things [is] the final word of the historical world-view. . . . Everything is in flux, nothing is permanent. Where are the means for overcoming the anarchy of beliefs that threatens to overwhelm us?"[53] To solve this problem, he attempted to measure this relativism; he was motivated in this endeavor by an "insatiable desire to understand"[54] and his goal was to overcome it through himself: "It is not the relative nature of every world-view that is the final word of the mind which has actually run through them all, but rather the sovereignty of the mind over each one of them and at the same time the positive awareness that among the different ways in which the mind moves, the one reality of the world is there for us."[55] Thus: "By taking this standpoint toward all types of world-views," he believes he can simultaneously embrace and overcome the demon of historical consciousness. "The expansion of the self, its surrendering to objectivity also gives the individual an expansion of his entire vitality, peace amidst the fluctuation of situations, stability."[56] Did he in fact attain this? He who remarked on the position of his friend Count Yorck with the following words: "How great indeed is the power of a great personality to make a world-view believable. Does my own historical viewpoint not appear as unfruitful skepticism if I judge it by such a life? Where is this same power in my world-view?"

As we know now, relativism cannot be overcome with the approach that Dilthey adopted. The reason for this lies in the structure of historical consciousness itself. We can devote ourselves wholeheartedly to researching the world of ideas of English Puritanism, for example, and attempt to understand it; we can marvel at its intellectual willpower, the energy of "inner-wordly asceticism," and its powerful repercussions in the economic and political spheres. However, this will not give us the "security and stability" that the Puritans knew, because we cannot *become* Puritans by taking the path of interpretative understanding *(Verstehen)*. Herein lies one of Dilthey's gravest errors, which is difficult to recognize but which comes to light quite clearly in his statement that "the experience of one's own situation and the imitation of another situation or of another individuality are identical as far as the essence of the process is concerned."[57] If this were true, then to reexperience and imagine the psychical energy of another would be for this same energy to arise in oneself, whereas in fact there is no greater gap than that between imagined will and real will.

Thus, modern man's astonishing ability to re-create and imagine the world view of distant or ancient peoples down to the finest details may be applied in two directions. On the one hand, it can serve as a method for the purely objective, scientific analysis of cultural systems. In this case, then, the "idées directrices" are understood as part of a cultural whole and will often have a clear, logical relationship to the economic, sociological, and environmental facts. Such studies are usually most successful with primitive cultures in

which there is little differentiation; however, this limitation is not fundamental. The relative nature of values, morals, of institutions, and dominant
ideas is really first discovered in the broad field of the ethnological and
social sciences. There it is dealt with in such a way that universal statements
are dispensed with altogether or are only conceived of as admitted hypotheses and that the descriptions of the individual social bodies or cultures
bring out the context in which all these features determined each other
reciprocally and established each other in a historically unique "integration." This is the method pursued in one of the best-known works of descriptive cultural research—Ruth Benedict's *Patterns of Culture*.

The cultural science patterned after Dilthey takes a different approach to
the breadth of material that has become visible historically and understandable psychologically. Here, the analysis of world views systematizes the lack
of belief in dominant symbols; these directing systems and dominant ideas
(*Leitideen*) appear as "possible truths" precisely because of this lack of
belief coupled with the need to believe. One can mentally transfer oneself
into these possible truths, create them through a process of appropriation,
in the hope that this nonactive assimilation of life-contents represented in
the mind will make it possible to achieve the standpoint of "sovereignty of
the mind over each one of them." In Dilthey, this search for ultimate motives
is quite conscious but it is in fact hopeless, because this situation rules out
the possibility that the imagined and reexperienced ideas themselves could
actually become motives. This is a *fallacia intrinseca* in the state of reflection:
in the modern, "super-conscious" (*überbewusst*) and isolated soul, all things
can be understood in the sphere of the mind and imagination where they
are, however, objectified, stripped of power, and weakened as far as motivation is concerned. This attitude then argues that the mind (*this* mind)
enjoys an absolute superiority, for as reflection moves back and forth it can,
because it is the only thing left, appear as the "sovereignty of the mind."
The sovereignty of the mind which is achieved by running through all the
possible world views in one's mind is based on the simple fact that one can
do this at all. This is indeed not a convincing argument. Reflection can only
reflect mental images; the inner life of the thinker becomes itself a mental
image, and the soul a *sujet de fiction* (Mme de Stael), so that "the experience
of one's own situation and the imitation of another situation are identical
as far as the essence of the process is concerned." The belief in the sovereignty
of the mind which is achieved via this route is in fact simply the hypostasi-
zation of the state of reflection itself. If it were carried out with conviction,
it would lead to an all-encompassing irony, to an attitude of a "Grand-

seigneur de la Pensée" and to the "noble smile of d'Alembert," which Dilthey so hated and which he managed to escape only because the science of his times could still function as a substitute religion for him. There is some justification to this insofar as science had its own real institutional connection and the institutions of science at that time still supported a specific and intact set of morals.

In looking over our discussion thus far, we can conclude that since the possibility for this attitude of consciousness arose, the objective cultural sciences can be successfully pursued as purely empirical disciplines. This is achieved when in the thinker's own consciousness, the truths and values that were formerly dogmatic (that is, that qualified as metaphysical reality) are shattered, at least on a virtual level. Until this point is reached, it is impossible to understand strange, dominant ideas as anything other than false doctrines; it is therefore impossible to study these with the "disinterested interest" that one has for factual things. Different morals and religions can be recreated in the mind if the way has at least been cleared for the subjectification of one's own beliefs, if this has already begun to become fluid to a certain degree in the medium of the subjective (psychological) and historical. As long as the metaphysical and empirical structures of consciousness continue to interact with each other within one's own consciousness, a state of aporia will exist, a dilemma, the expression of which is the problem of relativism. The diversity among—indeed, the opposition between—different religions, moral, and legal systems which empirical consciousness finds collides with the residue of the firmly held belief in metaphysical consciousness that there can be only one truth. Dilthey's philosophy represents a classical attempt to avoid this dilemma basically by proposing to abolish both consciousnesses in higher reflection. However, this higher reflection remains without substance, so that, in fact, it proves nothing more than that this reflection itself is possible.

It is also possible to achieve the complete neutrality and freedom of movement of empirical science. A broad field of comparative cultural science with a sociological foundation opens up with the expressed claim of finally liberating itself from the limited perspectives and bounds of the norms of one's own culture. For "today, whether it is a question of imperialism, or of race prejudice, or of a comparison between Christianity and paganism, we are still preoccupied with the uniqueness . . . of our own institutions and achievements, our own civilizations."[58]

When one has analyzed a number of societies or cultures, the need arises for universal concepts; the form of thought that immediately suggests itself is the teleological, as we have already discussed. We find this most clearly with Malinowski, the distinguished researcher of primitive cultures, whenever he moves into the realm of the formulation of theories. The "first axiom" of his theory states: "Culture is essentially an instrumental apparatus by which man is put in a position the better to cope with the concrete specific problems that face him in his environment in the course of the satisfaction of his needs."[59] We should note that Jhering reached this view of the problem as early as 1877: "The ultimate purpose of the state, as of law, is the creation and securing of the conditions necessary for society's existence." Jhering did not use the image of the instrumental apparatus but rather that of the "octopus of the law" *(Rechtspolyp)*. "All law is nothing more than one single creation with a purpose, a powerful octopus of law with countless tentacles called legal maxims, each of which wants, intends, and strives for something."[60] In accordance with this scheme, such thinkers as Bergson, Scheler, and others, conceive of religion as Nature's design of man in order to equip the human being better for survival.

If what we have said so far is correct, then it is clear how we should continue: we must begin with this aporia, with the interaction of two supposedly heterogeneous intellectual authorities. And we must attempt to reach this goal analytically, with the aid of a philosophical examination of the categories of human existence and behavior. The first step is to draw a clear line between the two authorities *(Instanzen)* of the mind. This line does *not* lie between the instrumental-technical consciousness and the historical-psychological consciousness, as the separation between natural and cultural sciences *(Natur- und Geisteswissenschaften)* might suggest to us. Instead, these belong on the same side and are opposed to the *ideative* consciousness, which is in itself "nonscientific" (and not just "unscientific"). The instrumental and the historical consciousness share the common feature that they can propose no ultimate purpose and that no ways of behavior can follow from them in which an ultimate purpose could be pursued. Strictly speaking, the historical-psychological consciousness can be understood as resulting from a change in the inner life brought about by the breakdown of institutions and by social disintegration. It represents a sort of compensatory movement. This disintegration was in turn brought about by the unrestricted expression of instrumental behavior. For this reason, a philosophical analysis of the deeper social problems must first bracket out those ways of thinking that immediately suggest themselves—those forms of thought that both forms of consciousness present to us as self-evident. This is an important point. Thus, one might first attempt to understand institutions such as the family, the law, etc., as arising from rational purposeful action. This was Malinowski's method and we know that it leads to the scheme of presumed instincts that are gratified through goal-conscious behavior. This method has failed completely because it can obviously explain only what it has already assumed.

The next possible course is that adopted by Bergson, Scheler, Beth, and the majority of recent thinkers who seek to explain these institutions in terms of a primary, subjective expediency *(primäre, subjektive Zweckmässigkeit)*. The method here is to reduce religion, for example, to its "idea-content" and to stress the "encouraging," relieving, and vitalizing effect of this "fabulatory function" (Bergson) on the subjective inner life of the human being. This interpretation is the historical psychological one. It appears quite convincing but it cannot really approach the objective institutions and the categories hidden within these, as I myself realized after Hauriou pointed it out and after a thorough analysis of the fundamental social structures. Both these approaches are dangerous in the sense that they seem to compromise teleological thought in general; however, as we shall soon see, teleological thinking is indispensable to a third (ontological) form, which is revealed only after the forms previously discussed have been bracketed. The suggestion of instrumental behavior has become so powerful in our modern culture that we are only now beginning to broaden our view of it to include its inner, at first seemingly contradictory, consequences. In my book *Man in the Age of Technology* (German edition, 1957; English edition, 1980), I have shown that the representative modern psychical states, reflected a thousandfold in literature, are themselves the counterparts to disintegrated societies. These formations, which are conscious to a great degree and which respond to themselves and thereby differentiate themselves, turn the soul itself into a *sujet de fiction* and are the complementary mechanisms of the instrumental consciousness.

We have discussed these well-known views in order to go one step further. The empirical or objectified *(versachlicht)* consciousness of the human being—or more precisely, the instrumental aspect of his mind—has apparently undergone a type of intense growth as a result of the unpredictable consequences which have never before appeared in history and which are in fact ontologically "random," so to speak. This growth runs parallel to that experienced by the drive to posses and consume *(Konsumtrieb)*. On the basis of all the cultures before our own, we could not have predicated that human intelligence would be able to penetrate the laws of the material world to such a fantastically great degree, as testified to by the endless series of man's astonishing inventions. That cultures become overspecialized in certain single directions, that they can construct superstructures upon one-sided subjects and can invest so much energy into these that they actually endanger themselves, is nothing new to one who studies cultures and is, moreover, completely predictable given the "undetermined nature" of the human being. For example, the culture of the Zuñis in New Mexico, which has been studied for over 60 years, has basically "fossilized" itself, so to speak, through its overdevelopment of rituals. However, until now, no culture became specialized with the incredible dynamic that characterizes our own, with such a world-wide reach, and at such a great cost in catastrophes.

By identifying the functions of instrumental consciousness, we have not yet, however, thoroughly measured the realm of the human mind, not even if we accept the hypothesis discussed that the modern, "understanding" (*verstehend*), psychologically appropriative and descriptive, historical consciousness is the partner of the instrumental consciousness and arose as a sort of repercussion. From a philosophical point of view, the battle that raged at the beginning of this century between the natural and cultural sciences has significance only as a foreground; it did not extend to those intellectual acts and ways of behavior determined by impulses in which human beings cultivate nature within themselves. When we call this consciousness (described earlier as the metaphysical consciousness) the *ideative* consciousness, we are expressing that its creative power comes to light in the *founding of institutions* which are basically centered around an *idée directrice,* a directing idea. Instrumental consciousness, on the other hand, is tailored to the categories of inorganic material; it exploits Nature, just as understanding consciousness exploits history. However, both these authorities of the mind, the instrumental (along with its "appendix," the interpretative understanding consciousness) and the ideative, stand toward each other in a relationship described by Hartmann as "opposing realities" (*Realrepugnanz*). They represent contradictory tendencies which carry on their struggle in the arena of man's inner life. One makes gains only at the expense of the other.

Hartmann's *Realrepugnanz* is not a logical contradiction but is rather the collision of opposing tendencies or determinations which consists of real conflict.[61] In Nature, all dynamic balances are forms of adjusting to conflicting elements. Antagonistic forces are built into the organic process with a complexity that we can hardly grasp: the anti-auxins counteract the auxins, specific hormones act against other hormones, which they repress or place in a dynamic balance. Man's impulses represent a field of conflict because different groups of heterogeneous impulses are always competing with each other to find expression in behavior. Psychology has indicated what might result from this conflict (ambivalence, repression, for example). The conflict between duty and inclination is an especially familiar example of opposing realities, which appear in the higher realm of the mind whenever emotion comes into conflict with social obligation.

It has not often been noted that different authorities are at work in the human mind. Bergson made this point when he accused psychology of "postulating certain general faculties of perception, interpretation, comprehension, without enquiring whether the mechanisms that come into play are not different, according as the faculties apply to persons or things, or according as the intelligence is immersed or not in the social environment."[62] Not only are there different "mechanisms" at work here, but these mechanisms are in fact antagonistic—one inhibits or even destroys the other.

At this point in our discussion I would like to confine myself to pointing out that there are very specific, noninstrumental acts of the ideative consciousness from which institutions are developed. I would like to illustrate this point through an analysis of totemism—the social worship of animals—which is one of the few cultural forms that can justifiably be accorded a universal human significance. Its existence has been confirmed among North and South American Indians, in countless "primitive" tribal groups in Africa, North and East Asia, in the South Seas, and in Australia. The early high cultures (especially in Egypt, the classical land of animal deities, but also in Mexico and China) show phenomena that can be traced only to more ancient, prehistorical totemism. Even among the Greeks, traces of totemism can be discovered: for example, Erinys was originally a deity in horse form from Thelpusa in Arcadia; in Brauron in Attica, a festival is held in which Artemis is represented in the shape of a bear.[63] However, if there is one cult that can be shown to extend back to the Paleolithic, to the Riss-Würm interglacial, then it is the bear cult of the Mousterian.

What then is totemism, apart from being the "object of a never-ending conflict"?[64] There are a great number of theories on this point which Freud[65] has divided into the following groups: nominalistic theories that focus on "naming," sociological and psychoanalytic theories, on up to the most superficial of psychological theories based on a shallow understanding, one of which van der Leeuw describes: "If man, as a hunter, was so driven by the necessity of survival and his occupation which remains unchanged from day to day, that he could think only of the animal which represents simultaneously his enemy and his food source, if man merges, in a manner of speaking, with the animal, then it is only natural that this content of his consciousness would also press to be expressed." Of course it is not clear here why a daily routine that never changes would not just as easily have led to a trivialization of the entire complex.

Let us then ask ourselves what a theory of totemism must include. The fundamental points are, of course, as follows: there are groups that identify themselves with specific animals and bear their names; the totem animal is seen as the ancestor of the group; the group is usually forbidden to kill or eat the totem animal. The theory must also take into account that totemism is an age-old phenomenon, that it represents a structure of prehistorical consciousness, of which one thing can be said with great probability—that this consciousness was overwhelmingly oriented toward the external world—that is, it was a reflexive self-awareness only to a minor degree.

At this point, the identification of the self with the animal—the enacted transformation of oneself into the animal—should be understood literally. I have referred often in this book to the great anthropological importance of Mead's discovery that "taking the role of the other," or "imitation," if you like, leads to self-awareness. Then, totemism would primarily be the most primitive, as yet indirect, realization of self-awareness. By identifying with something beyond himself, the individual achieves a contrasting self-awareness which he can hold onto in a more or less permanent *representation* of another being. The primitive consciousness, directed toward the external world, achieves self-awareness only indirectly—that is, in the process of representing the non-ego *(Nicht-Ich)* and in the process set in motion by this representation in which one's own self becomes an object which another represents. We can observe an analogous phenomenon today in children's "role-playing," in which the ego confronts itself in another and thereby becomes conscious of itself. This form of consciousness is a social configuration which can also be realized in the direct behavior of human beings toward each other, in reciprocal "imitation." Totemism, however, is characterized further by the fact that all the members of a group, which already exists in itself, identify with the *same* non-ego, and thus do not imitate each other directly but rather enact the same role of a third party toward each other. This non-ego must therefore lie outside of the group; indeed, it cannot possibly be another person who would become active himself and once more reduce this reciprocal relationship to the level of direct imitation. A living, nearby but passive point of reference must instead be found; here the already present feeling of the vital importance of the presence and continued existence of animal life for mankind serves as the substratum. Gerald Heard once made the insightful remark in this context that all parasitical relationships strive toward a stabilization of the symbiosis.

Because the individual participants all identify with the same animal, however, representing it in the same way for each other, they realize indirectly a self-awareness of their objective unity as a group. Hence, in the mimetical enactment, the objective concept of "our group" enters consciousness much earlier than it is abstractly understood. This concept goes far beyond any experience of "we" *(Wir-Erlebnis)* that is purely emotional or that is achieved through direct, common behavior; it is part of a reflection of a higher degree and can be achieved when the externally directed consciousness interpolates a behavior that is in itself reflexive (i.e., the incorporation of oneself into something else). The way this concept of "our group" is later understood is connected to the point of reference of the entire structure—the totem animal—and focuses on the obvious idea that all are descended from this animal. From an empirical viewpoint this idea is, of course, false or fictitious (as, incidentally, are most of the later genealogical myths). Nonetheless, it does have a reality *sui generis,* as the schematization of a very complex behavior in a *concrete* concept to which experiences of obligation can be connected, which would not follow from the reflected, abstract concept of "our group." At this point, probably for the first time in the history of mankind, an awareness of the objective community is created as a direct result of the identical self-awareness of all participants. This fact has been developed by the high, transnatural religions and has furthermore apparently proven to be difficult for modern consciousness to hold onto; in contrast to earlier times, its most developed forms now tend to isolate the individual. In prehistoric times, which are the focus of our discussion, the most developed phase was that in which self-awareness developed from an external basis and was realized through the incorporation of the self into another. Because the self-awareness of all members intersected at the same external point of reference, an awareness of the objective unity of the group consequently arose and was expressed in the idea of a common descent from the same animal.

Until this point, this process has remained a movement within consciousness. It has more profound aspects, however. Productive structures of consciousness are productive in both a theoretical and a practical sense: they always provide starting points which serve to orient the need for obligation. All obligations are in essence acts of self-denial which we can consider from two perspectives. First, they express the fact that when man confronts himself in this way, he encounters the issue of his own will power. The human being must form attitudes toward himself and consequently also against himself; to engage in a specific behavior directed toward the external world, he must wrestle with another, equally possible one within himself. Second, related to the reduction of instincts in man, the other side of man's consciousness and the plasticity of his impulses, there is a pervasive absence of truly instinctive inhibitory mechanisms. As a being of Nature, the human being is virtually without restraint. Asceticism is thus one of the fundamental phenomena that are part of man's spiritual process of coming to terms with his own constitution; it is therefore, as Durkheim realized, an essential element of religion. The experiences of obligation of the protomagic consciousness are linked to an *external* object of appeal—in this case to the totem animal—and they find therein the point of departure for an ascetic restrictive behavior: it is forbidden to kill or eat the totem animal. It is possible to analyze the "external" origin of these experiences of obligation and to study asceticism (taboo) as one of the possible determinants of obligation.[66]

We have now arrived at a point where the method pursued thus far of *Verstehen,* or reenactment on a psychological level, is of no further use. In understanding an action that is an end in itself, we only gain the insight that this behavior is one of many possible behaviors and it thereby loses its quality as a value in itself because it appears relative. In contrast, an action that has an obligatory quality to it is *exclusive,* and can result only when other possibilities have been checked. To understand willed acts one must therefore enact them on a real level in order to transcend a merely imagined behavior. The factual consequences that follow from real group behavior can therefore be deduced neither from the point of view of psychological *Verstehen* nor from that of an empirical (sociological) assessment of the newly occurring changes. Our examination must then take a *philosophical* route and make use of ontological categories. The ontological category appropriate in this context is that of "secondary, objective expediency" *(sekundäre objektive Zweckmässigkeit).*

As we have described it thus far, the totemistic structure of behavior could have a merely transitory significance. It might develop at many points and on many occasions, but it could dissolve later into other forms of behavior. This behavior had an immanent expediency which, when it was actually reenacted, became objective secondarily; this expediency made totemism a dominant institution for many centuries. The individual members of the group all identify with the same animal and therein discover not only an awareness but also a common point where this self-awareness converges. The obligation which all are under not to kill or eat the animal represents the form in which this awareness can be translated into an obligation—that is, into an ascetic act. For these reasons, this killing taboo simultaneously forbids the group's members to kill and eat anyone within the group itself, since each individual has identified with the totem in relation to each other. This means that the unity of the group, which was imagined, now becomes a reality because of the deep obligations that lie in this behavior. We can therefore understand totemism as that worldwide cultural form by means of which mankind overcomes *anthropophagy;* this accounts for its stability and its incredible power. The pre-totemic groups should be viewed as unstable and fluctuating because of the ever-present possibility of killing and eating other members of the group itself: *Sinanthropus pekinensis,* for example, was an anthropophage.

The ban on killing and eating the totem animal implies therefore that the same taboo applies toward each member of the group. In other words, through this indirect self-awareness of the group, the unity of the group becomes conceivable and in the same movement is actually created because the ascetic obligations that are linked to this type of consciousness follow the associative pathways of this consciousness down to its very consequences. Furthermore, as a result of this same totemistic identification, the aggression toward neighboring groups of another totem can be channeled toward their totem animal which can be killed and the habit of anthropophagy can be restricted to rare, special cases in which, with great ceremony, the killing and consumption of the totem animal of one's own group is permitted.

The internal satisfaction of the group and its united front toward the outside world are of course the prerequisite for every stable tradition (that is, in essence, for culture itself) whether this tradition relates to the cult or to economic or political matters. Above all, this foundation makes possible a clear and stable regulation of sexual relations within the larger group. For this reason, the regulation of obligatory marriages has evolved from totemism. If enduring families are to be established, there must be some sort of restrictive regulation of sexual relations, which makes certain relationships taboo and others obligatory. At the same time there must be an equally restrictive regulation of bonds between families to set them off from competing communities and especially from higher federations. The most important of these factors is the incest taboo; second to it is the understanding of marriage as a deep obligation determined by the already existing totemistic groupings. The simplest form of both conditions is the rule of exogamy—that is, the taboo against sexual relations within one's own totem group of fictitious consanguinity and the requirement that a spouse be chosen from another totem group. The fundamental natural reality of sexual relations thereby becomes institutionalized; in other words, reproduction, which is "in itself" already a given fact, becomes the object of an ordered behavior of the group "for itself."

Our theory suggests that in the early age of totemism, the parallel identification with the totem animal must have been represented and preserved in a gradually ritualized behavior of the members toward each other. The unexpected and overwhelming objective expediency of this behavior served to stabilize it after the fact. Directing ideas do not simply remain in the mind: they must be reflected in real institutions and become part of the foundations of daily behavior. When this totemistic behavior became stereotypical, flattened out, and condensed to suggestions, because the vital energy was channelled into evaluating and processing the resulting obligations and secondary expediencies, the primary behavior had to become symbolic and had to be relieved of the concrete incarnation. This happened in the following manner: the originally totemistic contents of consciousness were developed into narrations of events and actions, which came to assume the form of events to such an extent that they actually began to replace the real, active group behavior. The "myths" of the "totem spirits" that arose in this fashion are numerous in Australia, for example, and most likely reflect earlier real ways of behavior of the groups. Thus, these myths are brimming with tales of the "migrations" of the totem spirits and above all, with endless accounts of "metamorphoses." The group members thereby preserve the memory of a fundamental discovery; it was precisely this metamorphosis of oneself into another being that constituted the first powerful step forward taken by self-awareness.

The development of animal husbandry and agricultural cultivation could not have come about in any other way. Even these institutions are secondary objective expediencies which were seized upon and made use of after a behavior with a totally different orientation surprisingly made them possible. That plants grow from seeds was all too obvious a fact not to have been noticed everywhere. However, this observation alone did not inevitably lead to farming; instead, the magical guarding of totem animals and totem plants had to occur first. Farming also demands an ascetic self-discipline which the instrumental consciousness would not naturally produce. Edward Hahn was well aware of this: "When well-meaning Europeans attempted to teach farming to primitive tribes, it was always the case that the greatest enemies of the new cultures proved to be those who stood to benefit by it. Either the seeds and roots destined for the fields would wind up in their stomachs, or, if the field had been planted under the direction of experts, the young, half-grown plants would be pulled up and consumed while nothing was set aside for cultivation."[67] Such discipline can apparently be imposed only by the force of a taboo, such as one relating to the protection of totem plants. Similarly, the exclusive guarding of *one* plant, keeping away anything that did not directly belong to it, can have arisen only from magical sources. Once such a behavior led to the discovery that cultivated plants can produce multiple yields, one could separate this secondary objective expediency from its original purpose and pursue it for its own sake, even if one was not always prepared for such an act of rationalization. Even today, there are South American Indian tribes who grow tobacco only for ritual purposes and in fact import the tobacco that they actually smoke.

If these analyses can sufficiently account for such original cultural creations, then this has important philosophical implications. Totemism is an example of a typically ideative, noninstrumental behavior. Neither indirect self-awareness, achieved by incorporating oneself into the non-ego, nor the resulting feeling of obligation, nor even its ascetic expression can be explained in terms of the instrumental categories of purpose, means, and need. Probably, needs originally become concrete through the *representation* of their gratification, not in the gratification itself. A direct psychological way of understanding totemism no longer exists for our consciousness. There can, however, be no doubt as to its extraordinary significance. We were able to reconstruct it only with the help of several methods that complemented each other: we used a few fundamental anthropological theories, as were developed in this book, a few highly probable assumptions about the state of prehistoric consciousness and social conditions, and the thoroughly ontological category of "secondary, objective expediency."

This category contains a deeper philosophical problem. How is it possible that a behavior that necessarily appears to the instrumental consciousness as imaginary nonetheless led to the most astonishing objective expediencies of Nature for man—expediencies that had remained hidden for a long time, indeed, that were present only virtually and that instrumental behavior would never have uncovered? This objective teleology is of a very special type. It is not the case here that expediencies that already exist in Nature, that are in fact abundant in the organic world, are recognized and made available; this actually constitutes the second step in the process. The first step lies in realizing that potential objective expediencies are first developed through the chains of consequences of an ideative behavior. The difficulty here is that our analytical consciousness can only approach in fragmentary fashion what we call organic "refinement." *(Veredelung)*. The cultivation of useful plants signifies a *qualitative* change which cannot be completely defined in terms of chromosomal changes, although these are all we can comprehend analytically. A similar situation exists as far as the "humanization" of the human being is concerned, which first became possible with the disappearance of anthropophagy. The group is first held together by specific systems of restraints; as in totemism, it is self-content and self-contained and so provides the setting in which the higher development not only of culture but also of man himself is encouraged. As Malinowski has argued,[68] the decisive effect of restrictive behavioral norms is that they "curb certain natural propensities...control human instincts and...impose a nonspontaneous compulsory behavior." This development apparently proved expedient for the spiritual as well as vital development of the human species.

We have identified the internal categories of ideative behavior as follows: incorporation *(Verkörperung)* (this should not be confused with "role," which is a concept popular among American sociologists, for example; it is actually a secondary derivative of incorporation); indirect self-awareness; indirect group awareness; obligation "from without" *(von aussen)*; asceticism; and the originally creative other ego *(Ich)* (here, the totem animal as ancestor). To borrow terms from Hartmann's new ontology, these categories must coincide *(sich decken)* with certain *potential,* overlapping categories in the organic and human world; they must conform to these and realize them in their execution, just as the categories of instrumental thinking approximate to a great degree those of inorganic nature. The achievement of such a coincidence is revealed in the astonishing objective expediency which is perceived as an affirmation of or blessing upon the particular behavior. The fundamental institutions serve the function of preserving this expediency, as we have illustrated in the examples of group satisfaction, of marriage and of agricultural cultivation.

R. Meister was therefore completely correct to stress that the basic characteristic of all cultural formations is their orientation toward continuance.[69] Of equal importance is Hauriou's discussed acknowledgement of "incorporation" as a fundamental category of the theory of institutions. The real categories of life and the virtual objective expediencies contained within it are, of course, perceived only in part; they appear, however, to conform to the structures of ideative behavior to a great degree and in an indirect fashion. Indeed, real, objective, and thoroughly fundamental relationships are found in this noninstrumental, non-goal-conscious, ideative behavior, and in man's actions in opposition to his own impulses; these relationships thereby become conceivable as far as behavior is concerned, in an expediency that was not even originally intended. As we all know, animals know nothing about the periodic processes of "eating" and "mating"; instead, these processes run their course through instincts and behavior, behind the back of their consciousness, so to speak. In the human institutions of the family and of farming, these processes are not only lived but actually become the objects of goals and obligations. What had happened "in itself," now takes place "for itself," but also as a result of the ideative consciousness having developed completely different contents, which on the intellectual level were complete purposes and obligations for themselves. Instrumental consciousness did not create these institutions; as we know today from experience, this consciousness is completely unable to found stable, humanizing institutions. By pursuing the path of instrumental behavior, early hunting societies managed to find only an unsteady supply of food; they did not succeed in guaranteeing a stable source. For this reason, they resorted again and again to cannibalism, which, it cannot be denied, was directly expedient as a means toward an end. Nothing could have been more "practical." Once they began to tend totem animals and plants, they hit upon expediencies that allowed food to be institutionalized as an enduring structure, as a superindividual process. The stationary gratification of needs trivialized this fundamental drive to some extent and relieved man to undertake activities of a higher nature.

The institutions therefore preserved objective, overlapping expediencies; they crystallized these after ideative behavior revealed them. For this reason, their directing norm is invariably that idea by means of which the ideative consciousness first oriented itself. The strict, for the most part exogamous, marriage rules of primitive tribes are guided solely by the idea of the totem, which has since disintegrated in an array of almost exclusively classificatory designations and of numerous mythological tales, whose original content has degenerated into the obligation of eternal literal repetition. From a philosophical perspective, we believe that the primary complex relationship represented here between ideative behavior, the ascetic obligation, the thereby revealed unexpected ontological expediency, and the institutionalization of these under the aegis of one directing idea is the true nerve of religion. Our direct consciousness does not allow us to understand this relationship as anything but the image of a higher being (here, that of the totem ancestor) who has founded these institutions.

Now that we approach the end of our discussion, I would like to refer back to the critical remarks made at the beginning of this section. As a "pre-science" *(Vorwissenschaft)*, empirical research with a sociological orientation is indispensable. However, it only provides the starting points for special, cultural anthropological categories, some of which we discussed in this chapter and others of which (such as the "indefinite obligation," the "pro-tomagic" and the *tension stabilisée)* I have treated elsewhere.[70] The purpose of these efforts is a philosophical examination of social culture, above all, of the fundamental institutions including the directing ideas which are embodied within these. The psychological method of *Verstehen* played a part in this analysis only as a preliminary approach and had to be strictly controlled in its use. These psychological acts are never ends in themselves; they do not represent the direction in which this science will perfect itself. If one chooses this method and takes a few steps in approaching these deeper problems, one will very quickly come up against ontological categories, such as that of "secondary, objective expediency." This is a very important category in fundamental institutions and thereby also in religion. We can now understand why it is insufficient to propose a *direct* relation of religious *ideas* (in the purely subjective aspect) to the level of human impulses, as has been suggested by Bergson, Scheler, Beth, by myself in earlier editions, and by many other authors: A primary, subjective expediency cannot adequately copy the secondary objective one. It is telling that among the primitive religions, Bergson could conceive only of the "fabulatory function" and its subjectively expedient, relieving, "encouraging" effect, and among the higher forms, only the most individual one—mysticism. He could not conceive of religion as an institution and for this reason, he relegated it to sociology. It now appears probable that neither the instrumental consciousness nor one of its derivations—including the historical-psychological consciousness—is capable of founding enduring and stable institutions. All apologies for the cultural sciences might indeed lead to a glorification of the scholar's station but not, however, to new forms of social order. Dilthey's main error was his failure to recognize this fact.

As we have seen, enduring institutions are the products of highly complex human social behavior involving ideative acts as well as ascetic acts of self-discipline and restraint. Each step in the progress of human culture has also stabilized a new form of discipline. The solitary soul of reflecting man alone makes the unjustified claim to depths. "The only depths that one can justifiably lay claim to lie, according to ontic relationships, just as often towards the outside as towards the inside," wrote N. Hartmann.[71] For "higher philosophy treats the marriage between nature and the mind" (Novalis).[72]

Notes

Introduction

1. Friedrich Nietzsche, *Nietzsches Werke,* vol. 13 (Nachgelassene Werke) (Leipzig: Naumann, 1903).

2. Werner Heisenberg, *Die Einheit des naturwissenschaftlichen Weltbildes.* (Leipzig: Barth, 1942), p.32.

3. Nicolai Hartmann, *Blätter für deutsche Philosophie* 15, 1941.

4. Henri Bergson, *Creative Evolution* (Westport, Conn.: Greenwood Press, 1975), p.201.

5. Hans Freyer, *Weltgeschichte Europas* vol.1 (Wiesbaden: Dieterich, 1948), p.169.

6. Max Scheler, *Man's Place in Nature* (Boston: Beacon Press, 1961).

7. Scheler, *Man's Place,* p. 47.

8. Konrad Lorenz, "Über die Bildung des Instinkt begriffs," *Die Naturwissenschaften,* (1937), pp.19–21; "Über den Begriff der Instinkthandlung," *Folia Biotheoretica,* (1937), vol.2; "Vergleichende Verhaltensforschung," *Verhandlungen der Deutschen Zoologischen Gesellschaft,* (1939); "Die angeborenen Formen möglicher Erfahrung," *Zeitschrift für Tierpsychologie,* 5: 2; "Psychologie und Stammesgeschichte" in *Die Evolution der Organismen,* (1943); "Über das Toten von Artgenossen," *Jahrbuch der Max Planck-Gesellschaft,* (1955).

9. Lorenz, "Die angeborenen Formen," p.257.

10. Seitz, *Zeitschrift für Tierpsychologie,* 1940, vol.4.

11. Nikolaas Tinbergen, *Instinktlehre: Vergleichende Erforschung angeborenen Verhaltens* (Berlin, Hamburg: Parey, 1952).

12. Lorenz, "Die angeborenen Formen," p.292.

13. Frederik Jacobus Johannes Buytendijk, *Psychologie des animaux,* (Paris: Payot, 1928); *Blätter für Deutsche Philosophie,* 3: 33 ff.; *Die Neue Rundschau,* October, 1938.

14. Frederick J. J. Buytendijk, *Psychologie,* p.243; see ch.8, "La Pensée des animaux."

15. Lorenz, "Über den Begriff der Instinkthandlung."

16. Ibid.

17. Ibid, p.41.

18. Paul Guillaume, *La Formation des Habitudes* (Paris: Alcan, 1936), p.24.

19. Lorenz, "Über die Bildung des Instinktbegriffs," p.295.

20. Otto Storch, *Die Sonderstellung des Menschen in Lebensabspiel und Vererbung,* (Vienna, 1948).

21. Lorenz, "Psychologie und Stammesgeschichte," p.122 f.

22. Lorenz, "Über die Bildung des Instinktbegriffs," p.311.

23. Friedrich Schiller, "On Grace and Dignity," in *Essays Aesthetical and Philosophical* (London: G. Bell, 1884).

24. Johann Gottfried Herder, *Essay on the Origin of Language* (New York: Ungar, 1966), p.109.

25. Kant, *Idee zu einer allgemeinen Geschichte in weltbürgerlicher Absicht,* (Wiesbaden: Staadt, 1914).

26. Josef Pieper has called my attention to the fact that the anthropological problem defined here is described in the *Summa Theologica* by Thomas Aquinas (I, 76, 5): "The intellectual soul is the most perfect of souls. However, since the bodies of the other sensing beings (that is, of animals) have been provided by Nature with natural means of protection (fur instead of clothing and hoofs instead of shoes) as well as with their own weapons (such as claws, teeth, and horns), then it would appear that the intellectual soul should not have been united with such an imperfect body which lacks such natural means of defense." In his answer to this problem, Thomas Aquinas even makes mention of the "reduction of instincts": "The intellectual soul has infinite strength because it can comprehend the universal [world-openness!]. For this reason, Nature could not provide it with definite, instinctive beliefs.... Instead of all these things, the human being possesses reason and his hands, which are the tools of tools." A similar line of reasoning also appears, as A. Szalai has indicated to me, in Aquinas, *De regimine principum* I, 1.

27. Adolf Portman, "Die Ontogenese des Menschen als Problem der Evolutionsforschung," *Verhandlungen der Schweizerischen Naturforschenden Gesellschaft,* 1945; *Biologische Fragmente zu einer Lehre vom Menschen,* (Basel: Schwabe, 1944); "Zoologie und das neue Bild des Menschen," 1960.

28. Portman, *Biologische Fragmente,* p.45.

29. Ibid., p.47.

30. Ibid., pp.79, 81.

31. Ibid., p.80.

32. Ibid., p.12.

33. Portman, "Ontogenese des Menschen," p.2.

34. Hobbes, *De homina,* 10: 3.

35. Alfred Seidel, *Bewusstsein als Verhängnis,* (Bonn: F. Cohen, 1927); Scheler, *Man's Place.*

36. Portman, "Biologische Fragmente," pp.61–62.

37. Gerald Heard, *Social Substance of Religion,* (London: Allen & Unwin, 1931).

38. Georges Sorel, *De l'utilité du pragmatisme* (Paris, 1928).

39. Guillaume, *La Formation des habitudes,* p.27.

40. Maurice Pradines, *Traité de psychologie generale,* (Paris: Presses universitaires de France, 1946), 1: p.208.

41. Nicolai Hartmann, "Neue Anthropologie in Deutschland," *Blätter für deutsche Philosophie* (1941) 15: p. 163.

42. Maurice Pradines, *Philosophie de la sensation* (London and New York: Oxford, 1932), p.378.

43. Ibid.

44. Kant, *The Critique of Judgement.* (Oxford: Clarendon Press, 1969).

45. Nietzsche, *The Will to Power,* aphorism 289, p.163.

46. Ibid., aphorism 504, p.274.

47. See my essay "Die Resultate Schopenhauers," in Emge and van Schweinichen, eds., *Gedächtnisschrift für Arthur Schopenhauer,* (Berlin, 1938).

48. Nietzsche, *Will to Power,* aphorism 676, p.357.

49. See my book *Urmensch und Spätkultur: Philosophische Ergebnisse und Aussagen* (Bonn: Athenäum, 1956).

50. Theodor Ballauff, *Das Problem des Lebendigen* (Bonn: Humboldt, 1949), p.136.

51. Schopenhauer, *Über den Willen in der Natur,* chapter entitled "Vergleichende Anatomie" (3rd ed rev. Leipzig, 1867).

52. Jakob Johan von Uexküll, *Umwelt und Innenwelt der Tiere,* (Berlin: Springer, 1909); *Bausteine zu einer biologischen Weltanschauung,* (Munich: Bruckmann, 1913); with Kriszat, *Streifzüge durch die Umwelten von Tieren und Menschen,* (Hamburg: Rowohlt, 1956).

53. Henry Fairfield Osborn, *The Origin and Evolution of Life,* (NY: Scribners, 1917).

54. Buytendijk, *Psychologie,* p.74.

55. Ibid., p.96.

56. Uexküll, *Zeitschrift für die gesamte Naturwissenschaften,* 1:7.

57. Richard Woltereck, *Grundzüge einer allgemeinen Biologie,* (Stuttgart: Enke, 1932), pp. 42, 220 ff.

58. Uexküll, *Theoretical Biology* (London: K. Paul, Trench, Trubner, & Co.: 1926); Brock, *Sudhoffs Archiv* (1935), vol. 27; Herman Weber, "Zur neueren Entwickelung der Umweltlehre J. v. Uexkülls," *Die Naturwissenschaften* (1937), vol. 7; "Zur Fassung und Gliederung eines allgemein Umweltbegriffes," *Die Naturwissenschaften* (1939):38; "Der Umweltbegriff der Biologie und seine Anwendung," *Der Biologe* (1939), vol 8; "Zum gegenwärtigen Stand der allgemeinen Ökologie," *Die Naturwissenschaften* (1940):50–51; "Organismus und Umwelt," *Der Biologe* (1942), vol. 11.

59. Uexküll, *Niegeschaute Welten: Die Umwelten meiner Freunde.* (Berlin: Fischer, 1936).

60. Hermann Weber, "Zur Fassung und Gliederung."

61. See Egon von Eickstedt, *Rassenkunde und Rassengeschichte der Menschheit,* (Stuttgart: Enke, 1934), p.793 ff.

62. Gustav Neckel, *Kultur der alten Germanen,* (Potsdam: Akademische Verlagsgesellschaft, 1934), p. 181.

63. von Eickstedt, *Rassenkunde,* p.819.

64. Herder, *Essay on the Origin of Language,* p. 103.

65. Ibid., p. 104.

66. Ibid., pp. 104–105; p. 104.

67. Ibid., p. 105.

68. Ibid., p. 107.

69. Ibid., pp. 105, 106.
70. Ibid., p. 108.
71. Ibid., pp. 109–110.

Part One

1. Mijsberg, "Über den Bau des urogenitalen Apparates bei den männlichen Primaten," *Verhandlungen der königlichen Akademi᷉ der Wissenschaft*, (Amsterdam, 1923).

2. cf. Wilhelm Burkamp, *Wirklichkeit und Sinn*, (Berlin: Junker und Dünnhaupt, 1938), vol.2.

3. Westenhöfer, *Das Problem der Menschwerdung*, 2d ed., 1935; "Das menschliche Kinn," *Archiv für Frauenkunde und Konst. Forschung*, (1924), vol. 10.

4. Adolf Naef, *Die Naturwissenschaften*, (1926), pp.89f., 445f., 472f.

5. Naef, "Der neue Menschenaffe," *Die Naturwissenschaften*, (1925), no. 33.

6. Kollman, *Archiv für Anthropologie*, (1906), vol. 5; *Korrespondenz der Deutschen anthropologischen Gesellschaft*, (1905), vol. 36.

7. Ranke, *Korrespondenz der Deutschen Anthropologischen Gesellschaft*, 1897.

8. Jacob Hermann Frederik Kohlbrugge, *Die morphologische Abstammung des Menschen*, (Stuttgart: Strecker & Schröder, 1908).

9. Hermann Klaatsch, *Das Werden der Menschheit und die Anfange der Kultur*, 3d ed., (Berlin: Bong, 1936).

10. Adloff, "Einige besondere Bildungen an den Zahnen des Menschen und ihre Bedeutung für die Vorgeschichte," *Anatomische Anzeiger* (1924), vol. 58.

11. Werth, "Diskussionsbemerkung," *Zeitschrift für Säugetierkunde* (1937), vol. 12.

12. See Adloff, "Das Gebiss der Menschen und der Anthropoiden und das Abstammungs problem," *Zeitschrift für Morphologie und Anthropologie*, (1927) vol. 26; "Der Eckzahn des Menschen und das Abstammungsproblem," *Zeitschrft für Anatomie und Entwicklungsgeschichte* (1931) 94; "Über die primitiven und die sogenannten pithecoiden Merkmale im Gebiss des rezenten und fossilen Menschen und ihre Bedeutung, "*Zeitschrift für Anatomie und Entwicklungsgeschichte* (1937), vol. 107; "Das Gebiss von Sinanthropus pekinensis," *Zeitschrift für Morphologie und Anthropologie* (1938), vol. 37.

13. S. Frechkop, "Considérations préliminaires sur l'évolution de la dentition des primates," *Notes sur les Mammiféres* 26, Bulletin Musée royal d'Histoire naturale de Belgique, 1940.

14. Adloff, "Erganzende Bemerkungen zur Beurteilung des Gebisses von Sinanthropus pekinensis," *Anatomischer Anzeiger* 91, 1941; "Odontologie und Anthropologie," *Zahnärztlicher Rundschau*, vol. 11, 1941.

15. Adloff, 1931 (see note 12).
16. Adloff, 1937, 1938 (see note 12).
17. Adloff, 1938, (see note 12).
18. Klaatsch, *Globus*, 1899, vol.76.
19. Osborn, "Fundamental Discoveries of the Last Decade in Human Evolu-

tion," *New York Academy of Medicine*, (April 1927); "Recent Discoveries Relating to the Origin and Antiquity of Man," *American Philosophical Society*, 1927; *Science* (1927), vol.65; "Recent discoveries in Human Evolution," *Medical Society of the County of Kings* (1927); "The Influence of Habit in the Evolution of Man and the Great Apes," *Bulletin of the New York Academy of Medicine* (1928) vol.4; "Influence of Bodily Locomotion in Separating Man from the Monkeys and Apes," *Scientific Monthly* (1928), vol.26.

20. Osborn (see note 19).

21. Osborn, "Recent Discoveries Relating to the Origin."

22. Osborn, ibid.

23. Osborn, ibid.

24. Osborn, ibid.

25. Osborn, *Human Biology* (1929) 1:1.

26. Frechkop, *Bulletin du Musée royal d'Histoire naturale de Belgique* (1937), vol. 13.

27. Frechkop, "Le pied de l'homme," *Mémoires du Musée royal d'Histoire naturale de Belgique*, series 2, no. 3, 1936.

28. Ibid, p.329.

29. Hancar, *Mitteilungen der Wiener Anthropologischen Gesellschaft*, 71, 2, 1941.

30. Henckel, "Das Primordialkranium von Tupaja und der Ursprung der Primaten," *Zeitschrift für Anatomie und Entwicklungsgeschichte*, (1928) vol. 86.

31. Bolk, "Vergleichende Untersuchungen an einem Fetus eines Gorillas und eines Schimpansen," *Zeitschrift für Anatomie und Entwicklungsgeschichte*, (1926), vol. 81; *Das Problem der Menschwerdung* (Jena), 1926.

32. Bolk, *Anatomischer Anzeiger*, vol. 24.

33. Bolk (see note 31).

34. cf. Bolk, "Zur Entwicklung und vergleichende Anatomie des Tractus urethro-vaginalis der Primaten," *Zeitschrift für Morphologie und Anthropologie* (1907), vol. 10.

35. An additional series of primitive features, in the sense of fetal states that man has preserved in contrast to the other primates, can be found in von Mijsberg's work, in *Abhandlungen der königlichen Akademie*, (Amsterdam, 1923), which supplements Bolk's research. The work is sound methodologically.

36. Lobosch, *Anatomischer Anzeiger* (1927), vol. 63.

37. Bolk, "Vergleichende Untersuchungen."

38. Versluys, *Hirngrösse und hormonales Geschehen bei der Menschwerdung*, (1939); Dubois, *Biologia generalis* (1930), vol. 6.

39. For more on this, see Grünthal, *Zur Frage der Entstehung des Menschenhirn*, (Basel and New York: 1948); Klatt, "Die theoretische Biologie und die Problematik der Schädelform," *Biologia generalis* (1949) 19:1; H. Spatz, *Gedanken über die Zukunft des Menschenhirns*, (1961).

40. Schindewolf, "Das Problem der Menschwerdung, ein paläontologischer Lösungsversuch," *Jahrbuch der preussischen geologischen Landesanstalt*, (1928) vol. 49, no.2; *Forschung und Fortschritt*, (1930), 6.

41. Bolk, "Vergleichende Untersuchungen," p.23.

42. Eugen Fischer, "Die Rassenmerkmale des Menschen als Domestikations-erscheinungen," *Zeitschrift für Morphologie und Anthropologie* (1914), vol. 18.

43. Max Hilzheimer, "Historisches und Kritisches zu Bolks Problem der Menschwerdung," *Anatomischer Anzeiger* vol. 62.

44. Hilzheimer, *Die Stammesgeschichte des Menschen* (Leipzig: Quelle and Meyer, 1926).

45. Lorenz, "Die angeborenen Formen"; "Durch Domestikation verursachte Störungen des arteigenen Verhaltens," *Zeitschrift für angewandte Psychologie* (1940), vol. 59.

46. For example, W.E. Mühlmann, *Geschichte der Anthropologie*, (Bonn: Universitätsverlag, 1948), p.193.

47. Lorenz, "Die angeborenen Formen," p.298.

48. Ibid., p. 297.

49. Georg Kraft, *Der Urmensch als Schöpfer: die geistige Welt des Eiszeitmenschen,* (Tübingen:Matthiesen, 1948), p.16.

50. Ibid., p.96.

51. Portmann, "Biologische Fragmente," p.134.

52. Cited in Portmann, p.35.

53. Portmann, "Biologische Fragmente," p.102; "Die Ontogenese des Menschen als Problem der Evolutionforschung," p.8.

54. Bernhard Rensch, *Neuere Probleme der Abstammungslehre,* 2d ed., (Stuttgart: Enke, 1954).

55. See, for example, W. Marinelli, *Die Abstammung des Menschen,* (Vienna, 1948), p.50.

56. Hans Weinert, *Entstehung der Menschenrassen,* (Stuttgart: Enke, 1938).

57. Weinert, *Der geistige Aufstieg der Menschheit: Vom Ursprung bis zur Gegenwart,* (Stuttgart: Enke, 1940), p.66.

58. Weinert, *Entstehung,* p.105.

59. Ibid., p.19.

60. *Das Werden der Menschheit.*

61. *Das Problem der Menschwerdung,* 1935; *Der Eigenweg des Menschen,* 1942.

62. *Urwelt, Sage, und Menschheit,* (Munich and Berlin: Oldenbourg, 1927); "Entwicklungslehre als anthropologisches-methaph. Problem, *"Blätter für deutsche Philosophie,* (1932), vol.6.

63. *Über Entstehung und Entwicklung des lebens,* 1933.

64. For Frechkop, see works cited above, in notes 13,26,27.

65. Klaatsch, *Korrespondenz–Blatt der deutschen Gesellschaft für Anthropologie,* 1899, p. 157.

66. von Koenigswald, "Neue Menschenaffen- und Vormenschenfunde," *Die Naturwissenschaften,* (1939).

67. Marinelli, *Abstammung,* p.46.

68. André Varagnac, ed., *Der Mensch der Urzeit,* 1960, p.16, p.19, p.54.

69. G. Heberer, *Natur und Volk*, (1960), 10:314.

70. Wilton M. Krogman, *Blick in die Wissenschaft*, vol. 2, 1949.

Part Two

1. Baldwin, *Die Entwicklung des Geistes beim Kinde und bei der Rasse*, (Berlin: Reuther, 1898), pp. 78–79.

2. Diderot, *Le rêve de d'Alembert*, (Paris: Didier, 1951).

3. Bichat, *Recherches physiologiques sur la vie et la mort*, (Paris, 1805), p.36.

4. Bostroem, "Störungen des Wollens," *Handbuch der Geisteskrankheiten*, vol. 2, no. 3.

5. Wilhelm von Humboldt, *Linguistic Variability and Intellectual Development* (Philadelphia: University of Pennsylvania Press, 1971).

6. Köhler, *Abhandlungen der preussischen Akademie der Wissenschaft*, 1917.

7. cf. Buytendijk, *Psychologie* p.80.

8. Metzger, *Psychologie: Die Entwicklung ihrer Grundannahmen seit der Einführung des Experiments* (Darmstadt: Steinkopff, 1968).

9. Lorenz, "Die angeborenen Formen," p.256.

10. Ibid., p.315.

11. Guillaume, *La Formation*, pp. 55–56.

12. Laurance Frederic Shaffer and Edward Shoben Jr., *The Psychology of Adjustment: A Dynamic and Experimental Approach to Personality and Mental Hygiene.* 2d ed., (Boston: Houghton-Mifflin, 1956).

13. Bertrand Russell, *Freedom and Organization* (London: Allen & Unwin, 1934).

14. cf. Lorenz, "Psychologie und Stammesgeschichte," p. 110, and the works of von Holst.

15. cf. Metzger, *Psychologie*, ch. 5, "Das Problem des Bezugssystems."

16. see M. Hertz, "beobachtungen an gefangenen Rabenvögeln," *Psychologische Forschung*, vol. 8.

17. see Eduard Baumgarten, *Der Pragmatismus*, (Frankfurt: Klostermann, 1938), pp.232, 236 f.

18. Nicolai Hartmann, *Grundzüge einer Metaphysik der Erkenntnis* (Berlin/ Leipzig: de Gruyter, 1925), p. 56.

19. Melchoir Palagyi, *Naturphilosophische Vorlesungen über die Grundprobleme des Bewusstseins und des Lebens* (Leipzig: Barth, 1924).

20. Arthur Schopenhauer, *The World as Will and Idea.* (London: Routledge, 1964).

21. Palagyi, *Naturphilosophische Vorlesungen*, p.116.

22. George Herbert Mead, *Mind, Self, and Society: From the Standpoint of a Social Behaviorist.* (Chicago: University of Chicago Press, 1972).

23. René Duret, *Les facteurs pratiques de la croyance dans la perception*, (Paris: Alcan, 1929), p. 134.

24. Egon Brunswik, *Wahrnehmung und Gegenstandswelt* (Leipzig and Vienna: Deuticke, 1934), pp.115, 125.

25. John Dewey, *The Quest for Certainty: A Study of the Relation of Knowledge and Action.* (New York: Minton, Blach, 1929), p.158.

26. Karl Bühler, *Sprachtheorie,* (Jena: Fischer, 1934), p.44 ff.

27. Bühler, "Die Axiomatik der Sprachwissenschaften," *Kantstudien* 1933, vol. 38.

28. See my essay, "Vom Wesen der Erfahrung," *Blätter für deutsche Philosophie,* vol. 10, no. 3.

29. Scheler, *Man's Place,* p.47.

30. Ibid.

31. Jean Przyluski, *L'Evolution humaine* (Paris: Presses universitaires de France, 1942).

32. Janet, *Nevroses et idées fixes* (Paris: Alcan, 1898).

33. Goldstein, *Monatschrift für Psychologie und Neurologie* 1923, vol. 54.

34. Buytendijk, *Wesen und Sinn des Spiels: das Spielen des Menschen und der Tiere als Erscheinungsform der Lebenstriebe* (Berlin: Wolff, 1933).

35. Aristotle, *De Anima.* (New York: Arno, 1976), p.155, p.91.

36. William Preyer, *Die Seele des Kindes,* (Leipzig: Grieben, 1895), p.882.

37. Hartmann, *Der Aufbau der realen Welt; Grundriss der allgemeinen Kategorienlehre,* (Meisenheim: Hain, 1949), p.569.

38. Palagyi, *Wahrnehmungslehre,* ed. by L. Klages, (Leipzig: Barth, 1925), p.94.

39. Mead, *Mind, Self, and Society,* p.340.

40. Schopenhauer, *World as Will and Idea,* p. 130.

41. Viktor von Weizsäcker, *Der Gestaltkreis: Theorie der Einheit von Wahrnehmen und Bewegen.* (Stuttgart: Thieme, 1947).

42. Storch, *Die Sonderstellung des Menschen;* "Erbmotorik und Erwerbmotorik," *Anzeige der österreichischen Akademie der Wissenschaften,* (1949),- vol.1.

43. P. Christian, "Die Willkürbewegung im Umgang mit beweglichen Mechanismen," Sitzungsberichte der Heidelberg Akademie der Wissenschaften, 1948.

44. Ibid., p.20.

45. Ibid.

46. Ibid., p.22f.

47. Humboldt, *Linguistic Variability,* p.19.

48. Lazarus Geiger, *Zur Entwicklungsgeschichte der Menschheit,* (Stuttgart: Cotta, 1871), p.24.

49. Otto Jespersen, *Language: Its Nature, Development, and Origin* (London: Allen and Unwin, 1922).

50. A.A. Grünbaum, "Aphasie und Motorik," *Zeitschrift für die gesamte Neurologie und Psychiatrie,* (1930) 130:385–412.

51. Herder, *Essay on the Origin.*

52. Ibid., p.115–116.

53. Hermann Ammann, "Die Sprachtheorie Arnold Gehlens," *Die Tatwelt* 17, (1941), vol. 17.

54. Groos, *Die Spiele des Menschen,* 1899.

55. Buytendijk, *Wesen und Sinn des Spiels,* p.88.

56. Kant, *Critique of Pure Reason* (London: Dent, 1964).

57. Mead, *Mind, Self, and Society*, p.138.
58. Ibid., p.151.
59. Ibid., p.154.
60. Brunswik, *Wahrnehmung und Gegenstandswelt*, p.207.
61. E. Jaensch, *Zeitschrift für Psychologie*, 88:144.
62. Wolfgang Köhler, *Intelligenzprüfungen an Menschenaffen*. (Berlin: Springer, 1921).
63. Metzger, *Psychologie*, 1954.
64. Johann Gottlieb Fichte, *Werke*, 1:424.
65. Julius Stenzel, *Philosophie der Sprache* (Munich and Berlin: Oldenbourg, 1934), p.26.
66. Jespersen, *Language*, p.152.
67. Noiré, *Der Ursprung der Sprache*, 1877.
68. Honoré Joseph Chavée, *Lexicologie indoeuropéenne* (Paris/Leipzig: Franck, 1849).
69. Noiré, *Der Ursprung*, p.332 f.
70. cf. Paul, *Prinzipien der Sprachgeschichte*, 70.
71. Noiré, *Der Ursprung*, p.356.
72. Ibid., p.341 f.
73. Jespersen, *Language*, p.115.
74. See my article, "Das Problem des Sprachursprungs," in *Forschungen und Fortschritte* (1938), pp.26–27.
75. Humboldt, *Linguistic Variability*, p.35.
76. Ammann, "Sprache und Wirklichkeit," *Blätter für deutsche Philosophie* vol. 12, no. 3.
77. Stenzel, *Philosophie der Sprache*, pp.35, p.36.
78. Humboldt, *Linguistic Variability*, pp.35–36.
79. Ammann, *Forschungen und Fortschritte* Vol 14, no. 25.
80. Humboldt, *Linguistic Variability*, p.164.
81. Ibid., p.164.
82. Fichte, "Über den Ursprung der Sprache," *Vorlesungen über Logik und Metaphysik*, 1797. *Nachlass*, (1937), 2: 173f.
83. More on this problem of word and sentence can be found in Kainz, *Sprachphilosophie*, 1:109f.
84. Grimm, *Deutsches Wörterbuch*, 1:1115.
85. Humboldt, *Linguistic Variability*, pp.37–38.
86. Stenzel, *Philosophie der Sprache*, 1934.
87. Weisgerber, "Die Bedeutungslehre — Ein Irrweg der Sprachwissenschaft?" *Germ.-Röm. Monatschrift* 15, 1927. See also his "Sprachwissenschaft und Philosophie zum Bedeutungsproblem," *Blätter für deutsche Philosophie*, vol. 4.
88. Ferdinand de Saussure, *Course in General Linguistics*, Rev. ed. (London: Fontana, 1974), p.112.
89. Humboldt, *Linguistic Variability*, p.111.
90. Weisgerber, "Sprachwissenschaft."
91. Jakob Segal, "Über das Vorstellen von Objekten und Situationen," (Stuttgart: Spemann, 1916).
92. Noiré, *Der Ursprung*, p.366, p.345.

93. Ibid., p.306.

94. Herder, *On the Origin*, p.117.

95. Novalis, *Werke*, 2:181.

96. Herder, *On the Origin*.

97. Ludwig Klages, *Vom Wesen des Bewusstseins* (Leipzig: Barth, 1921), p.33.

98. Plessner, *Die Stufen des Organischen und der Mensch*, 1928.

99. Mead, *Mind, Self, and Society*.

100. Ibid., p.47.

101. Ibid, p.47.

102. Guillaume, *La Formation*, p.85.

103. Mead, *Mind, Self, and Society*, pp.365–366.

104. Ibid., p.73.

105. Ibid., p.138.

106. Ibid., p.172.

107. Ibid., p. 175.

108. John Dewey, *Human Nature and Conduct* (New York: Modern Library, 1935), p.135.

109. Selz, *Zur Psychologie des produktiven Denkens und des Irrtums* (Bonn: 1922).

110. Sartre, *The Psychology of Imagination* (New York: Citadel Press, 1966).

111. Kainz, *Psychologie der Sprache*, 1:169.

112. Sigmund Freud, *Gesammelte kleine Schriften zur Neurosenlehre*, 1922 4:335.

113. Freud, *Schriften aus dem Nachlass*, 17:152.

114. Metzger, "Das Raumproblem in der Psychologie," Studium Generale (1957), vol. 10.

115. Kainz, *Psychologie*, 2:77.

116. Ibid., p.80.

117. Jespersen, *Language*, p.187.

118. Cited in Jespersen, *Language*, p.187–188.

119. Noiré, *Der Ursprung*.

120. Karl Vossler, *Gesammelte Aufsätze zur Sprachphilosophie*, (Munich: Hueber, 1923), p.214.

121. Ammann, "Sprache und Wirklichkeit," p.239.

122. Jespersen, *Language*, p.440 ff.

123. Fichte, *Vorlesungen über Logik und Metaphysik*, 1797.

124. Ibid.

125. Humboldt, *Linguistic Variability*, p.123.

126. Paul, *Prinzipien*, p.240.

127. Jakob Grimm, *Über den Ursprung der Sprache*, (Berlin: Dümmler, 1862).

128. Humboldt, *Linguistic Variability*, p.182.

129. Jespersen, *Language*, p.365.

130. Aristotle, *De Anima*.

131. Kainz, *Psychologie* 2:152.

132. Brugsch, *Religion und Mythologie der alten Ägypter* (Leipzig: J.C. Hinrichs, 1891).

133. Heinrich Winkler, *Der uralaltaische Sprachstamm, das Finnische und das Japanische* (Berlin: Dümmler, 1909).

134. Stenzel, *Philosophie der Sprache,* p.86f.

135. Paul, *Prinzipien,* p.69.

136. cf. Meinhof, *Die Sprache der Hamiten;* Westermann, *Handbuch der Ful-Sprache;* Reinisch, *Die Somalisprache.*

137. F.C.S. Schiller, *Studies in Humanism.*

138. Dewey, *Quest for Certainty,* p.152.

139. Gehlen, "Wirklichkeitsbegriff des Idealismus," Blätter für deutsche Philosophie, vol. 7.

140. Kant, *Critique of Pure Reason.*

141. Kant, *Reflexion,* no. 395.

142. F.H. Jacobi, vol. 4, p.153.

143. Novalis, *Werke,* 3:230; 2:87.

144. Nietzsche, *Daybreak,* (Cambridge: Cambridge University Press, 1982).

145. Fichte, *Werke,* vol. 2, p.169.

146. William James, *Pragmatism: A New Name for Some Old Ways of Thinking* (New York and London: Longman, Green, and Co.: 1943).

147. James, *The Will to Believe and Other Essays in Popular Philosophy* (New York: Dover, 1956). pp. 1–31.

148. Dewey, *The Quest for Certainty,* p.113.

149. Burkamp, *Wirklichkeit und Sinn,* 2:452.

150. Kant, *The Critique of Judgement* (Oxford: Clarendon Press, 1969), p.34.

151. Saussure, *Course in General Linguistics,* p. 114.

152. Friedrich Wilhelm Joseph von Schelling, *The Ages of the World* (New York: Columbia University Press, 1942).

153. von Weizsäcker, "Das Verhaltnis der Quantenmechanik zur Philosophie Kants," *Die Tatwelt* 3, 1941.

154. Dewey, *Quest for Certainty,* p.136.

155. Ibid., p.137.

156. Ibid., p.258.

157. Georges Sorel, *De l'utilité du pragmatisme,* (Paris: Librairie des sciences, 1928).

158. Vico, cited in Witzenmann, *Politische Akte und Sozialer Mythos.*

159. Nietzsche, *Human, All too Human* (New York: Russell & Russell, 1964), p.46.

160. Nietzsche, *Werke,* 11:23.

161. James, *Will to Believe,* pp. 1–31.

162. Vilfredo Pareto, *Trattato di sociologia generale,* translated as *The Mind and Society,* ed. by Arthur Livingston, (New York: Harcourt, Brace, 1935).

163. Hesiod, cited in Pareto.

164. Novalis, *Werke,* 3:97.

165. Aristotle, *The Ethics of Aristotle* (London: Penguin, 1973), p.91.

166. Karl Vossler, *Geist und Kultur in der Sprache,* (Heidelberg: Winter, 1925).

167. Herodotus, vol. 7.

168. *Grundrisse der Soziologie nach Vilfredo Pareto* (Karlsruhe: Braun, 1926).

169. Georg Gottfried Gervinus, *Geschichte der Deutschen Dichtung*, 5 vols. (Leipzig: Engelmann, 1871–1874).

170. Palagyi, *Wahrnehmungslehre*.

171. Segal, "Über das Vorstellen."

172. Lacroze, *La function de l'imagination*, 1938.

173. Sartre, "Structure intentionelle de l'image," *Revue de Metaphysique et de Morale* (1938) 45:543–609.

174. Sartre, *The Psychology of Imagination*.

175. Bergson, *The Two Sources of Morality and Religion* (New York: Doubleday, 1935).

176. Hans Kunz, *Die Anthropologische Bedeutung der Phantasie*, 2 vols. (Basel: 1946).

177. Herder, cited in Kunz, 1:131.

178. Palagyi, *Wahrnehmungslehre*, p.94.

179. G. Heard, *Social Substance of Religion*.

180. Sartre, *The Psychology of Imagination*, pp. 196–197.

181. Blondel, *Einführung in die Kollektivpsychologie*.

182. Hans Walter Gruhle, *Verstehende Psychologie*, (Stuttgart: Thieme, 1949), p.493.

183. Rothacker, "Tatkräfte und Wachstumskräfte," *Blätter für deutsche Philosophie*, vol.17.

184. Nietzsche, *The Will to Power*, aphorism 646, p.343.

185. Nietzsche, *Werke*, 13:230.

186. Rothacker, "Tatkräfte."

187. Kunz, *Die Anthropologische Bedeutung*, 1:133.

188. Nietzsche, *Will to Power*, aphorism 676.

189. Nietzsche, ibid.

190. See Becker in *Blätter für deutsche Philosophie*, 9,4; or Hofmiller "Das erste deutliche Zeichen des begonnenen Irrsins" in *Süddeutsches Monatsheft* (1931), vol.29.

191. Cicero, *De oratio*, 2:9.

192. Schelling, *Über das Verhaltnis der bildenden Kunste zur Natur*, 1807.

193. Schelling, *Philosophie der Kunst*, Nachlass, 1802–1805, p.31.

Part III

1. Shaffer and Shoben, *The Psychology of Adjustment*.

2. Hoffmann, *Das Problem des Charakteraufbaus*, 1926.

3. Fichte, *Werke*, 4:126.

4. G.W. Leibniz, *Theodicy* (London: Routledge and Kegan Paul, 1952), p.257.

5. Kant, *Critique of Pure Reason*, p.58f.

6. Aristotle, *Ethics*, p.91.

7. Nietzsche, *Nachlass*, 1869–1872, pp.180–181.

8. Buytendijk, *Wesen und Sinn des Spiels*, p.106.

9. Cicero, *Epistulae ad familiares* (Letters to his Friends); (Cambridge: Harvard University Press, 1958), 26:283.

10. Dewey, *Human Nature and Conduct.*

11. Novalis, *Werke,* 7:206.

12. Kant, *Critique of Judgement,* section 22 (83), p.94.

13. Hoffmann, *Das Problem des Charakteraufbaus,* p.178.

14. Frederik J.J. Buytendijk [with Helmuth Plessner] "Tier und Mensch." *Die Neue Rundschau,* (October 1938) 49:313–337.

15. In Buytendijk, *Wege zum Verstandnis der Tiere,* (Zurich and Leipzig: Niehans, 1939), p.126.

16. Aristotle, *Ethics,* p.88.

17. Ibid., p.105, for example.

18. Kant, *Critique of Judgement,* section 22 (83), p.95.

19. Bostroem, "Störungen des Wollens," *Handbuch der Geisteskrankheiten,* (1928), 2:15.

20. Nietzsche, *Will to Power,* pp.28–29.

21. Ibid., aphorism 692, p.369.

22. Ibid., aphorism 671, p.354.

23. Ibid., aphorism 644, p.342; aphorism 666, pp.351–352.

24. Ibid., aphorism 84, p.52.

25. Freyer, "Machiavelli und die Lehre vom Handeln," *Zeitschrift für deutsche Kulturphilosophie* (1938).

26. Aristotle, *Ethics,* p.103 ff.

27. Alexis Carrel, *Man the Unknown* (New York and London: Harper, 1935).

28. Ibid., p.221.

29. Ibid., p.227.

30. Ibid., p.231.

31. Homer, *The Odyssey* (New York: Harper and Row, 1965, 1967), Book 2, lines 270–275.

32. Panse, "Erbpathologie der Psycholpathien," *Handbuch der Erbbiologie des Menschen,* vol. 2.

33. Enke, "Die Persönlichkeitsradikale," *Allgemeine Zeitschrift für Psychiatrie,* (1934), vol. 102; "Warum Erziehung trotz Vererbung?" 1935.

34. Stumpfl, "Die erblichen Grundlagen der Persönlichkeit," *Handbuch der Erbbiologie, 1:415.*

35. Kroh, "Bericht no.14," Kongress der deutschen Gesellschaft für Psychology, 1935.

36. cf. Stumpfl, "Grundlagen," and Peters, "Bericht 8," Kongress exp. Psychology, 1924.

37. Hoffmann, "Vererbung und Seelenleben."

38. Stumpfl, in Schottky et al., *Die Persönlichkeit im Lichte der Erblehre,* 1936.

39. Stumpfl, *Handbuch der Erbbiologie,* p.425.

40. Enke, "Vortrag 56," Jahresversammlung der südwestdeutchen Psychiater, 1933.

41. Madame de Stael, *De L'Allemagne,* (1850) 2:28.

42. *Religione, id est cultu deorum,* Cicero, *De Natura Deorum,* (Cambridge: Harvard University Press, 1962), book 2, iii, p.130.

43. Maurice Hauriou, *La théorie de l'institution et de la fondation* in *La cité moderne et les transformations du droit* (Paris, 1925), cited in Carl Schmitt, *Die Drei Arten des rechtswissenschaftlichen Denkens.*

44. Gehlen, 3d ed., p.503 ff.

45. Schelling, *Philosophie der Kunst*, p.31.

46. Karl Beth, *Religion und Magie bei den Naturvölkern*, 1914, p.224.

47. Scheler, *Man's Place*, p.91.

48. Bergson, *The Two Sources*, p.138.

49. Kraft, *Der Urmensch als Schöpfer*, 1948, p.62.

50. Bergson, *The Two Sources*, p.101.

51. Hellpach, *Das Megethos*, 1947.

52. Dilthey, in E. Rothacker, ed., *Briefwechsel zwischen W. Dilthey und Graf Paul York von Wartenburg* (Halle, 1914).

53. Dilthey, *Gesammelte Schriften* (Leipzig, 1914) 5:9.

54. Ibid., 5:409.

55. Ibid., 5:406.

56. Ibid., 8:31.

57. Ibid., 5:277.

58. Ruth Benedict, *Patterns of Culture*, (Boston and New York: Houghton Mifflin, 1934), p.4.

59. Bronislaw Malinowski, *A Scientific Theory of Culture and Other Essays* (Chapel Hill, N.C.: University of North Carolina Press, 1944), p.150.

60. Jhering, *Zweck im Recht*, 1:417.

61. Hartmann, *Der Aufbau der realen Welt*, ch.32.

62. Bergson, *The Two Sources*, p. 106.

63. See H.J. Rose, *Ancient Greek Religion*, (London, 1946).

64. Van der Leeuw, *Phänomena der Religion*, 1933.

65. Freud, *Totem and Taboo.*

66. See *Urmensch und Spätkultur*, ch. 29.

67. Edward Hahn, *Die Entstehung der wirtschaftlichen Arbeit*, 1908.

68. Malinowski, *Crime and Custom in Savage Society* (London: Kegan Paul, Trench, Trubner), 1947.

69. R. Meister, 'Geistige Objektivierung und Resubjektivierung," *Wiener Zeitschrift für Philosophie, Psychologie, und Padagogik*, (1947) vol. 1(1).

70. *Urmensch und Spätkultur*, 1956.

71. Hartmann, *Der Aufbau der realen Welt*, p.44.

72. Novalis, *Fragmente*, p.471.

Index

European Perspectives: A Series of the Columbia University Press